May \
Do Con.

Tabr Khan

Lahore 2020

LAHORE

TALES WITHOUT END

LAHORE
TALES WITHOUT END

by

Majid Sheikh

SANG-E-MEEL PUBLICATIONS
LAHORE—PAKISTAN

954.9143   Majid Sheikh
          Lahore: Tales Without End/ Majid
        Sheikh.- Lahore: Sang-e-Meel Publications,
        2015.
          451pp.
          1. History - Lahore.   I. Title.

2015
Published by:
Afzaal Ahmad
Sang-e-Meel Publications,
Lahore.

ISBN-10: 969-35-2144-7
ISBN-13: 978-969-35-2144-3

Sang-e-Meel Publications
25 Shahrah-e-Pakistan (Lower Mall), Lahore-54000 PAKISTAN
Phones: 92-423-722-0100 / 92-423-722-8143 Fax: 92-423-724-5101
http://www.sang-e-meel.com e-mail: smp@sang-e-meel.com
PRINTED AT: HAJI HANIF & SONS PRINTERS, LAHORE.

Dedication

This book is dedicated to my parents, Hamid Sheikh and Violet Edith, whose caring made life worth loving. To my wife Rehana, for having tolerated me for so long. To my daughters, Sadia and Sehr, for being my greatest supporters and critics.

Dedicated to the people of Lahore, for being so unique and worth caring about.

Contents

8

Preface

The art of telling a tale will probably never die out. In this pastime lies the very essence of passing on to others, both old and young, the stories that our ancestors picked up, probably massaged it a bit to make it more edible, and passed on, depending on how strongly one felt about the issue at stake.

My father, Hamid Sheikh - or HS as he was known to his readers - was an avid storyteller. As Editor of the daily *The Civil & Military Gazette* of Lahore, he was known to describe his city better than anyone else in his times. In our childhood years we would listen to his stories with rapt attention. We really never knew just when or where he crossed that thin line that separates reality from a fib. It was engrossing stuff all the same, and we, all eight brothers and sisters, loved his stories. To all of us he passed on his passion for Lahore.

To add to his passion for telling us stories about Lahore, he would often take us on long walking expeditions through the old Walled City, where he welded his tales to the physical reality of the people and places that we came across. He seemed to intimately know almost every house, every lane, and every *mohallah*. At every turn there was a tale, a story grouted in the reality of the history of the city. Most of what I have to say in this book one has picked up from where he left off, as well as us, in 1971.

As a student of Government College, Lahore, for six happy years one cultivated friends with a shared interest in our heritage, our ancestors and the old Walled City. Those friends are still there for me to tap, to learn from, and to develop a greater understanding of where we are headed. Among these friends, numerous that they are, Ghazanfar Iqbal *alias* Sheero and Khalid Mahmood *alias* Khalidi, are special. Both of them possess immense knowledge of the old Walled City.

The origin of this first book, a collection of stories about Lahore, can squarely be placed on the shoulders of my guru, Mr. Zafar Iqbal Mirza, or ZIM to every journalist in the country. He called me in one day and virtually ordered me to write a weekly piece for the newspaper he was then editing, the daily *Dawn* of Lahore. He was an obedient understudy of my father in the 1960s, and he dared not say `No' to him. So tradition got the better of me, and the weekly column began to find readership, and, luckily, still does.

After almost six years of writing this column about the people, places, things and faces of Lahore, there was considerable pressure to publish it in book form. Providence has strange ways of assisting, for Dr. Fareeha Zafar and Abbas Rashid of the Society for the Advancement of Higher Education, Lahore, came to my assistance. They arranged the funds for the first edition and the burden of publishing was over. To them both one owes a special feeling of gratitude.

A few words about the contents you will read. These were all newspaper columns with the restriction of not exceeding 1,000 words. But a tale can surely be spun within this short space. All the facts one has tried to verify to the best of my ability. If, however, lapses exist, which they surely do, for them one apologise. But then Lahore is the city where the best stories are told. This book is a modest start, and one is hopeful it will promote the spirit of toleration that is the hallmark of the city. Along the way one has consulted many a book, as well as persons, all of whom have always been gracious. I must mention friends like Rafique Dogar and Fakir Syed Aijazuddin, whose superior knowledge one has tapped into.

Special mention must be made of the hundreds of unknown real life characters living in Lahore, some known to me, but most strangers, all of whom have always been willing to assist. Their comments, manners and ways inspire me to keep writing about Lahore, for the city would never be the same without them.

This second edition of the book is being published by Sang-e-Meel Publications, Lahore. They have a special place in the city as the publisher of books about the city and its history. They are an institution onto themselves, and surely deserve greater recognition.

Lastly, one must acknowledge the three lovely ladies in my life. Firstly is my wife Rehana, who one acknowledges for her stoic effort of tolerating my ways. Secondly, are my two daughters, Sadia and Sehr, both of whom have this ability to cut me down to size when my imagination goes astray, yet in the process love the tales that have been spun around them. To them one passes on the passion of Lahore, which they willing lap up.

Majid Sheikh
Lahore April, 2008.

*The **Ravi River** is a river in India and Pakistan. It is one of the five rivers which give Punjab its name. The Ravi was known as Parushani or Iravati to Indians in Vedic times and Hydraotes to the Ancient Greeks. It originates in the Himalayas in the Chamba district of Himachal Pradesh following a north-westerly course. It turns to the south-west, near Dalhousie, and then cuts a gorge in the Dhaola Dhar range entering the Punjab plain near Madhopur. It then flows along the Indo-Pakistan border for some distance before entering Pakistan and joining the Chenab river. The total length of the river is about 720 km. The waters of the Ravi river are allocated to India under the Indus Waters Treaty between India and Pakistan. It is also called 'The river of Lahore' since that great city is located on its banks.*

The Ravi's treasures

One of the great mystery stories in Lahore is about the River Ravi, which, legend has it, is a treasure-trove of unparalleled dimensions, and the secret underground tunnel from the Lahore Fort to the river. Every time a Lahori leaves the city, he relaxes only once he has seen the river. It remains an unprompted response even today.

You might be wondering why the Ravi is 'a treasure-trove of unparalleled dimensions', a rather colourful description of what has today become merely a small polluted stream in which buffaloes wallow. Instead of the mighty river, there exists an empty dusty desert. Merely looking at it is soul-wrenching, and all we do is blame the sins of man for the revenge of nature. The fact is that we have managed our water affairs very badly. The Ravi is a trickle because the Indians have taken our water away... or more accurately, we have agreed that they take our water away. Only when the rivers swell in the monsoons do they let the Ravi rage our way. We only see the rage, not the love, of our lifeline.

The story of the Ravi and its treasures started in the Vedas almost 5,000 years ago, when Ram and Sita, while sitting on the edge of the river at Lahore, described it as the retainer of the largest treasure known to man. That planted the seeds of a belief that exists even today. Since then our forefathers have believed that below the riverbed lie gold and silver, left over the ages by rulers and rich people, fleeing conquerors and invaders. Every time there was a turmoil, rumours of treasures being thrown in the Ravi surfaced. This gave rise to even more fanciful stories, which are even today believed as they are passed on from generation to generation.

The story about a tunnel originating from inside the Lahore Fort going all the way to Jehangir's Tomb, is a wilder version of this tale. Some people still believe that the tunnel went all the way to Delhi. Along this imagined route, it is believed, went most of the treasures when members of the Royal families fled when they were attacked or threatened. During the days of Akbar the Great, descriptions of those days tell us, gold coins were actually recovered from the river. Akbar's father hid them there when he fled Sher Shah Suri. That fired the imagination of the people to such an extent that during Akbar's days, people actually used to search the dry bed of the river before the monsoon swell.

Sher Shah Suri

But another two reasons have added to a renewed interest in searching the dry bed of the Ravi for treasures which, one never knows, might lie there. It is said that in the 1950ies, a British company offered to line the sides of the Ravi from the Indian border to ten miles downstream. The idea was the brainchild of the late Mr Zafarul Ahsan. It was supported by a dream to make the river the centre of Lahore, have a massive embankment on both sides and to develop the city in a planned manner.

The company, and documents testify to it, wanted the right to own anything found in the river. This fired the imagination of the bureaucrats who started believing that some treasure existed there. The contract was dropped and with the departure of the late Mr Ahsan, the ancient city of Lahore developed the way it did.

Of late, there have been a lot of people seen digging up the river-bed. Most of them are contracted people selling sand. But one newspaper report says that treasure hunters have started working on the bed. There is one occult 'master' in Mozang who claims he can assist people find such treasures. Suffice it to say, many a fool falls for such a scheme. All of which adds to the myth.

But the one about the tunnel right up to Delhi is the best one. We asked the Department of Archaeology for its comments. They said: "A tunnel exists no doubt, but it ends in one corner of the Fort. Having one right up to the river, or even Delhi, is pure fiction. It never existed in history". That was cold water over a beautiful myth. In my youth I asked my father about the tunnel, and he gave me an answer which cannot be reproduced here.

But scientific reality does not seem to matter in such affairs. With time the myths acquire the shape of a 'reality' that one does not feel like challenging. That is the fun of myths. They add to the beauty of life. But there is still hope for those who believe in the tunnel to Delhi theory. The beginning of the tunnel is from somewhere where a really dingy dungeon actually exists. It is a dungeon that needs to be developed into a major tourist attraction. That will certainly add to the myth, to the joy of living in Lahore.

Then one day, as I crossed the Ravi, it made me immensely sad to see the once great and immortal river almost gone, with nothing but a few buffaloes trying hard to bathe in the shallow polluted excuse of a stream that it has become.

The English poet Milton (1608-74) mentions Lahore among the cities seen by Adam from the hill of Paradise. Today we have managed to reduce it to what is probably the opposite of paradise. For us, whose forebears dwelt in the

Walled City before the dawn of history, nothing could be more painful. And as I stood in anguish I was reminded of the inscription on the tomb of Nur Jehan on the banks of the Ravi, which depicts what Lahore has become: "On the grave of us poor, there's neither a lamp nor a flower; no moth singes its wings, nor is a song of the nightingale (heard)". There she lies, in her dusty crumbling grave, still ignored, that great queen of the sub-continent, beside her Jahangir in his grand mausoleum, on the banks of a dying river, the very symbol of life to our ancient city, Lahore, that second largest city of the Mughal Empire, was described in 1641 by Friar Manrique Sebastian as: "a handsome and well-ordered city with large waterways... and the cleanliness of the streets surprised me much... the riches of the bazaars would equal the richest of any European mart". But today, as we face an immense water shortage, thanks primarily to our own inability to plan and live at peace with ourselves, and with mounting urban pollution, there is a need for planning to save Lahore from what surely awaits us. The speed of our urban decline is something we must face up to, and we must learn from what has happened in the past.

We know full well that this ancient city has been destroyed several times over, almost razed to the ground. Each time it has recovered and become an even greater city, thanks to its people. Mahmud Ghaznavi plundered it, 'golden hordes' of Mongols virtually raped this city, Babar put the city to the torch after a pitched battle against the brave Bhat Rajputs of Bhaati Gate. When the British took the city from the Sikhs, an officer recorded his impression:

"I visited the ruins of Lahore, which afforded a melancholic picture of fallen splendour... all was silence, solitude and gloom".

That is the way I felt this day standing on the banks of the Ravi, and I decided to walk in the middle

Mahmud Ghaznavi

of the river bed, a massive sandy desert, where save for a few buffaloes wallowing in the shallow stream that was once the river Ravi, there is not much to be seen, except for sand diggers who make a living out of the misfortune of this 'holy river' as the Vedas put it. For every Lahori it is certainly much more than holy. It is the life provider of Lahore. The question naturally springs to mind: 'Will Lahore rise again?' This piece is all about this question, the one we should be worried about today, and the one I would like all of you to ask yourself.

As an eternal optimist, I feel that as a city we have hit such a low that there is nothing much left for us but to climb back again. That has been the historic tradition of this ancient city of ours. The question is how will all this happen? Who will manage it? Who will lead? We must address these concerns in an enlightened manner.

Here it would not be out of place to mention that there is an ancient myth that says, "every time Lahore rises, it rises when the Ravi is made the centre of the city". It is a strange saying, but if we analyse how the Sikhs managed to develop the falling city, how even the British managed, we will see that the river had an important role to play in how the city was planned.

There is a plan lying in some old cupboard of the LDA, a plan acquired from the Lahore Improvement Trust, which acquired it from the British days, which was a futuristic plan of how Lahore should develop into the 21st century. Now the 21st century has arrived, it makes sense that the basics of this plan are thrown up for public discussion. We, the people of Lahore, must participate in what our city must become in the years to come if we are to hand over a reasonable place for our children and grandchildren to live in. But what does one do in a situation where local government means that even a microscopic Model Town Society is not allowed to function and ugly, surely illegal, disturbing offices and commercial plazas are springing up in this once 'model town' as the world of town planning calls it.

The reverse gear must be applied to this process, and the sooner it is done the better for everyone.

The plan envisages that both banks of the Ravi have huge embankments, which should, 20 miles downstream, form a barrage to store water in the rainy season in a massive lake. This 20 miles by one-mile lake should be the centre of Lahore. This will prevent the Eastwards slide of the city, bring the Walled City to the centre, and will provide the planner with an ideal chance to open up and plan correctly for a change. Wide boulevards and well-demarcated commercial and residential areas must be enforced. And while these massive plans are being put into force, the elected local authorities must enforce strict residential and commercial zones in the remaining 'infested' areas of the city, places like Gulberg, Model Town, Samnabad, and each and every locality of Lahore.

The writ of the law must prevail, surely, only by being responsible planners, with an eye on history and with a balanced view of what the ancient city stands for, can we make good for our mistakes.

The case of the forgotten ferries

There was a time, not very long ago, when besides the horse and bullock-drawn carriages plying the dusty roads emanating from Lahore, the main mass transport system feeding the city was the River Ravi. Sounds strange, but just as Lahore's railway station today is the main point of embarkation, in the past it was Khizri Gate, or Sheranwala Gate ... for this is where the ferry stopped.

The river snaked its way around the Walled City, touching Khizri Gate. Almost 250 years ago when the river decided to cut a new path, the ferry station became redundant. The river shifted to the west, almost on its present course, and the moat around Lahore was serviced by what came to be called the 'Buddha Ravi', Old Ravi. Soon even this source refused to oblige and the British filled in the moat. There are two versions as to the way the moat was filled in. One is that the British learned after the 1857 war of independence that the major cities should be made 'indefensible'. The second is that as the moat was drying up, it made better 'sanitary sense' to fili it up and prevent diseases from spreading. The British rulers encouraged the latter explanation.

The name Khizri Gate comes from the name of Khwaja Khizr, the patron saint of all fishermen and seafarers. Once the moat disappeared, the name also disappeared. It is amazing that not much research exists about the Walled City and its way of life as it has evolved over the centuries. Today, most people will be hard-pressed believing that in the not too distant past, a major portion of the city was served by a ferry. The names of streets, the professions followed in the immediate vicinity, the warehousing developments, the location of the major markets, the infrastructure etc., all evolved because of the location of the ferry. Like all great cities located on the bank of a great river, Lahore also developed and grew because of the river and the lay of the land. The mound and the river were the soul and the blood of the city. With time the highways and newer modes of transport began to take over this role.

The original timber market of Lahore was located just opposite the open spaces to the east of the Fort. Today truck axle and tyre rim dealers occupy these spaces. It was here that most of the boats were constructed. Even today a majority of carpenters live in areas around this gate. The lanes have interesting names, like 'Look Wali Gali', or 'Tar Lane', for here the shops handling the waterproofing of the boats were located. There is a Tar Lane in London that has a similar history. Then there is, slightly deeper inside the city, the 'Rassa Mandi' or the 'rope market'. From this place the ropes for the boats were provided. Inside Sheranwala Gate, on the street curving to the left as one heads towards Akbari, is the 'Sutar Mandi' or yarn market. Here the yarn for the looms that weaved the sails was sold. Even today in place of the canvas cloth woven on wooden looms, one can see the 'khaddar' looms working away. Names like 'Mauj Darya' and 'Mohallah Nilian' are all indicators of an era long gone by- the era when the ferry held an important place in the lives of the inhabitants of Lahore.

On the opposite side of the river lies Badami Bagh. It was here that the main boat manufacturers lived. Right up to Mughalpura just before where once the bend of the Ravi occurred, were small villages where fishermen lived. To the north lay the river forests of the Ravi, where it is said that once lived the fiercest dacoits of the sub-continent. When chased, they fled across the river on their boats and disappeared into the wilderness of Sheikhupura.

What did the ferry look like? Miniature paintings of that period and the drawings of foreign travellers of that era depict boats almost like those that sail on the River Nile in Egypt even today. These boats are known to have travelled down the river, bringing in spices and other exotic goods. Lahore served as a major market for such goods, feeding other cities around it.

This brings us to an important point, for along with the ferry was the life of the fishermen of the Ravi, whose fish was legendary for its excellent taste. Known for its 'Rahoo' and its 'Khagga' varieties among others, these freshwater fish have almost disappeared thanks to pollution and the river treaty with India, which has 'stolen' all the water of our sacred river from its inhabitants. The river has gone, the ferries have gone. Today no one would imagine that once this city of ours lived on and off the river ... and today we do not know even how to harness what little is left of it.

The lost boat bridge

Just how did the huge invading armies, with all those horses, carriages, cannons and the massive paraphernalia of war manage to cross the River Ravi at Lahore before the British built the first bridge across it when laying the railway line from Lahore to Peshawar? Surely this is a question that must have crossed the mind of every Lahori.

Just a few months ago, Fakir Syed Aijazuddin published a delightful book titled *Lahore Recollected* in which he reproduced a photograph of Lahore's 'Bridge of Boats' from J.H. Furneaux's *Glimpses of India*, published in 1895 in Bombay. If anything could easily satisfy my quest to visualize what stood across the river before the 'Shahdara' railway bridge was built, it was this one photograph. I had seen an old map of Lahore in which the location of the old boat bridge of Lahore was marked.

This map indicated the location with a dotted line. However, in the book by Aijazuddin, an equally interesting old map of Lahore shows the old boat bridge and its exact location. This prompted me to try to search for clues that remain of the old bridge, as well as try to retrace the old road that led to the original bridge of Lahore.

Before dwelling on my small adventure, it would not be out of place to reproduce a description of conditions while crossing the Ravi River by William Moorcroft when he crossed it on 15 May, 1820: " The road to Shahdara is intersected by three different branches of the Ravi, separated in the dry weather by intervals of half a mile; but in the rainy season the two most easterly branches are united, and form an expansive and rapid stream.... the first two branches are fordable, but the third, which is the principal one, has a ferry".

Bridge of Boats 1895

It is very clear that the western-most portion always did remain the main flow of the river, with the eastern ones becoming part of the flow in the monsoons. Today, these portions are known as the 'Buddha Ravi', while one still, though very much a highly polluted outfall, falls into the river. The last one is where once flowed the river round the walled city, major portions of which still remain there around the walls of the old city. If you have been a student of geography, you will immediately acknowledge that the eastern most river is the original flow, while the current river-bed is its natural 'shifting' bed.

A British map of 1867 shows the 'bridge of boats' connecting the two banks of the Ravi at Mirza Kamran's baradari. The map depicts this as 'Turgurwallee Baraduree'. The word 'turgurwallee' is a corruption of the word 'targarh' or wire house. Either this is the first 'telegraph' wire house set up by the British, or it is where the rope, or wire, of the boat bridge was secured.

Before the railway bridge was built, a British superintendent of bridges was stationed at the 'baradari', and it was there he had his residence. Later, this building was "fitted up as a Public Works Department rest house" as H.R. Goulding was to describe it.

With the Punjab annexed, the British started immediately building boat and 'pucca' bridges across all the rivers in the state to improve the movement of troops and trade. The boat bridge over the Ravi was "declared to be the best of its kind and adopted as a model" as one description puts it. This brings forth the possibility that a boat bridge existed across the river before the British captured Lahore in 1849.

There are numerous references of the Sikh period where Maharajah Ranjit Singh has been described as riding across the Ravi. Given that he had the assistance of French engineers, it is a possibility that they had constructed boat bridges to facilitate their army crossings rivers with speed.

However, Moorcroft does mention that a ferry existed in 1820. It would be safe to assume that the boat bridge, which the British mention in 1854 'the old boat bridge' does clearly mean that it was in place before the British annexed Lahore.

All these interesting pointers made me walk, on both sides of the bank, in a trek searching for clues to the old boat bridge. I walked through the Ravi Park and the northern portions of Mominpura to see where the landing stages would have been. The manner in which the roads lead does certainly point to the fact that they all converged on one point just south of Ravi Park. People of the area still call it 'Pul Morr' or bridge crossing. Even though the old railway bridge is almost half a mile to the north, and the Ravi Road crossing was later to be called by the same name.

This pointer led me through Mominpura and on to the edge of the current Bund Road. The crazy unplanned construction that has become Lahore has removed all traces of any old boat bridge. My guess is that the securing ground lies buried under the current Bund Road.

On the other side of the Ravi in Shahdara, the old road certainly does curve and hits a point, just opposite Kamran's baradari, which is also called 'Pul Morr'. It is clear that the 'baradari' once was part of the river's western bank. On the island there are definite signs of the boat bridge, with two solid brick structures now just on the surface of the eastern bank. On these were, probably, tied the ropes or wires of the old boat bridge.

The location of these fit exactly with the map description. Removed from the main road and the main line, there is no rational reason why these should be called 'targarh', except that they served as the staging post of the old boat bridge of Lahore.

There is even the possibility that the first telegraph wires across the Ravi were laid alongside the boat bridge, and that they were managed from the old 'targarh'. The story of Lahore's lost boat bridge needs to be told in greater detail, for it will always remain one of the enduring mysteries of the old city.

'Kacha kot' that became Lahore

Our search for the origins of the original Lahore has immense twists and turns. It's time period can be anything starting 2,000 B.C. onwards... at least carbon dating evidence of archaeological findings in the Lahore Fort do suggest this time period.

We learn from various sources that Lahore had many names, all of which changed over time. But the one name that does warrant research is 'kacha kot'. One of the two most probable sites of the 'original' Lahore is Mohallah Maulian. Let us explore this area in this brief piece. If we focus on Sootar Mandi - the yarn market - inside Lohari Gate, we can get a feel of what we are looking for. Sootar Mandi was once called Mohallah Chaileywala Hammam, and is located in what was once called Machli Hatta Gulzar, which is just off Chowk Chakla, Lahore's original red-light area.

As late as 1864, according to one source quoting Mufti Tajuddin, son of the well- known Mufti Imamuddin, the Lohari Mandi area was known among the old folk of the Walled City as 'kacha kot' - the mud fort. Why was this area called a 'mud fort' when we know that the original walls of the Lahore Fort, before Akbar the Great's days, were also made of mud? This is a question that must be explored.

To determine this it is important that one visits the old Walled City, observe the gradient of the land, the water (nullah's act as excellent guides of gradient and direction) flow and observe how 'mohallahs' and 'kuchas' and 'kattrahs' are structured. On Sundays, this is my favourite pastime. Standing at Chowk Sutar Mandi, if you observe the curve of Gali Pir Bola as it merges with Waachowali Bazaar, and then also the Lohari Bazaar where it merges with Chowk Lohari Mandi, and lastly Chowk Mati where it merges with Papar

Mandi, you can well imagine, if you close your eyes and transport yourself 3,500 years back, a small mud fort with a small dwelling. The setting is perfect. Once you open your eyes, it is time to observe, or look for, some evidence of a mud fort.

If you walk along Lohari Bazaar, just a short distance from Chowk Chakla (imagine, this beautiful name has been changed to a pious Chowk Bukhari) to the right you will see the street open a little, for on the right is a half-buried archway of 'pucca' bricks and mud. Could this be from the era, when Lahore was a mud fort? The evidence certainly does suggest that this could be an archway, or gateway, of the small original 'kacha kot' way back in time, a place that was to grow one day to become Lahore.

It is also possible, for we must not exclude any possibility, that this was the famous mud fort that was built by Malik Ayaz, the very first Muslim governor of Lahore. This is very probable because it is recorded history that Lohari Gate was the main entrance to Ayaz's mud fort. So no matter how you analyze recorded evidence, one thing is for sure, and that is, that Chowk Sutar Mandi was one important centre of Kacha Kot. The lay of the streets also suggest the boundaries.

In an earlier piece we had followed a similar theory, and come up with the proposition that during the times of Mughal Emperor Akbar, the original wall of the Walled City of Lahore was, on the western side, to the right of Bazaar Hakeeman in Bhatti Gate, and on the eastern side to the left of Shahalam Gate, which then curved eastwards and formed a 'kidney shaped' city that depended on the flow of the curving River Ravi. Thus the Lahore of the 'kacha kot' era has continued to expand in three major leaps of expansion, each with an almost 400 year gap. The eras of Raja Jaipal, of Akbar and of Maharajah Ranjit Singh mark the high points of this expansion.

But the expanding bubble definitely has its origins in three factors, they being (a) the way the Ravi has flown and how and when it has been changing its course, (b) the existence of the Lahore Fort and how power has flowed from the rulers, and (c) the manner in which the population and economy of the old original Walled City has changed over time, grown, or even shrunk, depending on invasions, droughts and famines in the countryside. The story of 'kacha kot' has been determined by these factors.

When walking through these streets, it is not hard to make out that the oldest buildings in the entire Walled City exist in this area. As one passes the old exquisite mosque known even now as Masjid Kohana Hammam Chaileywala, one is reminded that the area was named similarly once. There must have been a huge 'hammam' here once. The tomb of Pir Bola exists after which is named the 'gali'.

It is sad that we tend to change the names of streets and areas, and even cities, at the drop of a hat as if to stamp some sort of moral authority on time. All rulers love to block out history. It would be best to let history rest and emerge as times dictate. It would not be a bad idea to declare the entire Walled City as a protected area. Let us keep for the future the little that is left of 'kacha kot' - the mud fort that ultimately became the Walled City of Lahore.

Of Sita and Ashok

It might come as a surprise to most 'pucca Lahoris' that the Walled City is much older than many of them imagine. It has given birth to many creative movements. It has been the birthplace of some great religious movements. That is why the original inhabitants have a certain calm about matters of belief.

King Ashok

The origins of Lahore go back as far as time can be traced. Over 5,000 years ago, the famous poet Valmiki composed the famous Hindu epic Ramayana in Lahore. In this epic a pregnant Sita is located, during her second exile, in the Ravi area that "curls around the mound that has been inhabited since centuries". Research shows that her son Loh, or Lahu was reared on the mound that later was to take his name Lahore. There has always been a controversy as to where exactly did Sita live on the mound, or in Lahore. One version, which is popular with academics, puts the location where the Lahore Fort stands today, just next to where the road curls upwards from Haathi Darwaza.

This version is lent credence by the fact that the temple of Lahu still exists inside the fort. The second version, much fancied by scholars living inside the Walled City puts it near the Paniwala Talab. The fact is that these two locations are merely 500 yards apart, and both are salient, overlooking the rest of the city. And as the location of major portions of the Rig-Veda, the ancient Hindu shastras was composed on the banks of the river Ravi at Lahore, one can say with considerable confidence that the Hindu religion, in large part, sprang up and was nurtured by the people of this great city.

But then it might also come as a surprise that Lahore in particular, and the Punjab in general, played a major role in spreading Buddhism in the sub-continent. Not that Buddha came here, but Chandragupta Maurya, grandfather of the mighty King Ashoka, both resident Lahoris, spread Buddhism after leading a revolt triggered by the murder in 318 B.C. of Raja Porus, then a Greek ally, by jealous Greek officers who had earlier served under Alexander. Raja Porus, whose original name was Paurava (Porus being its Greek corruption) had become an ally of Alexander after being defeated by the Greek armies in 327 BC on the banks of River Jhelum, It was there that the seven-feet tall and dark Porus, captured after being wounded, uttered those famous words that he "be treated as a king should be". So impressed was Alexander, some accounts suggest that he was actually frightened, that he decreed that he remain king of his territories. His murder nine years later brought about the collapse of the Greek empire.

With Lahore as the capital, the official religion of the Punjab was Buddhism. The recent 'fatwa' by the Taliban of Afghanistan to destroy Buddhist statues should be seen in the light of the fact that Ashoka's empire on the western side included Kandahar, called Kurukshetrea in the Vedas and that during that era huge statues were made on his orders, the ones that are under threat today.

Sikhism also originated in the Punjab, though not particularly in Lahore alone. Its founder Nanak was born at Talwandi on the Ravi in the Sharaqpur area just outside Lahore. But in its history, the Sikh religion reached its zenith when Guru Gobind Singh turned the peaceful believers of both Islam and Hinduism into a warrior race. Lahore was the capital of the Khalsa Empire, and even today it is spiritually very much on their minds.

But then people practising other religions also came to Lahore. The Tartars and the Huns of Massagetae, who believed in their own gods came and attacked Lahore. It is said that the Jats, perhaps the most numerous ethnic group of the Punjab, were actually Huns.

Given such a history, it is no surprise that Lahore was the place where the very first mosque in the Punjab was built over 1,023 years ago in the year 977 A.D. after Raja Jaipal of Lahore was defeated by Subuktagin, father of Sultan Mahmud of Ghazni. Its location is claimed to be the Sunehri Masjid inside the fort. This mosque has been rebuilt a number of times, but experts believe that this was the very first mosque built in the Punjab. So the very first mosque and the very first temple exist side by side inside the Fort.

The various religions' relationship with Lahore has resulted in the people acquiring a very special and sensitive way of interpreting them, one based on humanity and tolerance. In Islam the Sufis have always held sway over the hearts and minds of the people. Their influence has been continuous and complete. That is what makes the people of the Walled City liberal at heart, and 'disdainful of courtly sycophancy'. Even today, when other smaller towns and cities could probably be held hostage by clerics; the Walled City of Lahore seems to reject any form of extremism. Old civilizations have a calm about them, for they have the ability to see beyond the immediate threat.

Lahore and its indigo history

When you enter Lahore's walled city through Lohari Gate, probably the oldest 'darwaza' after the now demolished Taxali Gate, the road runs for about 400 yards and enters an opening known once as Chowk Chakla, the original red-light district of the city. Taxali was then a culturally upper class area. To the left, or north-west, it heads and joins the edge of Tehsil Bazaar. To the right, heading north-east, it meanders along the Sootar Mandi, the yarn market of old.

Shah Jahan

As we move along we notice two lanes off this 'mandi' that are called 'Nilli Gali' and 'Rangwali Gali'. These two lanes interest us. Let us start our story from the year 1633. Mughal Emperor Shah Jahan imposed a Royal 'farman' making indigo a state monopoly. In the indigo market of Lahore, just off Lohari Gate, the crier announced the emperor's decision. Little did he know that decision laid the foundations of European colonialism in the subcontinent.

The royal edict also confirmed the sale of indigo throughout the empire for three years to a Hindu merchant called Manohar Das, who had a huge shop in Lohari Gate, but who also operated his business in Agra and Surat. He was to be assisted by a loan from the royal coffers which would share the profit that might accrue. Official estimates mentioned that it would be the largest money earning scheme in the empire.

Agra and Lahore were then the two major indigo markets of the subcontinent, with other important markets being Multan, Allahabad, Surat and Delhi. But Lahore was by far the largest, and Agra, in terms of quality, held sway. The Indian subcontinent was the oldest centre of indigo dyeing in the old world. It was a primary supplier of indigo to Europe as early as the Graeco-Roman era. The association of the western portion of the subcontinent with indigo is reflected in the Greek word for the dye, which was indikon the Romans used the term indicum, which passed into Italian dialect and eventually into English as the word indigo.

The Greek sage Periplus, writing in 80-90 AD, mentions indigo and its connection with the River Ravi. He writes: "This River (Sinthus, *i.e.* Indus) has 7 mouths and it has none of them navigable except the middle one only, on which there is a coast mart called Barbaricon (Lehar, or Lahore) articles imported into this mart are. On the other hand there are exported Costus, Bdellium and Indian Black (Indigo)."

The increasing interest of the strong Dutch and English merchant community in indigo had made the emperor act to increase his revenues. It was, 400 years ago, the biggest export sector of the sub-continent in terms of value. This 'royal farman' hit the world indigo trade hard, and the Dutch and the English merchant companies, who operated their ships along the coasts of the subcontinent, entered a solemn agreement on Nov 19, 1633 to break this monopoly.

They decided that no European would purchase indigo for one year, except at their own very low price, and that the purchase of indigo was to be a joint venture. The Dutch and the English solemnly pledged not to accept indigo as freight. The Portuguese also abided by this agreement. The indigo embargo was tightly in place.

The very first Europeans to import indigo were the Portuguese whose agents worked all over the sub-continent, especially in Lahore, Agra, Ahmadabad and Multan. They moved their product to Surat, from where it was carried to Lisbon by the Portuguese and further sold to dyers in Holland. But, with the formation of the Dutch and the English East India companies, there began a rivalry for the monopoly of its trade.

This 'European' combination compelled Emperor Shah Jahan to dissolve his partnership with Manohar Das on April 14, 1635. The Moghal Empire had wilted to European pressure for the very first time. From then onwards the pressure would never cease. With indigo came cotton from Punjab. In the south they had managed to wrest the spice trade, with the Portuguese, the Dutch, the French, and finally the English playing out their roles. But indigo had a very special role to play in the Lahore of the Mughal era.

Marco Polo, writing in the 13th century, mentions: "that at colium they make an abundant quantity of very fine indigo. This is made of a certain herb which is gathered and (after the roots have been removed) is put into great vessels upon which they pour water and then leave it till the whole of the plant is decomposed".An English trader called William Finch, writing in his diary on August 30, 1609, mentioned three varieties of indigo produced during that time, with the main and best variety being Biana, also a village near Agra, and it sold 400 years ago for Rs. 25 per maund.

William Finch has again described the three varieties of indigo prepared in Biana. The first year's crop was known as note (naudha, young plant), the second year's crop was jari, sprouting from the roots and was considered the best. The third year's crop was khunti and was the worst of the three. Another indigo merchant writing about the trade in India says: "I have indeed on more than one occasion observed that if an egg is placed in the morning near one of these indigo sifters, in the evening, when one of them breaks the egg, it is altogether blue inside, so penetrating is the dust of indigo".

One characteristic of indigo trade was a keen sense of competition between the Dutch and the English for its monopoly. In 1637, the Dutch were found paying more for indigo at Ahmadabad in order to frustrate the attempts of the English. Another letter written by the English factors on May 29, 1619 to the company ran as follows "the high price of indigo is entirely due to the competition between the English and the Dutch and to their allowing the ships to be used by the native merchants for its transportation, for although it was not very useful to send Biana over land to Persia *via* Lahore, no one would dream of it otherwise."

It would come as a surprise to many, that Arab, especially Egyptian, traders were transporting indigo to the Middle East for over 2,000 years before the Europeans completely took over this business. Even the mummies preserved in the pyramids of Egypt have indigo dyed cotton fabrics used in them.

It would also come as a surprise to many that the sails of the ships of Christopher Columbus had indigo dyed canvas. So the indigo of Lahore and Agra could be said to be witness to the discovery of the so-called New World. In Scotland the nearest thing to indigo is the 'woad' plant, which is even today used in traditional Scottish checks and tweeds.

The use of indigo in woven fabrics was also taking place well over 600 years ago. For example the pants worn by Indian sailors were canvas dyed in indigo. It was manufactured in the city of Dhunga near Ahmadabad. From there came the world 'dungaree'. The French, who were always master weavers, were producing special weaves like serge. The city of Nimes is even today known as the textile centre of France. The Serge of Nimes, or 'serge de Nimes' went on to be called denim.

The French soldiers fighting the British in the Americas used denim. This denim was also worn by Italian sailors and working men, especially in Genoa, their main port. From Genoa the denim trousers worn were called jeans. It is amazing how a product produced mainly in western India, or Lahore, Agra, Ahmadabad and Multan, travelled all over the world and evolved into the world's most worn garment.

Once synthetic indigo was formulated by a German scientist called Bayaer in the 19th century, the demand for natural indigo dye fell. By the time the British took over the indigo business demand began to die down, especially after the plant was being grown in other parts of the world. The only place now where natural indigo is produced and used in Pakistan is in Sindh and Multan, where the traditional 'ajrak' is indigo-dyed.

In Lahore, it has ceased as a business. The names of streets in the walled city are now merely remembered by the older people. Street names are being changed. Chowk Chakla is now called Chowk Bukhari. But as Pakistan has the world's best medium staple cotton, indigo-dyeing is returning as more denim plants are set up. The sad thing is that the dye is now imported. A sad twist in the land and city that gave the world so much indigo dye.

The 'shroud' over Lahore's antiquity

We all know that Lahore's history is shrouded in antiquity. But then which were the very first dwellings that came to be known as Lahore? A search for an answer to this question can be an endless pursuit. There are some definite clues that need much more research, especially archaeological research.

In 1959, the department of archaeology carried out an "archaeological strata analysis" of a site inside the Lahore Fort. A 52-foot deep sample was taken and every foot carbon-dated. The findings were dramatic to say the least. In this sample, scientists found three specific layers of definite proof of dwellings, each one almost 700 to 800 years older than the one above.

The lowest, found at almost 45 feet, had "fine brick earlier occupation compacted soil". The estimate was that this was a 3,000-year old dwelling. Experts had then suggested that a much deeper sample needed to be taken also, from other sites, especially from mounds that were higher than the one that came to be known as the Lahore Fort.

There is a generally accepted theory that the very first dwellings that we know as Lahore started from where the citadel of the city stands. The existence of the Temple of Lahu inside the fort, and the fact that he was the son of Rama and Sita, do support this theory. But then this does not have any support from any written text from the Pre-Islamic era. The very first mention of this 'fact' was made by the famous Hindu historian, Sujan Rai Bhandari, in 1695-96 in his famous discourse *Khulasat-at-Tawarikh*. Though he quotes from folklore and other sources, the timeframe of the existence of the legendary Raja Ram Chandra is difficult to pinpoint. One source puts it at 5300 BC, another in 2200 BC. Thus antiquity, in this case, has become a matter of perception. Our interest lies solely in scientific proof.

A second 'archaeological strata study' was undertaken in the Haveli of Raja Dhayan Singh. The reason for this was that its site is slightly higher than the mound of the Lahore Fort. This carbon-dating study showed even more clearly the antiquity of Lahore, with human dwellings being found at four levels. But then such a research was not carried forward.

This research was followed by a study carried out by PEPAC in 1988, in which a considerable number of Pakistani and foreign experts participated. A topographical survey of the walled city showed that the two highest points in Lahore were the Paniwala Talaab at Choona Mandi, and the Mohallah Maulian, just north of the Papar Mandi.

These findings coincide perfectly with another historical document, which happens to be the oldest written authentic document, of the Pre-Islamic era, about Lahore. Written by an anonymous writer in AD 982 and called *Hudud-al-Alam,* this rare document lies in the British

Museum. It was translated by V. Minorsky into English and published in London in 1927.

In this rare book, Lahore is referred to as a small 'shahr' town with "impressive temples, large markets and huge orchards". It points out to "two major markets around which dwellings exist", and it also points out to "the mud walls that enclose these two dwellings to make it one". Thus, it seems, the walled city of Lahore could be much older than the citadel itself.

That is why there is need for archaeological research at different points inside the walled city, and outside, and to take samples from much deeper depths. The scientific record could then piece together an impressive scientific history of Lahore. This could prove to be the building blocks of a truly authentic history of the city.

It is important that we have an idea of what Lahore looked liked before the Muslim invaders came to this city. The writings in *Hudud-al-Alam* clearly demarcate the outer walls of the city. On one side is the western wall that runs along where today we have the Bazaar Hakeeman. If you have been to the old walled city, you will notice that all streets that turn off eastwards are all on an incline.

This is where logic seems to suggest and a research by Mufti Ghulam Sarwar Lahori in the 19th century also mentions this, the original western wall was. So Bazaar Hakeeman today runs outside where the ancient walls existed.

On the southern side the old mud wall ran very much inside where the present wall exists. On the northern side the wall starts from the top of the 'tibba' that is today known as Tibbi Chowk. The word Tibbi is derived from the word 'tibba', meaning a mound. The wall then ran along this high mound and turned southwards at where today we have the Rang Mahal Chowk at Gumti Bazaar. The word 'gumti' means a curved mound. The eastern wall ran, as evidence shows us, just to the west of the main Shahalami road right up to Said Mitha Bazaar.

If you walk along the road starting from Shahalam Gate, you will notice that all the streets to the west are inclined. On this incline was the old mud wall. In this way the ancient walled city of Lahore existed within this area. The River Arvada (Ravi) flowed around this city as mentioned in Sujan Rai Bhandari's book. It might interest readers to know that in *Hudud-al-Alam,* the Shahalami area is referred to as 'rarra maidan' - barren ground. This ancient Lahore was only one-third of the old walled city of Lahore that we know today.

Just as proof of this, it might also strike the reader that the graves of the early Muslims are all outside this area that we call ancient Lahore. The Muslims always buried their dead outside cities. For example, the graves of Malik Ayaz, Syed Ali Hujwairi, Syed Zanjani, Sadr Dewan, etc., are all outside the areas we have mentioned. Thus Bhatti, Lahori and Mori gates are the oldest of the 13 gates we have today. The rest came later. Also that Mori Gate was specifically made by the Hindu population to take their dead outside to cremate on the river that flowed outside.

So we have a faint outline of where the oldest dwellings of Lahore sprung up some time in the midst of antiquity. There is need for genuine archaeological research inside the walled city to determine just what our past was. As man goes into space to learn about our past in terms of millions of years, surely it makes sense for us to learn something about our past just a few thousand years down the road to antiquity.

Lohari or Lahori an ancient legacy

The 13 gates of the old walled city of Lahore, or 12 plus a 'mori' as goes the popular saying, all have a history of their own. Within each gate live a people, distinctly different from others living inside the other gates. The way they speak, their tone and tenor, the drawl, even the expressions, definitely vary, and in this variation they revel. It is their identity.

It is about time that each gate be examined separately, for its history and culture is unique. The starting point has to be Lohari Gate or Lohari Darwaza as it is commonly known for this is the southern-most gate of the walled city. This is where my friend Syed Sikander Shah, a former banker and now gentleman-at-large, comes in. He always claims that his ancestral Icchara, starting from Miani Sahib, is where the original Lahore dwelt over 1,500 years ago. Therefore, our Icchara cousins claim that the real name was Lahori Gate and not Lohari Gate, as it faced Lahore in the pre-Muslim era, which they claim is the original village of Lahore. However, history tells us that Raja Jaipal fought from behind the ramparts of this gate, and when he failed his people in defeating Mahmud in two major battles to the West of the Indus, he came to Lahore and performed the Hindu sacrifice of 'Johar' or devotion by cremating himself, an act of supreme valour in the eyes of the Hindu Chauhan Rajput rajas of Lahore. The site of the actual cremation is between Mori Gate and Lohari Gate. It is ironic that he remains, for obvious reasons, an unacknowledged first original hero of our city.

The exact and precise location of Jaipal's Lahore is probably at Paniwala Talab, or the nearby Mohallah Maulian. In *Tarikh-e-Lahore* Kanhaiyya Lal claims, at one place, that the city was an open city without fortifications, yet at another place he claims that Jaipal fought Mahmud of Ghazni from behind the walls of the city and its closed gates. The walls were huge mud walls. He claims that Lohari Darwaza was the oldest gate of the city, though there is also ample evidence to support the fact that 'Mori Darwaza' is even older. Standing between Mori Gate and Shahalami Gate, it faces the Anarkali Bazaar to the south. Outside the gate, to the right, is the famous Muslim Masjid. To the left is a commercial building. Just who allowed them permission to build seems to be a closed chapter, for the Ancient Monuments Act seems to least interest our city 'fathers'.

After Jaipal, Lahore was ruled by his son Anandpal. When Mahmud finally did capture in 1021 and put Lahore to the sword, the first Muslim Governor, Ayaz Malik, quickly rebuilt the devastated Lohari Gate. According to H.R. Goulding, Lohari Gate was the only gate rebuilt and one source claims that the gate was rebuilt within one day, to protect the Muslims invaders from the original army of Lahore retaking it. Hence the tradition that it was the only gate that faced Lahore, and had top military priority. One can imagine even today that if 2,000 soldiers started building a mud wall and gate, it could be done within a day. This claim definitely adds a lot of myth to this most ancient of gates, as it was the main, if not the only gate, of ancient Lahore. According to Al-Biruni: "The sovereignity of India became extinct once Lahore finally fell in 1022, a year after it was tortured. This time it was completely plundered and no descendant remained to light a fire on the hearth".

The importance of Lohari Gate can also be gauged from the fact that the first Muslim ruler of the sub-continent, Qutbuddin Aibak, left Lohari Gate to play polo outside it, and fell from his horse and died. He lies buried just outside the gate which was once a garden of Lohari Gate, but now is part of Anarkali Bazaar. It was during the times of Akbar the Great that the gate was rebuilt in burnt brick and a 'drawbridge' installed. I remember in my youth my grandmother telling me about the three remaining drawbridges that she had seen herself. One of them was the Lohari Gate drawbridge. But that is another story.

Emperor Akbar enlarged the city to somewhat near its present size, though the outer walls were along bazaars Hakeeman and Shahalami. It was in later years that it expanded to its present position, for beyond Shahalami was known as 'rarra maidan'. Even from this point of view, it makes ample sense that Lohari Gate was the main gate of Lahore. When Mughal rule weakened and the

King Akbar

Sikhs, Marathas and Afghans kept attacking Lahore, all gates were walled up except Lohari, Delhi and Khizri, now known as Sheranwala, as that was the ferry station of old Lahore.

Behind the gate is Lohari Mandi, or the blacksmiths' market. This is a strange name, for the blacksmiths actually exist between Lohari and Shahalami. It goes without saying that, perhaps, Lohari Bazaar is one of the oldest markets of the old walled city. The main bazaar inside the gate runs up to what was once known as Chowk Chakla, or the Prostitutes Square. Other references tell us that this was the original red-light area of Lahore. With time it moved northwards near Chowk Jhanda, and then on to Tibbi Bazaar. Here it rested for many centuries, till President Ayub Khan, advised as he was by 'pious religious pirs' decided to ban the oldest profession. Thus from Chowk Chakla of over 1,000 years old, the profession moved outside the walled city towards Shahdara and then Allama Iqbal Town and now even to posh areas. Containment has never been the strength of our city fathers, for acceptance of ground realities is not the norm. Chowk Chakla was renamed Chowk Bukhari. Here the bazaar bifurcates and one heads towards Sootar Mandi while the other heads towards Chowk Jhanda, on to Said Mittha Bazaar and then to Hira Mandi. The right branch extends to Rang Mahal.

The beauty of Chowk Chakla is that it extends from the first crossing in Lohari Bazaar right up to the baradari of Wazir Khan. Even today there is a huge haveli, opposite the Sheikh Mubarak Ali bookshop, called 'Kanjaran-de-haveli'. It now has been renovated and the oldest profession is nowhere in sight. At Chowk Chakla one can see the 'Baghicha Masjid Kharasian', built in 1606, where the original 'katba' inscription in Persian by the calligrapher Abdullah al-Hussaini still adorns the staircase. Next to it are the stables of Maharajah Kharrak Singh, and then there is the Temple of Krishna Maharaj, with four statues of Shiva, Parvati, Ganesh and Surya. It was in its heydays one of the most beautiful temples in Lahore, the city that gave birth to Rama, his wife

Sita, and their sons Lahu and Kasu, for from Lahu came the word Lahore. No other area of Lahore has so much history packed into it as does the streets and gate of Lohari ... for each one is a separate story, and there is also in the main bazaar a haveli called 'Dastaango Haveli'. So the story continues, as it has over thousands of years.

History comes full circle

We live in strange times, and a lot of us seem baffled by what is happening around us. Current analyses seem inadequate and unconvincing. Every 10 experts have 11 theories. Probably it seems appropriate that we go over our past to understand what awaits us in the immediate future.

The last time we were faced with foreign armies on our soil was when the British had taken the whole of India minus the Punjab. The Punjab was from Ferozepur to the Khyber and from the Sindh border to Kashmir. The Hindustanis, or the *purbias* as we knew them then, were in the east, busy helping the British plan for the invasion of the Punjab. To the west, the crafty Maharajah Ranjit Singh had actually helped the British capture Afghanistan. The situation was so very similar to what it is today. The raiding and looting Afghans had been humbled. So in a way, our western border was secure, or so we imagined. The modern indigenous army was a match for anything that the British could throw at them, and that is what kept them at bay. An uneasy peace prevailed. To the north was Kashmir where an uneasy rebellion existed and the the Dogras were waiting to flex their muscles. To the south was Sindh where the British had managed to establish their stranglehold. In short, the British had surrounded the Punjab and the imperial Lahore darbar was uneasy.

In the Lahore Fort, the court of Ranjit Singh was in session. A British cartographer was showing him a map of India. The entire sub-continent was red save for the portion that represented the Punjab. The completely illiterate one-eyed Ranjit Singh asked his foreign minister, Fakir

Azizuddin, whose descendants' Fakirkhana still exists as a museum in Bazaar Hakeeman inside Bhatti Gate, what did the red colour mean. On being told it was the area under British control, he turned towards his courtiers and said: *"Eik roz sab lal ho jaiga"* (one day the entire map will be red). Within 10 years, by the spring of 1849, his prediction had come true.

What Ranjit Singh had managed in his reign was to bring a completely divided nation of warring tribes into a solidly welded nation. It was strong and prosperous, and most important; it ceased forever to be the cockpit of foreign armies fighting their battles on foreign soil. But wise as he was, his greatest fault was that no one else thrived to succeed him. It was the classic banyan tree casting its shadow over everything that was under its fold. Within 10 years the Punjab had been enslaved again.

There are a lot of theories going around that the Afghans have always managed to, eventually, beat back all invaders. In the case of the Lahore Darbar, the Maharajah gave clear instructions to his military commander Sheikh Bassan, that he should be as ruthless as possible when dealing with the Afghans; not to strike any deal, and once he had assisted the British establish their control, he was to pull out all troops. So swift and ruthless was the thrust from the Khyber that within days Kabul fell. The British took their time coming up from Kandahar, where Shah Shuja was helping them regain his throne. In the end, a Punjabi expeditionary force had to be sent to further assist them. This managed to crush the Afghans and a victory parade was held in Kabul.

At this point the wise foreign minister Fakir Azizuddin recommended that only Muslim soldiers parade in Kabul, and that once the parade was over, they should head home. "Never stay in Kabul, for you will soon have nothing left to bring back". Ranjit Singh followed his advice, and after the parade he left a small trade office there and the rest of his army returned immediately. What happened to the British afterwards we all know.

There has always been a distinct difference between the manner in which the armies of Kabul and the armies of Lahore conducted themselves. The Afghans were basically in the business of looting, and in the process they killed and raped. The Punjabis were never in this business. If they acquired territory they immediately left after making sure that they got an annual return for their protection. The Lahore Darbar had made sure that they remained in the business of economic consolidation at home. They were the first *swadeshis* and set into motion a movement that preached pride in all things *desi*. A century later Mahatma Gandhi, relaunched the *swadeshi* movement.

If we are to analyse the behaviour patterns of the Afghans and the Pakistanis today, one cannot help noticing that the same trends still exist, but in slightly differing variations. The Afghans to the west still have their extremist way of doing things, which is their right to do, as long as it does not affect the people of the Indus Valley, who remain basically moderate. The current situation has seen the vast majority wanting to desperately plug 'immoderates' among us. To the east remain the *purbias,* planning and plotting away. What they say they do not mean and what they mean they do not say. Nothing could be more non-Punjabi than this. Today, history has come full circle, and there is many a lesson to be learnt from it. But then as a well-known American said: "History is crap".

Famines in Lahore

Over the last 2,000 years, Lahore, and the Punjab, have been hit by almost 20 major famines, with a major famine being classified as one lasting more than three consecutive years. For the most the granaries of Lahore held out hope, but there have been grim times in the past, much grimmer than we can ever imagine today.

If we look up the records and consult various history books, we will notice that Lahore has faced a major famine after almost every 100 years on the average. The worst one lasted almost six years, and things were so bad that people wanting to get into the city were shut out and starvation reached a level where people had to resort to cannibalism to survive. Such a situation is difficult to imagine today, but this has happened thrice in our history. Every time the famine crossed the four-year mark, reports of cannibalism surfaced.

We must research and record these gruesome events to understand who we are, and what we have been through. In a way it also is the underlying reason of the way we behave even today as a collective lot. Lahore is definitely about magnificent buildings, with a history a few cities on earth can parallel; it is also about gardens, about poets, about universities. But more importantly, Lahore is about people. This city is what it is because of the people who have lived, and continue to live here. That is why what befell them needs to be told so that it never happens again. We have a habit of blotting out the scars in our collective lives, and the scars left by terrible famines need to be seen, to be felt, to be believed today.

These famines have certainly not been fleeting moments in our history, which goes back thousands of years. A lot of our folk songs, our collective behaviour patterns, all flow from such terrible events. The first recorded famine to hit Lahore was in the year 650. Though famine existed throughout the sub-continent in that year, people from far and wide in the Punjab came to Lahore and surrounded it thinking that its granaries had food for them. The Hindu Rajput Raja certainly was well stocked and he helped his subjects considerably. But people were dying on the streets, of sheer hunger. The next major famine to hit Lahore was in the year 879, when the granaries inside the city were attacked, and because of the law and order collapse, the famine spread. In the process the population had to be quelled with force by the Bhat Raja. Once order was restored, food was made available.

But the worst famine to hit Lahore was in 941, and it continued till the year 1022. This hit the entire Punjab as well as the entire sub-continent, and people died by the millions. One estimate is that 35 per cent of the population of the Punjab died in that famine. The population fell drastically and every day scores of dead would be found on the streets, dead from sheer hunger and exhaustion. To add to our miseries, our Afghan 'brothers' launched their first major invasion, ruthlessly killing whoever stood in their way. They removed to Afghanistan a major portion of our scarce wheat and rice, even though our textbooks say they came to spread Islam.

Then there was, finally, relief, and a bumper crop followed after major floods hit the city and its surrounding areas. The land was well fertilized and for many a year bumper crops were reported. The granaries remained full and life returned to normal. In a way these prosperous times led Lahore to becoming a great city. The rise of Lahore owes itself to the prosperity that bumper crops brought. This remains the pattern even today.

But by 1148 another famine hit Lahore, and it continued till 1159. Though it had spread all over India, where its effect was far greater, Lahore suffered as thousands died on its streets. Two good years followed and, before confidence could return, in 1162 another famine hit the city. Foreign invasions and famines seemed to come hand in hand. In 1344-45 the Great famine in India took place, when the Mughal emperor was unable to obtain the necessaries for his own household. The famine continued for years and millions perished. In 1396 right up to 1407, The Durga Devi famine in India, lasting 12 years, took place. Lahore was devastated.

But then super floods followed and life again returned to normal. The granaries of Lahore were known to be the largest in the sub-continent and the Mughals for this reason took a special interest in Lahore. Then came the Great Famine of Bengal from 1769 to 1770, and a third of the population (10,000,000) perished. It was a tragedy beyond comprehension. In this time period Lahore managed well, though in 1798 it had a very dry year. But in 1783 'The Chalisa Famine' took place affecting Lahore and Jammu, where thousands died. Though the city of Lahore managed to ration its wheat and maintain law and order, it was during this famine that the Kashmiri population moved to Lahore. Today we have a major Kashmiri population because of that famine.

In 1790 The Doji Bara, or skull famine, hit India. It was so called because the people died in such numbers that they could not be buried. According to tradition this was one of the severest famines ever known. This famine lasted four years and in this also cases of cannibalism were reported. It was during this time period that Lahore's Mori Gate was built to remove the hundreds of dead for cremation on the River Ravi that flowed outside its walls.

After the 'skull famine' followed a series of major famines, which research now tell us took place because the British were taking over major stocks of our grains. This aspect of British imperialism has never been discussed. In 1838 an "intense famine hit North-West Provinces (United Provinces) of India in which 800,000 perished."

In 1861 another major famine hit Northwest India in which 500,000 died of starvation. In 1866 a major famine hit Bengal and Orissa in which one million perished. In 1869 a major famine affected Rajputana; one million and a half perished. In 1876 a major famine hit central and western India in which 5,000,000 died. Lahore was badly hit and its granaries were almost empty.

In 1897 yet another famine came about, while in 1899 right up to 1901 the last major famine hit Lahore. In this famine over one million people died in the subcontinent. Our people have seen terrible times. Famines have fashioned the way we behave, our insecurities are more 'famine related' than anything else. Thanks to modern transportation famines are a thing of the past, at least in Pakistan, unless we make a right royal mess of the way we manage our scarce water resources. But then that is politics. Imagine.

Basant and the Sufi saint

Few would know that Basant Panchami, the ancient spring festival that is celebrated with such gusto in Lahore, is also celebrated by the Muslims of the sub-continent at the dargah of Nizamuddin Aulia at Delhi, every year. This 700-year-old colourful tradition is attributed to the Sufis, especially the Chishti saint and his disciple, Hazrat Amir Khusrau, who were probably the first Muslims to have rejoiced at the celebration of Basant.

Hazrat Nizamuddin Aulia

Legend has it that the Chishti saint experienced Basant in Lahore during a visit to the shrine of Hazrat Data Ganj Bakhsh, and willed that his disciples celebrate life and spring with the same gusto as was done in that city. However, the celebration was confined to the dargah of the saint, and to this day it is celebrated with kite flying, feasting, recitals of classical music, especially 'raag basant', and with light raags. Later, however, the dargah added 'qawalis' to the fare. One imagines that the spirit of the day was being dampened by the conservatives that took over the establishment of the dargah.

Two interesting changes have taken place in Lahore and Delhi over the last five years. In Lahore, the conservative religious extreme, which seems to have established a 'monopoly' on the morality of the population, (much as it is detested) has sought to kill off the very festival itself. In Delhi, which had over the centuries almost killed the festival because of the sway of the conservatives, have managed to turn this Lahori festival into a major money-spinning event.

My guess is that over the next few years, Basant Panchami will become one of India's main tourist attractions. It is almost like our sporting industry in Sialkot has been hijacked by a fake Sialkot in India. In the case of Basant, I firmly believe that this is an occasion that is impossible to hijack.

The beauty of Basant lies in the fact that it is truly a festival of the people, be they blue, black or white, be they be of any religious hue. Spring has this ability to bring out the optimists in us. It is an unprompted response. One cannot help it. Unlike the warrior extremists who see life in black and white terms only, it were the great Sufi saints of the sub-continent who

Hazrat Amir Khusrau

vividly saw the people, especially the poor, in colourful shades and tones. From Data Ganj Bakhsh to Hazrat Nizamuddin Aulia to Bulleh Shah, all of them saw the beauty of the inner spirit in the changing shades of spring, the bursting into life of the yellow flowers in our mustard fields.

The basic fact remains, irrespective of whom or what one worships, that our fortunes are firmly rooted in our land. The starting point is the fact spring means that the sun will soon dry our wheat and we will be assured food for another year. Let alone the ancient religions of the Jains or the Hindus or the Buddhists, all of which flourished in Lahore in their day, the Muslim saints gave it new meaning. The Sikhs celebrate it as 'Baisakhi' on the fifth day of 'Basaikh' in the lunar calendar. The ban on kites over most of the year has badly damaged this ancient festival. The reason is solely the use of metal wires, which is surely an unsporting tactic in a sport that is all about being happy. One cannot be happy and unfair at the same time. That is why if one were to concentrate on nabbing 'wire users' only, and to punish them in a nice sort of way, by making them ride donkeys with blackened faces, maybe then the 'law' would be enforced.

It would make greater sense if the population were asked to participate in nabbing wire flyers and handing them over to the police. On this the authorities need everyone's support. On banning, they do not deserve any support. It is silly to ban kite flying just because a few cheat at it. If that logic is followed, then every sport, including the most enjoyable one, would be banned.

In our youth, before night kite flying started, we loved making paper lantern balloons. At night the entire old walled city of Lahore would have paper lanterns floating in the sky. It was an exquisite experience. Lahore on Basant will be as beautiful, or as ugly, as we make it. I wish the Indians the best of luck in their effort to cash in on Basant. There is need for us, Lahoris, to use the occasion not to ban visits, or dull any celebration, but to take it to new heights. I for one will be enjoying myself.

Data Darbar, where there is something for everyone

When anyone talks of Lahore, at some point there has to be a mention of Data Ganj Bakhsh. He died in the year 465 AH and today it is 1,429 Hijri, almost 964 lunar years, or over 900 Gregorian years. That is a very long time and life around his shrine has been the same. But what is life really like around his shrine?

Data Darbar

We all know about him and most of us, at some stage, out of sheer curiosity or out of reverence, have visited the place. For the last 32 years as a journalist who lived just round the corner from the shrine, one has seen kings, presidents, prime ministers, governors; ministers and various other luminaries come and go.

But then beggars and pickpockets are also present in exceedingly large numbers, not to speak of the hungry or the lost. The pious are there and so are the crooks, probably more of the latter than the former. What goes on around this shrine is also part of the history of this city, and in days gone by Data Ganj Bakhsh was known as Ali Makhdum Ganj Bakhsh Hujwairi Lahori, for this is the way people in other lands know him. Who was he, after all, and why is he so respected almost a thousand years after his death?

Data Ganj Bakhsh came to Lahore in AH 431 from Ghazni in Afghanistan and he came with Sultan Mas'ud, the son of Sultan Mahmood Ghazni. He originally belonged to Hujwairi, and because of this, it became part of his name. Interestingly enough, the earlier accounts call him Sheikh Ali Makhdum Ghaznavi Lahori, and not Hujwairi, surely because he came with Mahmood Ghaznavi's son. The first wave of Muslim conquerors from the west saw the riches of the sub-continent being looted by the Afghani hordes. After the death of Mahmood Ghaznavi, came his son and the second wave of conquests. But with them also came many a saint whose sole objective was to spread the word of God, and among the first to come was Data Ganj Bakhsh. It would interest even an avid Lahori who claims the man as his own, to know that his ancestors are well marked on his grave. It reads: Here lies Sheikh Ali, son of Syed Usman, son of Syed Ali, son of Syed Abdur Rahman, son of Syed Abdullah, son of Syed Abul Hasan Ali, son of Syed Hasan, son of Syed Zaid Shaheed, son of Imam Hasan, son of Ali Murtaza, which is to say that Sheikh Ali Makhdum Ganj Bakhsh Hujwairi Lahori was just eight generations down the line from the Holy Prophet (peace be upon him).

But in matters of religious apprenticeship, he was a student (mureed) of Khwaja Abul Fazl, who was a student of Sheikh Ali Jafri, who learnt from Sheikh Shibli, who was a student of Junaid Baghdadi, who was a student of Syed Saqti, who was a student of Maruf Karkhi, who learnt from Dawud Tai, who learnt from Habib Ajmi, who was a student of Hasan of Basra, who was a student of Ali Murtaza. Complicated as this lineage is, it led to the birth of Sheikh Ali Makhdum, now known all over the world as Data Ganj Bakhsh.

So there he came to Lahore and planted himself in a small mud house just outside Bhatti Gate in AH 431. In those days, so the legend goes, a powerful Hindu magician was the religious leader of the population of Lahore, who were almost all Hindus or Jains. This magician challenged the young scholar and it is claimed, though I would tend to disbelieve any such assertion, that the magician actually flew in the air over the hut of Ali Hujwairi. The saint dismissed such displays as 'showing off' and after reciting the last two 'quls,' he blew towards the magician who fell to the ground and ran away. Word to this effect spread through the city, which was then enclosed in mud walls, and soon people, almost all Hindus, came to seek his blessings. It was then that he decided to stay on and serve the people with his knowledge and deep understanding of the human psyche. In a way, Lahore came to him, and he adopted it, and it was then that it was said that, "kings and beggars are alike before the saint." Almost 900 years later, it is still true.

The best thing is that people of every religion came here. Imagine that great scholars and saints like Khwaja Moinuddin Chishti of Ajmer and Khwaja Farid of Pakpattan spent considerable time at this shrine in meditation and prayer. It was only during the time of Maharajah Ranjit Singh that the outer madrassah was vandalized for its exquisite marble and engravings. But then the Sikhs did this to almost every shrine or tomb in Lahore. A day after the marble was removed, the Maharajah began to vomit, as one account puts it. He was advised to appease the saint for the damage done to the outer building. So the Maharajah set an annual income for the shrine and from then onwards always paid his respects when he passed that way. During the time of Z.A. Bhutto a grand outer building came up, and the Shah of Iran sent an exquisite door of gold and turquoise, which one can see even today. Nawaz Sharif went the full distance by rebuilding an entire mosque, and a beautiful one at that.

And if you look at the edges of all this grandeur, you will see extreme poverty. It is a haven for pickpockets and kidnappers. During my days as a young crime reporter, our team unearthed a 'school of pickpockets' that had an elementary textbook on ways to pick pockets and the language used by them. We had then alleged that it was run by the police, but that was almost 25 years ago. Nothing came of the story. I learn that even today the area is auctioned out to such rascals, to use a Victorian phrase. And then there are the cookery houses. You can buy a whole 'deg' of sweet rice, or meat or 'pilau' to distribute among the poor, who roam around the area in large numbers. For the hungry, it is a guaranteed meal. For everyone there is something there. So it has been for over 900 years. The shrine of Data Ganj Bakhsh is something to everyone... and that is the way it will always be.

If wishes were horses

In our youth my father loved going, just for a few hours, to the annual Mela that accompanies the Urs of Hazrat Madho Lal Hussain near the Shalimar Gardens. For him it was a reminder of happier days spent 'in a higher state'. Knowing him they were definitely not of the spiritual kind. He was too sane for that.

On the way back he would bring us a few mud-baked horses, and his comment every time was: "Make your wishes and the horses will deliver". These were the mud-baked horses 'khuggoo ghorray' from the shrine of Ghorray Shah, the child saint of Lahore. The popular myth is that if one brought the child saint his favourite pastime horses be it real or be it simple mud-baked ones, any wish made at his shrine is fulfilled. There are thousands, if not hundreds of thousands, of people who believe that the child saint delivers, for he is pure of heart. At the annual Urs celebration of Lahore's patron child saint, people leave behind thousands of 'khuggoo ghorray', some beautifully painted, and others just plain baked clay red, each person making their own wish.

Who was this child saint? The grandfather of the child saint was a holy man, a saint, who came from Uch in Sindh to Lahore almost 400 years ago. His name was Syed Usman Shah and he was considered among the learned religious persons in Lahore in those days. However, he suffered from Parkinson's disease, which in the local language is called 'Choolay' or tremors. In Punjabi and Urdu it is called 'Raasha'. Because of this disease he was known in Lahore as Choolay Shah, or, more respectfully, as Choolay Shah Bukhari. Such was the fame of the man, and so influential was he, that on his death he was buried inside the Lahore Fort. Many a miracle is ascribed to this old saint and scholar.

The son of Choolay Shah, by the name of Syed Shah Muhammad, acquired the seat 'gaddi' of his father. He was also known for his scholarship and respected in the city as a holy man. His son, born in 997 Hijra (AH), was named Syed Bahauddin Shah, but soon came to be lovingly called Choolan Shah, meaning the Shah who plays on swings. The name was, obviously, a clever derivative from the name of his grandfather 'Choolay' Shah. The people of Lahore excel in naming people after one attribute or the other, always having a touch of humour to it, yet vivid and sensitive in its rendition.

As soon as Choolan Shah began to talk and walk about, it became clear this child was a special gifted one. Even his own mother began to inform her husband that everything the child wishes, or says, happens. The father, himself a religious scholar with a large following because of Choolay Shah, always prayed to Allah to protect the child and do what is best for him. At the age of five, Bahauddin Shah took a liking for horses and learnt to ride them with great skill. But as he did not have his own horse, he asked people to allow him to ride theirs.

The people of Lahore respected the wishes of the son of a saintly scholar, and often allowed him to ride their horses. After the ride, he would inform them that if they had a wish, they could tell him. Those who did were immediately informed that the wish would be granted. Probably he was copying his father, who dealt with people coming to him for solutions to their problems. But very soon everyone realized that every time Choolan Shah told people that their wish would be granted, it actually was.

Among the poor who did not own horses, people presented him with mud-baked horses known as 'khuggoo ghorray', their wishes were granted. His fame spread in the city and the environs, and soon his father learned that he was granting wishes to people for riding their horses. He called his son and severely scolded him. It is said, so the story goes, that he told his son that instead of granting wishes to people at this young age, it would be better if he dropped dead. The heart-broken child is said to have looked skyward, fell on his knees crying, and died there and then, much to the shock of the angry father. The father, so the legend goes, asked Allah's forgiveness and was 'instructed' to bury him on the spot Allah took his life away, for the child had asked the Almighty to take his life away, and his wish was never turned down. It is a powerful story to say the least.

So Syed Bahauddin Shah *alias* Choolan Shah alias Ghorray Shah, the child saint of Lahore, was buried at the very spot he died in the year 1003 Hijra (AH). His shrine is just before the Shalimar Gardens when coming from the Engineering University on a street to the left side of the road. The street is called Ghooray Gali. Today a huge shrine exists where hundreds come every day to present the little child saint with a mud toy horse. Thousands of mud toy horses lie piled around the grave of this saintly child. It is a beautiful gesture which most people, especially children, in Lahore make at least once in a lifetime. The belief is that he still grants wishes when he gets his toy horse.

The curse of Gazoroni

In the walled city of Lahore it has happened a number of times; it happened to a Mughal prince, it happened to Maharajah Ranjit Singh himself, it happened to a British army commander, it happened also to a well-known Pakistani mayor. Old folk call it the 'Gazoroni Curse'.

When the ruler of Lahore, Wazir Khan, decided to build the famous mosque that today bears his name, he was looking for a place that constituted the centre of the city as it was then. In those days the elite looked towards Delhi for inspiration, just as we, today, look towards Islamabad, not that there is much inspiration there. So Delhi Darwaza (gate) and the road to the Lahore Fort was the most important boulevard in the city. If you have noted, it is the straightest road in the walled city.

The caravans that arrived from the east landed up in the 'serais' that were located around a open space opposite the location where today stands Wazir Khan's Mosque, at the very end of the Kashmiri Bazaar as it winds its way towards the mosque from Rang Mahal. In, days gone by, this was the epicenter of the walled city, the business centre, the storytellers' dwellings, where the famous Lahori hand-written leather-bound books were sold, where the horses and camels rested at the nearby 'nakkaskhana', where the serais were.

The subedar of Lahore, Nawab Wazir Khan, had built a beautiful haveli at the edge of Taxali Gate, which touched the old gate wall. On one side he built a beautiful small mosque, which is also called the Taxali Wazir Khan Mosque.

The British demolished the western wall of Lahore to remove any danger of the city raising a siege against them, with the 1857 siege of Delhi weighing heavily on their minds. In the process, they also demolished the beautiful haveli. However, the mosque was left alone and even today it stands, though in a very rundown condition.

Shrine of Syed Garozoni

But being a subedar, he wanted to build a bigger mosque, and he had the finest skilled workers at his disposal. His advisers pointed out to the open space, but it had one major flaw, and that being that in the middle of the land selected stood the grave of Mizra Syed Ishaque Gazoroni, also known popularly as 'Miran Badshah'. At this grave every year a sort of Urs took place, and both Hindus and Muslims revered him locally as a saint.

The clever and powerful subedar set about planning his mosque by first seeking the advice of the well-known Hindu pundits and Muslim ulema of Lahore. All of them advised that there was no problem as long as the grave was not damaged or entrance to it not restricted, and that the remains of this saint were respected. One pundit, as one source puts it, claimed that he had communicated with the spirit of the dead saint and he was happy that a mosque was being built there. And so in these circumstances, the exquisite and beautiful mosque of Wazir Khan was built on the grave of Syed Gazoroni or Syed Miran Badshah. The architects designed it in such a fashion that it incorporated the grave, which is actually in the basement of the mosque. In fact, this mosque is built on a grave, just like the Governor's House.

Once a Mughal prince, or so legend has it, walked about admiring the new mosque, and he took fancy to a Hindu devotee of Miran Badshah. It is not known what exactly the prince did, but the fact is that he fell ill, and it was only after he returned to seek the saint's forgiveness that he recovered. This was excellent stuff put out by the 'mujawars' of the grave of Syed Gazoroni, and so his legend grew in the walled city. A visit to the mosque also meant that everyone called on the saint and left their offerings to him, though in reality the 'mujawar' filled his coffers.

In the days when Maharajah Ranjit Singh took over the city and converted almost all its mosques into ammunition dumps, he ordered that the mosque of Wazir Khan be left to him as he wanted to use it as his pleasure palace. Once he had set it up he took his favourite keep, Moran, there and both of them spent the whole day drinking and, naturally, enjoying themselves. When he was about to leave, a strong and sharp pain arose in his entire body, and the Maharajah doubled up.

This incident has been quoted by three different scholars of the Sikh era. For three days and three nights the Maharajah was in acute pain and there were fears that he might die. At the same time Moran also suffered the same fate. The very best 'hakeems' and vaids tried everything possible on both of them, but to no effect. The fear of food poisoning passed as it was maintained that if it were poison, in three days it would have had its effect Yet no sign appeared of any illness, just a sharp pain in the entire body, especially the stomach, of both the Maharajah and Moran. The mujawar of Syed Gazoroni appeared before the Maharajah and informed him that as he had enjoyed himself inside the mosque, the curse of the saint was upon him.

The Hindu and Muslim seers working for the maharajah did their calculations and confirmed that it was indeed the Curse of Gazoroni: and the only way out was to return to the mosque, repent his acts and restore the mosque to its original use. This the Maharajah did, and offered 101 'degs' of rice for the poor, and till the day he died, a monthly stipend was sent for the upkeep of the mosque. It may come as a surprise that while the Badshahi Mosque remained a stable and an ammunition dump, like almost all the other mosques inside the walled city, the Wazir Khan Mosque was the sole one functioning for prayers for the Muslims of Lahore.

Moran made a promise to build a new mosque for the Muslims, and she built the beautiful 'Moran de Masjid', which even today stands as testimony to her devotion to Syed Gazoroni. Much later a British army commander, who had heard of the story of the maharajah and the saint, met the same fate and he also apologised and took his leave of Lahore. A well-known mayor of Lahore tried to take over the mujawar contract and in the process insulted the saint. He also suffered considerably. And so stories of Syed Gazoroni and his powers within the Wazir Khan's Mosque are still told inside the walled city, and they add to the mystique of the most beautiful mosque in Lahore.

Facts and fiction of the seers at Nila Gumbad

Almost every person living in Lahore, or its environs, knows about Nila Gumbad. Yet very few have ever bothered to stop, go into the building and explore what lies within. It is a very simple, yet exceptionally beautiful structure, and is only second in beauty to the Nila Gumbad of Delhi, though its history is far more intriguing.

The mosque called Nila Gumbad was originally a mausoleum of Sheikh Abdul Razzaq Makki. This seer migrated to Lahore in the times of the Mughal Emperor Humayun from the holy city of Mecca in Arabia. In Lahore he became a pupil of Meeran Muhammad Shah Mauj Darya Bukhari. In the world of Sufi

Nila Gumbad

exploration he is known to have achieved a special status. His following grew to such an extent that thousands are known to have devoted themselves to serving Sheikh Makki. Almost the entire business community of Lahore could be counted among his followers. The Sufi saint died in the year 1084 Hijrah and was buried in the place now known as Nila Gumbad.

His followers built the mausoleum, which was surrounded by beautiful gardens. The main building has three domes, the main one being of blue tiles, the inner portions were lined with copper. It was in its days said to rival the Nila Gumbad of Delhi, with many believing that it was much more beautiful. On the walls were precious stones and very expensive fresco decorations. The advent of Sikh rule in Lahore in 1799 saw the buildings face terrible times. Maharajah Ranjit Singh visited the place and ordered that the graves not be disturbed, but that the copper and all the precious stones be removed. He also ordered that the blue tiles and the red sandstone outside be also removed and sent to Amritsar.

Once this damage was dome, he ordered that the placed be handed over to the Sikh Army, who were to use it as an ammunition dump. To one side he ordered that a small armament factory be made, and so on the lawns of the mausoleum of Sheikh Makki, rifle manufacturing started. For a full half a century such was the fate of Nila Gumbad. With the advent of the British in 1849, the ammunition factory was, naturally, closed and the ammunition dump removed. As they set up their military cantonment in the present Old Anarkali, they got the mausoleum whitewashed and converted it into a posh restaurant for the officers of the East India Company. It was known by many as the 'Company Langar'. Some old people inside the walled city still refer to this place as such.

When the cantonment was shifted to the Mian Mir Cantonment, a Muslim food contractor by the name of Munshi Najmuddin 'Doubleroti Thakedar' moved an application with the British authorities claiming that the place was a mosque, and as such he would like to invest to restore it. The British handed over Nila Gumbad to him. It must be said that he and the business community of Lahore contributed and got the building restored. With the original precious stones missing, it remains, still, a shadow of its original class. Today the building is officially called the Masjid Najmuddin, though the people still call it Nila Gumbad Masjid.

But more important than the grave of Sheikh Makki is a grave just outside the mosque, which is that of Khawaja Muhammad Saeed Lahori. The small room built outside the mosque has three graves, they being those of Khawaja Lahori, of Haji Obaidullah and of Abdur Rahman, a nephew of Khawaja Lahori. So in one compound lie five very important religious persons of Lahore, each with a history all their own, yet today forgotten. The fifth grave is that of

Hazrat Shah Sharf.

Hazrat Shah Sharf was a well-known Sufi seer in the days of Aurangzeb, who was known for his immense powers of the 'unknown'. Many a miracle is attributed to him. He was buried in a beautiful tomb just near Bhatti Gate. When Maharajah Ranjit Singh came to power, he immediately started rebuilding the fallen walls of the old city. In his expansion plans the tomb of Shah Sharf was a hindrance. He orderéd that the tomb be demolished.

At this junction the famous Fakir family of Bazaar Hakeeman requested the new Sikh ruler to shift the remains of the saint to another place, lest some evil befell his curse. The Maharajah agreed and when the grave was dug, almost 125 years after being buried, the body of Shah Sharf was found to be fresh and warm. Reference to this can be found in the accounts of the fakir family, as well as to an account in the official records. Inside the old walled city, people still talk about this incident.

The body was reburied in the compound that we today call Nila Gumbad. The business community of old Lahore still visits the grave in large numbers. A lot can be written about Shah Sharf and his miracles, but that is another subject. Now we dwell on the last of the seers buried in the Nila Gumbad. Who was Khawaja Lahori ?

Khawaja Muhammad Saeed Lahori was a saint of the Qadriyya tradition, who was known for his immense power over the unseen as one account puts it. He travelled a lot and settled for some time in Kabul. There Ahmad Shah Durrani developed an immense respect for his religious knowledge and skill. During the third attack by Ahmad Shah on Lahore, he came along and just when he had ordered that the entire population be put to death for resisting him and the city be torched, this saint sent a small note to the King of Kabul, in which he said "Do not bother Allah's followers and their saints". This prompted Ahmad Shah to halt the pillage of Lahore, and he came to him and sought forgiveness. Later he also assisted in preventing the slaughter of Sikhs in Lahore in Mohallah Dolawari. He died in 1181 Hijrah.

Ironically, the Sikhs pillaged his tomb when Maharajah Ranjit Singh came to power. Many in Lahore believe that many a curse on Sikh places of worship are because they have not still apologized for the insults inflicted on Khawaja Sahib, a person who worked so hard to prevent many a Sikh slaughter. But then such are the myths of history, an amalgam of fact and fiction.

The moderate saint called Mian Wadda

Just a mile to the south of the Shalimar Gardens, midway from the Lahore Canal, a small road turns inside westwards and curves to a large opening in the centre of which is a massive and ancient banyan tree. On one side is an old gateway, the gateway to the 'Dars' of Mian Wadda, an important saint of Lahore.

The 'Dars', or 'darsgah', call it a school, of Mian Wadda the elder is a monument built in the age of Akbar the Great. Its construction took three years and was completed in the year 1008 Hijra. It has for the last 400 years been a leading madrassah in Lahore teaching students the Quran and Fiqh. During the days of Aurangzeb it faced difficulties, as also in the days after the death of Maharajah Ranjit Singh when the compound was the centre of a major battle among the Sikhs. But over time and through days good and bad, mostly bad, it has stuck to its tradition of open debate.

Once you enter the gateway, you will notice a number of buildings, all of the Akbar-era. In the gardens that once existed around the Dars, graves have filled the green spaces. The main building still has a row of 'hujras', in which scholars, locally called 'dervishes', lived and studied and taught their students. In the once lush gardens, these dervishes and their pupils debated the finer points of Islamic law and its practices.

To one side is a beautiful little mosque, while on the

opposite side is a small animal-driven flour rnill, its old grinding stones can still be seen intact. So the two aspects of life, the godly and the earthly, are represented by these beautiful structures. In its hey days, it would have been a very peaceful place, surrounded by huge banyan trees.

To the centre is a small building that has the grave of Sheikh Muhammad Ismail, the man known as Mian Wadda, and the person who founded this exquisite school of Quranic learning. To one side is the grave of Sheikh Jan Muhammad, on the other are two more graves, that of Sheikh Noor Muhammad and Hafiz Muhammad Saleh.

These were the three pupils of Sheikh Ismail, who originally belonged to Targraan in the Potohar plateau. By caste he was a Khokhar, and they were tillers of the sandy lands to which his ancestors belonged. One account tells us that his father's name was Fatehullah, son of Abdullah, son of Sarfraz Khan. It is said that Fatehullah, his father, learnt the Quran at a very early age and studied Fiqh.

Another account narrates that Fatehullah was a 'hafiz' of the Quran and spent long hours in deep meditation. It is said that he had a huge following at his village Chabba on the banks of the river Chenab. On his death, he was buried in his village. During his life time he made sure that his son Ismail, who was born in the year 995 Hijra, was educated in every aspect of life. He was a 'hafiz' at the age of five and recited the Quran in a most melodious tone. He was made a pupil of Makhdum Abdul Karim of Langar Makhdum on the Chenab.

He lived in his madrassah and learned Fiqh. Being of the Suhrawardy school of thought in Islamic jurisprudence, he went on to reach the highest levels of Islamic learning available in his environment. It was then that his teacher informed him that he should go to Lahore and pray at the 'darbar' of Ali Hujwairi and Allah will show him his way forward, for he predicted that he was to reach even greater pinnacles of learning.

So it was that Sheikh Hafiz Muhammad Ismail came to Lahore and settled in a small village Telpura, a little distance from where the famous Shalimar Gardens was to be built, and from where he could see the outer walls of the city. It was here that he set up his Dars, and within no time it grew into a huge school.

People of every religion flocked to him, for it is said that he performed many a miracle. He died in 1095 Hijra at the ripe age of 100 years. It is said that he had once mentioned that in a dream he was informed that he will die exactly at the age of 100, not a minute before or after, and so it seems his dream came true.

Many a miracle is ascribed to Sheikh Muhammad Ismail, who in his old age was known more by the name of Mian Wadday - the revered elder. This name stuck to his Dars, and even today it is known by this name. Just as he had performed 'miracles', so people of all faiths believed that by making a promise to the saint, their promises would be fulfilled if they fed the blind and the poor at his grave every Thursday. Ironically, the Sikh community of Lahore was a great admirer of Mian Wadday, and during the reign of Maharajah Ranjit Singh, his Dars was well looked after and provided for.

But when the infighting between the Sikhs broke out after the death of Maharajah Ranjit Singh, the raja of Jammu, Raja Sujeet Singh, battled it out with the forces of the darbar. Cannons were fired at his forces camped in the Dars, and the Kashmiri attacker was killed in battle here. Along with his forces, hundreds of dervish scholars of the Quran also perished in the battle.

When the British took over, the famous Muhammad Sultan, the contractor, bought a lot of land for the upkeep of the Dars. He restored the buildings in the shape that we see today. However, when he was asked by a dervish to return all stolen bricks from the various destroyed mosques of Lahore, he refused and a curse is said to have followed. We all know that he died a pauper, for in his desperation he also sold off the land.

So with time the Dars of Mian Wadday flourishes. People still come to make their promises. The blind are fed every Thursday. Graves have filled up the garden. Portions of which have been encroached upon by the land mafia. But the teaching goes on. The message of moderation survives. The blind of Lahore still go there to become a 'hafiz'. The banyan tree is said to be over 400 years old. In their own wisdom, people still make their secret wishes. Such is the power of a wish.

The 'zannani waal' and the 'Zanjani waal'

There is a saying in the old walled city of Lahore that the area between the 'zannani waal' (women's bend) and the 'Zanjani waal' (the bend of Zanjani) is protected for the women of Lahore. One had always wondered what and why this saying existed. The story is interesting.

The triangle that forms the land between Hospital Road, Bansaanwala Bazaar and the Circular Road is the area that, a portion of, was once part of Rattan Chand's garden. Many people in the old walled city still remember the tank of Rattan Chand outside Shahalami Gate and the gardens around it. This particular portion was always the special garden for women. But there is more than mere myth to this story. Our story has four aspects to it. First is the 'zannani waal', then there is the 'Zanjani waal', then there is the building of a women's hospital by the British in between, and, lastly, there is the sad story of what has happened to this magnificent hospital.

The 'zannani waal' pertains to the shape of Hospital Road itself. Starting from the Mayo Hospital Chowk, it winds its way in a steady curve to meet Circular Road. In days of old this was a garden where Qutbuddin Aibak played polo much before the West discovered the game of 'chaugan'. He fell from his horse and died on this bend, and was buried just a few yards off the 'waal'. There is a story, probably mere myth, which says that the king treated his women badly, and his fall, so the legend goes, was the curse of a woman.

Many years later, a very pious woman by the name of Dai Laado (the nurse Laadoo) of Prince Salim, who was later to become the Mughal Emperor Jahangir, used to feed the little baby prince. As the prince was educated by Shah Saleem Chishti of Fatehpur Sikri, Dai Laadoo was always available at the service of the prince. Chishti informed the prince that Dai Laadoo was an exceptional woman in the eyes of Allah, so she should be built a special mosque where she spends her life praying. So the mosque of Dai Laadoo came up. In 1119 AH she died and it continued to be used as a mosque.

Many years later as the Mughal Empire crumbled, a Hindu 'jogi' by the name of Basantgar and his followers took over the mosque and for 40 years remained in control of it. When the British came to power, a team led by Mehr Shah Fakir Qadri, who claimed a divine call to reclaim the mosque of a very pious woman, applied to the authorities to get the place back. On delay he led his followers and took over the mosque. Since then it has been used for prayers, and it is still an essential part of the daily prayers to pray for the welfare of the women of Lahore.

On the other side of the triangle lies the very first Muslim saint to come to Lahore. He was Hazrat Husain Zanjani. It was around the time of his death that Data Ganj Bakhsh was asked to come to Lahore, and when he entered Lahori Gate he saw the funeral procession of Hazrat Zanjani. On seeing this, Data Ganj Bakhsh understood why he had been sent to Lahore by the Almighty. It is said that every Thursday, Data Ganj Bakhsh would come to say 'fateha' at the grave of Zanjani, and he would, so the story goes, also pray that the women of Lahore be protected.

We then move ahead and see that on assuming power in 1849, the British planned a medical college and hospital in Lahore. The idea for its establishment was placed before the imperial Government but was postponed because of the 1857 war of independence. Keeping in view both the need for such a medical college and the financial constraints, a Lahore Medical College was established. It was situated in Artillery Barracks at the present site of Government College Lahore, with a hospital located in a stable near the present Tibbi Police Station in Taxali Gate, nearly a mile from the College.

Dr J.B. Scriven of General Hospital Calcutta, was nominated Principal of the college which after Calcutta was to be the second such institute in the entire sub-continent. Admissions opened in October, 1860, with separate courses in English and Hindi. In 1868, the Senate of the University of Dublin granted students of the Lahore Medical School privileges similar to those granted to students of English Schools, who have not passed the College of Surgeons of England.

The present famous Mayo Hospital was completed in 1870 and was opened in 1871. Pudon was the architect and Kanhiyya Lal was the engineer. It was named after the Earl of Mayo, the then Viceroy. Built in Italian style, double storied, bricked with Delhi stone brackets, the cost was Rs 1,58,951. Meanwhile the Lahore Medical School was shifted to the Railway Hostel near Mayo Hospital.

In 1887 the Lady Aitchison College was also constructed. This was to assume the shape of a hospital dedicated to the care of women. The first college day was held in the library on 5th Nov. 1888. Also the Lady Lyall's Home was founded in Nov. 1889 to accommodate 30 ladies. With the official affiliation of the college with Punjab University in 1906, the primary science teaching was handed over to Government College Lahore. However, on 31st of July, 1910, the government approved the proposal of setting up the King Edward's Medical College at its present site, and attached Mayo, Albert Victor and Lady Aitchison hospitals to the college.

So with time the grounds that tradition held was dedicated to the protection and care of women took the shape of the largest women's hospital in the Punjab. Lady Aitchison, after whom the hospital was named, reflected the wishes of the women of Lahore who wanted to be treated and cared by women only. As long as the British were here, this rule held sway. Women expecting children used to prefer this hospital. It built a strong reputation for excellence as a women's only hospital, and women of Lahore felt safe coming here. Sadly, this is no longer the case.

With time more and more male doctors started getting themselves posted here, with a situation today that there are fewer female than male doctors in this 'women's only' hospital. Many women in the old walled city have complained about this matter, and this is best left to the health department bureaucrats to sort out.

So one sees that over time, this triangle remains the realm of women, where they are cared for, and looked after. To one side is the mosque of Dai Laadoo, on the other side the grave of Hazrat Zanjani. In between is the hospital that cares for the women of Lahore. One only hopes that the wishes of the hospital founders, and the very valid wishes of the women of Lahore, are respected.

Mystique of the six pious ladies

Of all the graves and mausoleums in the Punjab, there is not one to match the mystery and mystique of the six pious ladies of Lahore. Known popularly as Bibi Pak Daman, the six graves have always remained an enigma. The beauty of this puzzle is that it is the one place in Lahore where all differences among all sects simply disappear. It is the picture of hope in an age of darkness.

Located just off Durand Road, opposite Queen Mary's College at Garhi Shahu, the graveyard has a small mausoleum and besides the other graves, the six most prominent are those of the six Bibis. The graveyard can be approached from Empress Road, too, but one has to walk through the narrow lane to reach a small mosque. The lane up to the mausoleum has an array of shops, all catering to the various beliefs that people have.

There are two versions as to who these six ladies are. One is the popular version, while the other is the researched version of scholars. Both versions have their appeal and their flaws, so it is best to narrate both as simply as is possible, and leave the reader to make up her or his own mind.

The popular version goes like this: It is claimed that the mausoleum on the six graves was build almost 1,000 years ago, so the legend goes, by the Afghan invader Mahmud of Ghazni and his followers, on the grave of Ruqqaya, claimed to be the daughter of the fourth caliph of Islam, Hazrat Ali Ibn Abi Talib, a cousin and son-in-law of the Holy Prophet (pbuh), and wife of Muslim Ibn Aqil, an emissary of Hazrat Imam Husain to Kufa. Another legend has it that the mausoleum actually holds the graves of six ladies from the Holy Prophet's household, including that of Ruqayya, with the remaining being Ibn-e-Aqeel's sister and daughters.

According to legend - and so the tombstone on the main grave says - Bibi Haj lies buried here. Popular belief is that Bibi Haj was the name of Ruqayya, and she along with some companions came to Lahore after the tragedy of Karbala. It is said that the Hindu Raja who then ruled Lahore on hearing of the news of their arrival summoned them to his court. As they were purdah observing ladies they prayed to God for death.

The earth, thereupon opened and the pious lady and her companion ladies were buried alive. There is some controversy about this legend for it is held that no lady related to Hazrat Ali was named Bibi Haj. Moreover, it is argued that after the tragedy of Karbala, there was no point in any Muslim ladies coming to Lahore, which was ruled by the Hindus.

However, in his book on Lahore, Kanhiyya Lal lists them as being six sisters, having the names Bibi Haj, Bibi Taj, Bibi Nur, Bibi Hur, Bibi Gauhar and Bibi Shahnaz, all of whom, the legend goes, fled Mecca after the massacre at Karbala on the 10th day of Muharram in 61AH (October 10, AD 680). Today, these are the very names written on the six graves. Nowhere does the word Ruqayya appear on any tombstone, though everyone present refers to the grave of Bibi Haj as that of Ruqayya.

To one side is a tablet which states that "Data Ganj Baksh stood at this place when offering fateha every week for the six Bibis". This reinforces the belief that the graves are over 1,000 years old. If this is true, then these are the very first graves of Muslims in Lahore, and represent, probably, the oldest Muslim graves in the entire sub-continent.

As there is no written proof, or even mention of any such movement of the women of the household of the Holy Prophet (pbuh) in the aftermath of the massacre, for this reason some scholars consider Ruqqaya to have been the daughter of Syed Ahmad Tokhta, who lived in Lahore in the 12th century. A mention of this fact has been made by Kanhiyya Lal, who says that in the 12th century AD, an Arab by the name of Syed Abid Zahid Waliullah Tokhta, came and settled in Lahore. He died in the year 604 Hijra and was buried inside of the walled city in Mohallah Chahal Bibian in Akbari Gate.

His grave is still there and the date of his death is given on the tombstone as 604 Hijra. To check this out, I visited the grave, and it seemed to depict its age. The grave once had a fine mausoleum, which was damaged extensively by Maharajah Ranjit Singh. The graveyard was flattened by the Sikh ruler, and on it was built the haveli of Ghulam Mohyuddin Shah Pirzada, who was kind enough to leave the grave of Syed Tokhta intact.

To this day lies the grave of Syed Tokhta on one side of a small house built in a side street on the now demolished

Haveli Pirzadan. There are again some scholars who hold that the daughter of Syed Ahmad Tokhta was married to the ruler of Kech Mekran and she died there and never came to Lahore. We find that Hazrat Ismail whose shrine is on Hall Road came to Lahore before the conquest of Lahore by the Muslims. It is probable that some Muslim ladies might have also come to Lahore during that period, and though not actually related to Hazrat Ali, they might have been Syed.

The six daughters of Syed Tokhta moved inside the walled city and settled in a haveli near the present graveyard of Bibi Pak Daman. They were known for their piety, and they all, so the claim goes, remained unmarried. For this reason, they were all referred to as Pak Daman Bibi in the singular sense. In the year 615 Hijra, when the Afghan invader Sultan Jalaluddin Khurasani sacked Lahore, the adjoining areas were also subjected to loot and rape, as was the Timurid tradition after a victory in battle. Fearing the worst, the six sisters, so legend goes, got together to pray for their chastity.

At that moment an earthquake struck, opening the ground to bury the six sisters and their maids, saving them from disgrace. Afterwards, local people seeing the clothes of the sisters sticking out of the ground, gave them a proper burial. These graves still exist in two portions. On one side are the graves of Haj, Taj and Noor, while in another compound are the graves of Hur, Gauhar and Shahnaz. The graves of the maids are also on the outer perimeter of these graves.

Saint or sinner: the tomb mystery deepens

Who lies there, a saint or a sinner? For almost 345 years exists a mystery that just cannot be solved. Under the dining hall of the beautiful Governor's House of Lahore, lies a tomb in which lies either Muhammad Qasim Khan, a cousin of the Mughal Emperor Akbar who led the slaughter of Kashmiris, or the saint Syed Badruddin Gilani, the 'pir' of Emperor Shah Jahan.

Probably no other person has written about Lahore with greater detail than Kanhiyya Lal. His classic *Tareekh-e-Lahore* has been reprinted by the Majlis Taraqqi-e-Adab, and he mentions the tomb in the Governor's House as that of Syed Badruddin Gilani, who died in 1661. Kanhiyya Lal goes on to say that the tomb was built a few years later by his descendants. There is, however, some confusion about dates as he claims that the tomb was built in the era of Shah Jahan, yet the time period is that of Emperor Aurangzeb.

This version has been backed by the well-known researcher Muhammad Tufail in the Lahore Number of the magazine Naqush printed in 1961. This is considered an authentic research piece. Kanhiyya Lal in his version goes on to say that the saint founded a 'mohallah' just west of the tomb, where he also built a mosque. Traces of this are mentioned in the description of Donald Town in the Punjab Gazetteer in the chapter on the extension of the Lawrence Gardens. So considerable material exists to pin down the tomb as that of Syed Badruddin Gilani.

But then there are other researchers like T.H. Thornton, J.L. Kipling, Syed Muhammad Latif and also Col. H.R. Goulding, all of whom state in clear terms that the tomb belongs to Muhammad Qasim Khan, a maternal cousin of the Emperor Akbar, but who died, or was murdered, in the same time period. No details of Qasim Khan, or at least details with some reasonable proof, of this gentleman exist.

However, Maulvi Nur Ahmed Chishti in his famous *Tahkeeqat-e-Chishti* claims, and adds to the confusion, that there was a gentleman by the name of Qasim Khan Mir Bahr, known in the Mughal court of Akbar as Chaman Ara-e-Khurasan Ajlah, who was highly respected and was responsible for the bloody conquest of Kashmir. So pleased was the emperor that he was appointed the Subedar (Governor) of Kabul, but given the terrible tribal rivalries he was recalled to Lahore. Here the well-known Chaman Ara-e-Khurasan, so Chishti claims, was murdered by another person by the name of Zaman Khan, son of Shah Rukh

Mirza. One source claims the recall and assassination was engineered by the Mughal court. The date of the assassination is approximately 1660. Blochmann in his translation of *Ain-e-Akbari* translates Chaman Ara-e-Khurasan as Governor of Kabul. The title 'Ajlah' means a raft maker, like in boat making.

However, Chishti describes the 'gumbad' of Qasim Khan as being between Anarkali and Sanda, and west of the 'Aslah Khana' armoury. He also describes the tomb in great detail, none of which match the tomb at the Governor's House. This definitive version has added to the mystery. From the location and description it seems he is describing the shrine of Hazrat Mauj Darya on Nabha Road. Maulvi Nur Ahmad Chishti was known for his accuracy, and that is why there are considerable doubts as to the version that the tomb belongs to Qasim Khan.

It must be mentioned that both Syed Muhammad Latif and Muhammad Baqir in *Past and Present Lahore*, printed in 1952, mention a garden of Mahdi Qasim Khan, both claim it being located on the banks of the Chuta Ravi and close to Karbala Gamay Shah. Latif locates it to the south west of the shrine of Data Ganj Bakhsh. But then he goes on to claim that Mahdi Qasim Khan was murdered in 1592, and that a tomb was raised in his memory by Akbar. Given this description and the details of Maulvi Nur Ahmad Chishti, one surmises that the tomb in the Governor's House is not that of Qasim Khan. There is some proof that it is also not that of Mahdi Qasim Khan. But then the description of Chishti also suffers from some inconsistency, and that is why other researchers believe that the chances of the tomb being that of Qasim Khan are more credible.

But the descriptions of Kanhiyya Lal on the matter seems more logical, and that is why the claim of Syed Badruddin Gilani has really never been refuted. But then come to think of it the claim of it belonging to Qasim Khan has never been refuted. What hits one is the lack of any evidence from well-known and well-documented histories and chronicles of the Mughal era. No less than 29 Qasim Khan's existed in the Lahore court of Akbar, some of whom, like our present day bureaucrats, served more than three emperors. The strongest case is that of a Qasim Khan who was in the service of Murad Begum, also known as Mughlani Begum, and he held the title of Jamadar. Here it must be added that no proof of any of them being buried in the tomb, or site, exists.

In many ways the claim of Syed Badruddin Gilani is the strongest, and as is the case with most such pious men, their descendants manage to build tombs to make economic or social gains in society. The case for a Qasim Khan is also very strong, and much more widely believed. As social scientists we cannot pinpoint the person who lies buried underneath the dining hall of the Governor's House. It will remain, forever, a mystery. Or will until some researcher finds the much needed evidence.

The balcony of Chajjoo Bhagat

Lahore has always had an exceptionally deep connection with the mystic. The eternal search for truth remains part of the Lahori character, and men who sought the truth have always been respected. One such seer was a man named Chajjoo Sahaf.

Most people in the old city remember Chajjoo Sahaf with reference to his balcony, or Chubbara as it is known. Chajjoo Sahaf underwent a transformation from a sahaf goldsmith to become Chajjoo Bhagat. Born inside the walled city almost 450 years ago in the days when Emperor Shah Jahan was reigning, he belonged to the elite Bhat Rajput clan, and, in all probability, was originally called Chajjoo Bhatti.

He had a goldsmith's shop inside the walled city and was known as an honest and God-fearing man. His interest in the world around him led him to start a search within himself for what was the 'ultimate' truth. The stage was set for him to seek out sages, and it was during his free hours that he would spend long hours with well-known men of his times.

Among his many friends were Hazrat Mian Mir, Balla Pir Lahori, Washah Balla Dal and Sheikh Ismail, also known as Mian Waddah. There is no doubt that such company is a rare honour in any age or time, and it was under the influence of such men that Chajjoo Sahaf began to question the issues of life and death. As he was a man of means, he decided to spend more time on his search for truth. By this time he had built a house just outside the walled city in the Gowalmandi area. If you happen to head from Gowalmandi Chowk along Railway Road, just 200 yards ahead is a building with a huge balcony jutting out. This is the 'Chubbara of Chajjoo Bhagat'.

Chajjoo decided to lodge on the first floor and cut off all entry to his balcony except for a ladder, which he would lower when the need arose. From there he would observe the world and think about the issues that bothered him. He would leave in the evening to discuss issues with his friends, and return at night, or early in the morning, to his position on his balcony. The stories about Chajjoo abound as to his mystical and occult powers.

But being a Bhagat, he was sworn never to drink alcohol, eat meat, tell lies and to worship only the Almighty. He believed that the Almighty, no matter how you address him, could be reached by searching within oneself, for this search gives man immense power. It was a simple message, but one that appealed to every religious belief.

As time passed, the fame of Chajjoo Bhagat spread far and wide. One legend has it that once an official of the Mughal court came to him with a purse of gold coins. He implored him to examine them and tell him whether they were real or fake. Chajjoo smiled as he took the purse and said: "Your intentions are not clean, and visiting me will change your life". He examined the gold and informed the courtier that they were all genuine. Once the purse had been returned, the courtier accused Chajjoo of stealing one coin.

This accusation he rejected and told him to go away. Very soon, the court guards arrived and searched the entire premises. Nothing was found. On this, the courtier beat up Chajjoo Bhagat and left asking him to make good his loss within a few days.

The legend goes on to say that when the courtier reached his home, he found his dear wife twisting and turning in pain as if she was being beaten up. She had very soon reached the point of dying when she was told that the courtier had the same day beaten up Chajjoo Bhagat for stealing a gold coin. The wife promptly confessed to stealing the coin. On this, the courtier rushed to Chajjoo to beg forgiveness, which he promptly gave.

There are other such stories about this remarkable bhagat, who soon began to be recognized as a Sufi sage. But all the people who came to him were asked to leave and search within themselves. "Do not waste your time on a mortal like me, search for the beautiful human within you", he would advise.

When Chajjoo Bhagat died in 1054 AH, the same courtier who had whipped him built a marble temple at the place where he used to spend his time. The balcony was never touched. Over time other Hindu priests lay claim to his lineage and made good money out of his name. In the evenings, hymns and qawwalis used to be sung there, and one learns from several elders inside the old city that one could never make out to which religion he belonged. The universality of the appeal of Chajjoo Bhagat continues to this day.

At the time of the partition of the Punjab, people occupied the house of Chajjoo, but no one dared to touch the balcony. With time it began to decay. During the 'dark ages' of the Zia era, several 'men of God' tried to burn down the balcony. Locals inform us that it just would not catch fire. In the end an old-timer from the walled city told the mob of the story of the royal courtier and how they risked injuring themselves.

An eyewitness of this scene confessed that within a few minutes everyone left the place never to attempt to harm the balcony of Chajjoo Bhagat. The house of the priest who led the mob burnt down a week later, or so the legend goes in the area.

Hazrat Mian Mir is said to have advised a pupil of his: "Go to meet Chajjoo Bhagat if you want to know the ways of the Almighty, for you will never make out his religion because he is a man in search of the Almighty". In this age and time when we have learnt to hate others with such vehemence, it makes sense to remember what Chajjoo Bhagat said: "Why preach, why not cleanse ourselves first?"

Lahore loses three who made a difference

Lahore is about people truly remarkable people - the simple, the unknown Lahoris, all of them from one mohallah or the other of the old walled city. Some make a name, others pass away unknown. But they all remain remarkable, a model of calm in these days of 'undue haste'.

At the funeral of Abdullah Malik, one got to meet journalists of every age, of every inclination, of every hue and shade, friends that had not been met for almost 25 years when *The Pakistan Times* was the only English-language newspaper, and *Imroze* was a sister Urdu daily of a class that few can imagine today. Abdullah Malik wrote in both  of them and they were both progressive in every sense of word. Once again, that entire 'family' of journalists of Lahore had gathered like they used to in those days when tolerance was an expected virtue. The imam at the namaz-i-janaza conducted the longest funeral prayer I have ever experienced, and everyone had a word or two to say about that. Controversy in the house of Abdullah Malik is the accepted norm, and religion was a deeply personal matter, never discussed as an issue, at least never publicly. That was bad manners.

Abdullah Malik

Funerals bring people of a lifetime together like no other occasion does. Everything is forgiven. It is a remarkable social binder in our social scheme of things. The man from Kucha Chabbaksawaran, the original cavalry precinct that Kakkayzai area where people are known to be born to argue, but in the end fold up every argument in great dignity, just as Abdullah Malik had

Usdat Daman

managed to fold up a full life like very few do manage. For that matter he had always been a man of great dignity, and his utter Lahori upbringing ensured that he had no complexes. Ejaz Batalvi, now looking rather weak, was telling former president Rafiq Tarar: "He belonged to a class and age where the demarcation was clear. Initially either you were for the British or you were against them and for freedom. Later on, either you were for freedom and democracy or you were against it. He was clear-headed and simple". The bearded former president nodded in agreement, if not awe, at probably Pakistan's most respected lawyer and teacher.

I have had the opportunity of seeing and meeting Abdullah Malik since I was a little child, for he was a friend of my father and lived just across the road from my grandfather's house in J-Block in Model Town. My grandmother had taught him inside the walled city as a schoolteacher, and Malik Sahib was ever so respectful. Even when she was old and tottered over to get an injection from the doctor, he would remain standing till she left, his head bowed in immense respect. He was a remarkable old Lahori to the core.

Faiz Ahmad Faiz

But then his funeral also brought back memories of another funeral I had attended in November, 1984, in the same graveyard in G-Block, Model Town, that of Faiz Ahmad Faiz. What I remember most was the way in which another very great Punjabi poet arrived to attend to his departed friend, and I am talking about that great Lahori poet, Ustad Daman. The great man was very ill, almost unable to walk. But he managed to attend the funeral in a rickshaw. Those who had seen his wrestler-like figure in better days could not believe their eyes to see the skeleton-like Daman arriving with the help of two people. There was a close friendship between Faiz and Daman and only a few days prior to Faiz's death both of them had attended a dinner together at Munnoo Bhai's residence. At Faiz's funeral, Ustad Daman kept repeating that it was his turn now. He joined his friend in death only 13 days later on December 3.

Ustad Daman, whose real name was Chiragh Din, belonged to Lahori Gate, inside the old city. He adopted Damdam as his pseudonym, following in the footsteps of his mentor Ustad Hamdam but changed it to Daman after some time. Daman was first introduced to public recital of his poetry from the stage of the All India Congress at a meeting held at Mochi Gate. The star speaker of the gathering was Jawaharlal Nehru, who developed a personal rapport with Daman instantly. Many years later when Daman went to Delhi to participate in an Indo-Pak mushaira, he stole the show with his verses that brought tears to the eyes of the audience. 'Lali akhian di pai dasdi ai roay tuosi vio, roay asi vi aan' (The redness of the eyes tells us, that both of us have wept).

The partition of the Punjab had jolted Daman badly. He felt shattered by the loss of friends and pupils, many of them being Hindus and Sikhs. His miseries were compounded by the death of his wife at the same time in riot-stricken Lahore. It is said that Daman had to hire labourers to carry her coffin to the graveyard. The incident made him an introvert and he shifted to a closet in the city. In Delhi, Pandit Nehru virtually begged Ustad Daman, even to the extent of touching his feet, to stay on in India, promising him a handsome pension and a life of great respect. But Daman was a Lahori to the core, and like every self-respecting Lahori, he could not do without the city. He returned to utter poverty and oppression. He lived the rest of his life as a hermit.

At the funeral of Abdullah Malik I stood watching the place where the great Ustad had alighted from that rickshaw. I remember Abdullah Malik once telling me, with reference to this incident: "A day will come, when we are not around, when the people of Lahore will lament the way our illiterate elite rulers have treated the finest men and women of this city". 'Aya-naan azaadian huthon barbad Hona -Hoaye Tusi wi o, ho-aye usi wi aaa'n.'

Of Kipling and Kim

One of the enduring legacies of the Raj, one that is remembered with fondness, is the legacy of Rudyard Kipling and his famous character Kim, which also is the title of one of his books. We have a Kim's Gun on The Mall, the popular name of which still remains Bhangianwali Toap - the cannon of the Bhangis.

Rudyard, as we all known, was the son of Mr. Lockwood Kipling, the principal of the Lahore School of Arts, now known as the National College of Arts, and in between also known as the Mayo School of Arts, named after Lord Mayo, after

Rudyard Kipling

whom is also named the Mayo Hospital, Lahore. Initially, Rudyard Kipling was made to volunteer for the Volunteer Corp. He was enlisted in 'B' Company of the 1st Punjab Volunteers, but when the young Kipling never turned up for parade, the commandant, Col Goulding, made 'Volunteer Kipling' make good the 'capitation grant' which he had failed to earn.

The amount was remitted "under cover of a frank letter expressing regret for neglect of duty". He was not cut out to be a soldier. He tried other pursuits, but because he was "disqualified for any of the public services because of his defective eyesight", his father approached Sir David Mason, the then managing proprietor of the *Civil and Military*

Gazette, Lahore, to let "the lad try his hand at journalism" as he was very fond of writing "long and strange tales".

He was appointed at Rs.100 a month and immediately he set about producing a short story. As it was Christmas time, it was strange that in the Christmas number, the four Kiplings, father, mother, son and daughter, each contributed a piece. According to a description by H. R. Goulding, that particular edition of the *C&MG* was auctioned at Sotheby's for a very handsome sum. But Rudyard described his appointment in rather grim terms. After his first piece, an old English journalist informed him that one starts journalism by "cutting telegrams and pasting and cutting stories". So it was no easy baptism for the great writer of English literature that was to emerge from Lahore.

The break for Rudyard Kipling, the journalist, came when the Amir of Afghanistan came to visit India in 1885. Rudyard joined the party at Peshawar and stayed with them till Rawalpindi. His racy and imaginative accounts of the Afghan king made him get noticed, and there was no looking back. From there, he began to write about the 'Great Game', the British-Russian rivalry over Afghanistan and the urge to reach warm waters. His description of that rivalry has coloured the way Europeans still look upon this region.

The novel Kim is considered among his finest contributions. The character of Kim has always fascinated people. Who really was Kim? Considerable research has been carried out into the character of the English boy Kim who used to roam about in Anarkali Bazaar, and used to play on the huge cannon, the Bhangianwali Toap, that stands outside the Lahore Museum. One version is that Kim was actually based on the character of a certain Mr F. Beatty, a police officer who retired in Quetta in 1922. Mr. Beatty's father was among

Kim's Gun in Lahore

the very first English people to come to Lahore after the Sikhs were defeated in 1849.

He was a clerk in the East India Company, and lived in the barracks that were demolished and made way for the Punjab University Old Campus building. The young Beatty used to play with Indian boys, or 'chokras' as one description tells us, and used to behave and 'swear' like the natives. He was often seen sitting atop the old cannon, and as Rudyard lived in quarters just opposite this, he must have been acquainted with the little Beatty. Even if he did not know him personally, it would have been difficult to miss this young 'brat', as one description of Beatty says.

When F. Beatty joined the police, he was posted in Balochistan, and helped in no small manner, through his sheer reckless ways, in making Baloch friends and keeping the peace in the then wild Quetta. His 'Indian ways' certainly did help him considerably in getting to know the people of this land. The adventures of Beatty must surely have reached Rudyard Kipling, and that was material enough for him to conjure up a tale worth telling. The interesting thing is that one newspaper description calls Beatty the 'Beauty of Balochistan'.

Here it would be interesting to introduce yet another character by the name of Brian. It was rumoured that Brian was born of a British father and a Lahori mother. The father was a clerk in the East India Company and lived near where today is the Kapurthala House. The Anglo-Indian was very fair and had blonde hair, and used to roam about the streets barefooted. He could speak chaste English, as well as chaste Punjabi.

During the day he would drive a 'tikka garri' owned by his widowed mother. So the young orphan Brian played on the famous cannon, as did Beatty, and it is anyone's guess as to which of the two was really the real Kim. Not enough is known about what happened to Brian, for there is a good possibility that he took up some official job and used his ability to deal with all types of races and languages. What is known is that one of his sisters married a Hindu clerk in the Company.

Here it must be remembered that the British, till the time the East India Company was in power, integrated very well with the local population. It was only when the British crown took over administration after the 1857 uprising that separate development became an official policy. So Kim was the product of those well-integrated days, a product that was to assist the British so well in the days that followed.

The stories of Kipling and Kim have a fascination all their own. One has to visit Lahore to understand the nature of this fascination. The places and things mentioned in Kim are all there, and that is why this is a very real legacy, one that needs to be better understood.

How the C&MG shaped Winston Churchill's Life

Very few people are aware of the vast array of men who have come to Lahore, and later in life made a name in history. Among the better known who stand out in the Raj are the Kiplings, father and son, and Sir Winston Leonard Spencer Churchill, the famous British prime minister during the Second World War, and orator par excellence.

While researching on Lahore, two most interesting sources have intrigued me considerably. First, there are (the *Kipling Papers)* which are focused primarily on Lahore and, second, are the complete papers on Churchill during his stay in India. My daughter, who is at Cambridge, has sent me considerable material on Sir Winston and his forays into journalism and Lahore's leading newspaper *The Civil & Military Gazette*. This is an important aspect of the life of Lahore that has not been researched enough. It would do justice to our ancient city if this aspect was also

Sir Winston

touched upon for two reasons. First, to provoke further research on important aspects of our city, and second, to add to the knowledge of experts who contribute to our newspapers on this subject.

The experience of Winston Churchill in British India laid the foundations on which he based his worldview. His 'inborn hate' for all things Russian was born out of his experiences in the North West Frontier, as were his intelligence forays into Russian-dominated Afghanistan, the sort of stuff that made up Kipling's work. Thus as a correspondent of the *C&MG,* he experienced the 'Big Game' for world domination and the race for the hot waters of the Indian Ocean. For the rest of his life, he struggled to win that Big Game, even though his battles were fought from afar in distant locations.

The Battle of Waterloo shot the House of the Duke of Marlborough into prominence, again after falling from grace, so to say, in the happenings of the English Civil War. He was no Roundhead, but Royal to his fingernails. Born in 1874, he went to Sandhurst and graduated in 1894 to join the 4th Hussars. His first brief experience of battle was with Spanish forces fighting guerillas in Cuba. After a short stint, he returned home and was sent to India. There he immediately went into action with the Indian Army against the restless tribesmen in the famous Malakand Expedition in the NWFP. It was then that the young Winston turned up in Lahore one day on the steps of the daily *The Civil & Military Gazette,* and was assigned the job of a war correspondent in the North West Frontier, a dual career as soldier and journalist. This was to be the beginning of a brilliant career as a journalist, among other things, which saw him report from India, Afghanistan, Sudan, and lastly from South Africa.

The first major series of reports were on the Malakand Field Force, followed by another excellent series on the exploits of the Tirah expeditionary force. Also of special mention were a series of pieces based on his 'intelligence expeditions' deep into Afghanistan and right up to

Samarkand. These pieces constitute of 21 dispatches that were later printed in book form. The quality of these dispatches have been mentioned in the *Kipling Papers* in the British Museum. They provide an ample understanding of how the British were thinking in those days. But where does Lahore fit into the story of Winston Churchill? This is explained by Kipling's diary:

"Today I was visited by the son of Lord Randolph Churchill, the youngest son of the seventh Duke of Marlborough. He is a dashing officer in the Hussars, is charming, gay, ebullient and endearing. He will make an excellent war correspondent, for he is located in the middle of where the action is." And so the journalistic writing career of another great Englishman started in Lahore. As a young schoolboy I remember my father, who was the editor of the *Gazette,* telling me that I was sitting in the chair where once Winston Churchill sat. So his story has always fascinated me.

Churchill's experiences as a war correspondent for *The Civil & Military Gazette* resulted in the very first publication of the great man. Titled *The Story of the Malakand Field Force,* the book was an instant success, and laid the foundations of a career that was to see him reach heights very few manage in a lifetime. It also launched his literary career. The first edition mentions the role of the *C&MG* in the writing of the hook. His second book is called the *River War,* based on his experiences in Sudan, where he was part of General Kitchner's expeditionary force. He fought the 'fanatical dervishes' in one of the last of the classical battles that managed cavalry charges. It also instilled in him a deep suspicion of all things Muslim, a seed probably planted in his experiences in the NWFP and Afghanistan, which later in life led him to support the cause of Israel. Ironically, the script of this second book was vetted by Kipling in Lahore. This was followed by a novel, and then Churchill went to South Africa to cover the Boer War for the

London *Morning Post*. His dispatches were lifted from the *Post* and reprinted with his permission by the *C&MG*. He was captured within a month, escaped and became world famous for his description of his escapade. This was the beginning of his political career. The rest is history.

Sir Winston Churchill wrote a lot about Lahore in his books and letters. He described it as "a city with a soul, that has a mind of its own, its beauty is there to be seen for it draws you to it." In a letter to a friend in Lahore, he writes: "I envy you, for you savour the delights of Lahore." But the real passion of young Winston was his love for polo. The records of the Lahore Polo Club have a special mention of his exploits in the field. Later in life, he was to mention, when Pakistan came into being, that he would always remember, among scores of other experiences about India, how much he enjoyed his polo in Lahore.

Young Winston loved to ride hard, but after his polo matches he would ride slowly along the new 'tanned' road being built from the Cantonment at Mian Mir to the Exhibition Hall. His early diaries have special mention of these experiences. The *Thandi Sarak* certainly played a formative role in the shaping of one of the world's greatest statesmen.

The pioneering Sarla Thakral

The place was the Lahore Flying Club at Walton. The year was 1936. A beautiful young 21-year old woman of Lahore's well-known Sharma family, dressed smartly in a hand-woven cotton sari, approached the new Gypsy Moth aircraft standing near the hangar. She entered the cockpit, fixed her eye goggles, started the engine and headed towards the runway. A few minutes she was airborne - solo. The very first woman pilot of the sub-continent had flown into history.

Mrs. Sarla Thakral is today 89 and lives in Delhi. In December she will be 90 years old and can proudly claim to be the world's oldest living woman pilot. The story of this Lahore girl is a fascinating tale of determination, for even today she is a much sought after person. Her story of personal tragedy she dismisses as just part of life, for she is determined to push ahead. In India there are numerous people interested in her costume and jewellery designs. She is a favourite designer with the National School of Drama students, whose institute is barely a kilometer away from her house in Delhi's Bengali Market. "Every morning I wake up and chart out my day's plans. If there is plenty of work I feel very happy, otherwise I feel a precious day has been wasted," she says.

Sarla Thakral

Recalling that day back in 1936, this young 21 year-old Lahorite did the unthinkable. She entered the cockpit of a Gypsy Moth and flew into history as undivided India's first lady pilot. Dressed in a smart hand-woven cotton sari with the 'pallu' demurely in place, the dainty 21 year-old confidently ascended the steps of the Gypsy Moth - a two-seater aircraft. Once in the cockpit she strapped her glasses around her eyes and took off into the blue skies.

"In Lahore in 1936 most people still associated flying with birds, for very few cars plied the roads. The nascent aeroplanes were considered the greatest miracle of science. There were only a handful of male pilots in the whole of India. For women, of course flying was unthinkable". With only nine hours of flying, Sarla was confident enough to take that solo flight, and having once flown, she was an instant celebrity.

Maharajahs, kings, princes, political leaders and the media wanted to meet her. "The feeling was the same all across undivided India. It was extraordinary," says the now 89-year-old Sarla as she remembers those glorious days. "People from different States began to claim me as one of their own," she laughs, and adds with a twinkle, "pur Lahore Lahore aye".

In those days the fear of flying in machines that crashed more than they flew ran deep. Flying meant inviting death. But then more and more reliable machines were coming in. When the British opened the Delhi Flying Club to Indians in 1929, only a handful of local students wanted to fly. One of them was P. D. Sharma, Sarla's future husband. Once married, far from telling his wife to sit at home and wait on him as was expected of a proper Indian woman in those days, Sharma persuaded his wife to train as a pilot. His family after all had nine pilots already and they were all supportive of the decision.

"In fact it wasn't so much my husband. My father-in-law was even more enthusiastic and got me enrolled in the flying club," says Sarla and adds, "I knew I was breaching a strictly male bastion, but I must say the men, they never made me feel out of place." In those days she could take flying lessons for Rs. 30 an hour. "Learning flying was cheap because not many wanted to risk their lives," she says. Sarla obtained her 'A' license when she accumulated over 1,000 hours of flying. She was now readying herself to apply for the group 'B' license that would authorise her to fly as a commercial pilot. But when she was undergoing training in Jodhpur, tragedy struck. Her husband died in a crash in 1939.

Jodhpur Flying Club closed down soon afterwards with the outbreak of the Second World War. Widowed at 24 years of age, Sarla returned to her hometown Lahore. She abandoned her plans to become a commercial pilot and ventured into diverse fields excelling in each one of them. To distract herself she joined the Mayo School of Arts in Lahore, now known as the National College of Arts. But her parents re-married her and she settled down in Lahore as a housewife.

In the flames of 1947 she left her city and her memories and settled in Delhi after Partition. It was there that her degree in arts from Lahore came in handy. She succeeded in establishing herself as a painter of renown with most of the big galleries exhibiting her works. Most of her water colours have followed the Bengali School of Art. Another feature of her paintings was that almost all of them depict women.

Along with paintings she also began designing clothes and costume jewellery and became an instant hit. She supplied her jewellery designs to several cottage industries for over 20 years. She had also started textile printing and her sari prints were a rage with the fashionable crowd. In the fifties she could virtually count the who's who of Delhi as her clients including Vijaylaxmi Pandit.

Today Sarla Thakral lives alone, without even domestic help to do her chores. Fuelled with so much creativity and undying energy she says she wants to keep on doing something till she can. She has, naturally aged, but her soul still flies. Known affectionately as 'Mati' by her clients, very few realise that the lady from Lahore, who stitches and designs their clothes, was once a celebrated pilot whose pictures were routinely published in newspapers for her daredevil achievement as the sub-continent's first flying superwoman.

She remembers Lahore as "that great city with a greater soul than many realise", she says with great fondness. "When many Indians returned after the cricket matches recently from Lahore, there were stories of how kind and open the people of Lahore had been to them. Most people felt that Indians would not be able to reciprocate such kindness. Little do they know that a part of Lahore lives in India too, and we will make them feel at home too."

Capturing the image of Lahore

When one thinks of photography in context of Lahore, the name of 'chaacha' F.E. Chaudhry springs to mind. When Pakistan came into being, he was nearing his 40th birthday and was recognized as a top photographer. This year was his 95th, and he remains alert, full of beans and, probably, the oldest living Lahori, let alone an icon in Pakistani photo-journalism.

As a child I recollect my elder brother and myself 'pinching', we called it borrowing, his Quickly moped every time he came to our house. We learned to ride motorcycles at his expense. When my father was sacked as Editor of the *Civil & Military Gazette,* Lahore, two days after suffering a major heart attack, he left money under the old

F.E.Chaudhry

man's pillow and then led a huge protest campaign against the owner for being callous. But then the owner was a businessman and a sick Editor was of no use to him. In those days a heart attack meant the end of a career, and it took my father two years to return to work.

But the career of F.E. Chaudhry as a photographer is another story. He definitely is the pioneer of Pakistani photojournalism. So good was he at his craft that at official functions he would sit and get up just once to take a picture, just one snap and his work was done. Others would click a whole reel to select their best. But not F.E. Just one picture was enough. He had learnt his craft from the 'Masters', for before him a long line of distinguished photographers had come and gone.

Photography arrived in Lahore in the 1840s. No record of those days is known today. But some were of the architecture, people and landscape of the Punjab. Felice Beato, an Italian-born photographer who travelled through India between 1857 and 1888, took beautifully detailed photographs of the Golden Temple and of Lahore after the fall of the Sikhs. These were the very first photographs of Lahore that exist today.

A few years later, in 1864, Samuel Bourne, the most famous commercial photographer in India at the time, took photographs of Amritsar and Lahore, which included Maharajah Ranjit Singh's *marrhi,* his marble pavilion, and

Lahore Fort. While in Srinagar he captured a stunning image of Colonel Alexander Gardner, known to have been in Ranjit Singh's court in 1831, dressed in a tartan suit and matching turban. The people of the Punjab, including Sikh soldiers, maharajahs and Akalis were also frequently photographed. Bourne's work is known for its sheer beauty and balance, for black and white photography has its own artistic value.

But the first photographer to set up business in Lahore was William Bartholomew, who was an 'apothecary'. He set up his business inside the Lahore Fort in 1849, and then later moved to where the Lower Mall is today. On the death of William Bartholomew, his assistant, James Craddock, became the main photographer of Lahore. He set up the first photographer's shop on The Mall, and was the official photographer to the British East India Company, and later to the British government.

But then came the famous Irish photographer William Henry Burke. Born in Peshawar in 1861, he grew up to become his photographer father's main apprentice. Willie got married in 1887 and soon became the branch manager for photographer James Craddock in Lahore. William Burke set up business at the hill station of Ooty in 1911 and also in Madras in 1913. Pictures by him in the India Office collection date from 1910-35.

One of the more important state events Burke photographed was the Rawalpindi Darbar of March 1885, at which Amir Abdur Rahman of Afghanistan met with the viceroy of India, Lord Dufferin. While there he met the young journalist from the Lahore-based *Civil and Military Gazette*. Kipling was apparently impressed by Burke's photography, and was responsible for luring him to come and live in Lahore. Kipling went on to work for six months in Simla, where again he may have come across Burke; by this time Simla had replaced Murree as the fashionable hill station and summer seat of the viceroy. One reason for this may have been the frequent cholera outbreaks with which Murree was plagued.

In July 1885, Burke opened a branch studio in Lahore, and this gradually became the centre of his business. He moved to Lahore to live and to bring up his children, although he still kept the Murree and Rawalpindi studios open. He also continued to make photography expeditions to the frontier areas, and to photograph the Punjab Frontier Force of the Queens Own Corps of Guides, based at Mardan. During the Second Afghan War in 1879, Kipling and Burke covered it and for the first time brought to the British and Indian reading public first-hand accounts of the happenings there. Burke died in Lahore in 1899.

But then there came to Lahore an array of brilliant photographers. The names of W. Baker, A. Sache, Fred Bremner and James Rickalton are well known to researchers. To follow them were a long line of Indians. With the advent of the 20th century, a number of photography shops opened in Lahore. They all used the glass plate cameras, which even today can be seen operating in the Mayo Hospital Crossing near Hospital Road. With rapid changes in technology came photo-journalism, and all over the world an entirely new breed of men emerged, all of them dedicated to capturing on celluloid moments that could be cherished later.

It was in that new rare breed of men that was born F.E. Chaudhry. He started his career as a schoolmaster at the St. Anthony's High School, Lahore, and soon became the chief photographer of *The Pakistan Times* of Lahore. A pioneer in Pakistani photo-journalism, he retired from active service when the newspaper closed in the 1980s. With him also came to an end an era, almost entirely dedicated to capturing the world we see in black and white. At the age of 95, he represents the very finest traditions of journalism that we have seen. It has been a long march from the Italian Felice Beato to the Pakistani F.E. Chaudhry. Maybe some day their entire world will be put together to present the mosaic that Lahore even today is.

The gift from Adolf Hitler

The first time I heard of the 'Khaksars' was from my neighbour Haji Abdur Rahman, a gentleman of the type they do not make any more. As a teenager I experienced my first sight of him after Eid prayers at the Badshahi Mosque. My father whispered in my ear: "He was a friend of Hitler". The awe of Mashriqi had set in.

Adolf Hitler

Just last week, my friend Syed Sikander Shah lamented the fact that Pakistan is probably the only country that loves to forget its heroes. He mentioned Mashriqi, and being a true Icchra dweller he subtly pushed forward the proposition that Mashriqi had a beautiful car presented to him by Adolf Hitler. That was bait enough for me to set off on a hunt for the gift from Adolf Hitler. On Thursday evening I walked through the narrow streets towards Zaildar Road.

Just before the main crossing, among the hundreds of vendors, is a cemented house with a red flag. A forbidding grey iron door awaits. I pushed open the small gate and before me, just as in a showcase, stood a rust battered car. There is no doubt about its vintage, for it is of the very highest order. I had managed to reach the car that the Fuhrer had presented to "a mind of the very highest calibre, a man whose integrity can lead India to great glory".

Just next to the old decaying masterpiece is the grave of Allama Inayatullah Khan Mashriqi and his wife. It is simplicity itself. His grandson is constructing a research library over the grave. Work stopped long ago, for money is scarce among these exceptionally honest followers of the great Allama, and they are not given to asking ... begging they call it. It is a desolate place. It makes one think about how we honour our greatest minds.

The car is a 1942 model Renault-Benz. For those not interested in vintage cars, let me inform that when the Nazi forces took over France, they manufactured a limited number of high quality Pullman versions of the Mercedes Benz. As they were made in the Renault factory, the car was named a Renault Benz. On the decaying front the name Renault is boldly written. The tyres, now decayed, are on old spoke wheels. There is a starting handle very much in place just below the front grill.

I climbed into the driving seat, those beautiful leather seats had decayed, and below the seat the chassis is very much intact. The chassis number is 381967. I shot off an email to the Renault company and promptly got a reply that the car chassis number, according to their archives, was a gift given by Adolf Hitler to Mr Inayatullah Khan Mashriqi of Lahore, India. It was one of only 1,000 produced in the world, and was a Pullman six-seater class of the Renault Nervasport. It was a 4278cc-powered super luxury version.

The original paint was cream on the engine and sides, and black on the wheel covers, front lights and back. The present condition is such that rust has eaten into the entire paintwork. Adolf Hitler himself had six of them, and he presented over 150 of them to honoured guests from all over the world. He even presented Field Marshal Rommel with one after his triumphant return from the African campaign in the Second World War.

The company had offered US$100,000 to the Mashriqi family for the car, but they refused as ownership was disputed. That was way back in the 1970s. Since then a new generation has come forth, and there seems little interest in this million dollar vintage car. Locals report that till recently it was in a garage with "pigeons living in it". It had become a reflection of our times.

Just who exactly was Allama Mashriqi? I rang up five middle-aged 'educated' persons, and only one of them had a faint clue about the great man. The man labelled as "the great test brain of British India" belonged to Lahore, and yet

Lahore does not know, or own, him. In case you label him with Hitler, let me inform you that Cambridge University and the British newspapers of the 1930s called him a "genius of untold possibilities".

The fact is that he was a liberal scientific person who expounded the theory that the "cultural ethos and history of India is such, that the people behave exactly in direct proportion to the behaviour of their leaders. To imagine that the people do not know what their leaders are up to is a gross fallacy. They get to know every detail".

Allama Mashriqi was born in a wealthy family of goldsmiths on August 25, 1888, in Amritsar and died on August 27, 1963 in Lahore. A brilliant student, he set new academic records that stunned everybody in Britain and the sub-continent. He completed his masters' degree in mathematics in one year at the age of 19. He joined the Cambridge University and completed his Tripose barely in four years.

Though he passed all subjects with distinction, his real fame was his ability in mathematics. Due to his academic achievements, he earned a 'Foundation Scholar' and 'Wrangler' from Cambridge University. *The Times of London* and *The Daily Telegraph* wrote editorials on "this brilliant mathematician from Lahore".

After completing his education at the age of 24, he came back to India and served in different government positions under British rule. Keeping in view his personality, it was not a surprise even for British officials when he slapped the then British deputy commissioner, Peshawar, for using slanderous and abusive language.

He even did not shut his mouth as a 'government official' on the massacre of Pathans in the Kissa Khwani Bazaar, Peshawar, on April 23, 1930, and revealed the truth of mishandling the situation by writing in British papers about the reality of the situation. These columns shocked the British public. When Punjabi leaders criticized him for his views, he wrote: "The British government has hired my knowledge for the salary and not my heart or conscience". It was in this context that he refused kinghthood.

In 1931, Allama Mashriqi founded the Khaksar Tehrik (Movement of the Humble) and abandoned the luxurious life that he was used to. The ideology of his party was based on egalitarianism. There was no status quo and no wall between the privileged and the unprivileged. Allama Mashriqi was among those people who accepted the hard fact that "Pakistan would face immense racial and provincial prejudices because of the supremacy of feudalism and class-based bureaucracy". The end result of this equation is total and complete disintegration. If they are removed, the end result will be prosperity of untold proportions.

The choice is stark. The mathematician instinct wrote in 1953: "East Pakistan, by my calculations, will declare its independence in 1970". He did not live to see that day. He also warned not to take the Kashmir issue to the UN, because we would never be able to liberate it from India. "Accept this fact now and you will be better off. It must remain a Pakistani province, and we must struggle to regain portions of our lost province, or one day we will accept the partition of Kashmir like we accepted the partition of the Punjab".

Need one say more about this remarkable Lahori who lived in a small, obscure lane in Icchra. Years later his nephew, the great Akhtar Hamid Khan set up the Orangi Project. The ideas of the great man were at work. The results were astounding. That Adolf Hitler presented him with the very best car did not come as a surprise to the British. The condition of that very rare car today is for all to see. It is about time that it was taken over by the State, restored and exhibited in a science museum. I can already hear a loud silence.

The origins of Sam Browne's belt

There was a time when the name Sam Browne was the buzz word in Lahore. Everyone knew of him, or about him. The Sikh empire had just been crushed in 1849 by the British at Chillianwala in Gujrat, in a ferocious battle that almost cost them their Empire. The first cantonment had been established inside the Lahore Fort, which was the last city to fall to the British as they consolidated their hold.

The badly battered British force was finding housing in the Old Anarkali cantonment difficult when Lt. Sam Browne rode into Lahore with his sowars. By the time he retired he was known as Gen Sir Samuel James Browne, VC, GCB, KCSI. There are three plaques in his memory today. One is the marker at his cremated ashes in the Rhye Cemetery on the Island of Wight, the second honouring him is at St. Paul's Cathedral in London and the third is at the Lahore Cathedral on The Mall. For the British he carved a name in history as a "fearless leader of men on horses". For Lahore, he was the fearless person who used local knowledge and expertise to be known as the man who gave the world the famous Sam Browne belt.

Sir Samuel James Browne

Sam Browne was born in Barrackpore in India on October 3, 1824, the son of a surgeon in the Bengal Medical Service of the East India Company. He joined the 46th Bengal Native Infantry as a subaltern, participating in action at Ramnagar and Sadulapur. It was only when he was thrust into action at Chillianwala, and a few months later at nearby Gujrat, that he experienced the force of the Punjabi soldier. For the rest of his life, he lived in awe of them, and it was to Lahore that he was sent to raise "horsemen of the highest order". It was Sam Browne's opinion that he had never heard or seen such bravery as he had experienced against the 'Fauj-e-Khas' at Chillianwala, and it was his opinion that these very men had to be won over. His assessment served the British well for another 100 years.

In 1849, he was made a lieutenant and asked to raise a cavalry force, to be designated the 2nd Punjab Irregular Cavalry and later incorporated into the regular force. For this, he came to Lahore, living in the Old Anarkali area. He started locating all the old cavalry men of the 'Fauj-e-Khas' from inside the walled city. He would command this unit for the next five years. Half a century later in 1904, the unit would be redesignated as the 22nd Sam Browne's Cavalry in his honour.

Browne led the 2nd Punjab in several engagements, and was decorated for action during the Bozdar Expedition, in 1857, being promoted to captain. Browne won the Victoria Cross on August 31, 1858, for action near Seerporah during the war of independence, known also as the Indian Mutiny. Browne, now a major, charged and captured a rebel gun, accompanied by only a single sowar. He lost his left arm but earned a Victoria Cross. One of the defenders severed his left arm with a sword.

Some time after this incident, he began to wear the accoutrement which bears his name, as compensation for the difficulty his disability caused by wearing his officer's sword. One account states that his Sikh orderly presented him with a belt that was worn by the 'Fauj-e-Khas' of Maharajah Ranjit Singh, for this elite force, led as it was by a French general from Napoleon's defeated army, had come up with a belt and a supporting belt, to hold a sword, a dagger (which all Sikhs wear), a pistol and two leather cases of ammunition. This makes up for a considerable weight, which a belt could not hold up.

The 'Fauj-e-Khas' design incorporated the sword belt that hung from the shoulder, as was worn by the French forces of Napoleon, while the traditional 'kamarband' of the sub-continent managed to hold a dagger and a pistol. To understand the 'kamarband' and its function, it is best to see drawings of soldiers in the Mughal armies and the Sikh 'misils' that followed them. The genius of Browne was that he incorporated both these belts to form one broad belt around the waist, supported by a thinner leather belt across the shoulder.

There is some dispute about the reasons for this 'invention'. One school of thought puts it down to Browne's disability, while the other puts it down to the fact that the virtual 'arsenal' that a cavalryman had to carry on himself made this essential. It was the addition of a pistol and ammunition to the sword and the dagger that made this 'invention' inevitable. Sam Browne, having lost his left arm, had difficultly in carrying his sword comfortably, whether mounted or dismounted, leaving his one hand free. Its design was also intended to carry a leather pistol holster where the weapon could be safely carried without the risk of accidental discharge, as the pistols of the day were inclined to do.

It seems that both these reasons played a part in this simple 'invention'. Later, the wearing of the Sam Browne belt would be adopted by other officers who knew Browne in India, but it was not to come into common use in the British Army until after his retirement. Browne's original belt is now on public display in the India Room of the Royal Military Academy, Sandhurst.

In those days, Lahore was known for its excellent leather products. Inside the walled city, just next to Kucha Chabaksawaran inside Mochi Gate, is a bazaar that sold belting and other equipment for horses. The particular finish, a glazed reddish brown finish, is typical to Lahore. The leather is definitely buffalo, which is not available in other parts of the world. It stands to good reason that the Sam Browne belt, now standard equipment to officers all over the world, was born out of the intense military city that Lahore had become. Today, there are companies in the West that specialise in the Sam Browne belts, mostly using cow leather. The original at the Royal Military Academy, Sandhurst, is made from buffalo leather.

The crazy Italian of Lahore

When Lahore adopts a man, the relationship is unique. One cannot say the attachment is magnetic, but it certainly defies logical explanation. One such man was an Italian, who rose to the post of governor of Lahore. He was, initially, made Qazi of the city, and then governor. He was all-powerful and he was feared like few have ever been.

Jean Baptiste Ventura was born in Italy some time in the very late 17th century. As a very young man he joined the Italian contingent that was raised to fight with the forces of Napoleon in Russia in 1812, and remained with the French forces as an outstanding officer. His final European battle was at Waterloo, after which he just walked away from the disarray. He was young and he was shattered, and as he was to record later, he felt sorry that everyone did not fight till death. Crazy is the only word any sane military analyst would use for a man like him.

But Ventura had other ideas, and when he walked away, he walked away. Historians tell us that he was "very martial to look at and a man with a fiercely independent streak", a sort of no-nonsense person who did the job given, irrespective of the methods employed. Yet he was a man of undoubted class. He returned to Italy, rested a while and then bade farewell to his family, gathered all the gold he could and set off for the 'Orient'. His long travels finally landed him in Lahore, which in those days after the fall of Napoleon was seen as the main centre of power that opposed imperial Britain. He would fight them there, the Maharajah Ranjit Singh was known far and wide, and the Punjabi Misls were revered as the finest army in Asia, at least Lord Roberts of India thought so.

In Lahore, the Maharajah made him wait for almost a year. He was sizing up this impressive man. Then Ranjit Singh made up his mind. Ventura entered the service of the Lahore Darbar in 1822. He was given command of a Sikh infantry regiment, and this regiment he trained himself like 'only tyrants do'. Very soon, it was known as the most fearless regiment of the Punjab army, and the soldiers admired this nonsense man, who led from the front, they liked him for his 'unpredictable' ways. He seldom punished offenders, but when he did it seemed unusually 'excessive'. But the Maharajah allowed him the freedom he needed, for the test would come in battle, and that test came in 1823 at the Battle of Nowshera. The Ventura Regiment put the Pathans not only to flight, but so ruthless was his drive and so merciless his methods, that many felt that battle actually opened up the road to Kabul, at least in the minds of the Pathans.

For this reason, Maharajah Ranjit Singh liked him and used him to good effect, though his actions often shocked and alarmed the maharajah every now and then. The maharajah always defended him with the remark:

"Garam khoon, damagh puttha, bandah mard hai" he is hot blooded, his mind odd, but he is a real man. Maharajah Ranjit Singh was convinced that this Italian, who it seems, had a slight French mannerism, was a born leader. In 1825, he was made head of two major campaigns, and this led to a major revolt among the Sikh sardars who thought that they had fought for years to earn that place, which an outsider had claimed. But Ranjit Singh insisted, and managed to get his way. It must be said that Gen Ventura stayed loyal to the Maharajah as long as he lived. He was given the title of 'Wafadar', a title to which he lived up to. The Maharajah ordered him to marry a Punjabi woman, but he flatly disagreed and said: "I will marry to obey your orders, but I will marry a woman I chose, not you." The maharajah loved his answer. Jean Baptiste Ventura married the petite daughter of a Frenchman living in Ludhiana, and kept her in a house built next to the tomb of Anarkali, away from the bustle of the city. That house is today part of the present secretariat complex, built by the French general as headquarters for the army of Maharajah Ranjit Singh.

But though he had a beautiful wife, he did never really bother about her. Instead he also kept a harem of his own near Chuna Mandi in a huge haveli which, according to one description, had "40 or 50 beautiful slave girls". It was known among the Lahore Court that they "all loved him and feared him". He was a crazy man by any description of the word. Soon he was made the Qazi of Lahore, and within a few months crime came to almost zero in the walled city of Lahore. He adopted the unique punishment of hanging thieves by one leg for two days. Odd, you will agree. One rapist he hung by the unmentionable till he died and he let his body hang for five days till it stank. When the governor protested to the maharajah, Ventura was made governor instead. The people loved the decision.

In that position he immediately set about improving the drainage system, and followed it with an emphasis on gardens and huge and beautiful buildings. The Italian in him was emerging. He can be said to have been a major influence in the way old Lahore, the old walled city, developed. By this time his own people were bothering Ranjit Singh. The maharajah felt the need to quell unrest among the Cheema and Chattha sardars in Wazirabad, Gujranwala and Daska, and so Ventura was sent as the governor of Wazirabad.

Ventura arrived quietly in Wazirabad. The locals laughed at the choice, because he had a fierce reputation of being fearlessly fair and honest. After two weeks of his arrival, he invited all the unruly landlords to a gathering in the main square of the city, and suddenly arrested over 20 known dacoits from among their followers. These he hung immediately by the neck to everyone's amazement and shock, and let their bodies rot in the sun for more than five days.

It was a sort of 'shock and awe' tactic that kept the Cheemas and the Chatthas in check for as long as Maharajah Ranjit Singh was in power. The Lahore Darbar was in turmoil over the incident, and the maharajah was himself very upset. He had expected some action, but not this. Ventura was summoned before the Khalsa sardars to explain his bizarre act.

He told the Maharajah: "You belong to Gujranwala. These people only fear force. Anything fine will not cut with them". The maharajah agreed and advised him to keep a softer touch. He smiled, begged leave and returned on horseback the same day to Wazirabad.

When Maharajah Ranjit Singh was nearing death in 1839, he was then posted in Peshawar after Hari Singh Nalwa had died. He rushed back and was one of the main mourners at his funeral, where he finally cried, with the famous comment: "It will be quite some time before another like him will rise".

Two years after the death of Ranjit Singh, Ventura could clearly see the end of the Sikh empire coming. He sold his house in Lahore in 1841, took his daughter, his money from the sale of his house, his gold and other possessions. He left behind his French wife and his harem:

"Impediments" he called them.

He went to France to live on his estate. "It's time to rest", he said, breathing his last on April 3, 1858. If ever a man had made Lahore his home, it was Gen Jean Baptiste Ventura the man who loved the work he did, but whose methods were definitely questionable. That is why he is known as the 'crazy Italian of Lahore'. When he walked away, he just - walked away.

The Death House and the leek

Over a thousand years ago, the population of the Walled City of Lahore was almost entirely Hindu. A thousand years later it is almost entirely Muslim. Two great civilizations 'met, learnt from one another, even joined hands to produce a new religion, and finally in one massive convulsion drew a line of hate'. Today we are ready to protect that line of hate.

Our gardener is a very old man called Puran. He is a quiet man and silently creates green life out of the earth that he plays with. Puran belongs to a village just near Wagah. His sisters married men living in villages just across the border before the line was drawn, the *leek* as he calls it in Punjabi. The *leek* was drawn not only across the land, but also across thousands of families like Pooran's. Last month, he got a letter from Dubai informing him that his last sister had died. He came over to meet me and sat listless on the floor in his white *dhoti*.

After a long, thoughtful silence he asked whether an atomic war would mean that all humans would vaporize. "Well, yes, it will be much more terrible than we humans can imagine," I told him. He shook his old head in disbelief that I had confirmed his worst fears. "That is what happens when we disgrace the dead, destroy places of worship and forget the past believing we are better than the others." He seemed very upset by his own condition and by the condition that surrounded all of us, and we got talking about the dead, about forms of worship and about the past.

He mentioned the Hindu Marghat, or the 'Death House' of the Hindus just outside the walled city since history had been recorded, and one popular myth that still lives inside the ancient Walled City is that even the Hindu deities Ram and Sita, and their sons Lahu and Kasu, were burned on logs of wood there.

In a way, Lahore, the Punjab and the Indus Valley have a very special place in Hindu religion, for it was primarily in these parts that their religion developed and grew into what it is today. On the banks of the River Ravi lived Ram, and just near his dwelling the Hindus cremated their dead. It was an efficient way of disposing off the dead, ensuring that no diseases were spread, or corpses stolen, or signs left for people to create new deities. From water had humans come and to water they returned. An interesting way of looking at life, and to be fair, scientifically correct too.

The Hindu Marghat outside Taxali and on the banks of the Old Ravi, known locally as 'Buddha Ravi,' had been functioning till about ten years ago. But then as the few dozen Hindus left in the city moved southwards, there was little work left for the person who looked after the marghat.

When he died it was closed, and in true tradition the 'qabza' groups moved in, razed it to the ground and now we have residential plots there. Bricks and concrete and small multistorey houses. So where do the Hindus now cremate their dead? The Sikhs also burn their dead, and Lahore has a few Sikhs still living inside the old Walled City. They now use an open space on the River Ravi far way from the local population and in the opposite direction of Shahdara. Near Shahdara on the banks of the Ravi, the Parsi community of Lahore, again dwindling in size, has their burial house, and they leave their dead to the elements in true Zoroastrian tradition. It used to be originally located at Rattigan Road, behind Central Model School, where they also had their delightful Parsi food at the house of Hylla and Behroze there and no such thing as hate ever dwelled in the hearts and minds of any one But besides Death Houses, Lahore was home to some of the oldest Hindu temples and some of the finest Sikh temples in the entire sub-continent. They existed in almost every street and lane of the Walled City. The heaviest concentration of Hindu temples was towards the southern parts of the city, especially at Mori, Bhati, Lohari and Mochi gates. Today barely a few can be recognized, and even if they are recognized, they have been converted into living quarters. If one were to walk the streets and observe the construction of houses, it would be easy to make out where these temples once existed. While it is true that there was just no one to look after them, and they fell into disrepair. The mandir and shivala of Hari Gian is one such place, as is the Devi Dowaza temple, both inside Mori Gate. One could name over a hundred such important temples, which were in place when the *leek* was drawn. Today, the rubble of history does not interest anyone in the land. But it would be in the fitness of things if the important ones were marked out, saved and left at that, as a mark of respect to a great religion that once thrived here in our city.

And so after a long chat over the dead and the living, my gardener Pooran left. His father had converted from Hinduism to Christianity and he actually migrated to Pakistan just five miles from Wagah for fear that Hindu priests would one day get at him. It must be said that he was not way off the mark. In a way it was a sensible economic decision. But the pain of the leek has always remained with him, and when he is gone and the newer generation, fed as it is on hate and without any experience of the prejudices of old, is in place, that line will be no different than the fate lines on our hands.

The rogue who ruled Lahore

The Walled City of Lahore has seen many a .tyrant, many a crazed woman, and even a 'eunuch' who ruled over it. Despots down to their bones, all of them. The Tartars also came, many a time, raped, pillaged and burned down the place. The city would just pick up the pieces and move on. What else could they do, that, is till Sikha Gakkhar hit them.

During the reign of the emperor Muhammad Shah, a Tughlaq, a governor or a Subedar as he was called then, governed Lahore from Delhi. Being removed from the centre of power and on the main route between the capital and Kabul, from where all the invaders normally used to come, Lahore's strategic importance lay in it being the last major military stop before anyone actually got to Delhi, to claim the throne of the sub-continent. To add to this military dimension was its economic importance, for it had, and still has, the largest and most important grain and goods market in the region. It was also a seat of learning. All these attractions proved enough for many an emperor, invader or pretender, who reached the conclusion that Lahore was a much more lucrative proposition than Delhi, for here the maidens were fairer and the music sweeter, not to talk of other matters. This combination proved for Sikha Gakkhar a fatal attraction.

The Gakkhar tribe dwells just below the foothills of the mountains in the north, and its main market town is even today called Gakkhar Mandi, near Sialkot. The Gakkhar tribe lives in this area and spreads right into the hills towards Hazara. From the foothills rose a man, tall, handsome, exceptionally brave and wild, who led an army of over a thousand, all mounted on horses whose sole objective was to loot and pillage and return to their lands with wealth and riches. Speed and force was their strategic advantage over the entrenched. Their forefathers had for centuries watched invaders come and go, and to them the way the Afghans had survived was to loot the sub-continent and take everything home. The rise of the Sikhs much later was also a result of Sikha Gakkhar's experiences, a Robin Hood of his day, who robbed the robbers from Afghanistan. Sikha Gakkhar visited Lahore many times and was convinced that the city could be taken and ruled. So he hit on a strategy, and that was to come in reasonable numbers, with overwhelming force, sit on the throne for a reasonable time, collect everything of value that could be carried away, and then make for the hills before the official army came.

Sikha Gakkhar came for the first time with his army from Hazara, where he had trained his men away from spies operating on the plains. He reached Lahore within a matter of three weeks, looting and pillaging almost every village and town on the way. He moved with great speed for his agents were posted along the main highways a week before the invasion, murdering anyone remotely looking like a spy or an agent of the crown. He entered Lahore for the first time in AH 795, killing the entire defending force and executing every official he could. Their heads were put on lances and displayed in the city streets to drive fear into the hearts of the people. His forces entered each and every house of the city, taking away everything of value, and if fancy caught them, any woman they thought was worth keeping.

Sikha Gakkhar and his men had a ball, for never in their lives had these peasants seen such splendour. Any person who complained of being mistreated was executed on the spot. Within two weeks of his taking Lahore, he had carted away over half the grain and spices in the markets to his hideouts in the hills of the Gakkhars. The emperor heard of the fall of Lahore and immediately dispatched a force under his son Prince Humayun to retake the city. But then as fate would have it, the emperor died even before the expeditionary force could enter the Punjab from Delhi, and the army was halted till a successor took the throne. This gave Sikha Gakkhar ideas of grandeur, for by then a small bureaucracy of locals had quickly risen to fill in the gap left by the initial killings.

In the streets of Lahore a saying arose:

"Forget your mothers and your daughters, hide your bread for Sikha is here." Even to this day many old folk in the city use this to describe the doings of a government. The new Emperor Sultan Mahmood Shah ascended the throne in AH 796 and he ordered an even bigger army to retake Lahore. Sikha Gakkhar grouped his forces to the east of the city, just near where today lies the area of Garhi Shahu. It was an intense battle and Sikha, very wisely, decided to retreat against a massive conventional force. He had already prepared his exit plan with his wealth and women, and as soon as night fell his forces disappeared towards the Jammu hills, crossing the River Ravi to trick the opposing army. Their speed and tactics made sure the Tughlaq forces would never be able to catch up with them.

In the hills of Jammu and Hazara, the now experienced Sikha Gakkhar regrouped and increased his army from his native lands stretching from Gujranwala right up to Hazara and Jammu. It was during his brief rule of Lahore that Gakkhar Mandi became a major grain market, and does remain so to this day. It is also because of Sikha Gakkhar that a few centuries later from Gujranwala, very near where Sikha lived, rose a Sikh leader who was to get together a force to rule not only Lahore, but the whole of the Punjab. The bureaucrats who had helped Sikha were punished, but not executed, and they remained in the city with their wealth and influence. They switched sides with ease.

It so happened that during this period Amir Timur had moved towards Delhi from the north to challenge the emperor, while his son, Prince Pir Muhammad, in a flanking movement had taken Multan after a stiff fight. A major change was in the offing in the sub-continent. As these huge armies prepared to do battle, Sikha Gakkhar got a signal from his bureaucrats and he moved in with lightening speed. He took Lahore within a matter of a few hours with a guile that left everyone dazed. Tyranny had returned with a vengeance, to Lahore and to Delhi, for there the forces of Timur had secured themselves.

On his way to Kashmir, Taimur was informed of the ways of Sikha Gakkhar, and he did not respond for a whole day. The mighty Taimur, a warrior known for his ruthless streak being a successor of Genghis Khan, was stunned by the tactics of this man. He called his council and discussed Sikha Gakkhar in detail and decided that a swift army of 10,000 of the fiercest horsemen ride out and surround Lahore. The order was that not one Gakkhar should leave the city alive. Sikha Gakkhar was trapped. A fierce fight took place in which the Gakkhars managed to defend themselves with honour. But Sikha had not accounted for the people of Lahore. As battle raged, the entire population attacked the Gakkhars, killing Sikha along with his favourite women and each and every Gakkhar. The rule of the wild man from the hills collapsed from within. But this is what happens when the rulers misread the people, or take their silence as a sign of weakness and so it happened with Sikha Gakkhar.

The legend of Billo and her ranis

Of late, a song by the name of Billo by that most creative of Punjabi singers, Ibrarul Haq, has been top of the pops. There is good reason for it to be there. The name Billo has a curious spell about it, with the attraction being grouted in Punjabi history, and for the people of Lahore it has a very special place.

Like all magnificent emperors in history, Ranjit Singh, also had his harem, though it was not as large in size as was that of the Mughals or the other rulers before him. While Maharajah Ranjit Singh ruled supreme over the land sitting atop his small room on the Shish Mahal, his harem was divided strictly into four categories. The first two had nine women each, the third had seven women and the fourth 21 women. The number of women in each group were selected by a band of Sikh and Muslim religious leaders who excelled in the 'science' of astrology and numerology.

The first category consisted of royal wives, all selected strictly in accordance with political needs of alliances and likes and dislikes. The second category comprised widows, who he also treated as his wives. The third was a select band of courtesans, all of them talented and educated women. The last group was an array of concubines. All these women were chosen for their beauty and came from all over his kingdom. It was normal for them to retire when they reached the age of 25, when newer and younger ones would be added. And so went on life in the royal household.

In Lahore, there was a woman of exceptional beauty by the name of Bashiran. She was an excellent singer and knew how to hold the Maharajah spellbound. Ranjit Singh called her Billo because she had light brown eyes like that of a cat. Her beauty was such that the whole of Lahore knew that Billo was out of bounds for all men except the Maharajah. She was, by all accounts, the favourite of the emperor, who had ordered an annual jagir of 8,000 rupees for her, double that given to any of the other women. Her strongest asset was her ability to sing ghazals from the *Diwan-i-Hafiz*, most of which she knew by heart. Her voice had a melody few could match. In the streets of Lahore any young beauty who had an ego larger than herself would be taunted as a 'Billo'. Such was the rage of Bashiran of Lahore. One account puts her residence as being one of the large havelis in Paniwala Talaab.

Another account narrates an interesting episode when one day Ranjit Singh, in a playful mood, offered Bashiran jewellery worth Rs.15,000 and a further jagir of Rs.4,000 if she could win the affection of his pious Muslim minister, Fakir Nuruddin. "No thank you, Maharajah", said Billo, "I fear I will be stricken blind for sinfully looking at that holy man."

However, Fakir Nuruddin's brother, Fakir Azizuddin, also a court minister, fell for her charms. One day when he went to see the Maharajah, he noticed that the king was busy listening to a ghazal by Hafiz. He stood by listening to the poetry and at one point was so overcome that he shouted 'Allah-o-Akbar' and jumped into a nearby water tank to cool off. Royal attendants jumped in to rescue him, for he fell unconscious. From that time onwards, whenever Fakir Azizuddin was announced in the Maharajah's presence, all music was stopped. The Maharajah would say: "Run away bharaus", bharau being the Punjabi name for cuckoo, but here meaning the musicians. This usage is still current inside the old city of Lahore.

Just a touch of odd detail about the sessions Maharajah Ranjit Singh used to have in the presence of Billo. The wine served at these sessions was made of the extraction of the choicest raisins, which were mixed with finely crushed pearls. Victor Jacquemont was to write much later that the wine was of the highest calibre, and the sessions with Billo did not smack of vulgarity, but were sober and had a class of their own. "The popular belief that they were orgies is far from the truth. The sessions were for the connoisseur and for those who love poetry and the arts."

In her prime, Billo had a troupe of about 40 young dancers. She had the ability to create mimes in the background while she sang, adding to the over-all effect of the ghazals she sang. Each of the girls was called 'Billo Rani', a usage that is still current in the Walled City. The clothes that Billo used for these 'ranis' is still current among girls following the profession in Tibbi in Lahore. Undoubtedly, Bashiran alias Billo of Lahore was a prima donna of her time. The legend lives on.

Creating a new image of Billo in the minds of the people of not only Lahore, but of the whole of the Punjab, goes to the credit of Ibrar-ul Haq. It would not be a bad idea if this creative genius could read more about the wondrous women and restore in the popular mind Billo's genius and talent.

The Cavalryman who made Ferozepur Road

Every time you turn on to Ferozepur Road from Mozang Chungi and head in the general direction of Model Town and beyond, spare a thought for Maj. Hodson, BA, of Trinity College, Cambridge. He was no ordinary person. The story of Ferozepur Road is an intriguing one, grouted in history as it is.

Lt. Hodson

When the British captured Lahore, the main road connecting the city to the rest of India was the Grand Trunk Road of Sher Shah Suri. Coming from Amritsar, the road curled just off the northern side of the Lahore Fort and headed towards Gujranwala and beyond right up to Peshawar. And though the whole of the Punjab was actually annexed in March, 1849, the British had managed to capture Lahore and its fort in 1848. It is for this very reason that the present Lahore Cantonment is located at Mian Mir, for this was the point where the British camped before capturing Lahore. The border of the Punjab started at the Sutlej, and the British viewed this area as critical for any flanking movement that its army would have to make in finally annexing the Punjab.

Col H.M. Lawrence, the man who actually reorganized the Corps of Guides in the ill-fated war of independence as we now call it, called Hodson, then a lieutenant, and told him that there was need to immediately build a good road right up to Kasur, or Kassoor Camp as the British called it, and onwards to the Sutlej. Lawrence told him: "Oh Hodson, we have agreed that you must take in hand the road to Ferozepur. You can start in a day or two, and you must finish it immediately". This was the total brief for the building of Ferozepur Road.

Hodson went on to make a big name for himself as the man who set up Hodson's Horse, the cavalry regiment that captured the Delhi Fort to bring the mutiny to an end. He was the man, along with his Punjabi Guides, who captured the emperor Pahadar Shah Zafar and his two sons and grandson Abu Bakht, from the tomb of Humayun. As promised he spared the life of the emperor, but deliberately shot dead the two sons of the emperor and his grandson and let their bodies rot in the sun on the 'chibotra' outside the Kotwali for over one day. He was later to write that he had deliberately wanted to end the house of Timur the Tartar. If you drive towards Lahore Defence and turn off the road coming from Gulberg, the regiment on the far-left corner has an old Hodson's Horse was and is still stationed, a unique piece of sub-continental history that we have never cared to tell our children.

The order was to start from the 'chungee' just outside the village of Mozang, then a small town outside Lahore. The road was basically meant to pass by the town of Kasur, which was then a Pathan stronghold and had been resisting the British, and head towards Ferozepur into British India.

Hodson was a tireless horseman, and riding 70 miles a day was normal for him. He is said to have ridden about all over India from the Chinese border to Kashmir and Kabul and Calcutta. One book acknowledges him as the man who rode more than any other Briton in the 150 years they were here. And so Hodson set out to survey the area from Mozang to Ferozepur. This legendary cavalryman became a road-builder. His life became telescopes, Gunter's chains, compasses, theodolites and the lot. His method of building the road was unique, a classic mixture of authority and grassroots democracy. He was later to write that the speed of the road building owed itself to the fact that everyone was fairly paid and everyone contributed good for them. It is worth studying his method.

Lt Hodson rode three times between Lahore and Ferozepur in a matter of two days, meeting all the 'sarpunchs' along the route. He then attended the meetings of the panchayats and argued with them that it was their duty to provide the men to build the road. He asked them for what would be a fair wage. After many a heated argument, a consensus was arrived at and work was started. As the Sikhs before the British had treated the poor villagers with ruthless savagery, the manner of Hodson was in sharp contrast. This the poor liked and they went out of their way to assist.

To find the best route, he lit fires at night and studied the curves in the road. It was almost a work of art for him. Hodson must have ridden the route almost once every day on horseback for three long hot months. Imagine a crazy Englishman galloping from Mozang to Kasur and then on to Ferozepur every day, and returning the same night. And while he was crazy to say the least, for his exploits in the 1857 war speak for themselves, the Punjabi labourers who worked for him were no less crazy. They were delighted to be paid daily and fairly, and also get good meals in the bargain. In three months and 21 days, the road was completed, a miracle even by modern engineering standards. His method was very logical and rooted in the logic of the land.

What he did was that he divided the entire road into 40 portions, and on each of them, he used the 'sarpunch' to find up to 700 able-bodied persons each to work at least 12 hours a day. Each district was given detailed workings of where the road was to be built, and Hodson went through the working of every district every day. His untiring stamina as a horseman paid off, stamina that was to have a telling effect in the critical days of the 1857 battles and the exploits of Hodson's Horse. Once the work was done, he was pleased to get out of the rut of road building and return to the life of a soldier on his horse.

If we are to build our motorways ourselves, with local help and local engineers and local contractors and local materials, it can certainly be done, and done very quickly. At least Hodson's experience tells us so, as does that of the Chinese after the 1949 Revolution. But then one has to be crazy to do anything useful in this beautiful land of ours.

The mystical miracles of Hasso Taelli

One had always wondered why Chowk Chanda (flag), inside Lohari Gate, so got its name. Many an incident over time had taken place there, but its real distinction lies in the fact that at this place a sage by the name Hasso Taelli ran a grain shop. Not much of a distinction one would imagine!

Hasso's real name was Sheikh Hasso, who was a 'taelli' (oil extractor) by caste. He was born and lived all his life inside Lohari Gate. He inherited a grain shop from his Sheikh father in the market opening now known as Chowk Chanda. It is, even today, a major grain market inside the walled city of Lahore. The approach to this market can be had by entering Mori Gate and taking the road swerving to the right. The other approach is by entering Lohari Gate and taking the left bend at the first crossing. Both end up at Chowk Chanda.

Hasso Taelli used to sit very quietly in his shop, silently observing people and reciting silently on his bead string. The time period was 955-1004 AH More often than not his eyes remained closed. Whenever a customer came to his shop, he would request him to weigh the grain himself. If a person refused to do so, he would not sell him anything. Very soon people began to notice that if they weighed more than what they paid for, by the time they got home the excess grain would vanish and they got only what they paid for. However, if they weighed the correct amount, or less than what they paid for, by the time they got home the grain would exceed in weight.

This might sound like a myth, but then numerous books on Lahore quote various incidents with regard to Hasso Taelli and this miracle. Very soon the people of Lahore got to know that trying to cheat Hasso Taelli was a futile pastime, and people started visiting him to seek cures to their problems. He would treat all such visits with the mere mention that they seek Allah's assistance and not his.

The fame of Hasso Taelli soon spread far and wide,

and he planted a flag in front of his shop to mark it. That flag post still stands there. In a lane just off the main grain market was a small resting room in which Hasso used to rest and pray. That small room is still there. Sheikh Hasso Taelli died in the year 1004, and was buried in a small graveyard near Icchara just near the grave of Hazrat Baba Shah Jamal. The reason he was buried so far away from his own home is because Hasso was a follower of Hazrat Shah Jamal, and he was one of his favourite pupils. The grave has been verified as that of Hasso Taelli by the famous Kanhiyya Lal in his book on Lahore. The grave is also marked as such.

But this is where a contradiction comes in. If you take the small road off Abbott Road, where today stands the passport office, there is a beautiful mosque near the gate. Inside on one side is a grave which says: "Syed Hussain, also known as Hasso Taelli". This means that a specific mention of the man and the correct dates are given. This is verified by the book of Allama Alam Faqiri titled *Tazkara Aulia-e-Lahore*. One would normally be inclined to believe that the Icchara grave is authentic as he was a disciple of Hazrat Shah Jamal. But then the Abbott Road grave also seems authentic, though no mention is made of this site by Maulvi Noor Ahmed Chishti in his book on Lahore. He remains silent over the exact site.

Hasso also had a deep understanding with Hazrat Shah Hussain, also known as Lal Hussain. In his lifetime Hazrat Lal Hussain used to say: "Hasso is Hussain and Hussain is Hasso and there is nothing more". The grave of Hasso is in a courtyard which also has the graves of Sheikh Saadullah Sattarposh and other well-known saints of their days. Such was status and fame of Hasso Taelli, the silent sage of Chowk Chanda.

If you ever go to Chowk Chanda, you will notice that people burn small oil lamps and candles in the small room where Hasso once sat. This is a tradition that was started by the followers of Madho Lal Hussain, who consider Hasso

Taelli as among the foremost seers of his age. Various miracles are attributed to him, though he always remained quiet about his powers.

Today Chowk Chanda continues to function as it has for hundreds of years, being a major grain market before the eastern portion of today's Akbari Mandi came up. From a historical point of view, it could well be the oldest grain market as it lies just to the east of the old and now forgotten western wall of Lahore. The flag post is almost 425 years old and is the mark of an ancient mystical tradition of Lahore. Much more research needs to be done on this remarkable saint of Lahore, for such men must not be forgotten.

The origins of Lahore's Rajput tribes

There is no doubt that before the Muslims invaded and captured Lahore, the city was Rajput in character and inhabited by two main tribes, the major ruling tribe of the Bhats, and the vastly different Solankis. The Rajput traditions of the city go back in antiquity, most of it left vague, more so by the scarring experience of the partition of the Punjab.

Most of the written history of Lahore started after the Afghans descended on the city almost 1,000 years ago, changing its character forever. The Muslim invader's religion, culture, eating habits and clothes were very different from the Rajput natives, and though mutual adjustments did take place, the invasion was to change forever the 'ancient' Lahore, the one we know so little about. In this piece I have tried to piece together a lose framework of the two main tribes of Lahore, their origin in mythology, or through the very strong verbal tradition that is part of the sub-continental way of recording history.

First a bit about the Solanki tribe. A British doctor, Henry Walter Bellew (1834-1892), a Pathan history specialist, writing in 1864, says that most Pakhtun tribal names were actually Rajput names, which had undergone changes over time. This gave rise to the theory that Hindus had occupied the region called Afghanistan before the 'foreigners' took it over. As civil surgeon in Peshawar, Dr. Bellew perfected his knowledge of the local languages. He was chief political officer in Kabul during the Second Afghan War. When he retired as India's surgeon-general, he was already an authority on oriental languages.

Dr. Bellew thinks the prefix Suleman is derived from Rajput Solan, which is today visible in Solankl. The Suri Pakhtun were people brought from Syria by the son of Seleukus (pronounced as Solankay), who ruled that part of Alexander's eastern empire. The Afridis are mentioned by Herodotus as 'Aparytai', brought to their present abode by Ghaznavi, but they came from the Afghan province of Maimana. Today most Solankis owe their geographical origins to the area between Sheikhupura and Gujrat in Pakistan.

The Rajput origin of the Solanki tribe, if we go back further in Rajput history, can be traced to a compilation of the Puranas known as 'Desh-v-Bhaga' (as T.H. Thornton describes it). This tribe moved to the Punjab and beyond from Anulhara Pattan in Rajputana. The word 'suraj' and 'sun' have the same origins, as has the word 'solar'. From this it seems that they were sun worshippers. The Solanki tribe, though a minor Lahore tribe, considered Lahore as their main capital, and mostly were traders. In later years they concentrated mainly in the area between Sheikhupura and Gujrat, with many moving beyond to live in the Frontier province. But they always retained their proud Rajput origins. One research even shows them as being related to the Khoja tribes that excelled in trading in Gujarat in India. These sub-tribes of the Solankis were to produce, much later in history, great men like Mahatama Gandhi and Mohammad Ali Jinnah.

But then when did the migration of the Solankis take place from Rajputana? Myth has it that the Kenek Sen, the famous Solar prince, migrated to Lahore almost 1,500 years ago. No exact date is possible, but they definitely came much after the Bhats, who were the rulers when they arrived and were welcome to stay in the city and beyond on the lands between the 'two great rivers'.

The main Rajput tribe of Lahore was always the Bhats, or Bhatis, or Bhattis as we spell them today. The famous Bhatti Gate of Lahore was named after this tribe. Of the ancient Bhats, the king Bhim Sen of Lahore is recorded as having gone into battle with 10,000 horsemen, a number that shows his economic clout over 1,200 years ago. Much later was to come Raja Jaipal of Lahore. His kingdom, so it is mentioned, stretched from "Sirhind to Lamghan, and from Kashmir to Multan". Almost 800 years later Maharajah Ranjit Singh was to rebuild the original Lahore empire exactly as Jaipal had chalked out for himself, only to lose it to the expanding British in 1849.

When Mahmud of Ghazni finally took Lahore, Raja Jaipal was to commit 'johar' self-immolation outside Mori Gate. This proud Bhat Chauhan Rajput was succeeded by his son Anandpal, who was then succeeded by another Jaipal, who had to flee in 1022 when Mahmood put the city to torch. This flight to Ajmer by Jaipal forever ended the Hindu Rajput kingdom of Lahore. Lahore was handed over to Malik Ayaz, and from there onwards a totally different strand of history begins.

But then where did the Bhats come from? History has it that they moved to Lahore almost 1750 years ago from Jaisalmer, establishing on the way a number of empires. This warrior race from Rajputana had other such tribes like the Bussas, Virks, etc. Today most of these Rajputs who converted to Islam live in Lahore and in the areas around Sheikhupura. The others went to India in 1947. Today Lahore is inhabited by a variety of people from all over the sub-continent and Afghanistan and beyond. The beautiful mix that constitutes the Lahori is what makes the city such a wonderful place. The city is because of them, not the other way round.

The Pen and the sword

Two statues that are no longer visible have always held a special allure for the people of Lahore. The first being of Lawrence and the other one of Queen Victoria. Both now lie in the deep 'dungeons' of Lahore Museum, for, it seems, we are afraid of displaying them. It is almost as if we are afraid of history.

Of the two, the one of Lawrence created a stir in its days. From 1911 onwards a movement started to get it removed from its plinth opposite the Lahore High Court on The Mall. It was felt that the words written underneath were an insult to the people of the sub-continent. The words were: "Will you be governed by the pen or the sword?" The Indian National Congress started a campaign to remove the statue, but the British held firmly on that the 'question' posed was not offensive. Come Pakistan and the first thing to fall was the statue. The 'wrong' had been removed, or so the belief went. But it would be interesting to see where this whole thing started.

According to H.R. Goulding, "in 1848 after the suppression of the rebellion of the Kangra hill chiefs, Mr. Robert Cust, Deputy Commissioner, acting under the orders of John Lawrence, then in charge of the newly acquired Trans-Sutlej territory, issued a proclamation which contained the passage: 'I have ruled this district three years by the sole agency of the pen, and, if necessary, I will rule it by the sword'." This proclamation was

Lord Lawrence

publicized by Cust, explaining to the headmen (or Lambardars) of the villages in the 'disaffected' parts of the district, to meet him as he marched to tackle the rebellion.

At each halting place along the route, a meeting of several villages was arranged. Cust put a pen and a sword on the table and asked the 'lambardars' to choose what they wished to be ruled by. Not a single meeting, and over 22 such meetings were held, went for the sword. The success of this policy yielded immense results for the British, who managed to crush the Kangra rebellion ruthlessly. In those days all rebels were put before a cannon and just blown away. Very soon, the people of the Punjab learned that rebellion was a one-way street. So it was no shocking news that all lambardars went for the pen. It is interesting that John Lawrence never uttered the words that have, over time, been ascribed to him.

The famous sculptor Sir Edgar Boehm in London built the statue. It was presented to the Lahore Municipality by the sculptor, and on the 30th of March, 1887, it was unveiled by the lieutenant governor, Sir Charles Aitchison. For the British, the statue represented the 'enlightened' aspects of their rule. In 1911, on a petition submitted by a citizen's committee, the municipality considered the proposal of removing the statue as it was seen to offend local sensitivities. The then deputy commissioner, R. Humphries, agreed with a proposal of Sir Louis Dane, the Lt. Governor, to leave the statue as it was. The matter was again brought up in 1920 just after the First World War had ended. A proposal was put forward to simply deface the words and leave the statue alone. This proposal soon gained currency, and as an agitation developed over the issue, people started demonstrating for the complete removal of the statue.

The British were deft at handling such issues. Initially, they put forward a proposal that the statue be removed to another place. This held the demonstrations off for some time. But then it was leaked to the Press that as the statue was built by a trust, there was nothing the government could do about it. The demonstrations started again. It was then decided to put the issue to a 'sub-committee' of the Lahore municipality, in which prominent Lahore personalities were represented. The entire activity went into low gear as the deliberations went on and on. After almost one year of consideration it was declared that the statue was "out and out a gift", and, therefore, the question of it being in trust did not exist. The commission, therefore, decided that the municipality was within its right to remove the statue.

On July 10, 1922, the Lahore municipality passed a resolution expressing the concern of the sub-committee, and the results of the discussion were passed on to the government for appropriate action. The government suggested that before the 'gift' statue was removed, it would only be fair to the name of Lawrence that a new statue be first built, which would replace the old one. It was suggested that two-thirds of the cost be borne by the government, and one-third by the Lahore municipality. The finance committee of the municipality rejected this on February 23, 1923. This impasse resulted in the following order being passed:

"In view of Government's refusal to share the expense of a new statue of Lord Lawrence, and in view of the financial stringency in the Municipality, it is resolved that the proposal to substitute a new statue in place of the older one be dropped and Government be requested to take over the statue". It was a masterly bureaucratic action. The agitation stopped, but continued to pick up once in a while.

Lord Lawrence kept standing with his pen and his sword in hand till the 14th of August 1947, on which day we knocked down the sword certainly, but then we also knocked down the pen in our lives. The deputy commissioner of Lahore, Mr. Zafarul Ahsan, who consigned the famous Lawrence to the godowns of the Lahore Museum, saved the statue.

The prince who became a pauper

There was a time when Lahore was ruled by Ahmad Shah Abdali's grandson Shah Zaman. The only aim of coming down from the mountains of Afghanistan was to loot and rob the people of this land of ours. Pretensions of Islamic aspirations came much later, years after they had died and gone - a convenient political twist to the 'accumulation of wealth' by any means.

There was a time when the people of Lahore in particular, and the Punjab in general, used a sentence to describe the uselessness of accumulating wealth, and that sentence was, "What you manage to eat or drink is yours, the rest belongs to Ahmad Shah". Such was their terror and the regularity with which these Afghan marauders came. The rise of Sikh power put an end to such Afghan ventures, especially after the ruthless general Hari Singh Nalwa went right up to Kabul to establish Punjab's writ. The cycle of historical claims had come full circle. Such was the ferocity of Nalwa that even today Afghan women scare their children by saying "stop crying or Nalwa will come".

One of the most interesting 'twists of fate' stories about the rulers of Lahore is that of Shah Zaman. Like his grandfather Abdali, and father Timur, every year the ruler of Kabul would descend on the Punjab and head for Lahore. Till the Indus they would not meet with much resistance. But once across the mighty river, initially the local rulers would try to stop them. But finding them too strong to stop, they would slink away and wait. The classic Punjabi guerilla tactic evolved over time. It sucked in the invader, prompted him to go towards Delhi and on the way back harassed the invader till he was stripped of the loot. The Sikh misls were masters of this tactic. The strategy in the end crushed the Afghans forever and established Punjabi rule over the Punjab.

The main problem for Afghan rulers was not fighting the Punjabis, but dealing with intrigue at home. It was brother against brother, and every time one set off for India, the other would try to usurp the throne. Shah Zaman had two ambitious brothers, who gave him no end of trouble. In 1796, when he invaded India for the third time, his brother Mahmud struck. And so it happened every year. Shah Zaman ruled Lahore with an iron hand, but in the end, his brothers got the better of him Mahmud managed to gouge out his eyes.

By the time Ranjit Singh managed to secure his position as Maharajah of the Punjab, Shah Zaman was again on the run from his brothers. Shah Shuja came to

Attock, where his gracious host, suspecting him of intrigue sent him in chains to Kashmir. But Ranjit Singh decided to give Shah Zaman and the family of Shuja asylum at Rawalpindi, where they again started to intrigue. They set up a government in exile. This led the crafty Ranjit to bring them to Lahore to keep a closer eye on them.

On Nov 11, 1811, Shah Zaman, a former ruler of Lahore, entered the Walled City. He had left as king and returned a virtual beggar. He was put up in an impressive 'haveli' in Bazaar Hakeeman and was guarded well. But the family's appetite for intrigue got the better of it. At that time, Ranjit was preparing for a grand wedding reception for his son and heir Kharrak Singh. It was the grandest wedding reception the city had ever seen. Rs. 236,000 was given to the bridegroom in cash, which by present day gold standard equivalent would be worth well over Rs200 million. The British East India Company presented a 'massive' cash gift of Rs.5,000.

But the purpose of Maharajah Ranjit Singh putting up Shah Zaman and the family of Shah Shuja as guests was much more than Afghan intrigue. His eye (and he had only one) was on the famous diamond from the Golconda mines, the Koh-i-Noor. The diamond was in the possession of his guests, or so it was suspected. It initially belonged to the Mughal emperors who got hold of it after it was mined and polished. Then the Persian invader Nadir Shah took the Koh-i-Nur and the Peacock throne from emperor Muhammad Shah in 1739. When in 1747 Nadir was assassinated, Ahmad Shah Abdali got hold of it. It then went to Taimur, and then to Shah Zaman. After him Shah Shuja and his wife Wafa Begum took possession. When he escaped from Kabul, the diamond was brought to Lahore. And it was from this family that the diamond was recovered by Ranjit Singh.

Wafa Begum had promised to hand over the diamond if her husband was welcomed and assisted in his efforts to reclaim his throne from his brother. So Shah Shuja was released from Shergarh and was welcomed in Lahore in grand style. He was escorted by Mohkam Chand, a loyal Ranjit aide. On the second day of their arrival, Ranjit Singh asked that the Afghans keep their part of the promise and hand over the famous diamond. The Afghans swore by the Quran that they did not possess it. Ranjit Singh tried for three days to make them keep their pledge, but the Afghans would not relent. Then on promise of helping them regain territory to the north of the Punjab, and for a price of Rs. 50,000, Shah Shuja said he would consider. On this the Punjabi exchanged turbans as a symbol of eternal friendship. On June 1, 1813, Shah Shuja handed over the diamond to the Maharajah. It had been with them all the time.

There are many versions about how the diamond was extracted. This version is from the diary of Mohkam Chand, who was present when the price was paid and the diamond received. It was also from Lahore that the British took the diamond that today remains in the possession of the British monarch. So the ruler of Lahore returned a virtual beggar, and sold a diamond for a price. On this rests the case of the Punjab Government, with Lahore as its capital, as being the real and rightful owners of this diamond. Will we ever get it back ... one has serious doubts. This is where legend comes in. There is a popular Lahori saying that the diamond will return to Lahore one day.

The Qizilbash Cossacks

If you drive along the Empress Road from the railway station towards the Shimla Pahari, the land on both sides of the road once all belonged, or was gifted by the British, to the Qizilbash family of Ali Raza Khan, the man who bailed the British out in Afghan wars. This gift is today part of a waqf, or trust.

At the beginning of the 19th century when the Raj was at its height, there were just a handful of Muslim wealthy families. The most important was the Fakir family of Bazaar Hakeeman, then there was the Kashmiri family of Nawab

Sheikh Imamuddin and Sheikh Ghulam Muhyuddin, and then there was the family known as the Nawabs of Multan, who originally belonged to Kandahar. But in terms of wealth, the Qizilbash family managed to acquire influence and wealth far beyond its numbers. Even today, their waqf property takes care of their dwindling influence.

When Qizilbash chief Raza Ali Khan first came to Lahore from Afghanistan, they were known locally as 'Kabuli Qizilbash'. With time, this description was dropped as the British for services rendered gave them the title 'Nawab'. They got the choicest lands taken over from the locals. One description describes Raza Ali Khan as "probably the most loyal subject of the British crown". When the British got stuck in Kabul, Raza Ali Khan bribed his way to assist the prisoners, and prevented them from being taken to Hazara. The Qizilbashes openly allied themselves with the British during the First Anglo-Afghan War (1838-1842). Amir Abdur Rahman accused them of being partisan to the enemy during his campaigns against the Hazaras in 1891-1893, declared them enemies of the state, and confiscated their property.

When the British launched their second offensive, Raza Ali Khan and his Qizilbash fighters joined hands with them against Muhammed Akbar Khan. In a way, he betrayed his own kind and on their defeat, came over to British India. In Kabul, his property was confiscated and his houses demolished. There was no going back for the Kabuli Qizilbash tribe and their leader.

During the campaign against the Sikhs, the Qizilbashes, who were excellent cavalry fighters, assisted the British in no small manner to crush the Lahore Court. They entered Lahore with them and took over major portions of the Mochi Gate area, where they built beautiful houses and established themselves as among the richest people in British Lahore. Earlier, in the 1846 campaigns against Kangra and Kashmir, the Qizilbash horsemen assisted Lord Lawrence in his campaigns. But it was in Lahore that they finally settled.

In 1857 Mohammed Raza Khan and Muhammed Taqi Khan with a thousand cavalry headed towards Delhi. They pledged not to charge a single penny from the British, i.e they declared themselves loyal to the British crown. The Qizilbash cavalry played a terrible part in that determining battle, when they cut down by the thousands Muslims trying to escape during the battle. The original Cossacks of the Caspian were among the most feared, for they made sure that the road between Delhi and Lahore remained open. This led them to involve themselves in considerable fighting as the Mughal Empire collapsed.

For their contribution, the British immediately in 1857 awarded them ownership of 147 villages to the south-east of Lahore. Raza Ali Khan was given a pension of Rs. 2,000 a year. They were allotted lands between Raiwind and Lahore, where they founded their own village at Ali Razabad. He was given the title of Nawab, and henceforth came to be known not as Kabuli Qizilbash Raza, but as Nawab Raza Ali Khan Qizilbash. His three sons, Nawazish Ali Khan, Nasir Ali Khan and Nisar Ali Khan, had also rendered sterling services to the British. Nawazish was with Lawrence when the campaign against Sardar Chattar Singh Attari was undertaken, and had it not been for the fierce Qizilbash swordsmen, the Khalsa warriors would have won the day. Since then Lawrence always had respect for these Caspian cavalrymen.

Nisar Ali Khan, after the death of his father, took over to looking after all lands and properties the British awarded the Qizilbash clan. One estimate is that this Kabuli-cum-Caspian Cossack accumulated more wealth than any other family in the Punjab. Nisar himself built an exquisite haveli inside Mochi Gate.

Today, the Qizilbash clan is a much-dwindled collection of families. The main landowners, the family of Nawab Muzaffar Ali Qizilbash, a former Punjab chief minister, still owns the Nawab Palace on Empress Road. They own a major chunk of the land on Empress Road, but all of it is waqf property. They also have huge landholdings on the Lahore-Raiwind Road. But their glory has definitely gone. No outstanding Qizilbash can be named today except for Dr. Muzaffar Qizilbash of the London School of Economics, a scholar more interested, and correctly so, in books and a quiet life than his fiery ancestors. A few have escaped to the cooler climes of the West.

The Rascal Chandu Shah

If you *ever* happen to be driving from The Mall into the Lahore Cantonment, you will reach a crossing opposite the Corps Commander's house, or Jinnah House. To the left is a memorial to the Sikh Pioneers, a regiment disbanded in 1947. I stood there and thought of Hodson's Horse, of the battlefields of the First and Second World Wars, of Guru Arjun Singh, and as my father used to say, of that rascal Chandu Shah.

Of all the military memorial structures in and around Lahore, there is none to rival this one. As you read the very long list of battlefields that the Sikh Pioneers, raised in Lahore in 1857, had been to and distinguished themselves in, one feels sorry for the loss of so many youth over a whole century. One is particularly struck by the story of a Pioneer resident of Lahore by the name of Risaldar Basharat Ali. Originally from Rohtak he served with Maj WSR Hodson, the man who founded the famous regiment called Hodson's Horse in Lahore and the man who captured the Emperor Bahadar Shah Zafar in 1857. Hodson went to Risaldar Basharat's village and shot him and his family. It was blamed on enemy action, but the Punjab District Gazetteers of 1878, quoting from the Rohtak Settlement report of Fanshaw 1878-79, tended to report that Hodson owed Risaldar Basharat a lot of money and instead of returning the loan, he killed him. The accusation stuck and the East India Company deep froze the case.

I remember almost 30 years ago, as a young student in my teens, walking through the battlefields of Belgium at

Ipiers and reading the names of Punjabi soldiers on a grand monument that still stands in their honour. Scores of names appear, with the place of birth of the dead soldier, and dotted at hundreds of places comes the name Lahore. Their blood still flows in those beautiful green fields at Ipiers, and Flanders, and several other places where the Punjabis fell. I remember reading a letter in Urdu in the museum at Ipiers from a mother from Mochi Gate to her son with the words:

Allah teray naal aye bachchay (God is with you, my son). I remember tears when I read those, and how excited I was that the martyrs from my city dot the battlefields of the world, I was sad in that why did a beautiful human from my city, let alone any other city, have to be there. The beautiful plaque in the Lahore Cantonment reminds me of all those that we lost. The monument also reminded me of Chandu Shah, a rich Hindu banker of Delhi who originally came from Lahore's Akbari Mandi area. He managed to get into the good books of Akbar the Great. My late father once, while walking with me through the Walled City pointed out a house and said: *Aay Chandu haramza-day da si* (This belonged to that bastard, Chandu). Now these were strong words coming from my father and I heard a story about Lahore's Chunna Mandi, which needs to be told. Chandu had a beautiful daughter for whom he just could not find a match. He insisted that the groom be a Punjabi from the Lahore-Amritsar area. His agents searched far and wide and ultimately they said that if there was a match it would surely be the son of Guru Arjun Dev, a handsome youth and named Hargobind. On hearing of this the Hindu banker remarked: "A brick baked with care in a castle is not meant to be used in a gutter." This remark still lives in the Sikh psyche.

But with time, circumstances made Chandu Shah change his mind, but now Guru Arjun refused, and that led Chandu to inform Akbar that the Holy Granth of the Sikhs was full of blasphemy. When in Lahore the Guru was summoned, but he sent two emissaries, Bhai Budha and Bhai Gurdas. The Holy Granth was opened and they recited:

From day and light God created the world.

The sky, the earth, trees and water are made by Him.

Forgetting God in avarice is like eating carrion.

The way the evil spirits kill and devour the dead. One must restrain oneself, Hell is the punishment otherwise. None will come to rescue when you depart.

God the Pure only knows what's in store for me

Nanak, my appeal of a slave is to You alone. (Tilang)

The Emperor Akbar heard this and was satisfied that there was nothing blasphemous in the verse. But Chandu Shah insisted that as the verse was quoted from memory it was not proof, let someone read the Granth. Akbar agreed and so the book was opened and the following verse was read:

You don't see God who dwells in your heart,

And you carry idols around your neck, A non-believer wanders about churning water, Ultimately dying in delusion. The idol you call God will drown with you, Oh ungrateful sinner, This boat of stone will not ferry you across.

Says Nanak, met the Guru who led me to God,

He who lives in water, earth, nether region and firmament. (Suhi)

The Emperor Akbar was delighted and from that day onwards whenever he came to Lahore, he stopped over to pay his respects to the Guru.

But Akbar died soon afterwards, and just because his son Khusrau happened to be the guest of Guru Arjun Singh, Chandu managed to get Emperor Jehangir to jail and torture Guru Arjun Singh. Chandu's young girl never married and tried to save Guru Arjun, but to no avail. The people of Lahore cursed Chandu Shah for years to come. Every time an elder passes by the house, he curses Chandu. That is why, probably, my father did the same. That is why they still say in the old, narrow and winding lanes of the Walled City:

Chandu chan nahi honda, beshak Shah hovay (Chandu can never shine, even if he is a Shah). Another translation by K.S. Duggal, however, translates this as:

"Chandu will never have a grandchild, even though he is a Shah." But in all honesty, I still feel sorry for his young daughter, for she bribed her way into Lahore Fort to apologize for her arrogant father.

The Roberts family of Lahore

Two major developments kept the Punjab from contributing to the 1857 war of independence; they were the telegraph and the Lahore Volunteers led by Arthur Austin Roberts, who was afterwards to become a judge of the Lahore Chief Court. The result was a mass surrender of the sepoys at the Mian Mir Cantonment.

Unlike the rest of India, the telegraph lines in the Punjab were never cut by the sepoys of the English East India Company, and communications flowed with ease about what was happening in Delhi. The fall of Delhi was kept a secret, for the British were lucky in getting the telegraphic information sent by the telegraph operator at Delhi which was received in the Punjab by both Lawrence, the chief commissioner, and by Montgomery, the financial commissioner, on May 12, 1857. Lawrence was a decisive person and he sent his spies immediately to the Mian Mir Cantonment, the portion we today call 'Saddar'. There was a sense of excitement in the bazaars, but what exactly was brewing Lawrence could not make out. It was this very vagueness that led him to strike first.

The native regiments at Lahore, they being the 16th Native Infantry, the 26th Native Infantry, the 49th Native Infantry and 8th Light Cavalry were all disarmed at four in the morning on May 13, 1857, by HM 81 Foot, which was stationed at Lahore. This was done in a totally unexpected manner since the sepoys were not aware of the Meerut outbreak or of the capture of Delhi by the sepoys. This decisive action secured Lahore for the British. But that was not the end. After disarming the Lahore regiments, half of the 81 Foot rode non-stop all night towards Amritsar and disarmed the 59th Native Infantry stationed there. That early morning strike on May 14, 1857, managed to contain any major outbreak of hostilities.

On May 14, a few disarmed sepoys in Lahore entered the Officers Colony at Saddar and killed a few British officers. They were swiftly captured and before the mutiny could take root, the British brought them to the main bazaar and blew them up from cannons to the utter amazement of the population. A similar undertaking was to take place at the Anarkali cantonment. Lahore remained the pillar of strength of the Company throughout the 'mutiny' and served as the headquarters of the forces set off to capture Delhi.

The commander of the Lahore Volunteers, a force raised in the city and disbanded in 1868, was led by the then commissioner of Lahore, a civil servant of Irish origin, who was to later become a judge of the Lahore High Court, then known as the Lahore Chief Court. The role of Arthur Austin Roberts remains a mystery to this day, for all mention of this man was suppressed in the 'Mutiny Record' of the Company and, later on, the British government. Arthur A. Roberts and his sons all served in Lahore in one way or the other, and to this family the Company and the British government owed a lot.

The Roberts originally belonged to Stradbally, Queens County (Laois), Ireland. The family moved to India during the potato famine of the 1790s, as the father of Roberts was a clerk in the East India Company. While a lot of the Irish were running westwards to the Americas under the cruelty of the English, the family of Arthur Roberts headed the other way, and it was in Benares (now known as Varanasi) that Arthur Austin Roberts was born on June 28, 1818. After his initial schooling in Calcutta, he went to

Hailebury College, in England in 1836, and then joined the Bengal Civil Service in 1837. He married Elizabeth Wood in 1841 in Calcutta and then moved to the Punjab with the forces of the East India Company during the reign of Maharajah Ranjit Singh. After Lahore was occupied in 1849, he moved here to head the civil service and by 1856, he was the commissioner. So if any person knew the Punjab best, it was Roberts.

Arthur Roberts set about organizing a network of informers, and as commissioner it was rumoured that he even knew each and every move that anyone of any importance made. It was this network that helped him to keep the Lahore police force intact in 1857, a force that ensured complete harmony during the entire 1857 war of independence. Anyone who was seen as a suspect was put before a cannon and blown up before an alarmed and frightened people. For his services in 1857, he was awarded a CB (Commander of the Bath).

Once the 'mutiny' was under control, Arthur Roberts immediately set about trying to prove what a just and fair administration the Company had to offer to the people. He was made judge of the Lahore Chief Court in 1866, and earned the respect of everyone by his fair judgments. For these services, he was awarded the Companion of Star of India. The British government by then had begun to plan the 'governance' of the State of Hyderabad through its Nizam. Roberts was sent there as the resident, where he died on May 10, 1868. The widow of Arthur Roberts moved to Waudlupe near Hawick, Scotland, where she died on June 7, 1905.

The three sons of Arthur Austin Roberts all served in the Punjab in Lahore, all of them with distinction. Arthur William Roberts (1842-1899), his first son, was born at Fort William, Bengal, India; educated at Harrow 1855-1857 and at East India College, 1857. He joined the 7th Dragoon Guards, 1858, was commissioned in the Bengal Cavalry in 1862, and entered the political department in the Punjab in 1864. He served against the Bikaner Uprising in 1881-82, and retired as a major-general in 1898.

The second son, Allan Scott Roberts (1845-1932), joined the Bengal Infantry, 1862, and served on the Punjab Commission, 1866-94. He retired as a Lt Col and moved to England. The third son, who for some reason remained unacknowledged, Stephen William Thomhill Roberts (1855-1897), served with the 27th Punjab Native Infantry; served at Jowaki, 1877, and Afghanistan. He died at Landikotal on June 16, 1879, aged 25. There is a tablet in the Lahore Cathedral which says: "to loving memory of Stephen William Thomhill Roberts, 27th P.N.I Probadoner died at lundi Kotul June 16, 1879, aged 25. Son of the late Arthur A. Roberts Esqre C.B., C.S.L, Bengal Civil Service."

The rule and reign of the Roberts family, especially the senior Roberts, had a telling effect on the way Lahore was administered just before and after the 1857 war of independence. While definitely ruthless in the execution of their decisions, they also tempered it with justice that was actually 'seen to be done'. His one noting on a judgment could still prove as guidance to officers today: "There is no point claiming to be honest. It is only when the populace perceives an officer to be honest, that he is free to administer effectively. Only then can law and order be maintained."

The roots of many a Lahore family

There was a time when the people of Lahore, especially the elite, took great pride in their roots, and almost every family had their 'shajara' - branches of the roots of a family - framed in their house. It was easy to trace the details of every family. This came in handy when a marriage was arranged, for it was considered a marriage not between two people, but of two families.

Tracing the roots of a family was no mean task, for it meant keeping track of every birth, death and marriage of a family. Every development meant an entire new branch being traced, and the sub-branches then took on a new meaning. This was no easy task, for as it was a two dimensional task, the third dimension had to be taken up in another shajara. For this reason every family had two shajara maps, one tracing the father's lineage, while the second traced the mother's lineage.

Even this had limitations, for come the third generation and it became too complex to record. For this reason Lahore had 'shajara' specialists, normally the 'munshi,' or assistant, of the family hakeem. Most of the 'shajjara munshis' sat in Bazaar Hakeeman, and they operated through the hakeems. These people kept records of the entire family, with a few working through barbers, who acted as informants.

It so happened that I wanted to search for my family roots, and a few elders pointed out to the fact that our entire family had been charted and recorded in a number of books. One strand of the family had Chishti roots, while the other has Sheikh roots. As I knew that the Sheikhs and the Chishtis inter-married a lot, one accepted that this was because of the family elders. A trip to the old city saw me discussing the issue with an elderly munshi who knew my father well.

He pointed out to a book printed at the turn of the last century, and after much searching, and thanks to some assistance from an aunt and a 'fourth removed' cousin, I managed to lay my hands on a book called *Yaadgar-e-Chishti,* written by Maulvi Nur Ahmad Chishti who had written this book specially for the British East India Company so as to 'educate' them about the people, families and customs of Lahore. This rare book was reprinted by the Majlis Taraki-i-Urdu, Lahore, in 1972, and is now a collector's item. The reprinted book has an update on families undertaken by Gauhar Naushahi.

Here it might be of interest to note that Maulvi Nur Ahmad Chishti was hired by the East India Company in 1849, the year the Sikh empire crumbled and the British took over Lahore, to teach the officials of the company Urdu and Persian. He impressed the new rulers so much that they requested that a book be compiled to be a standard text for all British officials coming to Lahore, a sort of get-through guide of Lahore and its people and families. So came about *Yadgar-e-Chishti.*

Among the numerous shajaras given in this book is the one of the Chishti family itself. At the head of this complex diagram is Maulvi Ziaul Haq, a religious scholar who served under the Mughal emperor Shah Jahan. His two children were Maulvi Muhammad Ibrahim Chishti and a daughter who was married off to a Mughal court official in Agra. His son was called Mirza Hidayatullah. Ibrahim Chishti had a son Maulvi Ghulam Hussain who further had five children.

We take up the line from Maulvi Ahmad Bakhsh Yakdil, a religious scholar who served the Lahore Darbar of Maharajah Ranjit Singh. Maulvi Yakdil had a huge family of 15 children, six of whom died at birth. In fact, of the seven first born, only one, Muhammad Ali, survived. Of the last eight, one died at birth. This makes a staggering seven dead at birth out of 15, providing a picture of the health standards before the British arrived in Lahore.

Maulvi Nur Ahmad Chishti was the ninth child of Maulvi Yakdil. One sister, Iqbal-un-Nisa, married Amir Bakhsh Sahaf, another well-known Lahore family. His brother Maulvi Muhammad Ali Chishti had a son Maulvi Hamid Ali Chishti, who had nine children. Not a single child died at birth.

This is the period at the end of the Sikh rule, by which time Lahore had a reasonable health system, put in place by French, Russian and Hungarian doctors, as well as an excellent 'hakmat' tradition, in which the famous Fakir family of Bazaar Hakeeman excelled. One grandson of Maulvi Hamid Ali Chishti was Abdul Qadir Chishti, the first Muslim shop owner in Anarkali Bazaar, whose shop China Mart sadly closed down last year after 115 years. His son Abdul Quddus Chishti died three years ago, and with him a tradition of Muslim entrepreneurial history.

One daughter of Maulvi Hamid Ali Chishti was Syeda Begum, my grandmother who married a Sheikh. Another daughter Zakia also married a Sheikh by the name of Abdul Salam, a police official and a cousin of my father. His son was the famous Dr Ahsanul Islam of Government College Lahore. One daughter Asghari Begum married a Makhdoom by the name of Muhammad Afzal, and her son was the famous Dr Muhammad Ajmal, an eminent psychologist and Principal of the Government College, Lahore.

It was seen by the 1970s that over 27 members of the family of Maulvi Hamid Ali Chishti were students of the Government College, Lahore, most of whom have gone into intellectual pursuits. It probably is in the genes, and that is why having a family shajara made sense to the elders of Lahore.

Another shajara of the mother of Maulvi Nur Ahmad Chishti is also given in the book, and it has a Sahaf lineage. In this complex diagram, we see another 21 children being students of the Government College, Lahore, by the 1970s. Here one sees the Siddiqui family marrying into the Sahaf family. Looking at various family shajaras one cannot avoid noticing that every one has a strong connection to another Lahore family.

According to the book itself, Maulvi Nur Ahmad Chishti does mention that before a marriage, the heads of the two families would go to their hakeem and consult them if the match was correct. Here the munshi would bring forth his books and break down the connection into 'blood lineage.' This, for me, was a remarkable discovery. In Lahore our elders were, even 200 years ago, in possession of family records to work out the way genes functioned. This is a field that needs much more research. There are scores of books lying with the family of old munshis of the various hakeems and barbers of Lahore.

In the west there is an immense interest in the roots of families, mostly because most westerners are of migrant origin. In a way this is also true of the Punjab and Lahore.

For example my dear friend Tahir Azam, more correctly Shahzada Tahir Azam, is of Royal Afghan lineage. His great grandfather ruled Kabul ... but that is another story of adventure and escapes that must be told.

The scoundrel who outlived the sage

When we think of Garhi Shahu, we think of the railway station, we think of the Christian community, we think of the Burt Institute and that wonderful dance club that no longer functions, and we think of the Convent of Jesus and Mary. But surely there is much much more to this place than we have ever cared to explore.

The pinnacle of fame for the Garhi Shahu area was during the British period when the rail track was laid, and being an engine driver was the 'in thing.' Initially all the engine drivers were British, and the Raj laid out beautiful residential colonies for them near the rail track, starting from the still superb Mayo Gardens to the Burt and to the other colonies on both side of the old Mayo Road, now renamed after Iqbal. Just why do we have to forget our history, one will never know. The British then started inducting into the railways Indian Christians, mostly of Portuguese origin from Goa. Lahore was full of D'Souzas, D'Sylvas and Ferrairas, not to speak of the fairer skinned British origin names like Burtons, Brians and Nibletts.

They were also inducted into the railway police, and later on into the Punjab police, and all of them served with distinction. Today, almost all of them have flown, for very valid reasons of our prejudices, to cooler climes. The social and cultural environment of Ghari Shahu was markedly different from the rest of Lahore, and it was a much sought after area.

But then the real story of the area must begin from the days of Emperor Shah Jahan, for during his reign an Arab sage by the name of Abul Khair came to Lahore. He was a well-known scholar of Islamic jurisprudence who had set off on his travels from Baghdad. On reaching the Punjab, he found the weather most agreeable to his temperament and decided to stay a while in Lahore. In those days, the area now known as Garhi Shahu was known as Mohallah Syedan, because in this area lived scholars like Syed Jan Muhammad Hazuri, after whom is named the famous Hazuri Bagh. The intellectual environment was much to his liking and he decided to settle down here.

During the reign of Emperor Aurangzeb, the fame of Abul Khair had spread far and wide, and the emperor wished that the maximum number of people should benefit from the sage. He ordered that a madrassah be built for Abul Khair and a suitable residence be arranged for the scholar. A maintenance fee was also ordered by a firman for the upkeep of the house and the madrassah. And so Abul Khair's institution was founded. Today it exists, empty and derelict on one edge of a small graveyard at the end of a small lane as the road curves towards the main Garhi Shahu crossing.

Abul Khair kept teaching in his madrassah till the age of 105, and on his death he was buried here, as were other well-known persons of that age. As the Mughal empire was folding and anarchy was slowly setting in, scholarship and learning were no longer on a premium. Lahore was ruled by three Sikhs before Maharajah Ranjit Singh finally managed to bring order for 40 odd years. During this period anarchy reigned supreme, and the madrassah was taken over by a 'khalifa' by the name of Muhammad Naeem, who taught there. On his death there was a void.

But anarchy has rules of its own, and it knows how to fill in voids on its own accord, just like in our times 'qabza groups' make a mockery of the law. In a way very little has changed. The house and madrassah that existed near the crossing of the present-day Garhi Shahu had many scoundrels with an eye on it. People started stealing bricks from the buildings of the madrassah. Groups of dacoits set upon the students of the madrassah and stripped them of their meagre belongings.

Then a real godfather by the name of Shahu came along with his gang of rustlers, and he took possession of the buildings meant to accommodate Abul Khair and his scholars. They would steal cattle and other things from the area and keep them there for safekeeping. If the owners came, for a small price they would return their goods. Otherwise, they would be sold.

This was the age when the three Sikh rulers were restricted to their small domains. In between there was no law. The gang of Shahu ruled supreme, and it was from him that the name Garhi Shahu came. The Sikhs called it by this name, and so did the British, and so do we, and there seems no reason why we should change its name just because Mr Shahu was a shady character and lived a life very much like many a 'respectable' citizen these days, and one does not say this in jest.

But the British changed the character of Garhi Shahu, for it was the hub of their entire effort to provide their forces and subjects with a means of communication that revolutionized life in a major way. Come to think of it, life is revolutionized by changes in the means of communication, like the internal combustion engine or the mobile telephone in their own time. But who would have ever thought that an area that came up to accommodate a most learned man never kept his name, and a complete scoundrel managed to keep his name alive because he was a genuine 'qabza group' leader. Strange are the twists of fate that we see in Lahore, for every brick has a story to tell.

The Shahalami of Rai Lakpat

If any portion of the old walled city of Lahore suffered the most during the ravages of the partition of the Punjab, it was the entire Shahalami Gate area. Along with the old historic gate with its wooden drawbridge over the moat, all the old havelis were burned down. In the carnage came the 'claim squads', who sold off the bricks. By September, 1947, it was ground zero.

The Shahalami gate got its name from Moazzam Shah, the second son of the last great Mughal emperor Aurangzeb, who died in 1707. Moazzam battled for the throne his younger brother Azin and ruled for five years, dying in Lahore in 1712. It was a formidable gate with huge wooden gates, which were shut at night. Even till the 1930s, it had a functioning drawbridge over the Ravi, part of which flowed round the walled city. At night the bridge was pulled up to keep outsiders away.

Inside the gate, the very first mohallah was known as Bazaar Hattar, At the very head of the bazaar were two magnificent havelis, considered by many as among the finest in the entire old walled city. The lane emerging from the bazaar is still called 'Lakpat da Phalla'. These were the havelis of Rai Lakpat; whose village Kot Lakpat is now part of the expanding Lahore. Lakpat Rai was among the richest men in the entire Lahore area and its suburbs, owing huge tracts of land, hundreds of shops inside Lahore's walled city and in Mauza Mozang and Mauza Ichhra. He also had huge food godowns in the Akbari Mandi (market) and stored his own wheat, rice and red chillies there. He was in the classic sense, a super hoarder, who picked up essential food items when they were cheapest, and sold them to the wholesale market when they were expensive. There is a tiny lane in Akbari Mandi still known as 'Lakpat di Arath'. Diwan Rai Lakpat and his brother Diwan Rai Jaspat built two huge havelis from the finest small bricks and used the finest lime mortar. Both the havelis were three-storey buildings with exquisite wooden balconies and in the middle of both buildings were huge courtyards. The date of construction can be gauged from the fact that they were built in the days when Nawab Zakariyya Khan was the governor of Lahore. On the sides of the main havelis were other smaller buildings, all meant   for   guests   and   for

Maharajah Ranjit Singh

entertainment. To entertain his special guests, Rai Lakpat built yet another haveli in the Paapar Mandi inside Shahalami.

His wealth can be gauged from the fact that when his eldest son got married, each and every person living inside the walled city of Lahore was presented with a bag of 'desi' sugar (shakkar) weighing two-and-a-half seers. Another source claims that one lakh (100,000) bags were made to be distributed in Lahore, Mozang and Ichhra. The entire Akbari Mandi's shakkar stock was purchased by the diwan as part of the celebration, which went on for a week.

During the Sikh era, Maharajah Ranjit Singh confiscated most of the buildings. The families of Rai Lakpat were seen as collaborators against the Sikhs. When the British took over in 1849, they decided to auction the property. Half of the property was picked up by Moallaf Katib, whose families started living there, while the other half was purchased by another Hindu businessman called Sohan Shah and his brothers, all of whom partitioned the portion to have their own smaller havelis. The two brothers* had property in Mozang, along with the famous Lakpat Talab (pond). The villagers saw that the owner and his sons were no more, and they knocked down the entire property and sold off the bricks. The pond of Jaspat Rai remained, though a gent by the name of Kallo, on orders from Maharajah Ranjit Singh, took over the property and sold it in smaller bits. It later transpired that he had posed as the only remaining relative of Rai Lakpat. Inside the walled city, the remaining havelis of Rai Lakpat were taken over and handed to the family of the Nawab of Multan, who had collaborated with him in conquering that city. The scoundrel Kallo tried to claim that, too, but the Sikh ruler forced him to give up his claim and passed a royal 'firman' giving the property to the Multani nawab's family. The interesting thing is that when the British took over, Kallo tried to reclaim the three havelis, especially the one in Papar Mandi, but the British thought it prudent not to oblige and passed orders to that effect, securing the claim of the Multani nawab family.

Then came the carnage of partition. Most of the killings in Lahore took place in the Shahalami area. A massive fire was started to flush out the rich traders. By the time the fire was put down, each and every constructed building, including the ancient gateway, had collapsed. In the carnage the claim mafia moved in. Bricks were sold by anyone who could remove them. In one massive fit of madness, one of Lahore's oldest portions was lost forever.

In its place came up the present Shahalami Bazaar. Concrete replaced the bricks of old. New faces started business with a work ethic that will yet take many years to mature. But then life goes on along new avenues. The historic gateway and its drawbridge are no more. The havelis are lost. Today we remember Rai Lakpat because of the name of his village, far removed as it is from the old walled city where once he distributed sweets on a scale never seen since.

The 'ghazi' of Lahore

His act made him a 'ghazi'. His hanging made him a 'shaheed'. The name of the 19-year old boy was Ilm Din, and he belonged to Mohallah Sirianwala, near Rang Mahal inside the old walled city of Lahore. Today he is called Ghazi Ilm Din Shaheed, and he lies buried in Miani Sahib, just near the Mozang end of the huge graveyard of Lahore. His story, and the legal drama that ensued, led as it was in the end by an astute barrister called Muhammad Ali Jinnah, needs to be reflected upon.

Our story begins in the year 1927. On the 7th of February the Sessions Judge, Lahore, sentenced a printer/publisher called Raj Pal, of Hospital Road, Lahore, whose printing works was just next to the Lady Aitchison Hospital, to six months rigorous imprisonment for publishing a booklet titled *Rangeela Rasool*, in which he had tried to make fun of the Prophet of Islam, Muhammad (pbuh). The British Government, on the protest of the Muslims of Lahore arrested the writer/printer and after a lengthy trial sentenced him to six months in jail under Section 153-A. He appealed against the sentence in the Lahore High Court before Mr. Justice Dilip Singh. The sentence was quashed as it was felt that Section 153-A was not maintainable. The judgment stated that under the meaning of the section, a "criticism of deceased religious leaders is not punishable. So free walked Mr. Raj Pal on the 4th of May, 1927.

Initially Mr. Raj Pal disappeared from Lahore. When tempers cooled he returned to his house. Twice he was attacked inside the walled city, and so he was given an armed guard. With time it was felt that even that was not needed. So life returned to normal and Mr. Raj Pal returned to his business on Hospital Road. Almost two years after Raj Pal walked out a free man, he was working in his Press when in walked a thin 19-year old boy. He walked up to Raj Pal and asked him a question. The printer turned to look for something in his cupboard. The day was the 6th of April, 1929. The 19-year old immediately pulled out a dagger and attacked him, killing him on the spot. He dropped the dagger and ran up a lane to the right of the printing works and ended up in a timber courtyard next to the grave of Hazrat Zanjani. People chased him and caught him and handed him over to the police, along with the murder weapon.

The witnesses and the murder weapon and the circumstances all led to the tacit conclusion that the insult because of the booklet had been avenged. A day by day trial took place and by the 22nd of May, 1929, Ilm Din was sentenced to death by the Sessions Court, Lahore, under Section 302. The Muslims of Lahore all got together and decided to appeal against the death sentence, and they turned towards Mr. Muhammad Ali Jinnah. The lawyer in the case was a well-known Lahore legal expert by the name of Farrukh Hussain. His son, Aftab, was to later become a Lahore High Court judge. Mr. Jinnah came to Lahore and filed the appeal before the Lahore High Court. But before filing the appeal, so accounts go, Mr. Jinnah met Ilm Din in jail.

He went over the circumstances and after much thought informed Mr. Ilm Din that he had actually committed the murder, and, therefore, to deny it was wrong. He asked him to confess the crime, and then he would defend him from that position best. Ilm Din, scared as he might have been at that moment, refused. The Muslims of the old walled city all stuck to their guns and kept the stance that he was innocent. One source claims that Mr. Jinnah forcefully informed them that unless Ilm Din confessed to the crime, he has a chance, otherwise he will be hanged. "Let us begin with the truth, then we will find reason why the truth took place", he is claimed to have said. Ilm Din stubbornly refused to confess to his act. The rumour was that Mr. Jinnah was a British/Congress agent and would get the lad strung up. It was in these circumstances that the appeal came up before Mr. Justice Broadway and Mr. Justice Johnstone.

Mr. Jinnah started his arguments with the contention that all the witnesses were tainted and unreliable, as they worked for, or were, in one way or another, under obligation to the deceased. He produced evidence to this effect. The prosecution contented that Ilm Din had purchased the knife with which he had murdered Raj Pal from the shop of Atma Ram, who happened to be related to Raj Pal. Atma Ram had appeared as a witness to this effect. Mr. Jinnah presented to the court two knives that looked similar to the 'murder weapon and informed the court that they had been purchased from an auction at a medical store. "The claim of Atma Ram, a relative of the deceased, is surely highly suspect", said Jinnah.

The other two witnesses were workers of Raj Pal. Mr. Jinnah cut them down to size, using the initial report lodged by one of them, Kidar Nath, who did not mention a claim made much later that Ilm Din had said on his capture that "he had sought revenge for the Prophet (pbuh)". Ilm Din had denied saying any such thing in court during cross examination. So Mr. Jinnah put forward the proposition that his booklet has nothing to do with this case, and that Ilm Din was wrongly implicated in this respect. There is no doubt that Mr. Jinnah had spun a stunning case, but then, it goes without doubt, that the bare essentials of the murder and the witnesses and the murder weapon and its source and the identification of Ilm Din by Atma Ram, who was not at the murder scene, all led to the conclusion arrived at by the Sessions Judge. The Lordships decided to reject the appeal. Mr. Jinnah then used his last trump card and asked for an adjournment of a day to consult his client. It was allowed.

One source claims that Mr. Jinnah put immense pressure on Ilm Din to confess to the crime and he would use the law to ensure that the death sentence was waived to a long imprisonment. "It is now merely a matter of choosing the better option", he is claimed to have informed Ilm Din. But Ilm Din baffled Mr. Jinnah by refusing to own up to his act. The world called him a 'ghazi' and the 'ghazi' refused to own up to his act. One account claims that Mr. Jinnah returned to the court with 'his hands tied behind his back'.

Here Mr. Jinnah took a completely new twist. He pleaded with his Lordships that the boy was merely 19-years old, and by the definition of the law not an adult (in those days an adult was 21 years or more). "The insult to the Holy Prophet (pbuh) had angered him and he was not in his senses. There is a very strong case for not considering the death sentence on a 19 year old boy". He quoted the Amir Vs Emperor case (AIR 1928 Lahore 531) and showed how such a young boy could not be sentenced to death. The judges contented that as the incident had taken place two years after the 'deliberate insult', therefore, the act was cold-blooded murder. The argument of his age was also dismissed. The appeal was dismissed and the sentence confirmed.

It remains a mystery as to why Ilm Din continued, till his last days, to refuse to own up to his act. The world outside made him a martyr, and to this day his act is sort of 'celebrated'. There is no doubt that Raj Pal was a silly person who deliberately set out to offend Muslim feelings.

Many feel he got what was his due. In a way both indulged in extreme positions, causing harm to themselves, as well as to the body politics of our sub-continent.

The 'thugs' of old have returned

Like all old civilizations, the one that exists inside the old city of Lahore had, and has, sinister sides to it. There are always crooks around like there are hyenas in the wild; there are pimps, and pickpockets and charlatans of every hue. They defy the establishment. And then there are the decent folk who dictate the pace of life. That is what makes life so livable, especially inside the walled city.

In the days of Akbar the Great, the new Mughal order had to grapple with a major law and order problem as crooks of old used religious excuses to gain a foothold in the new establishment. In the end, Akbar had to use force to establish peace that would last for another 200 years. Crooks of every hue were hanged just outside the fort walls as they were being reconstructed. The result was that considerable progress took place and Lahore was considered, along with Delhi, Multan and Calcutta, as among the best cities in the world. Commerce flourished and the bazaars were full of the finest things from as far off as China and Africa.

After the Mughals crumbled, thanks primarily to the policies of Aurangzeb; Lahore was again in the grip of crooks and charlatans. During the days of Aurangzeb, the occult arts flourished, even though he was said to be against them. Thanks to the sagacity of Maharajah Ranjit Singh, a new Punjabi order was established. He also set about hanging people, and just outside Lohari Gate, many a crook was strung up to the delight of the decent folk of the city. The underlying reasons for his success was that justice was actually dispensed, irrespective of creed or caste. Once his empire crumbled, the British moved in to establish order. They had to contend with, all over the sub-continent, with the 'thug' phenomenon, something that is emerging again, and that is why this piece is about thugs, a word that has found its way into the English lexicon. Such was the romance of the thug campaign.

In the 1800s, religious orders supported crooks known as thugs. Their modus operandi was strange. They fitted an old paisa coin, then minted in copper with a hole in the middle, at the end of a knotted silk handkerchief and in a strange technique they swung the coin at the head of an unsuspecting victim, knocking him out cold. Often, it was rumoured, that expert thugs could kill a man with one such swing, (in my youth we tried practising this swing, often ending up being given a good hiding by my parents, who impressed upon us that the thing actually hurt others). These thugs contributed half their gains to their religious order. It had no special religious learning in Lahore, though it was Hindu in essence and leans more towards the Hindu gods Kali and Shiva. Muslim versions of this movement had also emerged, and they thrived on the notion the "evil was essential if the poor were to have justice". Muslims began to have influence on this movement, thanks to their leaning towards the occult. The Hindus feared the occult, for it has always had a fascination for the people of the sub-continent, with Bengal being known as the home of black magic. Such charlatans abounded then, and such people still abound Lahore. The occult deserves a special piece. I visited one such champion inside Mochi Gate just this week, who actually made scores of stones rain down from a roof to prove that the occult existed. I was laughing but friends reassure me it is no laughing matter.

After 1857, in Lahore a major thug problem arose and Lawrence of the Lawrence Gardens fame, also known as the East India Company Gardens, or locally as Company Bagh, took matters in hand. He began to actually hunt them down like one hunts animals. Three major clashes with the thugs took place. One in Tehsil Bazaar just off Bazaar Hakeeman, one just outside Delhi Gate and one in the Shahi Mohalla next to the Badshahi Mosque.

In the first incident, Lawrence and his guards shot dead three thugs as they ran to attack his mounted party. In the second, a major battle followed after thugs attacked travellers. A major bloodbath took place and over 12 thugs and two Punjabi soldiers were killed. Their bodies were hung up for three days "till the stench was unbearable" outside the gate as a lesson to other thugs. That sobered up the population considerably.

The last clash took place in the last days of the thug campaign as the British hunted them down in their dens inside the Shahi Mohalla, which houses the red light area of the city. Two thugs were hung up for two days in the middle of the Tibbi Chowk. It is said that visitors refrained from going to the area for over a month. But slowly they returned to the delights they were seeking. That bloody campaign brought to an end the thug movement. It must be said that the thugs were a far bigger menace in Delhi and the south, where Hindu influence was all pervasive. But the British made an example of the thugs, and taught the people of Lahore how important it was to 'obey' the law. City elders say that after that a woman bedecked with all her jewellery could travel unharmed from Peshawar to Calcutta. This is a favourite phrase in old Lahore when discussing the law and order situation as it is today.

The walled city even today has its own style of crooks and charlatans. Behind these crooks were always influential people who supported them. In the British days, the local 'pehlwan' kept everyone in check. No one dare tease a woman of his area, and all crime was under his control. But all of them had other subtle means of organizing crime, for surely they had no other means of living well. With time this role shifted to the organized sector, where the police are the least trusted of all organizations. Again, just like in the days of Akbar and Ranjit Singh and Lawrence, organized crime is the dominant force, backed as it always has been by one religious hue or the other. The 'thugs' have returned, armed to the teeth with even the police fearing them. The fascination of Lahore has always been its people and how they have managed to blend with times. This is one aspect that needs to be studied in greater depth.

The unique man with the little red light

The ancient city of Lahore has always been about people first and foremost. Over time the actions of these unique people take their place in our collective psyche. Today's story is about one such very unique person, a person with the unique art of listening, and of making sure that every word, or musical note, listened to was in its correct place and time.

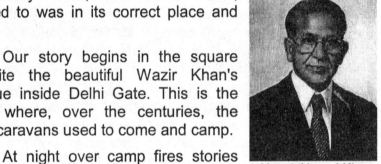

Our story begins in the square opposite the beautiful Wazir Khan's mosque inside Delhi Gate. This is the place where, over the centuries, the trade caravans used to come and camp.

At night over camp fires stories from all over the world were told and

Hayat Ahmad Khan

recorded. The mosque of Wazir Khan, undoubtedly the finest in Lahore, is where, some time in 1925, Ustad Bade Ghulam Ali Khan was reciting the Holy Quran.

He moved from verse to verse, as if his tone and tenor was designed for this celestial task. In one corner a little boy of four sat listening to the maestro. He lived just round the corner inside Delhi Gate, and every time the 'ustad' would come to recite the Holy Quran, he would find the little lad in rapt attention.

This is where the musical life of Hayat Ahmad Khan started. His long 83 year old journey of life ended last week. His is a story that must be told, little that he wished it to be.

The experience of listening to Bade Ghulam Ali Khan must have been a unique one for the boy to come every day, for all he did was listen. It was, as if, the musical words of the Almighty entered the very soul and spirit of the man the musicians of Pakistan learned to call 'Khan Sahib'.

The elders of Hayat Ahmad Khan belonged to an Afghan family that had fled the royal infightings of the Kabul court. They settled, initially, in the Soan Valley near Khushab at a village called Chak Kazian, named probably because they belonged to a family of 'kazis'.

Education, administration and business ran in the family, and as was the wont of such people, they happened to be very modern and religious in disposition. It might seem a dichotomy to many today, but till recently the mix went very well.

In the square opposite the mosque are a number of old buildings. One of them was owned by the grandfather of Hayat Ahmad Khan. Here sat the calligraphists, who recorded the stories of old and far away.

The hand-written pages were decorated with golden floral outlines, and after leather-binding the books would be sold as unique pieces of art. A few lie today in the best museums of the world.

Hayat Ahmad Khan grew up in the streets around the mosque of Wazir Khan inside the old walled city of Lahore. In his school and college days he was a good sportsman, being a champion in 100 metres swimming.

It was in those heady days, just before the making of Pakistan, that he met his wonderful wife Syeda Khanum, who happened to live just a few houses away. It was a match made 'in heaven', for their love affair never ceased. She backed him in his enterprises and he loved her more for doing so.

When she died a few years ago, Hayat Ahmad Khan was never the same. "Had it not been her desire that we save our music for the future children of our country, I would have loved to go with her. But I meet her every night that I sleep, and I always assure her that I will come soon," he mentioned to a friend. The mystic in him was emerging slowly. It was only the mention of Syeda Khanum that ever saw his eyes moisten and he would be a wee bit lost. To the world, however, he was a strict disciplinarian and a man with a mission.

From Delhi Gate the family moved to Davis Road. The family business was known as the Abdur Rahim Khan, the famous auctioneers and furniture mart on McLeod Road. It was, in its days, one of the city's major business house. The family tradition of education and business was very much intact.

Like his father, Hayat Ahmad Khan was also a businessman, and he maintained his office on McLeod Road, though most of his time was spent meeting musicians from all over the country.

He was among the very first to recognize that the future business opportunities lay in Japan and Germany. I once asked him how he had opted to do business with the defeated Japanese and Germans after the Second World War. "Oh, very simple. Culturally great nations cannot be killed by atom bombs. They have a habit of standing tall again. In that process business is always good." His reply stunned me. Here was a man who knew how to look beyond the horizon and through time.

The Japanese honoured this unique Lahori on his death like they have seldom honoured a foreign person. He had understood their psyche well, and more importantly, respected them like few in those days did. After one of his scores of visits to Japan, he set up the Japan Karate Association.

He had sown the seed and that was enough. He introduced an annual Japanese calender exhibition, showing the world that simple lines mean so much to those with an eye.

His daughter Lala Rukh, now a teacher in the National College of Arts, is also very frugal with her lines. Few understand her lines yet, but a time will surely come when the beauty and responsibility of the artist's line will be appreciated.

I remember as a young schoolboy going to the Pakistan Music Conference with my father, where we listened all night to Roshan Ara Begum. On the way back I got a lesson on why listening was the most important human trait.

"People have stopped listening to one another, which is why they are no longer communicating with one another." He spoke in general terms always. Many years later I recalled this conversation to Hayat Ahmad Khan while having dinner with him in an Islamabad hotel.

He got up and ordered me to hug him. Who was I to disobey? I mentioned Roshan Ara Begum as it was because of her that the All-Pakistan Music Conference (APMC) came about. The great classical music queen of the sub-continent had announced that she was giving up singing as people were no longer interested.

Hayat Ahmad Khan's time had come. He then had the foresight to see that the 'red light' had to be shown to the emerging forces of obscurantism, a force that was likely to rob us of one of our greatest traditions, the tradition of sub-continental classical music.

For the first time in 1959, over 45 years ago, the APMC started, and Hayat Ahmad Khan set the rules straight and simple. "We will start on time, and every performer, no matter how famous or great, or young or even a novice, will begin and end his performance on time".

The rules were simple and in 45 years he saw to it that the rules were never violated. To enforce these rules, he had a small red light installed in front of the performer. He operated the red light himself, and if anyone refused to see it, he would make sure that he was shown the red light. "The art of performing means discipline, and the APMC makes sure its proceedings are disciplined", he would inform everyone.

Over the years the greatest of our musicians, classical and semi-classical, have been through the routine set by the quiet man that Hayat Sahib was. He had learnt his music at the Ghandharav Mahahvidala Academy in India. He lived a full life in every respect. His interests were diverse. He was an avid hiker and mountaineer. He was among the very first to climb the K-36, also known as Siachin Glacier, not to speak of even higher peaks like Nanga Parbat, Trichmir and other similar peaks.

Recently, as his daughter Gul Rukh mentioned, a little child started crying during a classical music recital in the APMC. Everyone was irked. Hayat Sahib rushed to the distressed woman's help, saw her to the gate and instructed her strictly: "Comfort the little angel, and once he is quiet you must bring him back. Let him start his life listening to pure sounds". The woman did return and the child sat through the performance in rapt attention, just like the little child listening to Ustad Bade Ghulam Ali in the mosque of Wazir Khan almost 80 years ago. His unique role in our lives was that he saved sub-continental classical music from being forgotten. His work has been done, and done well. His red light worked. That is reward enough for a life well lived.

Unknown eunuchs

There can be no doubt that eunuchs have a strange appeal about them. And though our parents raised us to strictly ignore them as 'undesirables', one grew up always wondering whether they had the real stuff or not. In history, they have played a powerful role, both as defenders of the status quo, and also as a class that constantly pricked the conscious of the oppressing rulers.

If you happen to visit the shrine Data Ganj Bakhsh and walk along the left lane while facing the newly constructed mosque, you will reach the crossing of Bilal Ganj Road. If you head back towards Rattigan Road, the two lanes to the left house an entire area where live two communities ... the eunuchs of Lahore and the Pathan beggars of the shrine. Outsiders to this maze lane get the sternest looks one can imagine, for both these communities do not offer or give an inch. It is their territory, their haven, and within this fairly large area some of the strangest secrets of these communities are hidden.

When you go to the Lahore Fort from the Roshnai Gate end, which is the only gate open to the public, you have two ways in which to enter the historic place. The road curving upwards to the right is where the elephants went with their passengers towards the Divan-e-Aam and onwards towards the Divan-e-Khas. But if you take the huge stairways-cum-walkway that is to the left of the pathways, you will walk up and land just outside the Sheesh Mahal. As you walk along this stairway, you will notice in the walls a number of bullet marks. Signs point out some, the others you can easily find as you scan the walls. These are the scars of fighting that took place over 200 years ago and some even earlier. But where do bullets and eunuchs come in? Well, this is where one must understand the historic role of eunuchs in our royal families for none existed without eunuchs.

When fighting broke out for the control of Lahore after the death of Shah Alam the emperor after the death of Aurangzeb, the last of the great Muhgals, troops belonging to the grand nephew of the great king attacked and entered the fort from this side. As they rushed towards the harem area, which was guarded by a 'virtual army of eunuchs' who stood in the doorways and balconies of the walkway. As the soldiers rushed forward, the eunuchs flung themselves on the soldiers, some using knives to defend the women and the princesses of the harem. The account is a gruesome one of bloodshed as soldiers and eunuchs fought for every inch of the walkway. "In the end, the invaders had to reach the royal quarters from where the defending soldiers surrendered virtually without a fight". Later, after the death of Maharajah Ranjit Singh, the fort was fired upon from cannons mounted on the two front minarets of the Badshahi Mosque. Soldiers dared not enter the haram area, for it was rumoured that the eunuchs were more fearsome than the Sikh soldiers. This account is all the more believable because stories of the bravery of the eunuchs of Delhi had been circulating in Lahore when Captain Hodson captured the last Mughal Emperor Bahadur Shah Zafar on September 22, 1857. The personal dairy of Hodson records: "I was fortunate enough to capture the King and his favourite wife, today, more fortunate still, I have seized and destroyed the King's two sons and a grandson, the famous or infamous Abu Bukht. He was ferociously defended by a guard of eunuchs, all of whom were slain, in his defence. It goes to their credit that each one ferociously stood his ground."

The eunuchs of Lahore have a tradition under which they elect their 'king', who is replaced only on death. This election takes place in this area of Data Sahib. They guard their 'king' with a ferocious will, and not even the police are allowed to enter the area without the king's consent. Marriages among eunuchs take place with the consent of the king, and if anyone tries to break this bond of friendship, or call it what you like, then the eunuch community of Lahore strikes back. For this reason the police of Lahore have a tradition of never entering this area.

You might be wondering what the Pathan beggars of the shrine have to do with the eunuchs of Lahore. Legend has it that for over 200 years, ever since the Mughal patronage of the eunuchs of Lahore ended, one tenth of their takings have been given to the eunuch 'king', who spends it on his community's welfare. No verifiable records exist of this tradition, but verbal confirmation of this exists even today. It is a very closed society, which hopefully will open up as Pakistan and the world becomes more tolerant towards those whose preferences are 'dissimilar' to those of the average citizen. Even that is a moot point.

Jagga's sister Meedan

When I read the news that 'finally' Khushwant Singh's novel, *Train to Pakistan* was to be made into a film in India, I thought of Nimmo, and then I thought of Jagga, the womanizer-dacoit, and then I thought of Meedan. If ever there was a tantalizing woman, she was one.

During my college days we would walk to my friend Sheroo's house inside Bhatti Gate in the walled city, and often in order to reach the Data Darbar area we would walk towards the small makeshift bridge that crosses the old moat ... or nullah as everyone calls it ... at the extreme south-eastern corner of the walled city. As we walked along the nullah, we crossed a number of buffaloes tied there. These belonged to Meedan, probably her name was Hameeda and in typical Lahori, the name was spoken with a short jerk to make it sound sort of sensual. If the last portion of the name was dragged a bit, it certainly does add an extra sensual tone to the name.

But Meedan was no pushover. She was six-feet tall, broad, not fat at all, her body was so well proportioned from hard work that even at the age of 65-plus, she was magnificent. Probably when we were at college anything seemed exciting. But Meedan was one magnificent woman. My friend Sheroo was scared of her, and by scared I mean really scared. When I asked what the reason was, he said in my ear: "She is Jagga's sister." I stopped in my tracks. Now she looked menacing to me. I could not look her in the eye, and even though I am six-feet-two and rather recommendable, I was no match for Meedan. She could probably eat me for breakfast. Such was the fear she instilled in everyone who ever saw her.

Meedan owns a building on the south-east corner of the walled city's now dried moat. She is still there aged almost 98, and she still sits on her 'charpoy', the traditional cot woven with jute yarn. She still maintains a number of buffaloes and her voice can still be heard above all others. At age 98 she is still menacing, and she still holds court among her kin, for she is Meedan, Jagga's sister and that is enough to stop anyone in their tracks, just like in my case almost 27 years ago.

There was always a mystery as to how Meedan managed, for her life-style did not warrant her managing off the milk of the buffaloes she kept. Here was a story told to me by the Bhatti Gate police station SHO. He claimed that all the stolen buffaloes from nearby villages were sold to her for a pittance, and that she then sold them at a handsome profit. But no one, not even the SHO, ever dared ask her just where did she get her buffaloes from. When one daring police officer 'dared' to arrest her for possessing stolen property, she physically beat him up inside the Lahore District courts, and when she was jailed, it took four burly men to keep her in control.

But within an hour over 300 'gujjars' on their 'rehras' descended on the police station and all milk stopped flowing to the city for two days. A crisis had hit Lahore, for Meedan had been touched, so to say. Every gujjar in and around Lahore contributed one tola of gold to her cause. At the first hearing, the judge let her off and admonished the SHO for daring to try to 'molest' a lady.

On her being freed honourably, Meedan returned home in a huge procession. Outside the police station, she yelled a sort of war cry called a *barrhak* in local lingo. No one inside the station dared even look out of the window. I remember that all milk in the Bhatti Gate area was sold for free that day. No one dares tamper with Jagga's sister, not even today. Recently, my friend Sheroo informed me that she was still alive, and I ventured onto the old route. There she was, magnificent as ever, a tall strong woman of 98. She has that aura about her that makes everyone stay away from her, for she commands immense respect. She is a wise woman and advises her huge family on how to conduct themselves. She still keeps buffaloes inside the walled city, even though they are officially banned. But then she is Meedan, Jagga's sister. May she live to be a hundred and may she keep telling stories of how her brave brother sacrificed his life to save his love Nimmo on that train to Pakistan.

A lot of people are of the opinion that the entire story is a yarn. That Khushwant Singh, like all good Punjabis, is a great storyteller. Khushwant's 'Jagga' was not a Muslim.So how could Meedan claim to be Jagga's sister? This has baffled me. Could Jagga Dakoo and Jagga Gujjar be two different characters? Such is the legend of Jagga, dacoit, rustler, womanizer, drinker of the stiffest stuff on Allah's earth, and brave to a fault. No wonder Meedan still walks tall.

Just who was Bullaki Shah

When I started this column almost three years ago, I set forth certain parameters for discussing Lahore and the parameters were set firmly by my friend Sheroo of Bhatti Gate inside the walled city, with whom I still spend long hours walking through the lanes and streets discussing every issue under the sun.

The priority was people, places, things and faces ... after all, that is what memories are made of, and in that priority they shall remain. Today let us begin from the beginning, like all good stories. 'People' belong to 'places', they do 'things' over time and we call it history, and what they do has a 'face', and we examine that face and a memory is etched on our conscious mind, which makes its way to our unconscious memory, with the collective living on in the way we conduct our lives. Lahore and its people are unique, for history has etched them out like it does all cities and people.

One gent about whom I would love to write about, and about whom I do not know enough, is a person called Bullaki Shah, a Hindu money lender of Paniwala Talab. Of all Lahoris, this gent lives most in the minds of our elders who are still living in the walled city. Who was Bullaki Shah? I remember my father telling me that the grandson of Bullaki Shah, whom he called 'Lattoo Shah' or Ram Prakash was his classmate in Government College, Lahore, and that they both played cricket for the college. Now Lattoo and Mazhar

Ali Khan, the late distinguished journalist, were the only two students who came to college in their own cars. Only Lattoo wore silks and Mazhar Ali Khan wore 'khaddar', a trade mark till his dying day. So Bullaki Shah was definitely a very rich man, and at the time of the partition of the Punjab, he was said to be the richest man of Lahore. It is said that almost every rich landowner of the Punjab owed him money. One story even goes to the extent that the prime minister. Sir Khizr Hayat Tiwana, owed him considerable money. So partition was a sign of relief for the rich, who did not have to pay their debts, and who got richer in the claims loot that followed.

Bullaki Shah was a typical Lahori character. An old gent of considerable standing tells me that when Bullaki Shah learnt that his son was frequenting the dancers of Tibbi, he turned up one night to face his son at a 'mujra'. The son would give a five rupee note (a lot in those days) and Bullaki would give ten. That night the dancers went crazy with excitement as the money was flowing fast and furious as son and father competed, each doubling the other. They returned home empty-handed and the son learnt his lesson that he was just wasting his money, for the dancers were interested not in him but his money. A month later, a delegation of dancers called on Bullaki Shah to return his money and allow the young buck to frequent them. He took back his money and told them to buzz off.

There are other stories about Bullaki Shah, each more interesting than the other. But I am sure that our readers will be able to come up with a lot about Bullaki, for much more needs to be written about him. Then there are towering personalities like Sir Ganga Ram, whose contribution to our city remain unparalleled. That we have not honoured him enough, or at all, speaks volumes of our mental poverty. We have written about Sultan the contractor, and about Kanhiyya Lal, the engineer and chronicler par excellence, though much more needs to be known about them. But then there were people like Dyal Singh, Rattan Chand, Mela Ram and Sir Shah Din, all great Lahoris and all neglected. We need to know more about them and we need to honour them as sons of our city. We also should not forget martyrs like Lala Lajpat Rai and Bhagat Singh, who gave their lives for the independence of the sub-continent and not India alone. Why should we forget them just because they are not Muslims?

But then there were 'lesser mortals' than the rich and the mighty whose names still live on in the collective memory of the people even today. I remember as a young boy buying 'spinning tops' from Taj Din 'The Cabinet Maker', and later on the top maker. On his huge hands he could make a top spin and buzz with the flick of his huge fingers. He died almost 25 years ago, but he had been making tops on Lawrence Road since 1929. On the food front several names stand out. There was Khaleefa the kebab maker of Chuna Mandi. His grandsons still run his shop there, but the taste has gone. Quality needs to be constantly enhanced if names are to live.

Then there was Sardar the fish seller of Gowalmandi. His sons run the show now as they sell insipid farm fish as Ravi Rahu. The Ravi is now a trickle and so polluted that even a stubborn species like man would die of pollution, let alone a sensitive Rahu. Inside the walled city, still standing alone, is Shaukat Ali the only man left who produces Dal Kulchas. He still roams the streets and claims he has no one to take his torch forward. May be Lahore's famous Dal Kulcha will soon die out. We cannot forget two Fazals of Lahore, the 'barfi' maker of Lal Khooh, and Fazl the 'siree payey-wallah' of Tibbi Chowk. Both names have spread all over and outside Lahore and may both prosper. More needs to be known about them.

Lost people of our land

When Larry Niblett left Lahore for 'greener pastures' in the US, his celebrated father, the 'angrez' DIG (Traffic) of Lahore, Mr. Niblett, headed the other way to Australia. The loss of both these 'pucca' Lahori characters was immense.

But then father and son never did see eye to eye. In the end, they headed in opposite directions.

The senior Niblett we had seen since we started going to school. He was a smart police officer who brooked no nonsense.

I have three enduring images in my mind's eye of DIG Niblett. The first was when as a school-going student I violated the one-way traffic rule on Lawrence Road. He rode up on his motorcycle and stopped me. "You must be bloody well Larry's friend riding your bike up a one-way road, having no lights. I will confiscate your bicycle and send you to jail".

I trembled in fear at such an outcome. Imagine me, a school student, in jail, my father would kill me. "He bloody well should," roared the police officer Niblett. "Who is your father?" he asked. I told him so. "Oh, in that case I will give you a bloody good hiding", he said and got off his motorcycle. One clip round the head was enough to make me walk with my bicycle to school with the tyres having been deflated. I was ashamed of myself. In those days students used to be ashamed if Niblett stopped them. In the evening I told my mother about what had happened and got another good hiding. But she was kind enough not to tell my father, because Mr. Niblett had already phoned him and asked him to "educate the brat". Oh, I shall not narrate what followed. But then Lahore was like that, one big family where everyone cared.

My next image is as a student in Government College, Lahore. The anti-Ayub troubles had seen a massive crowd surround the Governor's House. The mad mob was baying for blood and the cry went out to storm the gates and take over the premises. The angry mob attacked. The gate chains were broken and the crowd began to surge in. This had never happened before in the history of the Governor's House. The police guards had fled. In the middle of the road, behind the gate, stood one man alone ... Mr. Niblett, then a DSP. Pistol in hand he shouted over the megaphone,

"Wapas chalay jao varna goli maar doon ga" (Leave or I will shoot you). The crowd surged. A shot rang out. The crowd stopped. Then three rapid shots whizzed over the head of the crowd hitting the walls. Panic. The crowd rushed back. More shots followed. Total panic as everyone rushed out. DSP Niblett had saved the Governor's House alone. What he did with his panic-stricken staff later is also history, like almost making them eat hay out of horse bags. Many years later he told me: "I never shoot to kill. The kids were doing the right thing, but in a wrong way". He remained a sensitive father to all the students of Lahore, and they feared and yet loved and respected him.

Several years later, his son Larry indulged in an illegality. The DIG was like a man gone mad. He personally arrested his own son, sent him on a three-day remand, ordered that he be given the terrible 'channa and one roti' diet as stipulated by law, then appeared before the judge and testified against his son and sent him to jail. Even the judge requested him to soften up. "No way my lord, the son of DIG Niblett would not have the easy way out". This glorious police officer saw to it that his name was not soiled. "If I had my way, I would lock him up and throw the keys away", he would say when reminded of the incident. But Larry was his father's son. He more than made amends, spent his time and apologized to his father. Ask any old police constable or officer in Lahore about DIG Niblett, and you will notice that they still pride themselves in the fact that he was one of them.

Just 30 years ago Lahore had such a healthy mix of religions and people. The Christians of Lahore made up a very lively portion of Lahore. The few remaining Anglo-Indians, or Eurasians as they were originally called, still contribute much more than their numbers. But then thousands have fled the rages of intolerance. But their hearts remain in Lahore. There they will remember the old Lahore, of fun and joy.

There are so many names I recall from the years gone by, a year senior to us in the St. Anthony's High School, Lahore, was a pretty girl called Perry Young. Then Gomes the boxer of Beadon Road. Peter Snell, of Temple Road, a close friend of my younger brother Karim. It makes one sad to see that the sons and daughters of our soil should have to be chased away by a set of beliefs that have been distorted beyond measure. Yet they remember their homeland with such fondness.

The people of the city of Lahore, both old and new, till very recently considered the inhabitants as a bunch of beautiful flowers, each person, each religion, each sect, complementing the other. Most of the original inhabitants had been lost to the Partition. Yet the city still had a healthy mix of religions and people with immense toleration. My old man called the new arrivals the '47' variety, and with time he scorned their 'claim mentality', a purely materialistic approach to life. He often cursed them for not understanding the ethos of Lahore, one of the seven great cities of the old world. There were Christians, Parsis, and even a few Hindus, with a few Sikhs living inside the walled city. The festivals of Eid, Christmas, Nauroze, Baisakhi belonged to everyone. The world was love, not hate and suspicion. We have come a long way up a one-way street. Probably against the one-way. And no DIG Niblett now serves to give us 'a clip', to bring us to our senses.

Famous 'akharas' and the tradition of Gama

One of the most historic wrestling matches ever to be held in Lahore was when an unknown 18-year old called Hari Singh, from Gujranwala, turned up at the Shahi Dangal in 1803, presided over by Maharajah Ranjit Singh, and who, in a series of fights, defeated the very finest wrestlers of the Punjab. He was named Nalwa, and he was to become the finest general in the Punjabi Army of the Lahore Darbar.

Many years later another 'Shahi Dangal' would capture the imagination of the entire people of the sub-continent. It was the 'dangal' between Rustum-e-Hind Gama Pehalwan of Lahore and the world champion Polish wrestler Zybisko in 1935, the legend of which, even today, is discussed in the winding streets of the old walled city of Lahore. By the time Ahmad Bakhsh Gama retired, he had defeated almost every champion of any sort in the world. His feats brought 'desi kushti' – sub-continental wrestling - to international sports and lend it immense credibility as an exceptionally fair sport for "honourable men of strength and agility" as he himself described it. In 1910, a wrestling match was organized for the award of the title 'Rustum-e-Hind', Gama defeated all the wrestlers and earned the title. Gama's last match was with the European champion J.C. Peterson, whom he defeated in just 45 seconds. He died in Lahore on 22nd May in 1960.

For thousands of years wrestling has been a royal sport, and over the centuries the finest wrestlers also became the finest generals. Be it ancient Greece, the Roman empire, Egypt of Cleopatra, or Iran, or the India-Pakistan sub-continent, wrestling has always been a part of national life. Even today the annual All-Punjab Dangal, held ever year at the wrestling stadium next to the Lahore Fort, attracts the finest young men from far off villages in the Punjab. Such is the allure of human strength. We all know that in times of old, often wars were decided by a single wrestling bout among enemies. The city of Lahore has a special tradition of wrestling, and as this tradition fades away, it is about time that we understood what it was, so that it could be revived.

All wrestlers were attached to a particular 'Akhara'. The word 'pit' is the nearest to describing this patch of loose earth. In local folklore these are legendary places. Lahore has three basic groups of pehalwans, they being 'Kalluwala', 'Nurwala' and 'Kotwala'. Each 'akhara' trains its own pehalwans, and then 'dangals' are held between different 'akharas'. At the turn of the century, Lahore had hundreds of such 'akharas', and with time they began to dwindle.

According to the *Naqush* Lahore Number, a 1962 print collector's item now and much in need of a rewrite, the major 'akharas' of Lahore were Akhara Khalifa Buta, the Akhara Gama and Imam Bakhsh on Mohni Road, the Akhara Takya Tajey Shah, the Akhara Chanan Qasai, Akhara Nathey Shah inside the walled city, then there was the Akhara Nazd Pul Misri Shah, and another famous one was the Akhara Veyam Shala, used by the famous Bholu Pehalwan, Aslam, Akram, Goga and Azam pehalwans. The Akhara Chowk Baraf Khana also had a fierce reputation. Among the other famous akharas were the Akhara Khalifa Bakhshi, the Akhara Jani Pehalwan and the Akhara Ghadu Shah, which was owned by Rustum-e-Zaman. Just outside the walled city, in the circular gardens, were two well-known akharas, both by the name Akhara Balmikian, one outside Bhatti Gate and the other outside Taxali Gate.

Over the last 56 years, ones that my late father called the 'Claim Mentality Years', which transformed into the 'qabza era' and today is popularly called the 'military plots era', all these akharas were taken over and converted into plots for sale. But the need for space to run 'desi kushti' remained and we have seen the emergence of Wrestling Clubs, a corporate name for the old family-run akharas.

Let me give you a few examples of these new wrestling clubs. The Akhara Haji Siddique Pehalwan in Shadbagh No. 2 is now called the Miran Wrestling Club, and in Kot Khawaja Saeed the Akhara Kala Jat Pehalwan is called the Kala Jat Wrestling Club. The Akhara Sadiq Pehalwan Meva Mandi Wallay is now called the Sadiq Wrestling Club, Sadiqabad, Lahore. One very famous and old akhara, the Akhara Sajjan Pehalwan in Shah Meran is now called the Sajjan Wrestling Club. One interesting name, the Akhara Billa Changar Pehalwan is called the Billa Wrestling Club, Shahdara. It is almost as if with the changing times, there is a rush for a new respectability, devoid of

Gama Pehalwan

the rich roots of wrestlers. The names might sound offensive today, but they bring with them – in just one small name - a long history of the origin and feats of a wrestler. For example the name Akhara Pappu Pehalwan Chardha Suraj (rising sun) is today called the Pappu Wrestling Club. There was a time when Pappu claimed he could challenge the siblings of Gama and Bholu, and in one well-known fight Pappu did 'chitt' defeat Aslam, only to lose in a return fight. On both occasions there were massive celebrations in the old city and sweets were distributed. Some odd fights also broke out between the supporters of the two wrestlers, not to speak of even more heinous events that followed. Such was the pride of being a wrestler in Lahore.

As a school-going boy I remember meeting Aacha Pehalwan, who was a neighbour. Once I was late from school and my mother had asked him if he had seen me. "No, but I will see him" was the response. Phew, that one light hand across my head still rings today. But then, mind you, the pehalwan of old was no hoodlum. He was the protector of his mohallah, and no crime dared take place in his territory. He was a huge loving man who sat outside the milk shop and downed them by the dozen. People would watch in awe. There were rumours, which probably they spread themselves, that a champion pehalwan ate at least the meat of a whole goat for a single meal. We know from former Test cricketers that in his prime, the Test cricketer Imran Khan could eat half a goat. I once mentioned this to Kala Pehalwan at his Akhara inside the walled city, and prompt came the reply: "Totally possible, see why the 'goris' flock to him". On this he held his ears as if seeking pardon from Allah for saying something rude.

The traditional pehalwan of Lahore was a supreme sportsman, forgiving by nature and a protector of the weak, a task in which he took great pride. For them their health was everything and they gave alms to protect themselves against the 'evil eye'. But then as the city has grown miles away from its centre, so has faded the ancient tradition of the Desi Pehalwan. His art is on the wane, even though in England the Punjabis have managed to revive it considerably. Maybe the cycle has come full circle, and we might yet see another Gama from Lahore fight another Zybisko from Europe in our city. That would be a crowd-puller, of this rest assured.

A Tiger of a man

We were five brothers and we mostly lived in our tree house in the lawn, hid in the pigeon cage for two days when the hairdresser came to circumcise us, kept the Ganga Ram Hospital emergency doctors busy with almost an injury a day. We were a fearsome lot ... but we feared just one thing, and that was when my father would say "Haria Ragla". That was just too much to digest and we would fall in line.

Just opposite the Lahore Fort is the samadhi of Maharajah Ranjit Singh and within the compound is the samadhi of an even more revered Punjabi, Guru Arjun Dev. Here once flowed the River Ravi and on its banks, for hundreds of years, the strongest and bravest of the land have wrestled in contests that go back thousands of years.

Just outside the samadhi and between the Circular Road is the Atique Stadium, named after the late Gen. Atiqur Rehman, a gentleman par excellence, a general in every sense of the word and undoubtedly the most honest governor that Punjab has ever had. He was very fond of wrestling and promoted the game. Just before the traditional 'Basant' festival begins in the first week of February, take place the annual *dangal* bouts to determine who is the strongest in the land.

Normally in the days gone by, wrestling was the main attraction, but before it came tent-pegging, fencing and horse racing. In the 1960s Gen. Atiqur Rehman brought these traditional sports into a new event called the Horse and Cattle Show, an event that is now fizzling out because of the 'uncaring' urban touch this basically rural sport got from organizers who made it more of a show than a sport. But wrestling remains where it has always been, just outside the samadhi of Guru Arjun and Maharajah Ranjit Singh.

Almost 200 years ago at this very place took place a most unusual *dangal*. Maharajah Ranjit Singh, who was himself a keen horseman and loved a fair sport, ruled the Punjab.

The year was 1805 and the Maharajah was the chief guest. After the preliminary rounds the finest wrestlers were battling it out when a young man aged 14 stepped forward from out of the crowd and boldly challenged one of the wrestlers who seemed destined to win the contest that year. His taunt in true Punjabi bravado was taken up by the crowd and the Maharajah asked the wrestler to teach the young brat a lesson or two in good manners. There was the usual banter as the youngster took off his kurta, tied up his 'dhoti' and got ready to meet a man twice his size.

Hari Singh Nalwa

The champion wrestler got hold of the youngster and before he knew what was happening the young boy threw the champion over his shoulder and pinned him down. He taunted him and moved aside. The angry wrestler returned and tried to grab the youngster, but like lightening the boy dived into his legs, picked him up and threw him aside. The crowd went wild. The Maharajah ordered the young boy to fight all the remaining wrestlers, which he did, and, won in record time.

The proud Punjabi calmly ambled up to the Maharajah and boldly said to him: "Maharaj, I can fight four of your best wrestlers together". The shrewd ruler was not one to let go such a delight, for he wanted the youngster humbled before the contest was over. So four of the best surrounded the boy. What followed will go down in history as the most amazing rise of a man those name even today is taken by mothers to scare their children... such has been the terror of the man who walked out of a crowd to shame the strongest of the land. Within a few minutes the boy had all four wrestlers on the ground.

Maharajah Ranjit Singh stood up, called the boy over and presented him with his most expensive diamond necklace. The man was Hari Singh, son of Sardar Gurdial Singh of the Gujranwala Sukerchakia Misl. He had ridden into Lahore alone on his horse to witness the annual wrestling bouts, and while watching come to the conclusion that he could beat all of them. The Maharajah ordered that Hari Singh to become his personal bodyguard, for he knew his father Gurdial Singh well.

So Hari Singh moved to Lahore and lived with the Maharajah, accompanying him on his trips. Within a few months, the Maharajah went on a hunting trip in the forests that once abounded on the banks of the Ravi. As the Maharajah and Hari Singh moved through the trees, a tiger emerged and attacked Hari Singh's horse. The young man fell down and the tiger pounced on him. To the amazement of Maharajah Ranjit Singh, the young Hari Singh threw off the tiger in a wrestling move, produced a dagger from his waist and in a lightening move he opened the tiger's stomach, killing him on the spot. But in the quick struggle Hari Singh lost his horse, and ignoring the Maharajah he lay down besides his horse and wept. Maharajah Ranjit Singh picked him up, consoled him, gave him the title of "Nalwa" the tiger slayer and presented him with ten of his finest horses. He also appointed the young man a general and asked him to set up an elite army called the 'Sherdil Fauj'.

With time Hari Singh Nalwa and his Sherdils from Lahore carved out a name for themselves, conquering the cruel Khans of Kasur, taming the Dogras of Kashmir, capturing the Multan Fort by using the Zamzama Gun — Kim's Gun — that now lies outside Lahore's Museum, and most importantly conquering the Pathans of the North West Frontier. He built the Jamrud Fort and such was his terror that even today, from Kabul to Attock, when Pathan women want to scare their children, all they have to say is *Haria Ragla* — Hari is coming. He died of injuries during a siege of Jamrud, which took place after the Pathans learned that Hari Singh Nalwa had died of injuries sustained during a sneak attack while hunting... but when his dead body was shown from the walls to give the impression that he was alive, the Pathans ran away. But Hari Singh was dead. In death his terror reigned supreme. Even today the spirit of that 14 year-old can be felt watching wrestling matches outside the samadhi of Ranjit Singh. Lets see who wins the next championship... a tradition of Lahore as old as time itself.

Dina Nath Brahmin ... the survivor

(The darbar of December 1845; the Maharajah Dulip Singh (1837-1893) is seated on a chair holding a gun, a pet lap dog at his feet and an attendant with a fly-whisk behind him. On the Maharajah's left sit Diwan Dina Nath and Fakir Nur ud-din holding a book and rosary; on his right sit Teja Singh with a rosary and Labha Singh with a sword and shield.)

The first time I heard his name was as a college student having tea in a Bhatti Gate eatery. The aged owner scolded a stingy customer calling him "Dina Nath Brahmin". That name sounded interesting, for it remained 'embedded' in my sub-conscious memory for a good 35 years, that is, till last week when I happened to be passing by Wazir Khan's mosque.

Dwellers of the old walled city connect this name to the two excellent havelis that stand just round the corner from the Wazir Khan's Mosque, and also to the samadhi of Dina Nath on the Ravi. Of the two havelis, one is known as 'Haveli Dina Nath', the second is known as 'Haveli Dina Nath Raja Kalanaur'. The first was built during the reign of Maharajah Ranjit Singh. The second during British rule, but before the 1857 war of independence.

He is important in history because he was one of three persons - a Muslim, a Sikh and a Hindu -- who formed a Council of Regency to administer the affairs of the Lahore Darbar in December 1846, before the East India Company took over completely in 1849. The other two being Fakiruddin and Teja Singh. Dewan Dina Nath was the president of the council.

But who was this Dina Nath whose name was still being used in the streets of old Lahore 147 years after he died. A bit of research into the 50-year time period (1807 to 1857) did bring forth interesting facts about this remarkable man who ruled Lahore directly for three years, and, indirectly, for almost a decade. For three decades he silently, yet very effectively, influenced the manner in which Lahore's various rulers, unpredictable as they were, went about their business. What is remarkable about this man was that he made virtually no enemies.

Dewan Dina Nath was a Kashmiri Pandit who migrated to Lahore in 1815. Known as an outstanding civil administrator and counselor of considerable influence at the Sikh court, he was the son of a Kashmiri Pandit, Bakht Mal, who had migrated to Delhi during the oppressive rule of the Afghan governors of the Kashmir valley. He was also closely related to the military accounts and keeper of the Privy Seal at Lahore, Dewan Ganga Ram (not to be confused with Sir Ganga Ram, who came much later), and it was because of him that Dina Nath came to Lahore.

At the instance of Dewan Ganga Ram, Maharajah Ranjit Singh invited Dina Nath to Lahore and offered him the post of 'mutasadi', or writer, in the department of military accounts. In 1826, when Dewan Ganga Ram died, Dina Nath succeeded him as the head of military accounts department and keeper of the Privy Seal. In 1834, when Dewan Bhavani Das passed away, the Maharajah made him the head of the civil and finance office and conferred upon him, in 1838, the honorary title of Dewan. By his ability and political acumen, Dina Nath rose to the highest position of power and influence in the affairs of the State. The scholar Lepel Griffin called him the 'Talleyrand of the Punjab'. The outstanding ability of Dewan Dina Nath was that he knew how to keep his ambition in check. He knew every face and name, and was constantly reassuring everyone of his "immense interest" in his or her welfare.

The most remarkable ability of Dewan Dina Nath was that he remained an exceptionally low profile person, yet his grip on the affairs of State, especially on financial matters, was 'iron-like'. The entire military depended on him for money. That is why a few scholars have even gone to the extent of suggesting that after Maharajah Ranjit Singh, he was probably the most powerful person in the Lahore Darbar.

In the turbulent days following Maharajah Ranjit Singh's death, he refused to take sides with Rani Chand Kaur or Kanvar Sher Singh. It was a dangerous balancing act, but he performed it with immense expertise, never letting real financial power slip from his hands. Upon his succession to the throne, Maharajah Sher Singh reposed his full trust in him. Dina Nath retained his position at the court during the reign of both Maharajah Hira Singh and Jawahar Singh, as well as during the regency of Maharani Jindan Kaur.

For a good ten years he firmly held the purse of the Punjab, a duty he performed with immense honesty. The one single quote one has been able to find ascribed to him is: "Greed invariably grows, till even the mightiest fall. So curb greed and enjoy the serenity of simplicity". It speaks much of the man whom the British were to later honour in ever possible way.

After the Anglo-Sikh War of 1845-46, the British nominated him a member of the Council of Regency established in Lahore for the minor king, Maharajah Dulip Singh. In November 1847, the title of the Raja of Kalanaur, with a jagir worth Rs. 20,000 annually, was conferred upon him. After the annexation of the Punjab in 1849, Dewan Dina Nath served under the British, who confirmed him in his jagirs worth about Rs. 50,000/- annually.

By the Treaty of Lahore, Sir Henry Lawrence was appointed the British resident in Lahore. A few months following the treaty, it was Dina Nath who informed a disillusioned Rani Jindan and Lal Singh about the true intentions of the British. In a way he was the man who informed the Sikh rulers that the British were here to stay.

When the Resident asked the Lahore Darbar to surrender Kashmir to Raja Gulab Singh, Lal Singh indirectly encouraged Imamuddin, the Darbar's Muslim Governor there, to resist. Lal Singh was exiled, on charges of conspiracy against the British Resident. Dewan Dina Nath remained neutral in the matter, for technically the end had not been reached.

With Pandit Dina Nath, now the Raja of Kalanaur, in saddle, hundreds of Kashmiri Pandits migrated to Lahore from Kashmir. He became the rallying factor of all these fresh immigrants and invariably helped them to influential careers. In the course of time, Pandit colonies sprang up in Lahore, the most famous of them being Krishan Nagar and Sant Nagar.

In view of the fact that Raja Dina Nath and other Kashmiri Pandit notables had succeeded in winning the confidence of the British conquerors, the East India Company meted out to them great encouragement, and made them recipients of many posts of trust and honour, which were, till then, kept closed to Indians. Till then there were very few Kashmiri Pandits residing in Lahore. Dewan Dina Nath died in Lahore in February 1857, just before the war of independence broke out and failed. He was cremated outside Mori Gate, and his ashes consigned to the River Ravi.

Dr Harlan's magical potion

Of all foreign adventurers who came to Lahore during the 40-year long reign of Maharajah Ranjit Singh, surely the most colourful was a mysterious American doctor by the name of Josiah Harlan. He was the man who promised the shrewd Maharajah a "magical potion to cure all his ills".

By the time the offer of the 'magical potion' was made, Dr Harlan was a well-known figure in the intrigue and politics of Lahore. He was a very close friend of the Maharajah's closest Minister, Fakir Azizuddin, and lived in one of the houses owned by the fakir family. If you know your way around the corner of Tehsil Bazaar and Bazaar Hakeeman deep inside Bhatti Gate, you will notice an old house with a British era nameplate of one of the Fakir family. In this house lived Dr Harlan and very soon he had a thriving practice.

Dr. Harlan

The Sikh ruler had a love-hate relationship with Harlan, who was probably the only person in that era to meet Maharajah Ranjit Singh on equal terms. Many thought he was too arrogant. When asked by Ranjit Singh to explain his insolence, Dr Harlan replied. "Because I belong to the United States of America, and more so to Pennsylvania".

In 1824, Dr Harlan enrolled for the Bengal Army, as they were short of surgeons during the Burmese War. How and why this American turned up there is not known. He served in Rangoon in 1823, then in Karnal with a regiment of Native infantry. He was on leave in Ludhiana in 1826 when he was informed that an order had been issued for the dismissal of temporary surgeons in the British Army.

In 1827, Harlan asked and got permission from the British authorities to cross the Sutlej, allegedly to go by land to Saint Petersburg. Proud of being "a free citizen of the United States," his plan was in fact to join Maharajah Ranjit Singh's service. However, the Maharajah did not allow Harlan to enter his territories.

So Harlan decided to go to Kabul through Bahawalpur, Kandahar and Ghazni in September 1827. He initially worked as an agent for Shah Shuja, the exiled king of Afghanistan who resided in British-held Ludhiana. Harlan's real motive was to try to recover the papers of William

Moorcroft and George Trebeck who had been murdered near Mazar-i-Sharif in northern Afghanistan while on a spying mission for the East India Company.

There Jabbar Khan, a Qizilbash Shia and stepbrother of Dost Mohammed Khan, the Emir of Kabul, welcomed him. Jabbar Khan was a close friend of the French officers in the Lahore service, and whatever Harlan did in Kabul was most certainly known to Gen Allard in Lahore, and, therefore, also to Maharajah Ranjit Singh. Through them Harlan managed to weave his way to Lahore. In early 1829, Dr. Harlan left Kabul and reached Lahore, where he set up his private practice in Bazaar Hakeeman. Even today, some old residents call the house 'Amreekan hakeem di Hatti'.

Ranjit Singh kept a strict eye on this American doctor. One day, he summoned him and offered him command of the Oms Brigade, as the French commander had just died. The elite regiments were stationed at Shahdara, on the right (north) bank of the Ravi. Dr. Harlan refused, saying that he was a medical practitioner and not a military man, and that he soon planned to return to the United States. The Maharajah did not believe him.

Realizing that he could not induce Harlan to join him as a military officer, the Maharajah offered him the position of governor of Nurpur and Jasrota, two Rajput principalities between Jammu and Kangra in December 1829. By March 1831, he was back in Lahore, recalled by the Maharajah because of growing complaints against him. In Lahore he took up residence with Gen Allard, who offered him protection.

In May 1832, Ranjit Singh appointed him governor of Gujrat and invested him with a *khilat* (dress of honour). He was even presented with an elephant and given the *sanad* conferring upon him the necessary authority for his government. A few months later he was called back to Lahore because of the complaints by infuriated zamindars.

In 1833-34, Shah Shuja, in an attempt to recover his throne, undertook his disastrous expedition to Kandahar. This fighting served as a diversion, for Maharajah Ranjit Singh sent Hari Singh Nalwa and Gen. Court with their elite brigades, who in a swift move recaptured Peshawar and its province up to the Khyber Pass. Mahmud Ghaznavi in 1001-1005 AD had annexed Peshawar from the Punjab.

Dost Muhammed Khan protested against this move, and in 1833 he made his first attempt to recapture Peshawar through a jihad against the 'kafir' Sikhs. British intelligence predicted that if Ranjit Singh were defeated, the whole Muslim population of Punjab would rise against the Sikhs. Well aware of this possibility, Ranjit Singh planned to encircle the entrance to the Khyber Pass. His strategy was to wait, let the invading Afghans come out of the Khyber and then encircle and destroy them entirely. For that he needed a plan to keep Dost Muhammed Khan busy. The tactic Ranjit Singh devised was to send a delegation to the Khan. He selected Fakir Syed Azizuddin, his trusted minister of foreign affairs, and his 'mysterious' American governor, Dr. Josiah Harlan for the job. That was on May 11,1835.

Amidst all this, Ranjit Singh was tightening the noose. Suddenly Dost Muhammad Khan was informed that the Afghan army was almost completely surrounded. Dost Mohammed Khan ordered Fakir Azizuddin and Josiah Harlan to be delivered to his brother Sultan Muhammad Khan to be kept as hostages. Already in the pay of Dr Harlan, Sultan Muhammad Khan simply sent them back to the Punjab. The master spy had shown his cards.

In April 1836 as Maharajah Ranjit Singh began to fall increasingly ill, Harlan promised to prepare a medical medicine for him at the exorbitant price of one lakh rupees: a price to be paid in advance "as he did not trust the Maharajah". The comment sent the Maharajah in a rage. Dr Harlan was immediately dismissed, paid his dues and escorted across the Sutlej to British territories.

In Ludhiana, he informed the East India Company of his desire to enter the service of Dost Muhammed Khan at Kabul. The Company record states: "His declared intention is to bring down the Peshawar an army to avenge himself on his former master Ranjit Singh for the injuries he has received at his hands". Dr Harlan retraced his journey to Kabul, where he trained the second regular infantry regiment. Overnight the American doctor had become a military man. He participated in the war to recapture Peshawar in 1837, which was saved by the heroic deeds of Hari Singh Nalwa, who was fatally wounded at Jamrud.

After Jamrud, Harlan was back in Kabul in the spring of 1839, just in time to meet with the British advance troop in the First Anglo-Afghan war. Dr Harlan was sent back to Ludhiana with the British forces in September 1839 after the capture of Kabul. He was transferred to Calcutta, and then sent back to the US at the expense of the East India Company.

Dr Harlan spent the next 30 years of his life in the United States. During the American Civil War in 1861, he raised a regiment for the Union Army, called Harlan's Light Cavalry, later known as the 11th Cavalry. He served as its colonel in the army of the Potomac until he retired due to ill health in 1862. Harlan moved to San Francisco where he again practiced as a physician. He died there in October 1871.

How the bhangis lost Lahore

Lahore has been ruled by the strangest of people — from the original Rajput Bhat rajas chivalrous and brave to a fault, to looting Afghan hordes to the invading Mughals to the indigenous Sikhs to the absolutely foreign British. In short spans, the city was even ruled by a nymphomaniac woman and a wise eunuch to say the least.

But definitely no rulers were as bizarre as the threesome 'Bhangi' sardars who ruled Lahore for ten years up to 1799. Ultimately, the entire population conspired to get them thrown out. The 'Bhangi' rulers were Chet Singh, Sahib Singh and Mohar Singh, and they ruled together, all three, at the same time by dividing Lahore into three zones of influence. They ruled together because all they did was drink *bhang* and indulge in pastimes this city has never seen since, nor had witnessed before. This preference for *bhang* resulted in them being called *bhangi,* and not because they belonged to the Gujrati Bhangi tribe, who were no small marauders and pestered everyone from Multan to Delhi.

These three gents ruled Lahore before Ranjit Singh was finally invited by the elite of the city, the Arain Mians of Lahore, to invade and establish his rule, an invitation he was glad to accept. The *bhangi* sardars were drunkards, womanizers and looted whomever and whatever they could lay their hands on. The loved to drink *bhang* and having done so, they would sleep for days on end. All three rulers would indulge in their pastimes together. As they did not know how to rule, they left the affairs of State to two leading Mians of Lahore, they being Mian Ashik Muhammad and Mian Muhkam Din. These two loyally served the *bhangi* sardars and managed to protect the population of the walled city from the transgressions of the *bhangis* and their wild Sikh soldiers as far as possible.

But then things took a turn for the worse when Mian Ashik Muhammad married his daughter to another rich Arain, Mian Badruddin. The *bhangi* sardars, so one account goes, decided that they had been wronged by not being consulted on the match. Another account states that Mohar Singh wanted to marry the young girl himself. A third account states that the money lending 'khatris' of Lahore did not like Badruddin, for he was strongly opposed to borrowing on interest from them, which the *bhangis* did by pledging almost every property in the walled city. A stage had been reached when the money lending 'khatris' virtually owned almost all property in Lahore. This led to considerable tension as the 'khatris' began to influence matters of State. In the end, large sections of the population, began to show sign of revolt, and the wild *bhangi* soldiers began to molest the families of the leading dissenters. In the end, five leading Muslim personalities, two Sikh sardars and a number of Hindu scholars of the walled city invited Ranjit Singh to take Lahore. They provided him with considerable intelligence on when to strike and which were the weak points. A plan to take the city from within was hatched, which was to operate once the rising Sikh leader had broken into the city.

The Muslims of Lahore, who then were in a minority, celebrated the coming of Maharajah Ranjit Singh. In return, the Sikh ruler made it a point to first visit the Badshahi Mosque, a move that paid him considerable dividends. Later, he used these very people to declare himself a 'maharajah'. He timed his entry to perfection, on the Tenth of Muharram, or July 7, 1799. Just one, interesting observation here. The army of Ranjit Singh assaulted from two sides... from Lahori Gate came the maharajah himself, while the first entry was made by his elite assault troops from Delhi Gate, and they were led by an exceptionally brave woman. Rani Sada Kaur, a beautiful sword-yielding woman who led by example.

The main army of Ranjit Singh approached Lahori Gate and managed to, on the night of the tenth of Muharram, breach the outer walls by blowing up a portion near Mori Gate. Forces within the city immediately overcame the guards at Lahori Gate, and the Sikh troops entered almost without a fight. At that very moment, Rani Sada Kaur and her assault troops, with assistance from the Muslims of Delhi Gate, managed to scale the walls and open the gates. Thus the forces of Ranjit Singh entered at the same time from the south and the east. The few soldiers defending the walls headed towards the Lahore Fort and gathered at the Hazuri Bagh. Seeing the city overrun, Sahib Singh and Mohar Singh decided to flee and left Chet Sigh to defend his own zone. Almost 500 soldiers of Chet Sigh seeing that it was useless to fight decided to surrender, while Chet Singh Bhangi was allowed to flee across the river.

And so with the support of the Muslims of Lahore, more so the Arain Mians of the city, Maharajah Ranjit Singh was able to establish his Punjabi empire and to build the strongest Punjabi army that ever was. The 'khatris' had to suffer, as all loans provided were declared null and void and all securities were taken over by the State. The Arain Mians were skillfully cast aside by the maharajah, as all those assisting a coup are done so even to this day. Ranjit Singh chose to manage his affairs through another Muslim family of Lahore, the Fakirs of Bazaar Hakeeman.

The new maharajah proved to be the opposite of what the *bhangis* stood for. Their priority was women, horses and governance in that order. Maharajah Ranjit Sigh reversed it and made it known publicly. His priority proved the correct way of going about things. In the ultimate analysis the ousted 'bhangis' played a major role in acting as British agents, who created discord among the Sikh sardars after the death of Ranjit Singh in 1839. It sounds so much like what is happening today, for who is the king and who is the kingmaker, it seems that line is too fine to determine.

Rattan Chand and his Shivala

The Lahore Darbar of Maharajah Ranjit Singh had an array of very talented men from all over the Punjab-men of letters, of arms, of commerce, and then there were scholars and analysts. He would consult at least three to four persons on any matter of importance before making up his mind.

The Maharajah liked to ask young and old, and often he would pose the most vexing questions to the numerous young children of courtiers that were present. His view was that the innocent often solved the most difficult problems. "Simplicity is not the virtue of those in intrigue", he would often comment. One of his favourite young child at court was a boy by the name of Rattan Chand, and the Maharajah called him Rattan Chand 'dhariwala' to distinguish him from a namesake. When he came of age, he was known as a wise young man, and was greatly respected for his views. He was officially called Lala Rattan Chand Dhariwala. He was appointed to various positions, all of which he served with distinction. After the death of the Maharajah in 1839, he continued to serve the Lahore Darbar and in 1846 was the postmaster-general of the Punjab in the dying days of Sikh rule. When the British took over in 1849, he worked for them and became the honorary magistrate of Lahore in 1862. He then went on to become a member of the Municipal Committee and was made a Dewan in 1865, where after he was described as Dewan Lala Rattan Chand Dhariwala.

During the reign preceding Maharajah Ranjit Singh, the area outside the Shahalami Gate had been laid waste by conflict. The various Sikh chiefs, who began constructing huge havelis inside the walled city, plundered the bricks from vacant houses. Very soon the area was a huge empty ground, and it was at that time that Lala Rattan Chand wanted to purchase it. He was opposed by Sikh chiefs who felt that too large and important a tract of land was being given to a mere boy. The maharajah decided not to allot it to anyone. One version has it that the maharajah promised that if it was allotted in his lifetime, it would be to him. As a special gesture, he allotted him a smaller piece to build a temple as a first step.

So Lala Rattan Chand set about levelling the wasteland and then he built a wall around his possession. On the four corners of the walls he built four structures with Sikh-style domes. In the middle he built a temple perched on a platform raised above the ground. The temple dome was raised to a considerable height, making it among the finest in Lahore. Outside, he built a series of houses and shops, and even before the British arrived, the road was being called Rattan Chand di Sarak.

The ten years after the death of the maharajah saw considerable fighting within the Lahore Darbar. In this period, Lala Rattan Chand consolidated his position and kept the status quo, thanks to his connections with the 'patwaris' of those days, all of whom feared him. When the British took over, he immediately switched sides, put in an application that the late Maharajah had promised him this additional land. The British immediately allotted him his 'promised' land.

The British were short of residential accommodation, and Lala Rattan Chand provided them with ample housing, "at very reasonable rates. Within a few months, he had managed to get allotted the entire gardens that were to make the garden, tank and temple of Rattan Chand a major feature of Lahore. Lala Rattan Chand was among the very first Punjabi bureaucrats to join the British administration of the East India Company.

The water tank was made in such a way that it surrounded the temple. The water for the Shivala was brought through an ingenious system of very small canals. The gardens laid out were well watered and green all the year round. Its fruit trees were well-known in the city and a nursery of sorts developed at this point, where today exists the dusty Bansaanwala Bazaar. Lala Rattan Chand died in 1872 and the road right up to the Mayo Hospital crossing was named after him. Once the Mayo Hospital was built, a major portion of the road was named Hospital Road.

After his death, his son Lala Bhagvan Das took over and he soon fell victim to commercial pressures to part with some of the residential houses and shops. With time this Shivala was seen to be a major obstruction to the expansion of commercial activities, and it were the Hindu traders of Shahalami who began to pressure the administration to take over the Shivala. But then came the partition of the Punjab and in the bloody riots, just like in the days preceding the Sikhs, the entire temple, Shivala and gardens were reduced to bricks and the 'claim brigade' took over. Today, there lie hundreds of small high houses, the dusty Bansaanwala Bazaar and the road now has three names, just one of these is Rattan Chand Road.

The 30-year rule of the 'three hakeems'

There is a 30-year period, before Maharajah Ranjit Singh came to power in 1799, which is known as the reign of the three hakeems. Who were these three hakeems and what role do they have in Lahore's history?

The three hakeems were basically three Sikh chieftains who lived and ruled Lahore in a curious triumvirate whose antics have become part of Lahori folklore. My investigation started almost three weeks ago when, while walking through a hot, dusty street on the outskirts of Lahore, I heard a vegetable vendor shouting to sell his ware: "Na Lehna Singh, na Dehna Singh, tammatar (tomatoes) asli Gujjar Singh". That stopped me in my track. What an amazing sentence to be used in the year 2005. I asked the old man where he had heard this 'marketing message'. He informed me that he was from an old Arain family of Shalimar that had sold vegetables for the last five generations, before which they were vegetable growers, and this was a common sentence used by the family. "But what does it mean?" I asked. "I have no idea," he said.

The words and sentences we inherit need to be investigated, for in it resides our history. Let us go back to the period when Ahmad Shah Abdali (1738-1767) in his 30-year reign invaded and captured Lahore a total of nine times, each time ransacking and looting, not to speak of the rape and murder that went with every invasion.

With each invasion, the hold of Abdali began to loosen as strife inside his own capital began to threaten his very base. He decided to give Lahore to a Bhangi sardar called Lehna Singh. But Lehna was no fool. He teamed up with another two Sikh chieftains to secure the environs around Lahore. So it was that the triumvirate of Lehna Singh, Suba Singh and Gujjar Singh came to occupy power in and around Lahore. For 30 long years they ruled supreme and kept paying the Afghan invader and his offspring an annual sum to keep them at bay.

The Lahore Fort and the Walled City and its gates went to Lehna Singh. He was, for formal purposes, the governor of Lahore, and was so recongized. The area between Amritsar and Lahore, or more correctly between the Shalimar Gardens and Lahore, went to Gujjar Singh, who built himself a small fort called Qila Gujjar Singh. Today, a few walls of that old fort can be seen in a street between today's Nicholson Road and Empress Road, which is still called Qila Gujjar Singh. To Suba Singh went the area to the south of the Walled City, and he resided in the garden of Zubeida Begum in Nawankot, where he built a small fort for himself. Thus the three Sikh chieftains ruled Lahore in peace for 30 long years, years in which their antics became the butt of many a Sikh joke that we still recall today. But why were they called the 'three hakeems'? The three chieftains cooperated very closely with one another, and often they would have orgies in which dancing women, or 'nautch girls' as the British liked to call them, entertained them. In these sessions, opium smoking was the norm. When asked why they used this drug, they laughed it off as a medicine recommended by hakeems. Thus they began to be called the three hakeems, a name that stuck to them.

The three chieftains imposed heavy taxes on the people, all in the name of paying the Afghans a heavy protection duty. In the process, they became one of the richest Sikh chieftains of all Khalsa Misls in Punjab. Their armies soon became known for the excesses they committed on the people, and very soon other Sikhs began to plan and plot their overthrow. But more than other Sikhs, the wealth of Lahore began to attract the Afghans themselves, who demanded a heavier protection fee. This the three refused on grounds of poverty. It was excuse enough for them to return in force.

In 1797, Shah Zaman, the grandson of Ahmad Shah, mustered a huge army to take Lahore, but he failed to do so, losing some heavy guns in the process in the River Jhelum. It was at this stage that Ranjit Singh, son of Maha Singh, and chief of the Sukherchakria Misl of Gujranwala, came to the assistance of the Afghans. The young crafty chieftain, against the advice of his elders, but on the urging of his mother-in-law, used his forces to retrieve eight of the 20 lost cannons of the Afghans from the Jhelum River and returned them in prime condition to Kabul. This pleased the Kabul Court which immediately gave permission to Ranjit Singh to become governor of Lahore. At that time, Lahore was under Chet Singh, son of Lehna Singh, and given the triumvirate around Lahore and their excellent spy network, it was no easy task.

Ranjit Singh realized that the Afghans were a spent force. So he set about infiltrating spies inside the Walled City. It took him two long years to plan this move, years in which he trained and developed his cavalry to move with immense speed, while also building enough firepower to blast his way into a heavily defended Lahore. In 1799, he moved his forces to a base camp about a mile from the southern Lahori Gate. His camp was on the grounds of the Baradari of Wazir Khan, where today is built the Lahore Museum. The Baradari still stands and houses the Punjab Public Library.

The spies managed to buy over most of the guards of the gates, while also spreading rumours that the attack was coming from Delhi Gate. Mock attacks at night were attempted to test each gate, which spread fear among the trapped inhabitants. Finally, when the attack did take place, it was a walkover as the spies had managed to buy over almost all guards. Those loyal to Chet Singh were killed. The three hakeems fled and Lahore welcomed Ranjit Singh, chief of the Sukherchakria Misl. The foundations of the Lahore Darbar were laid and a strong Punjab was to emerge from the crafty tactics of the young man from Gujranwala. The rule of the three hakeems saw Lahore prosper as a trading city, and with it the business community thrived, even though they were forced to pay more and more in taxes in the guise of protection money. The style of governance made the three famous for uttering the strangest of things, all of which gave the Sikhs an image from which they have still not recovered. The early morning opium parties reached their peak by the afternoon, which soon began to be called 'peak hour intoxication'. But these orgies aside, the triumvirate did, in reality, strengthen Lahore to the extent whereby the Afghan predatory yoke was removed forever, and Ranjit Singh managed to build a huge empire on those foundations. History still remains, unfairly, harsh on the three hakeems, even though even today their names are used by .. street vendors.

The curse on Sultan the contractor

In every disaster lies an opportunity. Every street, every brick of Lahore speaks a story of opportunities taken. One such tale is that of Muhammad Sultan the thekaydar, contractor, whose unique contribution to Lahore lies in his ability to use bricks from the ruins of war to reconstruct an array of new buildings and bazaars ... carving for himself a unique place in the annals of the city.

He started life as a poor man living inside Delhi Gate, working in the last days of Maharajah Ranjit Singh as a casual labourer in the markets. The Sikh era had seen hundreds of mosques going into disrepair, mainly because they were used as stables or ammunition depots. Once the British had defeated the Sikhs, all within ten years of the death of the Maharajah, they consolidated their power by beginning the construction of the Lahore Cantonment. Among the first contractors to be used by them was Muhammad Sultan of Delhi Gate. How this unknown and poor casual labourer became a contractor has remained an enduring myth among scholars of the British era, but one story goes on to say that he posed as a contractor and was given a small job of constructing a house in the cantonment among the hundreds planned.

Sultan moved swiftly, and the first thing he did was to buy out a few derelict mosques inside the old walled city. He then set about removing all the bricks from the mosques, and though many protested against this practice, he managed to feed the poor in large numbers to win the sympathies of the starving population. So good was Muhammad Sultan at finding old mosques and flattening them within days, that many predicted that a curse would soon fall on the man who specializes in "martyring mosques". But no such curse ever befell Sultan, for it seems that his wealth just kept on growing.

Among the first brand new British bungalows that came up in the Lahore Cantonment were those made by Sultan, and the quality of his work impressed the British, who started giving him more and more work. He demolished many a famous building of Lahore, including the famous Pari Mahal, Masjid Neem Bismil, Jahan Sarai, Chowk Shahzada Dara Shikoh, etc. But then he set about building his own Sarai Sultan just outside Delhi Gate. Along with this sarai, he built a small bazaar, and so small was it that the people of the walled city nicknamed it lunda bazaar, the crippled bazaar. Today that very bazaar is known as Landa Bazaar.

The particular skill of Sultan the Contractor was to find out from the elderly folk of the walled city about old buildings and how they were built. Once he was sure that considerable masonry work had been undertaken and that the structure of the building clearly showed that its foundations had a lot of bricks used in it, he would set about digging up the foundations.

One such building was the haveli of Wazir Khan also known as the Pari Mahal. It had considerable water courses under its gardens and its entire foundations had an intricate water channel system which made sure that throughout the hot summers exceptionally cold water was always available, and it was clean filtered water, the type of filter that existed outside the Shalimar Gardens. The gardens of this building provided Sultan with an exceptional collection of bricks. With these bricks, laid as they were with clay mortar and easy pickings for him, he made his immense fortune. The rule of thumb was that each worker had to produce at least 1,000 bricks a day to qualify for his daily wage.

All these bricks he used, as he did from other sites of derelict mosques all over Lahore, to build his serai and the lunda bazaar. Some of the best bricks he used in the construction of some of the finest houses in the old cantonment. A man of immense wealth with an army of friends who fed off him, Sultan went into high gear when the Prince of Wales visited Lahore in 1876. The entire Lunda Bazaar area was decorated and he spent a lot of money in the construction of special houses and rest houses, all from his own resources. To fill up the bazaar he invited traders from inside the walled city and for many years did not take any rent from them. By the time the Prince arrived, Sultan the Contractor was at his zenith.

But then like every fairy tale, the story of Sultan had its downside. He remained without any children from his wife, and she died before he did. Once his health began to give way, his lavish ways led him into a deficit from which he never recovered.

Very soon, all his property began to be sold off. The British government tried to assist him by helping to raise loans to pay off old ones, but when the chips were down, nothing but his own assets were left to bank upon. These he mortgaged with the Maharajah of Jammu, and to him they ultimately went, including his prized Pari Mahal, stripped as it was of its gardens. The rumour went round that the curse of demolishing mosques had caught up with Sultan the Contractor.

He died in debt and the son of his uncle got some share of some old shops constructed from the bricks of old Lahore mosques. He also died in circumstances unknown, and it was decided by the elderly of Delhi Gate that any money accruing from the shops of Sultan the Contractor would go to three old widows, who would pray to Allah to forgive him for his deeds. The rest is local legend, which says that ultimately these three women also fell into debt and refused to take the money that came their way. In this was their salvation. Here the story ends of a man who rose from the ashes of the destroyed Sikh empire, by selling the bricks of derelict mosques and ultimately died a pauper cursed by the legend of his own misdeeds, if you can call it so. I for one, do not.

The day the butchers had their noses cut off

It was a bizarre sight by any standards. If you enter the Delhi Gate of Lahore's Walled City, almost 50 yards down the main entrance there is a butcher's shop on the corner of a lane starting to the left. This is the beginning of Mohallah Qassaban - the Butchers Precinct. Almost 223 years ago at this point the noses and ears of the butchers of Lahore were cut off to avert a disaster.

This brutal act took place because the Walled City was surrounded by the combined forces of the Sikhs. They were threatening to attack and torch the city if the butchers of Lahore were not handed over to them. The governor, or *subedar* as he was known then, did not want to hand over his citizens to the bloodthirsty Sikhs, so he opted for a bizarre solution. He got hold of a few butchers, cut off their noses and ears, and presented the Sikhs with these 'presents' on a silver platter. He then opened Delhi Gate and the bleeding butchers, with their noses and ears cut off, were presented to the Sikh forces, who left in jubilation. A major crisis had been averted.

This amazing event in the history of Lahore happened in the reign of the Afghan invader, the Durrani Ahmad Shah, who had appointed a *subedar* by the name of Kabuli Mal. This strange event took place because the butchers of Lahore had over time developed an intense hatred for the Sikhs, who at every turn clashed with them. Every time these encounters were fierce, leading to considerable blood being spilled. The butchers knew how to slice a man in two with ease, and the Sikhs feared them. The Sikhs, because of sheer numbers, relished a battle with them to avenge old wounds. The last such clash of over 500 years of hatred took place during the partition of the Punjab in 1947, ending, hopefully, a sorry tale that needed to be wound up and put to rest.

The original enmity has its origin in the death of the Sikh guru Arjun on the banks of the River Ravi just outside the walls of the Lahore Fort. Sikh folklore has it that he dived into the river and disappeared forever in a 'divine act.' The Muslims think he died, while bathing in the river, from wounds received from torture in the Lahore Fort. But his death was blamed on the emperor Shah Jahan, who faced a popular rebellion. The royal forces rounded up militant followers of Guru Arjun from all over the Punjab. Of these, almost 9,000 were brought to Lahore in chains. The emperor ordered the butchers of Lahore to slaughter them just outside Yakki Gate, and for one whole week they were slaughtered. It was a massacre the Sikhs never forgot, and they decided to avenge the slaughter by killing the entire butcher community of Lahore. The siege of Lahore took place because of this original enmity.

The slaughter of the Sikhs by the butchers of Lahore led the Hindu population to press the emperor to remove all butchers, or cow slayers as they were called then, from the city. After considerable hesitation the emperor succumbed to this demand and he set them up outside Lahore in the place where today is located the Lahore Hide Market (Chamra Mandi). They were assisted considerably by the emperor and almost all of them built beautiful havelis, a few of which still survive, as well as a beautiful mosque, a rebuilt version of which still exists on the corner of the road going into the Hide Market. This arrangement worked well for some time. Problems started to arise as the power of the Muslims began to slide and Sikh militancy grew apace. The time for revenge had come for the great grandchildren of the original victims, and they targeted the butchers instead of the crown.

The Sikhs operating outside Lahore attacked the area, and the butchers counter-attacked with knives and hatchets in a brutal encounter that saw the Sikhs retreat with huge losses. They had never seen such an enemy, and this incident tended to unite the Sikhs, who by now had vowed to seek revenge for the original massacre. A second and larger attack took place, and again the battle was intense and bloody. The Sikhs again withdrew in the face of fierce knives and hatchets used with tremendous skill. After all what did they expect butchers fighting for their lives to do? Local legend has it that even the womenfolk of the butchers fought side by side wlth their men.

Subedar Kabuli Mal was at his wit's end as to how to resolve this enmity. The Sikhs would not discuss anything but the complete elimination of all butchers from Lahore, which was also part of their quasi-Hindu faith. The Muslim population of the city, which was a majority by this time, demanded their right to eat meat, and for that butchers were essential. The Durrani Ahmad Shah ordered. that the butchers be resettled inside the Walled City, and it was then that the entire population of butchers was resettled in Mohallah Qassaban. The incident of the siege of Lahore did not last for more than 36 hours, and the solution seems to have satisfied the crazed Sikhs, who felt the humiliation of the butchers was enough punishment for them.

The reign of Maharajah Ranjit Singh saw just one incident when this mohallah was attacked and the houses set on fire. The crafty Sikh ruler ordered that the Sikh chiefs of Lahore should either slaughter cows or leave the butchers alone. They never bothered the butchers after that. During the British rule no incident of any importance except for stray happenings by crazed individuals took place. But they certainly did erupt when the fires of hatred burned in Lahore in 1947.

The rape and massacre of Muslim girls from Lahore in an Amritsar girls hostel led to attacks on Sikhs. inside the Walled City. They formed a *jattha* and roamed around the Shahalami area. The first major attack on the Muslims was on the Mohallah Qassaban, where six butchers were slaughtered. The next night the butchers hit back with a vengeance. From that point onwards the blood never stopped flowing till each and every Sikh had fled this city of love and poetry. With their exit ended a feud that had needlessly cost hundreds and thousands of lives. It seems emperors never seem to understand that acts of evil never die. The Machiavellian Prince has also been advised never to butcher in the name of establishing his reign and rule. Better settlements are always possible. But it seems the Prince never learns.

The Europeans of Lahore

The rise of Maharajah Ranjit Singh saw the mercurial rise of an immense power, an army unmatched in technology, skill and bravery. Over 67 percent of all Punjabis were literate, thanks to the Punjabi 'qaida', which the British banned spreading despondency that still prevails.

For a full 40 years, the Darbar in Lahore was seen as one of the most exciting places in the East. Lahore, in the first half of the 18th century, was an exciting prospect, the only part of the sub-continent that had effectively halted the advancing British. In their first encounter, the Punjabis smashed the British with superior tactics, training and arms. For 40 years, they remained still, merely conspiring and waiting for Maharajah Ranjit Singh to die. Lahore held out hope, for the rulers were fair and secular. This image lured many a foreigner to Lahore, and it was the richer for all those who came and made this city their home.

The two most prominent foreigners in Lahore during this era were Gen Ventura, an Italian by birth, and Gen Allard, a Frenchman. They came to Lahore in 1822 to seek service in the Sikh army. Both had served under Napoleon in the imperial army of France. After Napoleon's defeat at Waterloo, they fled Europe to try their fortune in the East and landed in Lahore.

Ranjit Singh, although not educated, was exceptionally wise and intelligent. He had heard about the exploits of Napoleon. Ranjit Singh met these two European generals and showed them his troops on parade and sought their opinion. He heard them carefully and never said a word.

In April of 1822, they sent a letter to the Maharajah, asking for employment with his troops. The communication between these soldiers and the Maharajah was in French, through his trusted aide Faqir Nuruddin, of Bazaar Hakeeman inside Bhatti Gate, who knew many languages. The Maharajah wanted to make sure that these people did not have any contacts with the British. Once he was sure, he gave them command of 500 horsemen each. They were also to train all Sikh forces in the western method. Gen Ventura's army was called Fauj-i-Khas.

A bit later Gen Allard was also asked to raise a cavalry of fresh recruits. This new Punjabi cavalry learnt all the techniques which the army of Napoleon had mastered and they came to be feared and called the 'finest army in Asia' by Lord Roberts of India himself.

Maharajah Ranjit Singh made all the foreigners hired by him sign strict terms of employment, which, among other things, stated that in the case of a clash between the forces of the Maharajah and any European or other power, they would remain loyal to him. They were all bound by the agreement to wear a beard, abstain from beef and tobacco. All the Europeans were exceptionally well paid. To Ventura and Allard he provided excellent living quarters. When Gen Ventura married a Muslim Punjabi girl, the Maharajah gave him Rs. 40,000 as a gift and a small jagir. Gen Ventura built a beautiful French chateau outside Anarkali Bazaar.

Besides these, a large number of other Europeans were employed in various disciplines. One well-known person was a Hungarian by the name of Dr. Honigberger, who set up the first modern clinic just outside where today stands the gate of the Tibbi police station. He soon set up similar clinics in the city and in other smaller towns of the Punjab.

Gen. Avitable, an Italian, also joined him and was later appointed the Governor of Peshawar. Then there was Gen Court, a Frenchman, who organized the first scientific artillery of the Punjabi army. Dr Harlan, an American, initially assisted in the new medical clinics in Lahore, and was to later become a governor of Gujrat. Herr Henry Steinbach, a German, was made a battalion commander. He was a strict trainer of men and soon the Sikh soldiers feared him as he worked very hard to discipline them. 'Henry Sahib' was a feared man in the Punjabi army.

Senor Hurbon, a Spaniard, was an engineer who was to prove invaluable in organizing the Army's engineering corps. An important person to the huge European gathering was Dr. Benet, a Frenchman, who was surgeon-general of the Punjabi army. The trained staff of Benet made sure that every regiment of the Punjabi army had appropriate medical assistance. The battle at Chillianwala Bagh near Gujrat, when the British finally overcame the Punjabis in 1850, showed how well the medical staff conducted themselves. The battle had been savage and the Punjabis almost overcame the British, with casualties high on both sides.

A most interesting foreigner in Lahore of those days was Gen Viekenavitch, a Russian, who held a high rank in the artillery. He is credited with having trained the Punjabis in the advanced science of gun making. He set up his foundry inside the Lahore Fort, and this foundry provided the army with its new guns.

To add to this large group of foreigners, there were a number of Englishmen too. Well-known among them were Fitzroy, Gillmore, Leslie, Harvey, and Foulkes, though they were keenly watched at all times. Ranjit Singh maintained a cosmopolitan court and he made sure all of them had a nice time in every respect. All this added to the romance of Lahore in the eyes of foreigners. But he always kept a watchful eye on them and never let them have undue influence over him. It must be said that they all served him faithfully.

But it must also be said that Ranjit Singh treated the various Christian missionaries with polite detachment. He met them all, and all of them requested that they be allowed to open up churches and convent schools. All these requests he denied, and urged them to first open schools to teach the Punjabi language. Religion could come later, he always argued. He deemed this as critical to the opening up of the knowledge of the world to the people at large. The ruling Sikhs made up about 15 per cent of the population, the Hindus around 25 per cent, with the remaining 50 per cent being Muslims.

Victor Jacquemont, a French traveller, praised Ranjit Singh's powers of conversation and his shrewd judgment. He wrote: "Ranjit Singh is almost the first inquisitive Indian I have seen, but his curiosity makes up for the apathy of his whole nation. He asked me a hundred thousand questions about India, the English, Europe, Napoleon, this world in general and the other one, hell and paradise, the soul, God, the devil, and a thousand things besides."

The European of Lahore played a much greater role in the life of Lahore than most of us would like to confess. Probably more research needs to be done. Perhaps, there are still lessons for us to be learnt.

The horse that led Lahore to wars

It might sound amazing today that an entire street of the Walled City of Lahore was cleaned and scrubbed for two whole days just because a horse had to pass that way. It was no religious ceremony, but just the immense passion of a horseman who felt more comfortable in his saddle than on his feet. Almost 200 years ago when the Sukerchakian chief from Gujranwala, Ranjit Singh, declared himself the Maharajah of the Punjab in the Lahore Fort on Muharram 10, 1799, the day he conquered the city, he declared that any man with any pride must give top priority to his horses, his work and his women, in that order. If you have visited the Lahore Fort, you will notice to the left of the side entrance a

British military barrack. Before the British built this barrack, this was the stable of the Lahore Darbar.

At any one time Maharajah Ranjit Singh could keep almost 1,000 of the very finest horses there. When he ran out of space they went into the Hazuri Bagh, and when that was not enough the horses went into the Badshahi Masjid. Such was the craze of the man who ruled the Punjab for a full 40 years with an iron grip, and rule he did with great wisdom. For a beautiful horse, or a beautiful woman, he would go to any length, for once he got it into his head to acquire the 'filly', it became an obsession with him. Sounds rather logical to any Punjabi male chauvinist.

Asp-i-Laila

But one horse stands out from any other in the history of the Punjab and Lahore. The maharajah had heard a lot about this legendary horse and vowed to get it no matter what the cost. In the end it cost him "rupees 60 lakh and 12,000 soldiers," or so the traveller Baron Charles quotes Ranjit Singh having told him so himself. By current gold standards that would be almost Rs12 billion and a whole division of infantry. The accounts of the Fakir family of Bazaar Hakeeman also corroborate this figure, actually puts it even higher. What was, after all, so amazing about a horse that the Lahore Darbar went crazy to acquire it? After all, the maharajah had a large stable of Arabian thoroughbreds, not to speak of legendary horses like Gauharbar and Sufaid Pari, both of which are said to have "the speed of the wind". Not a single horse in his stable was then worth less than Rs. 20,000 by the rupees standard 200 years ago. A joke doing the rounds of Lahore then listed the price of the entire city of Lahore and the cost of the Maharajah's horses as being equal.

This legendary horse was known as Asp-i-Laila and belonged to the Barakzai tribe chiefs, either Dost

Muhammad or Yar Muhammad, it is not clear from a number of records consulted. It was a pure Persian breed, jet black in colour and a "sight to watch." Its speed was legendary in the whole of the Khyber Pass, and what intrigued Maharajah Ranjit Singh was the fact that it was known for its intelligence. The news of this 'great' horse reached the Lahore Darbar sometime in 1822. Immediately Ranjit Singh dispatched intelligence agents to find out where the horse was located. One account put it at Peshawar, while another stated that the Barakzais had heard of the interest of the maharajah from their agents in Lahore, and had shifted the horse to Kabul. This single horse led to a full scale war between the Punjab and Afghanistan.

In 1822, the maharajah sent his special minister Fakir Azizuddin to Peshawar to collect tribute from Yar Muhammad and among the gifts were some very fine horses. But Asp-i-Laila was not among them. On query, Yar Muhammad told him that he did not own the horse. This angered the maharajah who set up a whole team of agents to track down the horse. Once he was sure the horse was alive and well and in Yar Muhammad's possession, discreet negotiations were conducted. By 1828 the patience of the maharajah was exhausted and he sent a punitive force under Sardar Budh Singh Sandhawalia to acquire the horse. In the battle Budh Singh and hundreds of his solders were killed, but the Lahore Darbar won the battle after the two French generals Allard and Ventura, now buried in Lahore in Old Anarkali, were sent with another force to assist Budh Singh's force.

At the surrender the French generals were told that Asp-i-Laila was not there. In a rage, they arrested Yar Muhammad's brother and held him hostage. In the end, the fierce Pathans told the French generals that the horse was dead. This sent the maharajah into a fit of rage, and he sent another punitive expedition under Sardar Kharrak Singh to Peshawar, where his agents informed the horse now was. But before Kharrak Singh could reach Peshawar, Yar Muhammad was killed by his own tribe for fighting over a horse, and his brother Sultan Muhammad fled for his own safety.

In 1830, Maharajah Ranjit Singh installed Sultan Muhammad as governor of Peshawar. Gen Ventura at that point asked for Asp-i-Laila, which demand the new governor spurned. Gen Ventura immediately arrested the new governor in his own palace and informed him that within 24 hours he would be beheaded. Gen Ventura had built a fierce reputation for executing scores of dacoits in Wazirabad, and they took his word seriously. At this point Sultan Muhammad agreed to hand over the horse, and on doing so, "cried like a child." The horse was immediately carried to Lahore in a special carriage guarded by well over 500 soldiers.

It reached Lahore at the western Akbari Gate of the Lahore Fort, and the road that comes from Badami Bagh and curves around the fort was all cleaned and scrubbed for two days in advance, and the order was that not a single speck of dust should enter the horse's nostrils. And so Asp-i-Laila reached Lahore, and the Maharajah feasted his eyes on the horse and commented: "It has been worth the trouble." One account puts the colour as jet black, as the name Asp-i-Laila suggests, another makes it dark grey. But no matter what the colour was, the horse had the honour of not only wearing the Koh-i-Nur diamond around its neck on special occasions, but of also being the horse that was brought out on special occasions. It was also the last horse the Maharajah ever rode. He was lifted in illness and put in the saddle. Once there he was fine, for he was a natural horseman. No horse in history, so the legend then went, has had more spent on it than the acquisition of the Lahore Darbar.

The last heirs of the Lahore Darbar

Every morning a frail old woman in flowing clothes would board the Model Town bus, headed for the city. The conductor dared not ask for the fare, for he would be confronting the last ancestor of the Lahore Darbar's Royal family, Princess Bamba Sutherland Dulip Singh.

Last week I paid a visit to the Christian graveyard on the main Jail Road in Gulberg. The keeper escorted me to the grave of Princess Bamba Sutherland, who died on the 10th of March, 1957. Her father, Maharajah Dulip Singh, the last King of the Punjab, was born on 6 September 1838, occupied the throne at the age of five and was removed from the throne in 1849. The story of the last ruler of the Punjab is a sad one that must be studied, for it forms a major event in the history of Lahore. Lord Dalhousie put the young Maharajah under the charge of Dr. and Mrs. Login. He was baptized on 8 March 1853 and the unshorn hair he kept as a Sikh was cut as a part of denaturing process. He was deported to England on the steamer SS Hindustan on 19 April 1854, reaching London in end of May.

Maharajah Dulip Singh

Maharajah Dulip Singh was introduced to the Royal family at Windsor Palace and Queen Victoria felt infatuated with his youth and beauty. The Maharajah had come to Windsor on several occasions and the Queen got his portraits made by the celebrated court painter of Frankfurt, Franz Winterhalter in 1855. He made friends with Prince of Wales and enjoyed the company of princesses. Dulip Singh was provided an annual pension of 50,000 pounds in England. He purchased a large estate of 16,000 acres at Elveden in Suffolk and settled down as a country gentleman. It was during one such Winterhalter sitting that the Queen persuaded the Maharajah to gift her the Kohi-Noor diamond, which was already in their possession. His response to the request is debated. The end result was that Maharajah Dulip Singh was not allowed a public school or university education, but Prince Albert appointed tutors to teach him science, music and German and he became well versed in all. In 1863, he left London and settled down at Elveden estate in Suffolk.

The imprisoned Rani Jindan met her son in Calcutta on 16 January 1861, after thirteen and half years. She was shocked to discover Dulip as a clean-shaven young man and told him bluntly that she did not repent the loss of Sikh Kingdom so much as the loss of his Sikh faith. Dulip took Jindan to England where she died in 1863. She was cremated according to the Sikh rites in India and her ashes scattered in the waters of the Godavri river at Nasik, as Maharajah was banned to visit Punjab. On his return journey, the Maharajah stopped in Cairo and married a pretty girl named Bamba Muller. His marriage was solemnized as per Christian rites.

Rani Jindan told her son about a Guru's prophecy that he shall rule over India, but he did not believe. In 1883, Thakur Singh Sandhanwalia, a cousin of the Maharajah was sent to England. He convinced the Maharajah about the truth of the Guru's prophecy and prevailed upon him to return to the Sikh faith. This prophecy was broadcast mainly by the Kukas in Punjab who were fighting against the British Empire in India.

Convinced of the Guru's prophecy, Dulip Singh wrote an impassioned appeal on 25 March 1886 in the name of his countrymen. The Maharajah was dissuaded to visit India but he had resolved to do so. He set sail with his family but was detained at Aden on 21 April 1886. After a few days, his family returned to England. Maharajah Dulip Singh was administered Khande Di Pahul on 25 May 1886 at Aden but not allowed to visit India. Heart-broken and frustrated, he returned to Paris in July 1886.

In Paris, he set up his headquarters to start revolutionary activities against the British Empire. He met Irish rebels and Russian diplomats. He issued two proclamations from Paris, the first to the Sikhs and the second was addressed to "Brother Princes and Nobles and the people of beloved Hindustan", declaring himself as the Maharajah of Sikhs and exhorting them to revolt against the British Empire.

Maharajah Dulip Singh travelled to St. Petersburg, the Russian capital, under a false identity as Mr. Patrick Casey, the Irish rebel. He was accompanied by a young pretty girl, Ada Wetherill, whom he married in Paris after his return from Russia. Dulip Singh wrote a detailed letter to the Russian Czar on 10 May 1887, asking for his help in liberation of India. He also mentioned his Guru's prophecy in this letter. It was a masterly plan in tactics and geo-political warfare. The Czar made comments on its contents but did not adhere to the Maharajah's plan of action. Dulip Singh dispatched his emissary, Arur Singh, to India with letters of revolt addressed to Indian princes.

The British had penetrated the Maharajah's conspiracy with impeccable accuracy. All his letters were copied and dispatched to the office of Secretary of State for India in London by the French officer-in charge of the Maharajah in Paris. Arur Singh was captured in Calcutta and all the plans of the Maharajah were revealed by him during his interrogation. Thakur Singh Sandhanwalia acted as the Maharajah's Prime Minister-in-exile. He was based in Pondicherry, the French colony in India. He died -some believe poisoned - while the Maharajah was still negotiating his terms with the Russian Czar. His family jagir was confiscated by the British

Maharajah Dulip Singh returned to Paris and married Ada Douglas Wetherill, who also acted as a British spy during his sojourn in Russia. The network of British spies was so perfect that all his movements were reported to London and Simla simultaneously. He had eight children, six from his first wife and two girls from the second. All of them died issueless, confirming another prophecy of the Guru. Maharajah Dulip Singh, the last King of the Punjab, died in a Paris hotel on 21 October, 1893. He was buried in Elveden Estate cemetery, not as a Sikh but a Christian.

Maharajah Dulip Singh's six children from his first marriage were Princes Victor, Albert Edward and Frederick Dulip Singh and Princesses Catherine, Sophia and Bamba

Dulip Singh. The Maharajah wanted his eldest son to marry in India, but he did not agree calling the Maharajah "my idiotic father". Prince Victor studied at Eton and Cambridge where he met his true love, Anne Blanche of Coventry and married her. Maharajah Dulip Singh did not attend the marriage ceremony. Even Queen Victoria was not happy with Victor over this marriage. She treated Victor as her godson. She called Princess Anne, the pretty wife of Victor, to her audience and ordered her to leave England and to take a vow never to have children who would become the heir apparent of the Sikh Kingdom. The couple followed the royal command faithfully and never returned to England.

Prince Albert Edward Dulip Singh died at the young age of thirteen. Maharajah Dulip Singh came from Paris to see his ailing son and wept bitterly, but he returned and could not attend his funeral. Prince Frederick Dulip Singh was the most talented of all the Princes. He went to Cambridge and got an MA degree in history. He was a keen collector of old books, coins, stained glass, and other artifacts. He was very popular in Suffolk and was called the 'Black Prince'. He was a historian, an archaeologist, a philanthropist and a great lover of music. He was keen to promote the legacy of Maharajah Dulip Singh, and keeping this in view he donated all his art collection to set up the Ancient House Museum in Thetford, which is a living testimony to the family of Maharajah Dulip Singh. The British Royal family even today takes an immense interest in the museum. Frederick remained a bachelor all his life.

Of his three daughters, Princesses Catherine, Sophia, and Bamba Dulip Singh, Catherine was ranked as one of the most beautiful European princesses, but she did not marry. She spent most of her time in Germany with her governess Lina Schafer. Princess Sophia was the youngest of the three sisters, a firebrand like her father and became a leading figure fighting for the voting rights of women in England. During the First World War, Princess Sophia visited wounded Punjabi troops of the Indian Army and gave them mementos as a granddaughter of Maharajah Ranjit Singh.

Princess Bamba Dulip Singh was the most colorful character in the Maharajah Dulip Singh family. She was a rebel like her father and began styling herself as the 'Queen of the Punjab'. She frequently visited India and married Col. Sutherland, who became Principal at King Edward's Medical College, Lahore. Once Sophia and Bamba visited Lahore in 1924 and the crowds gathered from Punjab villages to see the daughters of their last Maharajah. The police dispersed the crowd, as it was thought to be politically too dangerous for the British Empire.

Princess Bamba shifted to Lahore in 1944. She never accepted the partition of Punjab and settled in Lahore, the capital of Sikh kingdom, as a permanent resident. She set up a museum in Lahore Fort, which is known as the Princess Bamba Collection. With her death in March 1957, the last member of the Royal family of Maharajah Ranjit Singh and Maharajah Dulip Singh passed into history. Not a single direct descendant of Maharajah Ranjit Singh exists, fulfilling an old Guru prophesy that the Sikh empire will vanish because it will have no children left. Even today most Sikhs believe this myth.

The story of Kita Paya the lunatic

The daughter of a very dear friend works in Lahore's Mental Hospital as a psychologist and she was telling me about this former well-known bureaucrat of Lahore, who is a patient there, and keeps shouting: "Lunatics of the world unite". I was wondering whether he should be released so that saner people listen to his advice.

The history of the 'Lunatic Asylum' of Lahore is interesting history. Perhaps it gained certain respectability *Dr. John Martin Honigberger* after Saadat Hassan Manto wrote his master piece, *Toba Tek Singh.* Manto also spent a few days there after a nervous breakdown, and was released after he pleaded that the laws regarding the functioning of the 'asylum' be given to him so that he could see if he was being treated properly. The superintendent immediately decided that this man was just too sensible to be declared a lunatic and released him after 'due diligence'. It was after his release that he wrote his masterpiece. *Nairang-i-Khyal,* a literary magazine, published a transcript of a dialogue Manto had with Prof. G.M. Asar, a close friend of his. The other participants in the dialogue, Muzaffar Ali Syed and Munir Ahmad Sheikh, all discussed the real reasons he ended up in the asylum. That is a story that must also be told, but not here. The first 'Lunatic Asylum' of Lahore was set up during the reign of Maharajah Ranjit Singh, who was the first to understand that lunacy was a curable illness. He asked his state physician, Dr. Honigberger, a German who had set up a practice just off Bazaar Hakeeman inside Bhatti Gate, just opposite the Tehsil Bazaar corner, and who lived in a house rented from the Fakir family, to set up an 'asylum' to cure a few patients belonging to the royal Punjabi family. In an old barrack that once stood where today stands the University Senate Hall and the Pharmacy department of the Punjab University Old Campus, the very first Lunatic Asylum of Lahore opened with eight patients. The exact date is not available, but it was about the time of the Maharajah's death and the time when Maharajah Dulip Singh came to the throne. Probably the period 1839-41 would be a safe guess. When the British annexed Lahore, they took over the asylum from Dr. Honigberger and on the first of May, 1849, the board of administration of the East India Company handed it over to a British doctor, Dr. Hathaway, who was the residency surgeon. By then the asylum had 12 patients. After just four years he wrote in to say that the location was most unsuitable, and in 1853, the Lahore Lunatic Asylum, as it was then known, was shifted to another barrack that was occupied by 'married artillerymen' in Anarkali. Here the Company decided, in 1861 that as the Delhi asylum was overcrowded, a majority of the patients be shifted to Lahore.

This increased their numbers considerably and very soon the asylum again ran out of space.

In 1876, the Lahore Mental Asylum, as it was renamed then, was again shifted to the haveli of Lehna Singh on the Lahore-Amritsar Road, just near the new Lahore railway station. In those days this haveli was considered as being a safe distance from the old walled city, and "here the patients could be looked after much better". This was an interesting reason for a problem that we all prefer to not look in the eye. Speaking of 'eyes', there is an interesting description of a visit to this asylum by Goulding who says: "On the entrance gateway of the serai, we were shown a framed photograph of a dangerous lunatic known as Kita Paya. Nothing was known of the antecedents of this wild looking creature... and the only answer to all questions he gave were 'Jo kita so paya' ". He goes on to describe another calm lunatic who informed everybody that he was the king of Delhi and that he had killed many *feringis* during the Mutiny. Such was the state of the patients at the turn of the 19th century.

Just a bit of history might interest the reader. The first mention of something like a mental hospital is at Dhar (near Mandu) in Madhya Pardesh, which was established by Mohammad Khilji (1436-1469) where Maulana Fazlullah Hakim was its physician. During British rule, the first asylum was established in Bombay in 1745 at a cost of Rs.125 and the second at Calcutta in 1784 which were meant for Europeans. The Indian Asylum Act of 1858 was replaced by the Lunacy Act of 1912. The term Lunatic Asylum was changed to Mental Hospital in 1922. At the time of partition in 1947, there were about 40 mental hospitals in India. Pakistan inherited two of them, at Lahore and Hyderabad.

The British built a new Lahore Mental Hospital on Jail Road, and in the year 1900 all the inmates of the Naulakha Mental Asylum were shifted there. This was the largest asylum in northern India, and patients from the entire north of sub-continent were brought here for treatment. Over 103 years have passed and the condition of the Lahore Mental Hospital is one of immense neglect. The 103-ycar old walls are in a state of disrepair, the gardens unkempt. I quite agree with the wild Sikh warrior called 'Kita Paya'. When Goulding saw this "fearsome object, with his matted hair and beard, and the glare of a wild beast in his bloodshot eyes" in 1861, little did he know that almost 150 years down the road, wé would still be paying just deserts. The warder then shouted "Hat Picche" and Kita Paya retreated. In a way that is what we still tell our people. It seems we are still not mature enough to look the problem in the eye. May be if the 'lunatics of the world unite' things might be very different.

The Story of Moyan di Mandi

In the dying days of the Moghal Empire and just before the Sikhs rose to power, between the newly emerging cattle market Gowalmandi outside the Shahalami Gate and the fiercely independent minded village of Mozang, a small posh enclave by the name of Mohallah Khojian emerged.

The Khoja community has always been one of business people. Even today they are entrepreneurs par excellence. One can imagine that they were, and still are, exceptionally wealthy people. Given the uncertain conditions inside the old walled city, these wealthy merchants decided to build their own little enclave Mohallah Khojian, protected from raiders and crazy rulers. The first step was to build a mosque, which was called 'Khojian di masjid', and around this mosque some palatial buildings were built. On the outside were low walls, which were guarded by chowkidars. In this way the rich merchants of Lahore, mostly with shops in Akbari Mandi, managed to build a haven for themselves. Every morning when the merchants rode in, the gates would be opened, for then it was a drawbridge.

There is some dispute as to where this 'mohallah' was located. One document puts it between Beadon and Hall Roads, while another description puts it squarely at the Regal crossing near Temple Road, named so because the first Freemason's Temple was built there, and amazingly not during British days, but at the end of the Sikh rule by a French officer in the army of Ranjit Singh. The story of the destruction of Mohallah Khojian, makes interesting reading, and it shows that just how helpless the business community becomes when the law and order situation breaks down, leading to the demise of states. As Machiavelli says that "when the trader is threatened, he manages to bring down the state in ways one cannot imagine, for he has strengths far greater than those of the state".

The emerging Sikh forces started raiding the mohallah, and each time the elders of the Khoja community would talk with the chieftains and give them a handsome purse. That kept the crazed Sikhs at bay for short periods. But then as the Sikhs jostled among themselves for power, each misl would try its hand at getting money from the rich Khojas, and each time they would manage something. With time the purses started to dwindle and this made the Sikhs think that they were being cheated by 'crafty traders'.

The Khojas decided that the time had come to take a stand, and when a Bhangi misl attacked, they faced the wrath of the well-armed young Khojas. The Sikh withdrew and met among themselves. The Khojas had to be taught a lesson. The verdict was that Mohallah Khojian had to be eradicated from the face of the earth And so three of the strongest Misls, the Bhangi, the Ramgariaas and the Kanahias gathered into one huge force and attacked Mohallah Khojian. The ruler of Lahore decided to stay away lest the crazed Sikhs should enter Lahore.

The Sikhs attacked with ferocity from all sides at the same time, and though they met with stiff resistance, they soon overwhelmed the locality, killing a lot of the leading merchants of Lahore. The younger elements withdrew to their mosque, while the raiding Sikhs captured all the havelis and mounted their guns on the rooftops. All the Khojas on the roof of the mosque were picked out and killed. Then a siege followed. All food to the mosque was stopped and in the time that followed the entire mohallah was ransacked and all the remaining Khojas were massacred. One account also states that a fight broke out among the Sikhs as they distributed the women among various chiefs. This account also states that long lines of bullock carts left the mohallah in every direction when the place was looted. This account states that in the end, the Sikhs entered the mosque and killed everyone. Another states that the few remaining Khojas surrendered and left the city. In this way Mohallah Khojian was left a deserted place.

By the time Maharajah Ranjit Singh came to power, he ordered that the entire place be demolished and the bricks used to rebuild the walls of the old city. Only the mosque was to be left intact. In this way where once stood a posh enclave of the rich was left a bullet-pocked mosque damaged by intense fighting. This mosque remained empty for almost 50 years and the area around it came to be known as 'Moyan di Mandi' or the 'marketplace of the dead', a usage that still prevails inside the walled city when meaning a place where nothing exists.

But this is not the end of the story. The dead do not die that easy. In 1865 when the British had established themselves after the unsuccessful war of 1857, a gentleman by the name of Syed Shamsi approached the British authorities at the district court and claimed that the mosque belonged to his family. He produced a number of witnesses and on the promise that he would remain loyal to the Raj, the deputy commissioner handed over the mosque to him in good faith.

For two years, Syed Shamsi led the prayer congregation and fulfilled all inspection clauses. Once the mosque was classified as having been handed over correctly and the deeds finalized, Syed Shamsi converted it into a house and rented it out to an English couple. When the English couple returned home he sold off the mosque, now converted into a house. One account states that the house was used for many years and was then demolished. And so in vagueness ends the story of Mohallah Khojian.

The man who designed the Taj

Who designed the Taj Mahal? Was it, one Italian architect Geranium Veronica, who visited India in that era, or was it the French silversmith Austin de Bordeaux, as the French like to believe or was it Ustad Ahmad of Lahore, the man on whom was conferred the title 'Nadir al-Asr' (the wonder of the age) by Emperor Shah Jahan,

Taj Mahal

The real architect of the Taj Mahal has always been shrouded in mystery. Documents of that era point to "architects from Lahore". The 17th century manuscript, *Diwan-i-Muhandis* discovered in the 1930s, is the oldest manuscript containing a collection of poems written by Lutfullah, including several verses in which he describes his father, Ustad Ahmad from Lahore, as the architect of the Taj Mahal and the Red Fort at Delhi. Ustad Ahmad was an engineer astrologer of Persian origin.

Another source claims that Ustad Ahmad was one of the architects of the Red Fort. There is considerable evidence to back this claim, and it is one acknowledged by the Indian government even today. Further evidence of other large projects undertaken by Ustad Ahmad exist strengthening the plausibility of the claim. It is interesting to note that Ustad Ahmad had a number of aliases: Ustad Khan Effendi, Ustad Muhammad Isa Khan and Isa Effendi.

The general consensus is that the design of the Taj Mahal cannot be ascribed to any single master in the way we can ascribe great architectural works to the creative genius of an outstanding master. It seems to be the product of an evolutionary process. The end result is "the perfected stage in the development of Mughal architecture" as one research paper puts it. But who was the man who started the process and gave the building its present shape? It is acknowledged that this man was Ustad Ahmad of Lahore. It was he who advised the Mughal court where to find the finest artisans that "existed on earth" and how to go about finding them and enticing them to work on the Taj. His strategy worked wonders, and the world saw the result.

From Turkey came Ismail Khan, a designer of hemispheres and "a genius in building domes". Another master of Lahore, Qazim Khan travelled to Agra to cast the solid gold finial that crowned the Turkish master's dome. In all probability it would have been Qazim who advised Ustad Ahmad on hiring the Turkish 'dome master'. Chiranjilal, a local lapidary from Delhi was chosen as the chief sculptor and mosaicist. Amanat Khan from Shiraz was the chief calligrapher, and this fact is attested on the Taj gateway where his name has been inscribed. Muhammad Hanif, yet another Lahori, was the 'supervisor of masons' while Mir Abdul Karim, a Kashmiri of Lahore handled the finances. There is every possibility that these men had worked with Ustad Ahmad in Lahore and he respected their craftsmanship.

But the Mughal court appointed Mukkarimat Khan of Shiraz to head the management of daily production. Sculptors form Bukhara, calligraphers from Syria and Persia, inlayers from south India, stone cutters from Balochistan, specialists in building turrets, another who carved only marble flowers-37 experts of various disciplines formed the creative nucleus, 12 of whom belonged to Lahore. To this core was added a labor force of 20,000 of the best workers and bricklayers from across north India. Such was the planning that was undertaken to build the Taj Mahal.

Of interest to us is Ustad Ahmad the "wonder of his age". Who was this man? Not much exists about him in textbooks, but the little that our research has shown is that he belonged to Mochi Gate, where he had a small yet beautiful house near the crossing now known as Chowk Nisar Haveli. This area in those days had a small beautiful garden with a small fountain in the middle. Around it were small beautiful brick houses. It must have been, without doubt an exquisite scene, beautiful and clean and not congested. With time the housing became more and more cramped and with constant invasions people preferred to stay within the walled city for protection.

If we are to believe the census carried out in 1883 by the British the walled city of Lahore had a population of 93,000. Today the official count is well over 5 million though some estimate it at being 7 million. If we have an idea of the growth over 120 years, earlier where the population would certainly not be above 5 million. In that sense, Lahore was a serene city of gardens, of educated peoples, of artisans and musicians and of men of letters. It was utopia and for this very reason Chaucer in his epic mentions Lahore as such.

In such an environment must have been born Ustad Ahmad probably the greatest architect produced by this city of ours. There is an urgent need for us to research more about this man to put his achievements including the Taj in its proper perspective.

The mystery of Lahore's Jews

In the walled city of Lahore, the phrase Baghdadi Chor is still used for a shrewd businessman. The phrase 'Saneechar Tailee' is now not used, but was till the 1940s, when Lahore's red light area had prostitutes known as 'yahoodi ke ladki'.

Very few of us know that Lahore, from the days of the Emperor Akbar, had a very small Jewish community, which soon established themselves as astute traders and money-lenders. By the time the British left, they were at their peak. At the turn of the 19th century, they were having a social impact on Lahore in that they began to control a major portion of the trade and financial sectors of Lahore. They, strangely, also had a solid grip on the prostitution business, which in those days, and even today in its own unique way, does exercise some control over the 'powers that be'. A few months before partition was announced, they all left Lahore and moved to Bombay (now Mumbai), where, 5,500 Jews still live. They are classified as 'Indian Jews' by Israel.

Who were these Jews and where did they come from? The sub-continent had a legacy of three distinct Jewish groups: the Bani Israel, the Cochin Jews and the White Jews from Europe. Each group practiced important elements of Judaism and had active synagogues. The Sephardic rites predominate among Indian Jews. According to an account on Jews in the sub-continent, printed in 1903 states: "The Bani Israel (Sons of Israel) live primarily in Bombay, Calcutta, Old Delhi, Ahmadabad and Lahore. The native language of the Bani Israel is Marathi, and most Punjabis mistake them for Gujarati Memons. The Cochin Jews of southern India speak Malayalam, while the White Jews came primarily with the British, and some also came from Europe during the days of the Sikhs".

Some research on the Jews of Lahore threw up an interesting observation by Bristow (page 195) who, while researching 'Jews and White Slavery' says: "The Jewish prostitution business extended from Europe across the world, where it sometimes overlapped with French, Italian, Chinese, and other rings. In the Punjabi (Indian) capital of Lahore, Jewish pimps were in the habit of leaving their women penniless only to reappear after workers had accumulated some money." To verify this claim, I visited an old friend in Tehsil Bazaar inside the walled city, who informs me that at the end of the First World War, Jewish money-lenders and pimps were a major force in Lahore. No person dared fool around with women 'owned' by a Jew, and no woman dared cheat a Jew.

According to a few old folk of the walled city, they had a place of worship in Tehsil Bazaar. I have tried my best to locate it, but have failed; save for some possibility that it may have been located in the Jain Manzil that still exists there. It would be interesting to dwell a bit on who were these Jews of Lahore.

The Bani Israel claim to be descended from Jews who. escaped persecution in Galilee in the 2nd century BC. The Bani Israel resemble the non-Jewish Maratha people in appearance and customs, which indicates intermarriage between Jews and Indians. The Bani Israel, however, maintained the practices of Jewish dietary laws, circumcision and observation of the Sabbath as a day of rest.

The Bani Israel say their ancestors were oil pressers in Galilee and they were descended from the survivors of a shipwreck. This could explain the term 'Saneechar Tailee'. In the 18th century, they were 'discovered' by Jewish traders from Baghdad, which explains the term 'Baghdadi Chor'. There are numerous references to Jewish Arab traders in the Akbari Gate Serai, where the camel caravans arrived from the West. At that time the Bani Israel were practising just a few outward forms of Judaism (which is how they were recognised), but had no scholars of their own. Jewish teachers from Baghdad and Cochin taught them mainstream Judaism in the 18th and 19th centuries.

Jewish merchants from Europe travelled to India in the mediaeval period for purposes of trade, but it is not clear whether they formed permanent settlements in South Asia. According to one research source: "The first reliable evidence of Jews living in India comes from the early 11th century. It is certain that the first Jewish settlements were centred along the western coast. Abraham Ibn Daud's 12th century reference to the Jews of India is unfortunately vague and we do not have further references to Indian Jews until several centuries later".

The first Jews in Cochin were the so-called 'Black Jews,' who spoke the Malayalam tongue. The 'White Jews' settled later, coming to India from Holland and Spain. A notable settlement of Spanish and Portuguese Jews starting in the 15th century was Goa, but the settlement eventually disappeared. In the 17th and 18th centuries, Cochin had an influx of Jewish settlers from the Middle East, North Africa and Spain.

The Jews of Cochin say that they came to Cranganore (south-west coast of India) after the destruction of the temple in 70 AD. They had, in effect, their own principality for many centuries until a chieftainship dispute broke out between two brothers in the 15th century. In 1524, the ruler of Calicut attacked the Jews of Cranganore on the pretext that they were 'tampering' with the pepper trade. Most Jews fled to Cochin and went under the protection of the Hindu Raja there. He granted them a site for their own town that later acquired the name 'Jew Town', by which it is still known.

Unfortunately for the Jews of Cochin, the Portuguese occupied it in the same period and indulged in persecution of the Jews until the Dutch displaced them. The Dutch Protestants were tolerant and the Jews prospered. In 1795, Cochin passed under the British sphere of influence.

Major migrations in the 16th and 17th century created important settlements of Jews from Iran, Afghanistan and Central Asia in northern India and Kashmir, with over 100 Jews moving to Lahore. By the late 18th century, Bombay had the largest Jewish community in India. Bani Israel Jews lived in Bombay, as did the Baghdadi and Iranian ones.

By the end of the 18th century, a third group of Indian Jews appears. They were the middle-eastern Jewish who came to India through trade. They established a network stretching from Aleppo to Baghdad and Basra to Surat and Bombay to Calcutta to Rangoon to Singapore to Hong Kong, and, eventually, as far as Kobe, Japan. There were strong family bonds among the traders in all these places.

Of all the Jews who came to Lahore, the Baghdadi ones were the most numerous, and they were mostly money-lenders and traders. Very soon, they entered other trading professions, gaining enough influence and confidence to enter the prostitution business. When the Raj folded, the Jews were the very first to leave, leaving behind mere words as threads from which one could piece together a story that is part of our history, and one day we will have to tell it.

The curse of the 'Choti memsahibs'

In our youth, we five brothers roamed the entire area of Bhatti Gate, the Data Darbar-Mohni Road tract right up to the river. On the eastern side we touched the Anarkali Bazaar-Government College area. After dark the District Courts were our playing field. We roamed fearlessly, but never once did we dare cross the path where exists the 'Curse of the Choti Memsahibs'.

Then, I decided to revisit the place at the edge of Mohni Road, just next to the akharra of the famous Gama Pehalwan, where sometimes we sneaked and posted ourselves near the eating area. It was always a rewarding experience. They respected us because of our father, for in those days people did respect the off-springs of the old families of Lahore. Just at the edge of the Old Christian graveyard on Circular Road-Mohni Road, is a dilapidated old dwelling whose roof has been broken ever since I remember.

No one dares, even today, enter the room, where once someone tried to build a shop and the very next day was found with his throat slit. His son, so the story goes, tried to complete the shop and the very next day his throat was also slit. Since then no one has dared to enter the place. Even the drug addicts who frequent the graveyard stay away.

On talking to a few old inhabitants of the area I learnt that they had heard from their elders that the two 'choti memsahibs' were buried here even before the British took over Lahore in 1849, and that they were murdered by a Sikh chief, who had slit the throats of one of the girls in a fit of rage on hearing the news that the Sikh rulers had signed away the sovereign rights of the State of the Punjab. The other child had died in an accident, though one person claimed that even she was murdered, but a month or two later. One version claimed that they were the children of illegitimate parents. The stories seem endless. So an investigation was needed.

I contacted the person who looks after the graveyard, and he thought I wanted to buy a marble statue or an old tombstone. When he heard of the curse of the 'choti memsahibs' he went pale in the face and refused to co-operate. I managed to calm him down and he took me to his room and showed me two broken tombstones. The first one read:" Edith Mary Welsford Carter, died 26 April, 1849, Lahore." The second one read: "Louisa Adams Carter, died 29 May, 1849, Lahore." So these were the two 'choti memsahibs' of Lahore. Just who were they and how did they end up in a Lahore graveyard even before the British officially took over Lahore?

It must be remembered that though the British took over in 1849, they had a small garrison inside the Lahore Fort much before the take-over. So British soldiers did live in Lahore, though they seldom ventured out lest they were murdered by Khalsa Sikhs. So the presence of the girls should not come as a surprise. But who was their father? This is where the colourful bit starts, and there is some substance to the rumours of the girls being murdered and the claim that the parents had some 'illegitimate' connection.

The father of the two girls was Lt.John Chilton Lambton Carter III. He was born in Cornwall in 1817 and joined the East India Company. He belonged to the 53rd Regiment of Foot and had fought in India before being sent to Lahore. His family was from Cornwall and had always served in the various armies of and from Britain. One of the girls died of a severe fever, so claims one record, and one was murdered by a Khalsa Sikh priest who cursed the family. Scared of the consequence, John Carter III fled Lahore and took his entire family to far away New Zealand, where even today his ancestors live.

The father of John Carter III was John Chilton Lambton Carter II. He was a Lt. Col. in the 44th Regiment and was killed fighting against Tipu Sultan. He lies buried in a military graveyard near the famous battlefield at Sringapatum. The father of Lt. Col. John Carter II was John

Chilton Lambton Carter I. He was an officer in the 32 Duke of Cornwall Regiment of Foot, and Lt. Carter died in the West Indies. One account says he was killed in battle, the other says he died in a shipwreck. This brings us to the point where we trace the original Carter.

The Chilton-Lambton family is even today a leading aristocratic family of Cornwall. In October 1750 was born a beautiful daughter to the head of this family, and she was named Harraton Chilton-Lambton. She was by all accounts a beautiful woman and just when her marriage was being arranged, she eloped with her servant, John Carter, the footman of the family post chaise. The Duke then, one account says, arranged for the local priest to set a curse on them, that whenever a girl is born in Harraton family, she meets a dreadful end.

That end was to take place almost a hundred years later. But then the fact is that John Carter was murdered a week after marrying Harraton in a London church. She promptly married a friend of her legally-wedded husband by the name of Robert Young. It was this 'illegitimate' man who acquired the name of John Carter, who with the Cornish aristocratic connections of Harraton, managed to get a commission in the Company army, and to leave England and Cornwall to safe faraway lands.

But the murder of the original John Carter in London also had to resurface. It so happened that the 'Carter' family did not have any girls till they came to Lahore, and it was here that Edith and Louisa were born, and it was here that they met their death. But just how does one end a curse, if there is such a thing in the first place.

Our research led us to New Zealand where John Chilton-Lambton Carter III had fled from the 'Curse of the Choti Memsahibs' of Lahore. He died in 1872. His grandson lost his small daughter in 1923 in what seemed like an accident. But then a Maori 'medicine man' approached the family and informed them that there was a curse on them.

They allowed him to drive the 'evil spirits' away as one account informs us. Since then the family has managed well. But in Lahore the 'Choti Memsahibs' lie. I have no idea whether the curse still holds. But the fact remains that the people living near their graves on Mohni Road still maintain a healthy respect for the little girls. May they rest in peace.

Mystique of the Lahore treasure

On March 10, 1957, in a run down house in Model Town, Lahore, died the last grandchild of the greatest ruler of the Punjab, Maharajah Ranjit Singh. The few remaining 'treasures' of the Lahore Darbar still left with Princess Bamba, mainly oil paintings of the 19th century, were 'gifted' to the government. They are today displayed in Rani Jindan's Palace in the Lahore Fort.

Princess Bamba died a virtual pauper. She refused to leave Lahore. Her father, Maharajah Dulip Singh, had been robbed of his 'rightful' treasures by the British government, leaving him to die m 1893 in Paris, as a bankrupt refugee. He spent the last days of his life trying to find out the exact extent of the

Princess Bamba Dulip Singh

treasure looted by the British when they officially took over the Lahore Fort on March 29, 1849. The eminent geologist Suzy Menkes states in her book on the British royal jewels that "the treasures accumulated from India by the British as gifts, or war booty, from the Indian Maharajahs, especially the massive one found in the Lahore Fort, are listed in a very secret manual kept by jewellers to the Royal family, Messrs Garrads & Co., and they are not willing to let the historians see the list, even a century after the demise of Queen Victoria". Why such secrecy?

There are compelling reasons to believe that it was the greatest and largest treasure ever found in history anywhere, by any conqueror, let alone the East India Company. Ironically, the people of Lahore, to whom this treasure actually belongs, know the least about it. That is why it makes sense to try to piece together some details. For reference, keep in mind the purchasing value of a single silver rupee. In Ranjit Singh's days for 10 silver rupees, you could buy a gold sovereign weighing seven grams. Today, ten grams of gold costs Rs. 6,990. This means that a silver rupee would today cost approximately Rs489.

A few years after Maharajah Ranjit Singh's death, famous historian Carl Steinbeck estimated that there were the "over eight crores silver rupees in cash that were officially accounted for in the Lahore Treasury inside the Lahore Fort by the East India Company". Then came the Lahore Jewellery Collection, probably the largest and most important ever in history. This was followed by a dazzling collection of "over 48,700 pure woollen Kashmiri shawls that were stacked in several rooms". Today, such a shawl would easily cost over Rs. 100.000 each, if not more. Then came an array of "other treasures, which alone were

Golden throne of Ranjit Singh

estimated at several crore rupees more," says Steinbeck in his book. In his comments he adds: "It was doubtful whether any royal family in Europe had so many jewels as the Court of Lahore".

Between 1849 and 1850, the treasures of the Lahore Darbar were looted by the British. The most famous and well-known jewels of Maharajah Ranjit Singh were taken away as "gifts to the British Sovereign Queen Victoria". The throne of Ranjit Singh is today in the Victoria and Albert

Museum at London. The famous diamond Koh-i-Nur is the star attraction in the display of British crown jewels in the Tower of London Museum. The famous Timur Ruby (283 carats), the second largest in the world and once occupying pride of place in the 17th century Peacock Throne of Emperor Shah Jahan, was kept for quite some time as one of the minor treasures, till one British officer recognized it as the Timur Ruby.

Maharajah Dulip Singh, the son of Maharajah Ranjit Singh, was brought up as a ward of the East India Company in England. Photographs exist showing him, standing next to Queen Victoria, in grand jewellery, a very small portion of the treasures of the Sikh empire that he had. Dulip Singh, in the later years, embarked on a campaign of trying to find out how much of the treasures had been taken away from the Lahore Treasury and with great difficulty succeeded in locating two of the seven catalogues that had been printed for sale at Lahore in 1849-50. No record could be found of the sum of money raised. The seven auctions of Maharajah Ranjit Singh's confiscated treasures were sold by Messrs Lattie Brothers, of Hays-on-Wyes, in the Diwan-i-Aam of the Lahore Fort, the last one starting on Monday, Dec 2, 1850, for five successive days.

The sale of 95 items of the second catalogue, out of 952 items listed, fetched Rs. 139,287 only. To realise the unbelievable throwaway prices (of these 95 items alone) at which the treasures were sold, page 56 of the catalogue describes item No 61, as "a magnificent jewelled dagger with belt inlaid with diamonds of purest water, the gold mounting sheath beautifully enamelled also inlaid with large diamonds and rubies attached with massive tassels of large pearls".

Then comes Item 70, "a magnificent Bajooband (armlet), the centre being a very large emerald of finest colour estimated to weigh 47 carats surrounded by very valuable rubies estimated to weigh 290 carats. At the end of the tassel was a very large sapphire. This ornament formerly belonged to Ahmad Shah, the founder of the Afghan Durrani Empire, and bears his name".

So what is the true extent of the Lahore Treasure? It is a reasonable estimate that minus the jewels, the current value of the treasure would be well over Rs. 78 billion. The jewels, including the Koh-i-nur and the Timur Ruby, and hundreds of major diamond pieces that it constituted, I will not venture to name a price. My calculator has betrayed me. So let the mystique of the world's largest and greatest treasure remain. The British definitely put in far less than what they took away in one year 1849-50, alone. The Bamba Collection is merely a "shade of a reminder of a glorious past", one we still do not acknowledge. Such is the power of bigotry.

The city's biggest explosion

There is no doubt that the walled city, over the centuries, has been burnt down, ravaged, looted and left in ruins. But then it has always bounced back to life. While external factors brought about these misfortunes, there have also been times when because of internal factors, considerable misfortune befell its inhabitants.

In the year 1809, or 1864 Bikrami, took place what can safely be described as the biggest explosion in the history of Lahore. The ruler of Lahore, and the Punjab, was Maharajah Ranjit Singh, and he had set about converting virtually every safe place into an arsenal and ordnance depot. All big mosques, including the famous Badshahi Mosque opposite the Lahore Fort, were put to military use. There were, according to one French writer, more ordnance depots in the walled city of Lahore than any other city in the world.

The Maharajah was armed to the teeth and was stocked with enough arms and ammunition to carry on a prolonged war with the fast expanding British forces in the East and the South, as well as the unpredictable Afghans to the North-West. His caution was understandable in the volatile circumstances that prevailed. Of the two largest havelis in Lahore undoubtedly, the largest was Haveli Mian Sahib, which, according to a description by Kanhiyya Lal, spread over two square miles. Another description of the Shah Jahan era claims that it was 'four kos' in spread. For those familiar with the old walled city, just one portion, the male section of the three-tier haveli was known as Rang Mahal, and it is from that era that the name Rang Mahal came. Built in the Mughal era, a small portion of the guest section was taken over by Maharajah Ranjit Singh and converted into an ammunition depot. But he took over the second largest haveli in Lahore completely, the 'Pathronwali Haveli' - the haveli of stone - in the Mochi gate area, whose name was Haveli Nawab Mian Khan. This haveli was known as the most beautiful residential building in the walled city, as its entire structure was laced with black stones.

The Haveli Nawab Mian Khan was taken over by the Sikh ruler and converted into an ordnance factory. In it's huge rooms were stored gunpowder and other materials for use in the making of bombs and ammunition. The entire place was supervised by 'foreign' experts in the manufacture of the latest artillery shells, and was a high security area. One can imagine that being the second largest house in the walled city in an age when the entire population was a mere 70,000, its size was, according to one estimate, almost "one kos if walked around". In the year 1809, in the tenth year of the rule of Maharajah Ranjit Singh, an explosion took place in one room, which immediately spread to the entire ordnance factory. There was then one massive explosion, which rocked the entire city in a jolt it had never experienced before, and probably never has since. The entire haveli went up and stones fell on almost each and every house of the city. According to one estimate, over 500 people were killed.

Kanhiyya Lal suggests that almost 200 people were killed instantly, while thousands of people were seriously injured. The entire Mochi Gate area looked like one massive bombed site and for years lay desolate. "Stones from the haveli were thrown five kos away", says one description of the explosion. The jolt brought hundreds of houses down, while flying stones damaged the entire area around the perimeter of the explosion.

This explosion, according to the notes of Gen. Ventura, saw the loss of two French engineers and one Russian artillery engineer, as well as many trained Punjabi craftsmen. The explosion completely erased from the face of Lahore the beautiful Haveli Nawab Mian Khan, or better known as the 'Pathronwali Haveli'. Two years after the explosion, people started taking over portions of the lost haveli, and with time, all traces of the famous building were lost forever.

The explosion of Haveli Nawab Mian Khan marked a change in the tactics of placing ordnance depots in populated areas inside the walled city. The Sikh ruler decided to use the large mosques, with the exception of the Wazir Khan Mosque. Almost all ordnance depots placed in residential areas were also moved out, and the building handed over to influential Sikh Misl sardars. This served a dual purpose, for while pleasing his allies, it also placed a major threat to the population out of harm's way, even though it was not taken well by the Muslim population of the city, which was in a majority. When the British took over Lahore, they presented a major portion of the area where once this haveli stood to their closest ally from Kabul. The entire area was rebuilt along old architectural lines, and most of the damaged buildings were also repaired. It was to become one of the finest residential areas of the walled city. Little do the people of this area know that their houses, as they exist today, were all built on a site where the biggest explosion in the history of Lahore took place.

The most expensive necklace

When the British annexed Lahore in 1849 and entered the fort, they were to find a treasure beyond their wildest imagination, one which in their centuries of plundering and invasions all over the world, they were to admit themselves was the finest on this third planet from the sun. Yet this treasure remains the least discussed and known.

We all know that they took the famous Koh-i-Nur diamond, which today is part of the British Crown. We all know that it belonged to the Lahore Darbar, and we all know that legend has it that it will one day return to Lahore. The Sikhs and the Indians have claimed it, though it makes eminent sense that it should lie in the Lahore Fort Museum -- or toshakhana.

Koh-i-Nur

It might amaze many to know that the original size of the Koh-i-Nur, when the ruler of Malwa owned it before the Mughal Babar hit our sub-continent, was an unbelievable 793 carats, which over time has been cut into several diamonds. When the British stole it from Lahore it weighed 186 carats. At the Great London Exhibition it was the centre of attraction and people complained (imagine) that it was not seen to show enough 'fire' as the experts had said it does. This made Queen Victoria order that it be cut to give 'more glitter' and reduce it to the 105.6 carats that it now is.

Maharajah Ranjit Singh fought a war in Kashmir on the promise of being presented the Koh-i-Nur diamond as the price for such an undertaking. He had earlier gone to war with the Afghans because he wanted to own the finest horse in the entire sub-continent. After losing almost 5,000 men he got his horse. For the Koh-i-Nur, he lost nearly 1,000 soldiers, but he managed to get the diamond in a deal that was clean and overboard. The diamond was entered into the records and registered as belonging to the Lahore Darbar. So legally it belongs to the government that rules Lahore.

But besides the Koh-i-Nur there has been a tendency to ignore, and ignore out of sheer ignorance, the other magnificent diamonds that comprised the Lahore Collection. This collection belonged to all the rulers who ever governed

Lahore, or the Punjab this side of the Sutlej. So these diamonds and the entire collection truly belong to the Punjab government in Pakistan.

This piece is about the most important diamond that is even today called the Lahore Diamond. Most people have probably never heard of it. Suffice it to say that besides the Koh-i-Nur, the next most important bag of diamonds, yes sir, a bag of diamonds as the records tell us, contained the Lahore Diamond as well as other important ones.

The toshakhana in the fort is where the records were kept of the Lahore treasures, and from there everything of value was handed over to Dr John Login, who made a list for the 'honourable' East India Company. The list includes the Koh-i-Nur, five bags of diamonds, 134 large gharras of gold jewellery and precious stones, a whole store full of expensive and rare Cashmere shawls and chogas, relics of the Holy Prophet (pbuh) including his shoes, walking stick, shirt, cap and pyjamas, as well as several locks of his hair.

Also taken in possession was the 'plume' of the last Sikh Guru, Gobind Singh, as well as the gold throne of Maharajah Ranjit Singh. Another item of interest among the thousands in the treasury was the jewel-encrusted saddle of Maharajah Ranjit Singh. Needless to add that over the last few years some relics of The Holy Prophet (pbuh) have been stolen by his followers. The saddle of the last Punjabi Maharajah has allegedly been stolen by a former 'ruler' who loved horses.

Our interest in this piece is about the next most precious diamond that the 'honourable' Company Sahib Bahadur stole and presented to the Royal family of Britain. This was a collection known as the Lahore Diamonds. If the Koh-i-Nur is worn on her head by the British Queen, on her neck is a magnificent necklace that is known as the Lahore Diamond Necklace, for its pendant is the magnificent Lahore Diamond.

The other diamonds and stones are all from the one bag that contained the Lahore Collection, said to have been stolen by Timur from the rich merchants of Lahore when he put the population to the sword and raped the women of this city. Since then this collection has remained in the Lahore Treasury, or the toshakhana.

The Lahore Diamond Necklace, now worn by Queen Elizabeth, is a 161-carat necklace, the one we know so little about. The main diamond is a 22.48-carat glittering diamond that was cut from an original 103-carat diamond by a master Dutch diamond cutter.

Queen Victoria had this necklace made in 1858 from 28 stones that she had removed from a Garter Badge and a ceremonial sword -- also removed from Lahore -- and she wore them when Winterhalter painted her portrait in 1859. The necklace added up to 161 carats, making it the world's most expensive necklace, with the nine largest stones weighing between 8.25 and 11.25 carats each. The pendant stone is known as the Lahore Diamond. The drops in the earnings come from the Timur ruby necklace, also taken from the Treasury of Lahore and presented to Queen Victoria by the 'Honourable' East India Company in 1851.

So each time the Queen of England, Scotland, Wales, Ireland and the Commonwealth and Colonies steps out all decked in her magnificent crown and glittering necklace and jewels, remember that almost the entire jewellery belongs to Lahore. The weak and the meek can only pray and hope that one day their treasures will be returned to the toshakhana of the Lahore Fort.

The horse and the 'nakkaskhana'

Before the internal combustion engine overtook our lives, existence in the Walled City of Lahore had two basic paces ... human and equestrian. Today, a variety of speeds, smells and sounds exist ... pleasant, neutral and some downright obnoxious.

We all tend to forget the immense contribution of the horse to life as we know it today. It would be interesting to see how the horse contributed to life in the Walled City over the last 1,000 years. Let us begin, as Lewis Carroll suggested, from the beginning. For me the beginning is how my father made me see the world and, more importantly, the ancient city in which our ancestors have lived over the centuries. He once took us to the Wazir Khan mosque. There he made us two brothers stand and close our eyes. "Imagine yourself in the times of the Mughal emperors, caravans from Samarkand stand before you in the courtyard outside this mosque, and beautiful horses stand all over. Merchants are selling all kinds of exotic ware. It is truly a bazaar of the East. Imagine. Imagine and then slowly open your eyes". The effect was magical. I can still feel that thrill of the courtyard today.

If you stand in the open space outside the Wazir Khan mosque, you can well imagine how life was then. Certainly a few major changes have taken places like plastic water-piping and plastic goods can be seen, as well as bicycles and motorcycles all over the place. But if you look hard enough, you can actually see where the horses stood and there is a beautiful water trough for the animals even today. Here stand tongas as they have stood for hundreds of years, and the lanes and mohallahs are still named after the horse.

The area just outside is known as the 'nakkaskhana', or the horse house, for here once stood a huge horse stable where horses were rested. A small portion of that 'nakkaskhana' still exists, only claimants in the 1947 deluge of refugees overtook it. The entire area to the east of the mosque is known as Mohallah Nakkas, or the Horse Mohallah. This is still a wide road on both sides of which people brought their horses to be sold. However, just outside Akbari Gate, which is where the road leads, was a very large ground, and this was known, and is still known, as 'Nakkas Mandi.' No horses are sold there today, but this is where the largest horse market of the Punjab once existed.

Just opposite it is the Landa Bazaar, which came up just as the Sikh period was drawing to a close, and here the huge havelis or palaces of the horse traders existed. With time these havelis were demolished to make way for commercialization. Eventually, with British imperialism creaming away our national wealth, the condition of the poor grew from bad to worse, and a huge secondhand clothes and shoes market sprang up. This is not only still thriving, but growing as actual poverty grows.

The condition of the horses was of paramount importance to the rulers. Be it the Mughals, the Sikhs or even the British, it seems that the welfare of the horse was a very important aspect of governance. The Sikhs appointed 'nakkas santris' who went round all over the city inspecting the physical condition of horses. One account, as quoted in the delightful book published by the Fakir family on 'The Real Ranjit Singh,' tells of how a man, who ruthlessly beat up his horse, was whipped publicly in the 'nakkashkhana' for one hour and made to sit with a blackened face backwards on the same horse, a lesson to others on how important the horse was to the Maharajah. An old saying in the Walled City even today describes being striped for striping a horse.

The British added to such punishment with even stricter checking, and adding a 15-day jail sentence as part of the law. Today it is common to see old wounded animals being beaten mercilessly and overloaded till they actually are left dangling in the air. The sad part is that today people actually laugh at such a situation, a sad reflection of the society we have become. It is hard to imagine that the horse, that favourite animal of our Holy Prophet (peace be upon him), is degraded and mistreated by a people whose ancestors prided in producing the speediest breed of horses in the Punjab.

The entire track from Akbari Gate curving round near Mochi Gate and going on towards Bhatti Gate was one long race track, where soldiers and kings raced and played polo and other games on horseback. The famous "Slave

Emperor" of India, Qutbuddin Aibak, died from a horsefall just outside Lahori Gate and is buried there. It was Mr Z.A. Bhutto who ordered that a tomb befitting the emperor be built on his modest and ignored grave in a small room in an insignificant and hidden house. But everywhere you look inside the Walled City, you will find traces of the contribution of the horse to our lives.

What is important today is for us to get together and honour the horse and his contribution to life in Lahore as we know it today. The old water troughs must not be knocked down in the name of development, or to make way for yet another ugly concrete structure. The old 'nakkaskhana' stables, now occupied by dozens of claimants, must be renovated and converted into a museum honouring the horse. The outer gardens of the Walled City, or the few that remain, must have their horse tracks restored and, perhaps, used as jogging tracks.

But as Lahore is a living museum with a history over not centuries, but thousands of years, there is a need to control what has replaced the horse. Today exceptionally noisy rickshaws ply inside the silent lanes, making life miserable. Secluded as it might seem, the passing of a rickshaw means that people in the same room cannot hear one another talk. Such is the misery of those living inside the Walled City. Just because they are very poor people, our system does not cater to their needs.

In another piece we talked of the famous horses of Maharajah Ranjit Singh, and how he waged a war with Afghanistan just to secure a horse, and how the dust was settled in the city so that the nostrils of the magnificent animal were not polluted. But then times have changed, only we are going towards disaster with both our eyes open, unlike the one-eyed Maharajah of the past.

Bhagat Singh and the circle of blood

There is one story about Lahore that is close to my heart and that is the story of Bhagat Singh, that great freedom fighter of Lahore and of this sub-continent. No amount of sectarian hatred can erase the memory of a man who walked tall in the streets of Lahore, and who was hanged in the now knocked down Central Jail.

There was a strange story we had heard about Bhagat Singh when we were small children. it was said that his ghost roamed around in the Shah Jamal area and near the shrine of Baba Shah Jamal. Many even claimed having seen an image of the saint talking to Bhagat Singh promising him revenge for the great injustice that had been done to him. I had heard of the story from our cook, who used to visit the shrine of Shah Jamal. My father was a storyteller par excellence. He never admitted that this was true, no matter how hard I pestered him. He always left the door of doubt open with a "maybe its true, maybe not, you will have to wait for the truth to come out one day." And the truth did come out one day.

Bhagat Singh

Not many people know that the area we know as Shadman and Shah Jamal was once known as Lehna Singh di Cchaoni, or the military cantonment of Lehna Singh. This was the place where Sardar Lehna Singh, one of the three chieftains who ruled Lahore just before Maharajah Ranjit Singh, forged his Punjab Empire to contain the spread of the British across the Sutlej. In the middle of this 'cantonment' was a huge house, just about where today exists the second roundabout coming from Jail Road. This is the roundabout nearest the shrine of Baba Shah Jamal, the sufi saint who lies buried just 200 yards from this point, and the reason the area is so called.

The legend goes that the Khans of Kasur, who were in league with the British to topple the Lahore Darbar, sent an envoy to negotiate with a Sikh chief to conspire the murder of Maharajah Ranjit Singh. During the discussions things went wrong and the head of the envoy was chopped off and sent to Kasur. The treachery of the Pathan rulers of Kasur had met its match. It is said that a seer had then predicted that the ghost of the envoy would seek revenge at this very place, and that the circle of revenge would not be completed with one killing alone. Chilling stuff. But then subsequent events were to prove that this prediction was true, and many say the circle of treachery still lives on.

The rule of the Sikhs gave way to the British, and the rulers of Kasur played their treacherous part all along. They had before them, through their mullahs, pestered the sufi saint Bulleh Shah, and had paid a heavy price for their bigotry. The house and cantonment of Lehna Singh was knocked down and in its place was built the largest jail in the Punjab, where long-term inmates, or death row servers, were imprisoned. At the place where the house of Lehna Singh was built came up the gallows, and here many a criminal and freedom fighter was hanged. The place of death continued to serve its purpose.

In 1928, the struggle to free our land from British rule was picking up, and during a procession in Lahore, just opposite the Lahore Museum, a well-known freedom fighter Lala Lajpat Rai was hit on the head during a police lathi-charge, resulting in his death. This sent a wave of anger all over the sub-continent and a young 21-year old revolutionary by the name of Bhagat Singh took it upon himself to seek revenge. On November 17, 1928, he positioned himself on the first floor window of the New Hostel of the Government College, and from there fired on what he thought was Mr Scott, a police official. Instead, he had shot dead the Assistant Superintendent of Police, Lahore, Mr Saunders. Bhagat Singh ran away to Calcutta, and then returned to Agra, where he allegedly set up a bomb-making concern. He was arrested while throwing bombs on the Legislative

Assembly that was passing the draconian Trade Disputes Bill. One account states that he gave himself up shouting that the British could never kill him, and that he was consigned to history and his blood would flow redder if he was killed.

Bhagat Singh was tried and sentenced to hang on October 7, 1930. The British feared this young man so much that not a single magistrate could be found in the whole of India to sign his death warrants. In the end, they turned to Kasur, where a loyal magistrate by the name of Nawab Muhammad Ahmad Khan later to be known as Kasuri, agreed to sign the necessary papers and supervise the hanging. Fearless and shouting slogans for the freedom of the sub-continent, the Ravian Bhagat Singh (one account says he was a student of the National College) was hanged on March 23, 1931, in the Lahore Central Jail at the place where once was the residence of Lehna Singh, where a relative of Nawab Muhammad Ahmad Khan Kasuri was killed for betraying the cause of the Punjab. Old timers say that all over the land not a single hearth fire burned that day.

Then comes an even stranger twist to this tale of blood. In 1975, in a now well-known assassination attempt on the son of Nawab Muhammad Ahmad Khan Kasuri, the old magistrate who had ordered the hanging of Bhagat Singh was himself shot dead at the very place where Lehna Singh's men beheaded a traitor from Kasur, where Bhagat Singh was hanged by the old magistrate. Revenge had come full circle and at the very same place. For that murder the famous Pakistani prime minister Z.A. Bhutto was to hang, keeping the circle of blood flowing. Where will it all end, we do not know ... maybe some seer will appear and tell us.

Remembering the martyrs of Mian Mir

It seems that a lot of people have not read the report by the British Government that investigated the reasons why the war of independence of 1857 took place and how it was stemmed, let alone the article by Sir Syed into the cause for the 'revolt', and the military assessment then carried out by the East India Company. Let me recount the role of Lahore in that massive movement.

The military assessment states "had Lahore not been secured, Delhi could not have been taken, and India would have been lost". This is also the view taken by the British Government report, though Sir Syed does not touch on these matters. Our interest lies in the role of Lahore in the 1857 war of independence. We must not forget that just eight years earlier, the Sikh Empire had been conquered by the British, with many Sikhs feeling that the Muslims had welcomed the fall of their Khalsa Army. To the East the battered remains of the decaying Mughal Empire had been conquered and the last Mughal emperor, Bahadar Shah Zafar, was recognized and pensioned off. It was a recipe for disaster, which saw gun greasing as an excuse to trigger things off.

As the revolt spread from the East of the sub-continent, the British immediately consolidated themselves in the Punjab. Intelligence reports told of a huge mutiny in Lahore and Ferozepur, for in these two stations the largest arsenals lay. Had these two stations fallen, the siege of Delhi would have not taken place and, probably, the War would have been won. Probably even greater confusion would have followed, but then discussing the 'ifs' of history is silly. So let's stick to the facts as they happened.

On the 13th of May, 1857, the sepoys had planned to take the Lahore Fort and the Lahore Cantonment, then based in Old Anarkali where today we have a Food Street. The treasury and arsenal were in the fort, while the European troops were in Old Anarkali. It was decided that during the morning parade the European officers would be killed and Lahore fort and the cantonment taken over. However, the British struck at 5.00 a.m. when three companies of Her Majesty's 81st Foot marched into the fort and relieved the native infantry, in the process asking them to leave their rifles and all arms and ammunition behind. The fort was secured.

In a similar action on the 13th of May, 1857, when the parade assembled at the Mian Mir grounds, where today we have the CMH and Saddar area, the parade was surrounded by 12 artillery guns and an impressive cavalry display. The guns were fired to remind everyone who was in charge and to the surprise of three regiments of native infantry and one light cavalry, everyone was asked to disarm and disband. The threat of utter destruction was called off and everyone piled their arms and marched off in utter shock and anger. Once the cavalry unbuckled their swords and threw them on the ground, the plan of the 13th of May had been smashed in Lahore.

On the 14th of May, 1957, intelligence reports told of the remaining sepoys in Mian Mir planning to desert and flee. This caused panic among the Europeans living in Old Anarkali and all the residents were collected at the Central Jail. On the morning of the 14th of May, all the artillery guns available and the entire 81st Foot were ready to kill anyone who fled. The native sepoys returned to their lines and the few who did run away were captured by the villagers living in the areas called the Majhas, near Kasur, and returned. Much to the advantage of the British, the Sikh villagers sided with them. A few younger Sikhs wanting to revive the old Khalsa glory were handed over. All the captured sepoys were tied to British guns and blown up in front of their colleagues. One such display took place at Mian Mir and the other one at Old Anarkali near the baradari of Wazir Khan. It sent shock waves throughout the city population and among the sepoys.

Thus Lahore and its environs had been secured. The East India Company immediately took massive defensive measures like filling the fort with six months of food provisions and blocking all gates except one for use. The old and magnificent Taxali Gate was also blown up and the walls on the western side of the old walled city flattened. A siege by the residents was thus prevented. A system of guarding the city was devised and a police officer called Subhan Khan led the effort. He was richly rewarded for his efforts. The Europeans organized a Company of 130 men on horses. The city was thus secured.

On the 26th and 27th of May, 1857, the Guides Corps, comprising mostly Sikhs, left Lahore on their march to Delhi. They were to play an important part in the fall of that city and the end of the War of Independence and the arrest of Bahadar Shah Zafar. To replace them a 'moveable column' under Brig. Neville Chamberlain arrived and on the 9th of June, 1857, two men of the 35th Native Infantry who spoke in strong terms were arrested and tied to the regiment guns and blown up in front of the regiment at the Old Anarkali parade ground. The official charge recorded was "intended mutiny". The city was stunned into silence.

For three weeks all was quiet as the siege of Delhi continued. On the 30th of June, 1857, the 26th Native Infantry managed to mutiny at Mian Mir in Lahore. They attacked the Officers Colony at Saddar and murdered Major Spencer, their commanding officer, a European NCO and others loyal to the British. Word of assistance frightened the troops and they fled thanks to a huge June dust storm. However, the Deputy Commissioner of Amritsar, Mr. Cooper, rushed after them with troops killing the entire fleeing men on the banks of the River Ravi. It was a massacre the likes of which had seldom been seen in Lahore. Today we do not even know about it. No memorial remembers those sons of the soil who died in the First War of Independence.

The last hope of an uprising came from the Kharrals to the South of Lahore, but the British moved swiftly and with the assistance of Sikh and even Muslim cavalry, all traces of the uprising in Lahore were smashed. For another 90 years nothing to match the martyrs of 1857 was to be seen, for in 1947 the people of the sub-continent killed one another, the frenzy of which we still live with.

The Letter from Givenchy

In my search for an ancient Jain temple, reputed to be among the oldest worship sites in the walled city of Lahore, which I finally located at the fag end of Tehsil Bazaar, off Bazaar Hakeeman, at the northern edge, of the Bhatti-Lahori divide, I met Allah Bakhsh.

At 95, Allah Bakhsh is a reasonably sprightly man. He lives with his sons and grandsons, and everyone in the area respects him for he belongs to the 'first big war' age as the people of the area refer to him. Having reassured himself that I meant no harm, he produced an old brownish postcard from his father... the father who never returned. It was the last letter he got from Givenchy. The date written was December 1914 and it was in English, a language his father never knew. The writer was 'Ameer Bux', a sepoy of the Lahore division, deployed at Givenchy in Pas de Calais, France. The very brief postcard speaks of his health, which is fine, and that "we go into battle soon. Please pray for me."

The walled city is a fascinating place, for within the walls live people who hold on to memories that are light years away from the reality of modern Lahore. For us, Givenchy is a famous perfume. For Allah Bakhsh, it is a precious memory, the last word from his father from an ancient battleground in France, near Calais. As long as the mother of Allah Bakhsh lived, she had a small pension of Rs. II and she died during the turmoil of partition in Tehsil Bazaar, after a roaming group of Sikhs butchered her. In return, a group of Muslims butchered two Sikh women the next day in the same bazaar. That the parents of Allah Bukhsh both died violent deaths in totally different circumstances at totally different places does strike one as strange.

The letter from Givenchy fascinated me, and I set about researching how did Lahoris end up fighting in remote France. A website about the village says:

"On the 18th of December, 1914, at the very beginning of the First World War, the Lahore Division battled fiercely with the Germans for possession of the legendary village of Givenchy in Pas de Calais, France. In five days of 'terrible' hand-to-hand fighting, over 4,000 stubborn Lahoris were martyred." The Germans lost over 2,000 men.

Fought on December 18-22, 1914, the Battle of Givenchy saw an initially advancing British force face strong opposition (and counter-attack) from a solidly entrenched German force around the village of Givenchy (in Pas-de-Calais, and which was held by the British). With the French under heavy pressure at Arras the order was given that the British force would provide relief by attacking the Germans around Givenchy, thus preventing a German reinforcement at Arras from that quarter at least for this task, the Lahore Division was chosen and thrust into battle. Perfect cannon fodder for the empire. Sharp fighting broke out on December 19 when Punjabi troops from the Lahore Division launched a attack, successfully capturing two lines of German trenches. However, their success was short-lived: a prompt and aggressive counteraction pushed the Punjabi troops back again.

The following day, the British force was caught somewhat by surprise by a heavy attack launched by the now reinforced Germans around Givenchy. The force of the German attack was clearly focussed on the trenches held by the same Lahore Division troops who had initiated operations on the previous day.

Defensive tactics were severely hampered by the conditions of the Lahore Division trenches. For five days, the Lahoris stood, without sleep; in severe cold in heavily waterlogged trenches. Consequently, the German force broke through, bayonetting the Lahoris by the hundred. They managed to occupy part of Givenchy. On this setback, two fresh British reserve battalions were brought into action, with the result that the village was back in British hands by December 20. The following day, a fresh influx of men relieved the Lahore Division, and the "line" was restored to its original position.

On August 6, 1914, the War Council asked the British Indian government to send two infantry divisions and a cavalry brigade to Egypt. The Lahore and the Meerut divisions were chosen, later followed by the Secunderabad cavalry brigade, which together formed the Indian Army Corps. The first elements of the Lahore Division were already on their way to the front. Their new destination was Marseilles, where they arrived, by the end of September. On its way to France, the Lahore Division left one of its brigades near the Suez Canal, and, as some units of the Jalandhar brigade left India by the end of September, it was only the Ferozepur brigade that was at full strength.

From Marseilles the Lahoris went north, over Orleans. The 47th Sikhs of the Jalandhar brigade while moving up to the front reached near Saint-Omer on October 20, 1914. On October 22, 1914, the Ferozepur brigade arrived in the 'new-born' Ypres Salient. They were sent to the trenches between Hollebeke in the north and Messines in the south. The first battalion of the Lahore Division that went into the firing line was the 57th Wilde's Rifles (even today along Walton Road, near the Cavalry Ground crossing point, you will see this regiment's fading name written on a wall). They were located at Wijtschate-Oosttaverne. Later, the entire Lahore Division was involved.

The 57th Wilde's Rifles and the 129th Balochis suffered heavy losses during the last two days of October 1914 (during the 1st battle of Ieper). The Wilde's Rifles lost 300 of 750 men, the Balochis had 240 men killed, wounded or taken prisoner. During the Second Battle of Ieper, the 47 Sikh Regiment from Lahore city itself fought alone on April 27,1915, and lost 348 men out of a total 444. These Lahori Sikhs even today have an honourable mention on a memorial at The Mall-Tufail Road crossing. Dr John Meire of Katholieke Universiteit, Belgium, writes in his book *Memories of the First World War In and Around Ieper*. "Between 24th

April and 1st May 1915 in a week's time, the Lahore Division had lost 30 per cent of the troops it had employed. 'It is finished with (Lahore) division', writes wounded Ishar Singh on 1st May 1915 to a friend in India. It appears on both sides there will be no survivors — then, when there is nobody, peace will prevail" (page 352). In about 14 months of fighting, the Indian Corps lost 34,252 men on the Western Front in France and Belgium. Of the Lahoris, Dr Meire says: "the Germans, in a famous message to their headquarters wrote:

'These crazy Lahore Division men just do not withdraw. They virtually invite our bayonets when surrounded'."

Many years ago, in 1972, when as a student I stood at the Menin Gate Memorial in Ieper, Belgium, I was shocked to revisit the trenches and the memorial. On these killing fields of Europe, the brave men from my city and land died and were buried. Yet today, no one remembers them. Yes there is Allah Bakhsh with his letter from Givenchy, but the Pakistan Army must send, every year, on December 22, to Menin Gate in Belgium, a bouquet of the beautiful red roses of Lahore to remember our ancestors. We must never forget our 'Unknown Soldiers.'

Lahore and the Komagata Maru

My father was always full of surprises. One day, and this must be some time in the 1960s, while we were both walking through a narrow lane inside Mochi Gate, he stopped outside a small house and said: "This is where the man who hired *Komagata Maru* lived. One day we must recognize him and his friends as our true heroes."

Komagata Maru had been lurking in my sub-conscious mind for years. Not many of us know that just before the First World War broke out, a group of Punjabis who had gone Westward to join the Californian gold rush and to freedom from British rule, gathered together to do something for their homeland. The majority of these people belonged to Jalandhar, Ludhiana and Lahore. Even today, a large number of Californian farmers are Punjabis from Lahore and its environs, and very successful and educated farmers they are at that. They are now fifth generation Americans.

In the true tradition of the 'rebel' immigrants of the US who finally managed to throw off the British yoke and gain freedom, these Indian or sub-continental immigrants decided that the time had come for them to set sail for their homeland and free their lands from the British. Mixed with this feeling was the desire to return home. A lot of them had migrated because the laws enforced by the British had dispossessed the poor farmers of their ancestral lands. Tall stories of gold nuggets were being printed in *The Civil and Military Gazette* of Lahore, and so a lot of educated Lahoris decided to migrate. By the turn of the last century, over 10,000 Punjabis are said to have reached America. If a Lahori can sell fish and chips in the Falklands, why not expect them to be in the Wild West?

1914. the Komagata Maru in Vancouver harbour surrounded by police boats.

California, more specifically San Francisco, was the scene for one of the most bizarre and memorable things done by any ethnic community in the United States. Most of them lived in the famous China Town. The Punjabi immigrants, who faced considerable racial discrimination, decided to create a revolutionary army, inspired as they were by the history of the land in which they were living. In what must surely be regarded as a far-fetched plan, they decided to invade India by sea. Imagine the year 1913 and Britain at the zenith of its power, and a small group of 'well-meaning patriots' deciding to invade South Asia and liberate in from the British. The Punjabis who organized it called their movement Ghaddar (alternately spelled Ghadar, or Ghadr). The name means 'mutiny' 'or revolt'.

In 1915, their plan had been fully formulated. Five boats, loaded with weapons and propaganda, set sail from various ports in California. The British intelligence agents had reached the conclusion that they were actually financed by the German war effort. These rebels had been collecting arms of every variety and were organizing like an army does. The logic was that if the American immigrants could do it, so could the hardy Punjabis. In 1913 was formed the Ghaddar (mutiny) Party, dedicated to the proposition that only an armed struggle could topple the British. The first gathering was at Astoria in 1913, where Sohan Singh Bhakna of Lahore was elected the chief of the Ghaddar Party. Lahoris have no time to find hidden meanings for what they intend, and so the word 'ghaddar' fitted in well with the traditions of the land and people where they dwelled.

In neighbouring Canada in the summer of 1914 the famous *Komagata Maru* saga unfolded. Kuldip Singh, a wealthy Indian businessman, had chartered the *Komagata Maru* and sailed the freighter from Hong Kong to Vancouver. On board were 376 Punjabis, 340 of them Sikhs, over half of them from Lahore. They were on their way to Canada where they hoped to immigrate and start a new life. When the *Komagata Maru* arrived at Vancouver, however, most of the passengers were detained on board. They waited for two months while immigration officials and the Indian community fought over their admission to the country.

The Canadian authorities had been alerted by the British who were already eyeing with suspicion the gathering of immigrants in the US and Canada in the wake of the formation of the Ghaddar Party. Despite these efforts, the battle was lost after the Supreme Court rejected all appeals and the *Komagata Maru* was forced to return. It was forced to sail for Calcutta. Upon arrival, police already alerted by the suspicious British authorities of the organizers' intentions, met it. As the passengers disembarked the police opened fire without any reason and 20 passengers were killed.

An estimated 8,000 Ghaddarites returned to India by sea to help the revolt. However, the British learnt about the plans of the Ghaddarites and promulgated an ordinance in 1914 empowering provincial governments to arrest people entering India. The Ghaddarites returning in big ships like *Komagata Maru, Namsang* and SS *Korea* were arrested. Many other Ghaddarites made it through the shores of Colombo, Madras and Bombay. The date of the uprising was fixed for Feb 21, 1913, which was advanced to Feb 19 at the last minute after the British got to know of their plans.

The authorities acted swiftly; they disarmed the Indian troops in the garrisons at Kohat, Bannu and Dinapur and interned the soldiers. Several leaders of the Ghaddar Party were arrested and imprisoned in Lahore. In the first Lahore Conspiracy Case, 24 Punjabis were ordered to be sent to the gallows. However, public protests followed and Viceroy Lord Harding himself intervened and converted the death sentence of 17 to life sentence. The seven Ghaddarites who were hanged included the fiery revolutionary Kartar Singh Sarabha, who belonged to Mochi Gate, Lahore. They were hanged at the Lahore Central Jail at the spot where today is the main Shah Jamal crossing. It is believed that at least 145 Ghaddarites were sent to the gallows and more than 304 were given sentences longer than 14 years in five Lahore Conspiracy cases. All of them died in 'Kala Pani' as the Andaman Islands were and are called.

He preferred death to defeat

Imagine the scene, just outside the walls of the old city of Lahore, in the area between Bhatti Gate and Mori Gate. The year is AD 996. The Punjabi ruler, soaked from head to toe in ghee, sets himself ablaze after suffering defeat repeatedly at the hands of foreign invaders.

In the history of this land of ours, and of Lahore in particular, two Punjabi rulers stand out. The first was Raja Jaipal of Lahore, while the second, Maharajah Ranjit Singh, the Sikh ruler, came almost 800 years later in 1799. We know so much more about Maharajah Ranjit Singh, that wise astute ruler who kept the British at bay, yet so little about Jaipal. Maybe it has to do with the fact that somehow history older than 1,000 years is no longer history for us. It has become an area over which we exercise a sort of self-censorship. But history is history and just will not go away, and the people of Lahore crave for leadership itself, let alone leaders with pride and honour.

Raja Jaipal of Lahore had a kingdom stretching from "Sirhind to Lamghan and from Kashmir to Mooltan" as the chroniclers of old used to say. According to Firishta, the Muslim historian, in AD 682, the Afghans of Kirman and Peshawar began to challenge the ruler of the Lahore court that was in the hands of a Rajput Chauhan prince. One account says that within the space of just five months, almost 70 battles were fought, and the Afghans, with the help of the Ghakkars of Khewra and Mianwali, managed to coerce the forces of Lahore to cede a large portion of their territory.

In AD 975, the forces of Subuktagin, who was then governor of Khurasan, decided that they should move beyond the Indus, to loot and conquer the sub-continent. For this they had to face the armies of the court of Lahore, led as they were by the proud Rajput ruler, Raja Jaipal. The Bhat Rajputs formed a major portion of the population and were very influential in the Lahore court. They advised that it was best to contain the wild Afghans and not to fight them. So negotiations took place and it was decided that peace was the best way out as Raja Jaipal reasoned that they had nothing to fight over. The Bhatis managed to avert the invasion.

When Subuktagin succeeded the throne of Ghazni, he decided that the riches of India were just too attractive for him to ignore, and thus started a series of invasions that were to change the very face of the sub-continent. When Subuktagin made his first move. Raja Jaipal prepared to face him at Lamghan. The swift Afghan horsemen were just too much for the conventional elephant-led forces of Lahore.

Ruler Raja Jaipal was defeated, but again decided to discuss peace, pleading that Subuktagin had violated his word of honour. But in defeat or against 'overwhelming' forces, logic and honour have no place. Such a situation is contained only at a price, and Raja Jaipal decided to pay that price. Subuktagin sent his emissaries to the walled city of Lahore to bring back the booty promised by Raja Jaipal, who in his fort decided to imprison the emissaries, refusing to pay the ransom agreed to. Instead, he decided to battle it out once again.

In the bloody clashes that followed, Subuktagin defeated the forces of Raja Jaipal and obliged him to surrender all territory west of the Indus. This was a double defeat and Jaipal returned to Lahore a broken man. One account tells us of him spending the whole night thinking of what to do next, and it was in the morning that all arrangements were made for the proud Rajput to undertake the ultimate 'Johar' ceremony. It is in essence the ultimate devotional act to the gods of war. Dressed in full battle dress and armed with his jewelled sword, Raja Jaipal came to the empty ground outside Bhatti Gate, just to the left of where today Mori Gate exists. He poured ghee all over himself and an attendant handed him a lit torch, with which the proud Raja set himself ablaze. According to folklore, the Raja did not utter a single cry of pain, asking his son to avenge the insult by the foreign forces.

And thus ended Jaipal's long and wise reign almost 1,000 years ago. The son of Jaipal remained true to his father's words and met the Afghans in battle at Peshawar, but was again defeated. His son also called Jaipal but referred to in history as Narjanpal, began to rule Lahore, till in A.D. 1022 the son of Subuktagin, known better as Mahmud of Ghazni, came down from Kashmir and seized Lahore almost without a fight. He decided to let his soldiers plunder Lahore. For seven days and nights rape and plunder reigned supreme. Raja Jaipal II fled to Ajmer, and the Rajput kingdom of Lahore and the Punjab was extinguished forever. It was only 800 years later, that the Punjabis managed to win back their freedom from the Afghans, only to lose it to the British again within a short period of 50 years. Every time you pass Circular Road near the Mori Gate, just pause to look for an old pipal tree in the garden that exists there today. That was, not very long ago, called the tree of Jaipal. Some call it the 'Johar tree' ... a tree that embodies the ritual that goes back to antiquity.

The forgotten killing fields

As you move eastwards from Roshnai Gate towards Yakki Gate, the road snakes inwards. Here once flowed the River Ravi. Just where the road turns inwards is a spot where died a man almost 400 years ago. His death was the determining moment in the history of northern India especially the Punjab,

The day was May 30, 1606, and a number of prisoners, shackled and beaten, were brought down from the deep dungeons of the Lahore Fort to have a much needed bath in the river. The man's sole fault was that he had played host to an honourable guest, prince Khusrau, brother of Emperor Jehangir. Once Khusrau had been silenced and Jehangir was firmly enthroned, he wanted to punish this tall handsome man for his hospitality.

The man was Arjun Mal, the fourth Guru of the Sikhs. So badly was Arjun tortured that he was unable to stand. As soon as he entered the cool water, life left this tall and sturdy man. The death of Arjun outside the walls of the Lahore Fort proved

Guru Arjun Dev

to be the catalyst for Nanak's new faith of 'peace' to turn away from "peace at any costs" to a faith that was to stand up and defend itself against an intolerance that was to reach its height much later during the nine invasions of Ahmad Shah Abdali.The end result was that the Sikhs founded their first and last empire in the Punjab which stretched from Kabul to Delhi and from Kashmir to Multan. Such was the impact of that remarkable man whom the cool waters of the Ravi delivered from his tormentors.

The Sikhs till then essentially belonged to a movement started by Guru Nanak to move beyond being a dogmatic 'brahmin' or a fundamentalist 'mullah'. He believed that there was One Master, who is Allah. That was the beginning and the end of the matter. The 'murder' of Arjun changed all this and the Sikhs evolved as "neither Hindu, nor Muslim, but a third community of their own". The Punjabi Jats of the doabas resolved to avenge Arjun's death and the militant Punjabi was born. From that point onwards a lot of blood flowed.

If you pause at the point where the wall of the Lahore Fort turns inwards towards the old city, just think of the hundreds of thousands that have passed that way, where Arjun died, on their way to be butchered in cold blood. Just stand there and imagine the various layers and layers of history as it passed that point next to the massive walls, for hundreds of thousands of men and women and children passed that point, all of whom died because of the manner in which Arjun had died at that spot.

Between 1739 and 1747, the Muslim governor of Lahore, Zakariyya Khan made the head hunting of Sikhs a favorite sport. He offered a 'massive' Rs. 50 per head for the scalp of a Sikh. Hundreds of thousands of Sikhs were caught and brought to Lahore in chains. They all passed that spot where Arjun had died. All of them were taken to the 'nakkas', or horse market, just outside the present Yakki Gate, where they were publicly slaughtered, their heads spiked on spears and paraded through the city Even today, the old folk of the walled city call this terrible place 'Shahidganj'. As a people, Pakistanis have no time for the martyrs of other religions, forgetting that they all belonged to this land of ours.

On October 14, 1745, the Sarbat Khalsa resolved to form small *jathas* of Punjabi horsemen into 25 regiments of cavalry. Their objective was to strike silently and hard, and after inflicting considerable damage to the enemy, to retreat and disappear. Then the Sikhs took on the Mughals and other invaders. They tired out the enemy to such an extent, that ultimately they founded their own empire. In 1746, after the Sikhs had refused to pay revenue to the government, all of them living around Lahore and inside the city were rounded up. Also a number of regiments were trapped on the banks of the Ravi north of Lahore. Over 7,000 Sikhs were killed, while almost 3,200 were chained and marched past the point where Arjun had fallen.

For eight days and nights, all the butchers of Lahore slaughtered these 3,200 men at Shahidganj by slitting open their throats. The June 1746 disaster is known as the 'Ghallughara' or 'The Holocaust'. Nowhere in the entire history of India, let alone the Punjab, has such a massive ethnic cleansing exercise been undertaken. It is said that from the Mahmud Buti village on the Ravi right up to Yakki Gate, the skulls and skeletons of these Sikhs could be found in the fields around Lahore for over 100 yeas later.

Yet today very few in Lahore know about our 'holocaust', bloody and gruesome as it was. From the blood of these Sikhs grew a virile and aggressive Punjabi nationalism. We ignore it because the Sikhs took the battle to the invaders and the foreigners. Even today vegetable farmers working in the fields next to the Ravi at Mahmood Buti Bund report finding skulls and human bones when they dig deeper than normal. The British-built rail track separates Shaheedganj outside Yakki Gate from Mahmood Buti and the Ravi next to it. Once the cool waters flowed right up to the city. In between lie the killing fields where the admirers of Arjun were slaughtered over the centuries by the thousand.

Hazrat Mian Mir pleaded in vain for Arjun. A verse of those days says it all:

"Those who think the blood of the Jat will be in vain
"Know not that

The Master knows best a heart when pure

Emperors rule only for as long as they live

For this Jat will reign as long as men walk tall."

The forgotten years of Lahore

There was a time when the inhabitants of Lahore were actually paid a monthly salary just to keep living in the Walled City. And all this happened because of the Khokhars, who constantly attacked the place, ravaged its people and places, and then moved on to attack and loot other smaller nearby towns. Their ancestors still live in the villages and towns right up to Sheikhupura.

Without any discourtesy to this tribe, even today the Punjab police consider the strip between Lahore and Sheikhupura as possessing the most dangerous dacoits and criminals in the entire province. Their role in the history of Lahore, and of the sub-continent, is very important, for they proved to be the catalysts for changes that have gone down in history as changes of outstanding importance. For over 250 years before Zahiruddin Babar invaded India, the ancient city changed hands many a time, and with each change the inhabitants were looted and the city pillaged. Things had become so bad, that it had become a natural reaction for the entire population to leave the city at the first rumour of an invasion. Along with the Khokhars, the Ghakkar tribe, which inhabited the lands between Gujranwala and Daska, also excelled in similar pastimes, and between them they made life miserable for the Lahoris.

After the assassination of Muhammad of Ghor, his successor Qutbuddin Aibak had himself crowned in Lahore. He set about trying to ward off threats from these two tribes, and to some extent managed to win considerable relief for the people of this city. After his death in a fall from his horse while playing 'Chaugan', a type of polo, he was buried just near Anarkali bazaar. His son Aram Bakhsh had himself crowned in Lahore. But his relative, Iltutmish, the ruler of Delhi, overcame him and Lahore was sidelined for almost 250 years, with Delhi considering the city as a buffer against any invasion from within or without India. During this period, Lahore suffered the most, and ironically, it is this period that has been most ignored by our historians, for these are the 'forgotten years'. Yet it is this period that is the most important in the history of the Walled City,

In AD 1241, during the reign of the ineffective Bahram Shah, the Mongols walked unopposed into a demoralized Lahore, and the pillage that followed remains unrivalled to date. The orders were that not a single woman should be spared and should be given over to the Mongol warriors. The entire population escaped into the countryside. For 30 long years, Lahore was a ghost city, "among those ruins even dogs and beggars dared not to roam around." During this long period, probably the darkest in the history of our ancient city, the rulers in Delhi dared not move to assist. These long years of isolation ingrained into the psyche of the Lahori a natural hatred for central rule.

It was only when Ghiasuddin Balban ascended the throne in Delhi in AD1266 that the restoration of Lahore was made a top priority. His squad roamed the countryside searching out the original inhabitants of Lahore and promising them a salary to live in their own city. He rebuilt the devastated Lahore Fort and built many buildings and mosques, some of which exist to this day. His son, Shahzada Muhammad, was made the governor of Lahore and poets like Amir Khusrau constantly accompanied the young prince around Lahore. A tradition of poetry and music was set into motion soon, with the areas of Taxali and Bhatti being the places where almost all the poets and musicians lived.

But then Lahore was attacked again by a Mongol horde led by Samar, known as "the bravest dog of all the dogs of Genghis Khan", who though initially defeated in battle, managed to surprise Prince Muhammad and forced him to approach the banks of the river Ravi, where he took Amir Khusrau prisoner. Sultan Balban prized Khusrau and negotiated his release. But the capture of Khusrau demoralized Balban, who at the age of 80 died of grief.

His death saw Lahore sink into a deep depression, and people started leaving the city again. The ghost city reappeared. The Khokhars again took to attacking Lahore, only this time the Mongols were there to tackle them. Delhi treated Lahore as an outpost. In AD 1398, Sheikha Khokhar surrendered to Taimur, only to rebel again on a slight sign of weakness shown by the Mongol tyrant. This incensed Timur, who ordered the complete plunder of Lahore and the surrounding areas. The operation was an awesome undertaking for its ferocity, for in its wake the Khokhar and Ghakkar. areas were put to the sword and their women taken slaves. After that every person who managed to reach Lahore did so "in the name of Timur."

In AD 1414, a Syed dynasty began ruling Lahore starting with Khizr Khan Syed. Their rule lasted almost 36 years during which time Lahore again slipped into a ghost city. The fires lit by Timur in Lahore, or so the legend goes, lasted for 100 years. There was a popular saying in those days that Lahore is a city where "except the owl of ill omen", nothing exists. By the time the Syeds had done with Lahore, it was almost without inhabitants. The feeling was of "hollow silence" as one description puts it. The crumbling Syeds gave way to the Lodhis, who just could not cope with the plundering Khokhars. They agonized Lahore governor Dulat Khan to such an extent that he invited the ruler of Kabul to invade and put the Khokhars to the sword just' like Timur had done earlier. The ruler of Kabul was Zaheeruddin Babar, who was just waiting for such an invitation, and as we all know, he came to stay.

From that moment onwards, the long agony of Lahore ended. It was rebuilt and the enduring legacy of Khusrau lived on to reach heights even the poet himself could not have imagined. If we Lahoris analyse our reaction to events even today, we will notice a detached cynicism to the rule of law as we know it. The origins of this Lahori trait probably lie in the three centuries of utter destruction that our forefathers faced before the Mughals came. The Sikhs and the British were also not able to change the lack of confidence Lahoris still have in central authority. Perhaps the habits of the Ghakkars and the Khokhars live in us. These forgotten 300 years of the city need to be researched in depth ... for these are the 'forgotten years' of Lahore.

The genocides in Baghdad and Lahore

It is so very difficult to think of anything else these days as we watch on television the planned genocide in Iraq. Day in and day out it happens and we simply pray that the thing ends. In a way, we have come to expect such genocide because of what is happening in Palestine. Genocide is genocide. Makes one think of Genghis Khan, the man who sacked and raped both Baghdad and Lahore almost 900 years ago.

I have been reading an old favourite, *Seven Pillars of Wisdom* by T.E. Lawrence, a.k.a Lawrence of Arabia, the man who delivered Arabia and the oil wealth of Arabs into British hands. He writes:

Genghis Khan

"I went up the Tigris with 100 Devon Territorials, young, clean, delightful fellows ... we were casting them into the fire to the worst of deaths, not to win the war, but that the corn and rice and oil of Mesopotamia might be ours".

This was his measured view, a view endorsed by Bernard Shaw, a view for which the establishment never forgave T.E. Lawrence. They finally declared him a "filthy homosexual" and consigned him to an air base at Karachi. But Lawrence was an irrepressible character, used to the desert and to the sensual, or so they claim, for his narrative does contain delightful portions of the sensual aspects of human existence. He would find one excuse or another to fly out of base on the old rickety aeroplanes to come to Lahore, "where life was sensitive, sensible, where men and women were lettered in the ways of life". He stayed at Garhi Shahu with an old Oxford friend, and there he relaxed as only he could.

Lawrence will live in legend as Lawrence of Arabia, the man who launched the mad scramble for the oil of the Arabs, who laid the foundations of the dangerous religious "pipe dream" of Israel, an idea so cruel that it has angered and violated an entire people. The present genocide promises to widen the scope of this violation. Human greed knows no bounds. But then if Lawrence came to Lahore, so did Genghis Khan ... and then Genghis Khan also went to Baghdad to burn all their books and their knowledge. The Arabs have always been a highly cultured people, and invaders have always left them poorer. The only way to beat them was to burn their books. This is exactly what he did in Lahore.

Genghis Khan, those original name was Temujin (1167-1227), was born the son of Yesukai, a Mongol chief and ruler of a large region between the Amur River and the Great Wall of China. At the age of 13 Temujin succeeded his father as tribal chief. By 1206, Temujin was master of almost all Mongolia. In that year, a convocation of the subjugated tribes proclaimed him Genghis Khan (Chinese cheng-sze, "precious warrior"; Turkish Khan, "lord"), leader of the united Mongol and Tatar tribes; the city of Karakorum was designated his capital. The Khan then began his conquest of China. By 1208, he had established a foothold inside the Great Wall, and in 1213 he led his armies south and west into the area dominated by the Juchen Chin (or Kin) dynasty (1122-1234), not stopping until he reached the Shantung Peninsula. In 1215, his armies captured Yenking (now

Beijing), the last Chin stronghold in northern China, and in 1218, the Korean Peninsula fell to the Mongols.

In 1219, in retaliation for the murder of some Mongol traders, the usual excuse to invade and such murders are normally stage managed, Genghis Khan turned his armies westward, invading a vast Turkish empire that included modern Iraq, Iran, and part of Western Turkestan. Looting and massacring, the Mongols swept through Turkestan and sacked the cities of Bukhara and Samarkand. He then conquered the cities of Peshawar and Lahore. In Lahore took place a ritual that had once before taken place in Baghdad. He ordered that before the men were slaughtered and the women raped, every book in Lahore be burned. Two other ancestors of Genghis Khan Timurlane and Babar also did the same to Lahore. Time changes very little in the behaviour of invaders. But be it Lawrence who displaced the Turks to deliver Arabia to the Sauds and to monarchy, or be it Genghis Khan who destroyed Baghdad and Lahore because he saw books and civil behaviour as a threat to his way of life, genocide is what we today remember them for.

And so the genocide continues, and it will be for genocide that they will be remembered in history, just like the Red Indians, the slaves from Africa, or more recently Vietnam. Most people think that after Baghdad, maybe the new Genghis Khan will head for Lahore. But then we have no oil, and who would want 140 million Pakistanis. In a way nothing changes, the genocide continues — only the ways become more refined and the explanation has a silken touch. But then, as the famous Original American — called Red Indian — saying goes: "He who speaks with a forked tongue, feels no sorrow". We live in immensely sad times.

The Nadir Shahi syndrome

When Khuli Khan of Kabul, or better known as Nadir Shah, came to Lahore in May 1738, he had within the space of less than 100 days put well over 200,000 men to the sword, a slaughter unparalleled in sub-continental history. The perpetuators being his Persian-speaking Tajiks, the Qizilbash Cossacks and the northern Caucasian Georgians.

When Nadir Shah left Lahore by the middle of February 1738, heading for Delhi, he vowed to teach the people of the Punjab, including Delhi, a lesson their future generations would never forget. The first person to try to stop him was Muhammad Shah, who in a battle near Karnal saw the crazed Nadir Shah put his army of 200,000 to flight. Thousands of prisoners were slaughtered and their heads piled on carts and driven around the Punjab countryside.

Nadir Shah

Over a hundred such carts were stationed outside Lahore's walled city. The order was to leave the slaughtered heads unburied so that the people of the city do not create hurdles for him when he returned from Delhi. The GT Road from the Shalimar Gardens to Badami Bagh had these carts parked on the roadside. Even today the old of the city cail that age "Nadir Shahi da sikka".

When the bloodthirsty king of Kabul hit Delhi on March 8, 1738, he climbed atop the main dome of the main mosque near the famed Chandni Chowk and drew out his sword, ordering that the slaughter continue till he put his sword back in its scabbard. It was a holocaust of unheard dimensions. When well over 100,000 inhabitants had been slaughtered a learned follower of the king threw himself at his feet and begged for forgiveness. The king put back his sword saying "My blood still boils for my thirst has yet to be quenched". For a good two months Nadir Shah consolidated himself ruthlessly, beheading any man who spoke his mind. The entire countryside was stunned. Then the loot began, the like of which has never since been seen. In May 1738, his forces began a phased withdrawal from Delhi and headed for Lahore carrying with him plunder that even today few can fathom.

One British historian estimates that Nadir Shah carried with him plunder to the amount of 87,000,000 sterling, approximately ten billion pounds by present day estimates. His army commanders and soldiers took another 12,000,000 sterling, or approximately two billion pounds by present estimates. There were also taken away 1,000 elephants, 7,000 fine horses, 10,000 camels, 130 writers, 200 masons, 300 stonecutters and 200 carpenters. All this wealth arrived in Lahore in May 1738, making it the richest city in the world for the period he was here.

At Lahore he left, permanently, a lot of his soldiers and administrators, foremost among them being members of the Qizilbash tribe. Even today they occupy major tracts of land and property in and around Lahore thanks to Nadir Shah, and later on because of their loyalty to the Sikh forces, and then to the British. It is said that when he headed for Kabul in May 1738, his forces were hit by flash floods in the River Ravi. Since that day rumours of gold coins and other treasures have become part of the folklore of Lahore.

But Nadir Shah's brutality saw the emergence of a Punjabi nationalism that was to reach its zenith in the person of Maharajah Ranjit Singh. For a full 40 years he ruled from his court in Lahore, meshing together a people who were to form the finest army in Asia. All this happened because the reply to brutality was initially with brutality, followed by years of peace and justice, and all this happened because in the end the wise Maharajah realized that only a secular approach could work. In a way, the same was true of the British who arrived with untold brutality and killing, but followed it with a just and secular dispensation.

It would be of interest to compare Nadir Shah, Maharajah Ranjit Singh and the Raj. All started off with extreme brutality. Like all looters who came from Kabul, the interest was solely to steal, and for that they had to murder and rape. There is a saying in the NWFP that Afghanistan is poor today because for over 200 years it has not been able to invade and loot the sub-continent.

Nadir Shah's pillage gave birth to Ranjit Singh. They devised tactics to loot the looters, becoming rich enough to form an army to conquer Lahore. In the end as they belonged to the land, they realized that only justice could prolong their rule. By the time the British arrived, they did exactly what the Sikhs did. In the end, moderation and justice prevailed.

The fight to be free is forever

On September 5, 1945, just three days after the Soviet army entered Berlin with Hitler committing suicide, a spirited Punjabi in full German army uniform was arrested and disarmed just 15 kilometres from Hitler's bunker. As the Russians arrested him, he shouted "Death to the British. We will free India". It seemed that the terrible fate that confronted his defeated army had not dampened his spirits.

The origins of this unbending young 'Nazi' fighter lay in the bloody massacre of Jallianwala Bagh in Amritsar. Troops under Brig-Gen REH Dyer opened fire on innocent Sikhs and Muslims on April 13, 1919, before the start of the annual Baisakhi mela. The British-led troops killed 379 persons and wounded over 2,000 in a massacre that was to change the course of Indian history. Among those killed was a Syed Khair Shah. The Syed family of Amritsar grieved over their loss and pledged to sacrifice their lives fighting the British and for the freedom of their country. The grandson of Syed Khair was born five years after the massacre, and grew up hating the British. Syed Wazir Ali Shah studied hard to matriculate and set off for Aligarh in 1939 to join the university, "for that was the only hope Muslims had of higher education".

In Delhi, a relative working in the GHQ Delhi put his name up for an Austrian Red Cross posting as an observer in a prisoner of war camp. The plucky young man impressed the Austrians and soon he was on a ship to Italy, from where he reached Austria by train. For one whole year he spent his days making sure the prisoners were looked after well. But then the cry for freedom that had its roots deep within him came through and he, along with a small group of Muslim, Sikh and Hindu Indians decided to join the German war effort. It was a decision taken for the land to which he belonged. The Nazis had managed to assemble a team of Indians to start a propaganda war against the British. The strategy suited Syed Wazir Ali and his great desire for winning freedom for India.

In 1941 Wazir Ali started off his propaganda war, and moved with the German Army wherever it went. He saw the war from the other side, working and fighting in Italy, France, Russia, Holland, Poland and all the other countries where the Second World War took place. They specialized in propaganda, and he said it straight and simple. With Syed Wazir Ali was a Sikh by the name of Partap Singh from Lahore. "He was an exciting person. In the middle of a broadcast he would often start swearing in choice Punjabi and had to be restrained". So deep was the hatred for the British that the Germans made sure the Indian Group moved with the regular and SS units whenever they faced a British unit, especially if Indian soldiers were in it. The idea was to demoralize them to surrender and fight against the British. And though history tells us that the Germans failed miserably in this effort, these freedom fighters continued to try to make sure the Germans won so that India could be free. Today this logic might seem warped, but to men like Syed Wazir Ali, "this was the path of every Indian freedom fighter".

After his arrest Wazir Ali was shifted to a prisoner of war camp in Poland. The orders of the Soviet Army were to shoot all such prisoners. It was only through sheer good luck that Shahji survived and in 1948 he was handed over to the American army. The Americans kept him for a year and after making sure of his story and his record in the German propaganda machinery and in the Austrian Red Cross, handed him over to the British.

"The British were delighted to get their hands on me and started proceedings to execute me for my role in the war, however small it might have been in the total effort". But then India was free by then and Pandit Nehru wanted the return of these "most respected of freedom fighters". The .frustrated British had no choice but to put them on a ship from their prisoner of war camp in Italy for them to land in Bombay in November, 1951.

"On the docks the bands were playing and the Hindu and Sikh freedom fighters were garlanded. Nehru was there to receive them. We had opted for Pakistan and we were not allowed to get off". So only two remaining Muslim freedom fighters, Syed Wazir Ali Shah of Lahore and Mr Ikram of Campbellpur (now Attock) had to return to Sicily and the prisoner of war camp. A year later they were put on a ship to Pakistan. What happened after that is something we should all be ashamed of ... for it makes grim reading.

At Karachi port in 1952 both Syed Wazir and Ikram were immediately arrested. They were taken to Multan Jail and put on trial for treason, punishable with death. Such was the fate that awaited our two honourable freedom fighters in the land that they fought so much to free. "I was treated as a criminal in my own land for fighting to free it" says Syed Wazir Ali. In the end he stood up and in defiance of the court procedure said: "I am a freedom fighter and I am not afraid of people like you against whom I fought. You cannot hang me so do whatever you want and do it quickly". Even today though age has made him slightly weaker, his spirit remains the same. "The Pakistan army decided to release me, but banned me from all government service", he says without any bitterness.

And so to Lahore came Syed Wazir Ali Shah in 1954, in utter ruin and in rage. No one was there to help him. "Poverty and rage was all that I had, but in true German spirit I decided to fight a battle for survival, with utter honesty and as a hard worker". He set up a small corner battery shop and named it Berlin, the place from where the Allied armies had captured him. His grandfather had been martyred, as had other members of his family at Jallianwala Bagh. All through the war he battled for the freedom of his land ... and when his own land disgraced him he did not give up and fought his own battle for survival. He did very well for himself and is sad that his country has forgotten the virtues of honesty and fair play. "This is a beautiful land, and we can still do wonders in a little time if we honestly try". But then who listens to men like Syed Wazir Ali anymore, or even bothers to pay respects to a man whose whole life has been dedicated to paying in blood to live on the soil of his ancestors. He is the last of a very special breed, and he still does not bend with the wind.

The mango tree of Gool Bharucha

In the year 1913, a young Parsi doctor, after graduating from a medical school in Bombay, came and settled in Said Mitha Bazaar inside the walled city of Lahore. It was the beginning of the legendary Dr. Edulji Pestonji Bharucha, a name every Lahori soon learnt to trust and respect.

The Parsi community of Lahore has seen its fair share of discrimination over the centuries. At the height of the Arab invasion of Iran 1,200 years ago, the original Zoroastrians, who refused to give up their ancient religion, left by land and sea, all heading eastwards. They came in traditional junks, crossed the Sea of Hurmuz off southern Iran and landed at a place called Sanjan, about 145 kilometers north of Mumbai. They also fled to the mountains in Afghanistan, eventually heading for Balochistan and the Punjab. Everywhere they went, the Hindu Rajput rulers welcomed them and gave them refuge.

According to the traditional account recorded in the *Kisseh-i-Sanjan,* after the Arab conquest of Iran, the ancestors of the present Indian Parsis took refuge in the mountainous districts of Kohistan in Khurasan for about 100 years. They then moved to the port city of Hurmuz in Iran, finally landing on the island of Div in southern Saurashtra. With the growing threat of an Arab invasion, the Parsis left Div and seeded on the west coast of India, near the place later to be known as Sanjan. It is here that the story of the sub-continent's Parsis begins.

The local Hindu Rajput Raja, known as Jadi Rana, permitted the Parsis to settle in his kingdom. Tradition states that the Parsis were sent a gift of milk by the Rajput ruler. The Parsis returned the milk after adding sugar, sending the message that they promised to sweeten the lives of everyone in the sub-continent. To this promise, every Parsi has always adhered. In Lahore, Raja Jaipal, the Rajput ruler, also welcomed them and allowed them to set up their 'Fire Temple'. Legend has it that it was near the Said Mitha Bazaar. It was here that Dr. Bharucha came, and he and his community have since sweetened the lives of Lahore with their honesty and hard work.

Dr Bharucha moved on to Anarkali Bazaar, and then to McLeod Road. Everywhere he went, his practice followed him. His sweet nature was legendary. The promise to Jadi Rana was still there. By the time Pakistan came about, there were a total of 56 Parsi families in Lahore with a population of 312. Today, there are only 25 of those families left with a population of only 45. Recently, the entire Pestonji family of seven migrated to Australia. Of the 25 families, there are 10 who are single persons, all unable to find an appropriate match. So basically just 15 families remain, and almost all their young children have migrated to the US and Australia.

Almost 80 per cent of the remaining 45 Parsis are over 60 years of age. The oldest is Mrs Maneckbai Framroze Cooper, who will be 100 in May. She is probably the oldest living Lahori. Her daughter Perin Boga is well-known in educational and drama circles. In business circles, where the Parsis once ruled supreme, the Kandawalas and the other families have all left. The tradition set by Dr Bharucha seems to be fizzling out. The oldest modern retail shop in Lahore was the Dinshaw Jamshedji store on Sarwar Road. Today, his grandson, Sarosh Challa, has sold most of the property and has restricted himself to running a small creamery, while his wife Aban makes the finest traditional cheese in Lahore, a far cry from the days of the Raj.

But the Bharucha family has managed to organize the Parsis, pushing them to get educated. Rustam Bharucha, a 'pucca' Lahori, went on to do his studies in automobile engineering in England, working with Leyland. Even he today, seems to be resigned to seeing his community in total disarray. But his wife, Gool Rustam Bharucha, is a fighter. She was born in Quetta where her father worked for the office of the controller of military accounts. When she was eight, her father was transferred to Amritsar. As his replacement was a day late, his departure on May 31, 1935, was delayed by a day. On that day a massive earthquake struck Quetta. Gool's entire family, her two parents and three sisters, were killed in the tragic events of the day. Little Gool was alone and landed up in Karachi.

She led a hard life, but managed to do well for herself. Gool wanted to marry Rustam Bharucha, and had to wait 13 years before the parents agreed. Three days before she married in 1965, she planted a mango tree, as per Parsi tradition, in a pot in Karachi. That pot she brought to Lahore and eventually when her husband bought a house in the newly-emerging Gulberg, she planted it in her lawn. A few years ago she sold her house to the Mother Teresa Trust, but only with the promise that the mango tree would never be cut down. The 'saintly' purchaser promised never to cut that magnificent mango tree. Today, the mango tree of Gool Bharucha is probably the finest and biggest in Lahore. It gives fruit every second year, and very sweet mangoes they are.

The 45 remaining Parsis of Lahore are destined to dwindle further. The environment we offer them is not attractive enough to bring their finest sons and daughters back. The tradition of Dr Bharucha of Said Mitha Bazaar will last as long as the mango tree of Gool Bharucha stands. What will happen then, I will not venture to suggest. But the thought makes me sad, very *sad.*

The Shahalami Plot

Lahore has, over the centuries, seen several religions being politically and socially dominant; Hinduism, Buddhism, Islam, Sikhism and Christianity. Conversion, therefore, has been a permanent topic in sub-continental politics. But the weirdest event in this regard happened to the Sikhs and it happened in Lahore.

Dr. Ambedkar

If you walk along the Shahalami Gate road leading to Rang Mahal, just after the Agha Khan clinic to the left, a narrow road climbs sharply and then twists into two lanes. To the left is a huge mansion. The year was 1935, Dr Ambedkar, the unchallenged leader of the 60 million untouchables in India, then almost over 50 per cent of the population of undivided India, was the guest of Sardar Baldev Singh, the Sikh leader. Along with him was the famous Master Tara Singh, the man who in March 1947 sparked off communal riots all over the Punjab. But in all fairness to the man, he represented Sikh interests, and knew full well that in the Hindu-Muslim grind for power, the Sikhs were being ignored. So he had to take a position that suited the Sikh community, and that he did, irrespective of whether we now agree with him or not, for now we have history to assist us.

The people of the Walled City have never been the fanatical sort. The arrival of Dr Ambedkar was reported in the local newspapers and for two days the leader of the 'untouchables' and the Sikh elite were in conference in that house in the Shahalami area. Soon rumours of all sorts began to float in the streets and lanes of the Walled City, which was a Muslim-majority area. One version is that the Muslim League leader of the Walled City, Dr. Amiruddin of Barud Khana, set about planting spies in and around that huge haveli. But nothing could be eked out of anyone. Even the British spy network had failed to pick up any clue.

Then Dr. Ambedkar left Lahore, and there was a long silence. After two weeks he expressed the desire that all 'untouchables' of India join Sikhism to rid themselves of the thousands of years of serfdom imposed by the caste-system. Hindu leaders like Dr Munje, president of the Hindu Mahasabha, totally agreed to this plan. The Shahalami meeting promised to change the very shape of sub-continental politics.

Mahatma Gandhi was the man most shaken. But in all fairness, so were the Muslims, who were now able to cope with the ways of their Hindu adversaries. Copies of Dr Ambedkar's correspondence with various Hindu leaders were brought to his notice. When Gandhi realized that the matter was close to finality, the case of the 'Shahalami Plot' as it was known, he released the whole correspondence in his newspaper titled *Young India*. This he did without the permission of any one of them. He 'warned' the untouchables that "joining Sikhism like this would permanently condemn them to apostasy from Hinduism".

After the Gandhi provocation and the announcement of the 'Shahalami Plot', Dr Ambedkar opened a direct dialogue with Sikh leaders to achieve his purpose, and the news spread throughout the country that the untouchables were on the verge of joining Sikhism. This is the time when the foundation of Khalsa College, Bombay, was laid so that it could function as the centre for the education of the 'untouchables' of southern India. At the time, even the Maharaja of Patiala, Sardar Bhupinder Singh, offered to marry his sister in the family of Dr Ambedkar to lend sense of pride to the untouchables joining Sikhism.

But then a joint Hindu and Muslim effort hatched another plot, and many people feel that that plot was hatched in the famous haveli of Mian Amiruddin at the Barud Khana. The Hindu merchants of the Walled City allegedly offered to finance a campaign to stop this effort. Mian Amiruddin later refuted that he had any thing to do with this 'Barood Khana Plot', but it seemed that the entire future of religious harmony was being played out in the Walled City.

It is said that the religious prayer leaders of Muslims and the Hindus, the maulvis and the pandits, were asked to keep hammering away from their pulpits that the Sikhs had decided to become 'churas' — sweepers, and that the 'churas' from south India were to take over the Sikh temples. So strong was the rumour that the Sikhs started demonstrating against this move. Even Sardar Baldev Singh and Master Tara Singh started openly saying that 'churas' would not be allowed inside their gurdwaras. Dr Ambedkar returned to Lahore and to the house in Shahalami to discuss the issue. He then went to the holy Sikh temple in Amritsar, where the Sikh religious leaders refused to let him in. That final act in Amritsar sealed the fate of the 'Shahalami Plot'. Such acute differences cropped up between Dr Ambedkar and Akali leaders that Dr Ambedkar and his followers became disenchanted with Sikhism and later joined Buddhism, a move that was to sharpen the Hindu-Muslim divide.

Sardar Indar Singh Karwal, advocate of the Chandigarh High Court, narrated this story in his book. He had sought to know the real reasons for this mishap from his neighbour in Lahore, Sardar Harbans Singh Jhalla, MA, LLB, and a High Court judge, who was then an eminent Akali leader. "You don't understand these things. Should we have handed over Darbar Sahib to the Churas by accepting 60 million untouchables into Sikhism?" Thus 69 million 'Ranghretas, Guru ka Betas' coming to the door of Sikhism were driven away unceremoniously.

One account also blamed Master Tara Singh for

trying to keep the leadership of the Sikhs in his hands. He was a fearless man from Rawalpindi, and when in March, 1947, he brandished his sword outside the Punjab Assembly building in Lahore, he set off Muslim-Hindu riots with his shouting of "Pakistan Murdabad". Lahore was always a peaceful city. But after that fateful day began the greatest exodus in the history of mankind, and Lahore was to be the centre of millions of untold stories — stories we are still afraid to tell.

When all was not quiet on the Western Front

The first time was in 1972 as a student while hitchhiking from Lahore to London. The second time was 25 years later with a Dutch friend. The third time was on Wednesday, August 7. There I was, a Lahori, visiting the dead of his ancient city. Each time it is an exceptionally moving moment, one that brings tears to my eyes.

Over 64,000 of them lie buried in Ypres in Belgium. The men of the Lahore Division of the Indian Army ... the cannon fodder of the British Empire. They are still honoured on the walls of Menin Gate, that magnificent monument built in memory of all those who died on the killing fields of Flanders and the Somme and at Ypres. The main memorial to the Lahore and Meerut Infantry Divisions of the Indian Army on the Western Front was designed by Sir Herbert Baker, and was opened in 1927 at Neuve Chapelle, the site of the bloodiest and most famous action in the opening years of the First World War.

The long casualty list consists almost entirely of names from the sub-continent, a vast majority of them belonging to the Lahore division. Sepoy Muhammad Ahmad of Mochi Gate in a letter to his parents writes: "This is not war, it is the ending of the world." His letter today is framed and hung up in the museum just outside Ypres. His name is also listed on Menin Gate. He lies somewhere in Ypres, for he never came home, like most of those 161,000 men, many of the Lahore and Meerut infantry divisions. The souls and spirits of almost five per cent of the youth of Lahore in those days lie in the battlefields of Ypres and Somme and Flanders.

Lahore Division brought to the Flanders front in London doubledecker buses, Oct.1914.

Very few of us really know just how much the city of Lahore and its suburbs suffered because of the First World War. Its youth actually disappeared. British military censorship managed to keep things in check, but the letters that did come through managed to contribute to the massive disturbances that took place in the Punjab in 1919. The 'patwaris' (revenue officials) of Lahore were given the task of finding strong young men in their 'patwar' and forcing them to join the army, or else lose their jobs. And so in August 1914 the first groups began to arrive in France and Belgium. Within a year over 161,000 Lahore and Meerut troops had arrived and the Lahoris were put into action at Ypres.

The month was October 1914 and the Germans attacked. The Lahoris defended and having made an exceptionally fierce defence were immediately asked to attack the German trenches. On that cold, wet, October evening, the attack began. The machine-guns rattled away and the Lahoris just went on and on, and they fell as they ran. From one battalion, the 47th Sikhs, of the 764 who began the attack, only 385 were left. The fighting shocked the Lahoris. It was ferocious. The end of the world was coming.

After four months of fierce fighting they were rested. The Lahore division was allowed to write home, but only if the company clerk wrote the letters. Those letters today offer glimpses of life on the Western Front. They very soon realized that their letters were censored, and so they used codes. One Lahore soldier wrote home: "the black pepper is very pungent, but only very few remain." One soldier belonging to Kot Abdul Malik wrote home in despair: "I am now even afraid of a glowworm that once I loved to catch in the village."

After being so rested they were again thrown into battle early in 1915. It was during this year that the fiercest and bloodiest trench battles took place. The Lahore and Meerut divisions provided half of the entire British and Allied forces that attacked in the famous Battle of Neuve Chapelle in March. The Lahore division was then withdrawn after achieving its objectives and thrown in for the second counter-attack in the Second Battle of Ypres in Belgium. They broke through with heavy losses but kept fighting till September. There just did not seem an end in sight of this, the bloodiest of wars. The Lahoris were withdrawn, rested for a few days and then thrown into the famous Battle of Loos in September 1915.

By this time the Meerut boys' morale had begun to flag and they were withdrawn, rested and sent to Mesopotamia. The war in the Middle East was hotting up and the British Empire needed them there. On the Somme the fighting was fierce and casualties high. The Lahoris were moved there. One Lahore division man wrote home in September, 1916, to his mother: "It is impossible that I return home alive. But do not grieve, for I shall die arms in hand, wearing a warrior's clothes. This will be a most happy death." The letter was never posted and now hangs in the museum next to the preserved trenches in the killing fields of Belgium.

Two Indian cavalry divisions, including the Lahore division, remained in Europe till March 1918. Once victory was in sight and blood had been let, the English moved in for the final kill. Five long years they had fought. And as I moved from letter to letter, trench to trench, monument to monument, I could feel the souls of city folk, my ancestors, reaching out, as if to ask how the city was doing. The streets and lanes and the mohallahs, seem to reach out to them. Our unsung boys, from the streets and mohallahs of Lahore, from the villages that dot our countryside around our city, all lie at Ypres. For them the end of the world had come.

But this was not enough. The Lahoris were moved in March 1918 to Palestine to take part in the offensive against the Turks ... but that is another story. But being a Lahori means doing something special. While in France and Belgium the soldiers met many a woman, and they have been described in various ways. But in ending this tale of blood and tears, it makes sense that the Lahori sense of humour is also described. Sepoy Karam Dad of Bhatti Gate married a beautiful French woman in 1917. The news dismayed his family. He wrote a stinging letter home, in which he explained: "What am I to do when the king of England has personally ordered me to marry the woman." That letter also hangs in the museum at Ypres. I wonder what became of Karam Dad?

The rebels of Mozang

When Babar conquered Kabul and set into motion his dream of conquering the Indian sub-continent, he faced a major rebellion from within his own Mughal tribe, and this was the tribe from the village of Mozang in Turkministan. The people of Mozang have never been pushovers, be it the Mozangis of Turkmenistan, or of Kabul or even of Lahore. They were related to a Cossack streak, and they prided themselves on their bravery. In my youth when we lived on Masson Road, just behind the Sir Ganga Ram Hospital in Lahore, bands of Mozangis passed through our Lovers' Lane, and we baited them to a fight and what a fight it used to be bats, hockey sticks and bricks, everything worked, and every time the Mozangis managed to get to their destination, Lawrence Gardens. We used to stop them because they used to jump over our house wall as a shortcut, and unfortunate was the person who tried to stop them. Years later when I happened to meet my professor of economics, Shoaib Hashmi, a diehard Mozangi, I truly understood what being a Mozangi meant.

There is a marked difference between a Lahori belonging to the Walled City, and that depends on which gate, or area you belong to, and a Mozangi. The former is a seeded confident lot, inclined to be a bit clannish and proud of his turf. The latter is an independent sort, prone to some adventurism. But opinions are opinions and no two people are the same. But the story of Mozang makes for the same blend of adventurism that marks the people who have lived and seen the rise and fall of Mauza Mozang.

It all started after Babar defeated the tribe of Mozang that had been critical of his conquering Kabul. Once the conquest had been completed, the Mozangis, instead of settling inside the old city of Kabul, set up their own village and called it Mozang. Ironically, that Mozang is now part of Kabul city. The Mozangis felt that they had been shortchanged by Babar and decided to challenge his authority. It was all over in one day as the new young emperor preempted any move the Cossacks of Mozang had in mind. Overnight the entire village fled towards India. Leading the band was a scholar of sorts, Pir Aziz, and he reached Lahore and set up camp outside Lahore. This was the beginning of Mauza Mozang.

Initially, it was an entirely Mughal community, but very soon the locals also began to dwell there as the Mughals were more organized. When Babar invaded Lahore, he first attacked the nearby Langar Khan, a Balochi village. So Mozang became a mix of Mughals and Balochis. It is said that Babar spared Mauza Mozang because he had met the founder of the Sikh faith, Guru Nanak, whom he had seen in a dream. The sage asked him to spare the 'mauza' and move on to greater glory. One account says that Babar had not forgotten the rebellion of the Mozangis, but strangely he spared them, and he benefited from the decision.

So Mauza Mozang developed into a growing village, and then a small town, but was sharply divided among the Mughals and Balochis. But this was not the end of the matter. The Mughal Empire saw the Mauza being invaded a number of times, especially during the reign of Shah Jahan and Aurangzeb, who hated the place because this was where the Sixth Guru, Hargobind Singh, was born. By this time over half the houses of Mauza Mozang lay empty and people considered it a dangerous place. It was during this period that the Arains of Lahore moved into Mozang. With time they became the dominant community, though the Mughals still maintained their hold over all things official. Thus a three-way division of communities came about in Mozang, the Arains, the Baloch and the original Mozangi Mughals. But no matter which community they belonged to, the people of this village were always a defiant lot. When Shah Jahan decided to butcher every Sikh in sight, it was the Sixth Sikh Guru from Mozang who decided to convert the peace loving Sikh community into a militant one. This was contrary to another Mozangi, the Fourth Sikh Guru, Ram Das, who completely belonged to Mozang, but who decided to settle inside the Walled City in a house in Bazaar Chuna Mandi. Ram Das was a completely docile pacifist and stuck to his own, even though he was also considerably harassed for his beliefs.

With the coming of the British the outer 'Chungi' toll station was established just outside Mozang for it was then officially made part of Lahore. Today, Mozang Chungi is a part of our history, though the toll station has moved almost 15 kilometres up the road towards Ferozepur. And though a typical Mozangi is an eccentric sort, they have produced some very fine minds; it might come as a surprise that Baba Farid, the Punjabi sage and the poet, was a Mozangi. The religious sage Abdullah Shah Qadri was a Mozangi, and his madrassah is the point where the Miani Sahib Graveyard began and is today Lahore's main graveyard. With time Mozang has become a central part of Lahore. Its streets and lanes hold intriguing stories of the days gone by.

Just for the record, we must not forget that 'mutton karahi', now a staple part of menus in every feast, started off in Mozang. It was a Balochi tradition, not a Lahori one, and it all started off in the Bhatti Tikka Shop, next to where my professor Shoaib Hashmi once lived. Prof Hashmi might now live in greener pastures, but at heart he is a Mozangi ... and no push over let me assure you.

The butchering of the 26th Native at Mian Mir

Two events about our history have always intrigued me since I was a child. First, how did a few thousand British manage to contain the entire sub-continent in the 1857 Mutiny? Second, what was the role of Lahore in the uprising?

When the mutiny broke out in Meerut on May 10, 1857, the army of the East India Company in the Punjab numbered approximately 60,000, of which only 10,000 were British soldiers. The Punjab had been annexed just 11 years earlier and top priority was given to raising the Guide Corps, which was raised in Lahore in 1846 by Henry Lawrence. The Guides constitute an elite regiment in the Pakistan Army today. The Guide's constituted the toughest brigands and even professional hunters were recruited. The idea was to raise a ruthless force that would quell the toughest opposition that India could throw at the British.

A very strong internal security apparatus was set up, the remains of which even today exist in the Punjab. The Punjab Police was trained to be ruthless, with its *khufia* branch coupled with the revived Mughal *chowkidara* system managing to bring about complete peace to a land that had seen ten years of total wildness after the death of Maharajah Ranjit Singh. Along with these reforms, the digging of canals, the setting up of seven commissions or divisions coupled with a five-tier system of administration starting from the tehsildar upwards to the divisional commissioner. Wide powers were given to the officers and special care taken to dispose off cases within the shortest possible time. The maxim that was followed was "rule by strength rather than precision". Lawrence got the very best and honest officers for the Punjab and invested heavily in improving its agriculture. Within ten years the "country of the Punjab" was a completely different place. In these ten years all arms were seized and destroyed. The Khalsa Army was no more and prosperity returned. To their surprise, the British found that Ranjit Singh had put into place an excellent education system. The British built on it with central model schools and colleges of excellence.

In this setting, the 1857 Mutiny took place. There was a natural mistrust between the Punjabis and the Hindustanis or *purabis* as they were called. The Punjabis blamed them for the fall of their country to the British, and to this day the mistrust remains. The British used this mistrust to devastating effect. A bumper crop and a very satisfied peasantry meant that the Punjabis as a whole did not see why they should join the mutiny. But most of the *purabis* did, as did a number of Punjabis.

Mystery fires broke out in the Lahore cantonment of Mian Mir. In the area where we have the Saddar Bazaar, revolt broke out. John Lawrence, the brother of Henry, decided that Lahore must be made an example of, and he set about trying to disarm the Punjabis.

The men of the 26th Native Infantry Regiment stationed at the Saddar area attacked their officers, who lived in the old Officers Colony of the Lahore Cantonment near Dharampura. Lawrence moved to disarm them. The regiment headed towards the river Ravi just half a mile to the north. A posse of the Punjab police chased them and in a terrible bloodbath 150 soldiers of the 26th Native were butchered. But the main body of the regiment moved towards a small island in the river, the one you can see from the old Ravi Bridge even today. Towards this the deputy commissioner F. Cooper, moved with his constables and hunted down another fifty, all of whom were shot dead after they had surrendered. On seeing the slaughter the remaining swam back to Lahore city, where the remaining 280 soldiers were all arrested and locked up in the Ajnala village police station.

Cooper wanted to make an example of these men and he invited the people of Lahore to witness the slaughter of the 'mutineers'. He brought out batches of ten men each and butchered them in broad daylight before a shocked audience. After a total of 237 men had been publicly butchered, the remaining 45 were locked up in one cell without any windows and no air to breathe. All the inmates died of suffocation. This case was worse than the 'Black Hole of Calcutta' story, but has never seen the light of day. Their bodies were brought out the next day, tied in front of cannons near the Lahore Fort and they were blown to pieces.

Subsequently, another 42 were captured and all of them were blown up alive from cannons placed outside the walls of the walled city. Thus the 26th Native Infantry was all butchered in the name of 'justice'. This incident spread terror in the Punjab, a terror that stood the British in good stead during the terrifying days of the 1857 Mutiny.

The resultant loyalty of the Punjabis, scared into submission, especially of the princes and rich zamindars, played a decisive role in saving the Punjab and the rest of India for the British. Sikh soldiers played a major role in defending almost every centre of British establishment. These very Sikh soldiers led the assault on Delhi, and it was Hodson and his Sikh horsemen from Lahore who arrested Bahadur Shah Zafar, his wife and sons. The Sikhs were amply rewarded for their services with lands and cash. From the irregular soldiers was also raised the Punjab Irregular Force, which later was to become famous as the Piffers.

Backed by these excellent Punjabi soldiers, and led by strategists who decided not to allow the mutineers to harass them, but rather fight pitched battles or defend themselves in fortified places, the British managed to destroy an essentially leaderless sub-continent. The classic Punjabi or Maratha harassment tactics were never used, providing the foreigner with an advantage they exploited to the fullest. In Delhi alone 600,000 soldiers were cramped into the small space of old Delhi. The Punjabi-British gunners contained them and then finished them off ruthlessly. That was the end of the 'Mutiny', and 100 years of relative peace returned to the sub-continent.

There are no signs put up for the men of the 26th Native Infantry of Lahore. However, just opposite of Corps Commanders House on The Mall is a magnificent signpost of the regiments that fought all over the world, and in the 1857 Mutiny, and who were posted in Lahore and served the British. That one signpost has history written all over it. Probably in the days to come, we might remember all those butchered for siding with their motherland. But that day seems still a long way away.

'Lahore Lahore Aye, Maaut Maaut Aye'

They belonged to different mohallahs of the old walled city of Lahore. In one fateful day, on the Third of September, 1879, the city lost 41 sons out of 69 killed. Their great grand children, now old men in their eighties, remember the respect they once commanded. They had a nameplate outside Mohallah Qassaban, inside Delhi Gate, that was removed in the 1920s after Jallianwala. They were the cannon fodder of the British Empire, unsung, forgotten, the ones who never came back.

In the old city they sing a couplet that goes: "Sarkar kay deewanay, jissay Kabul mein na mannay". This couplet I had heard a number of times in my youth, and recently on one of my walks through the old city, I happened to share a cup of tea with old Baba Rehmat, who lives in Tehsil Bazaar, near the old mosque. I often use him as a sounding board for old stories, and every time he comes up with a unique explanation.

When I asked him about the couplet, he referred to a massacre of the 'Lahore regiment' as he put it, in Kabul, 20 years after the 1857 war of independence. He calls it the 'wadah ghaddar'. "The mughals had become eunuchs, what else did you expect", he said scornfully. I researched the incident, met the great grand children of four Lahori soldiers, and the story makes remarkable reading, for we have lost just so much without learning anything from our losses. The decline continues.

The story of the 41 soldiers belonging to the old walled city out of the 69 Indians who never returned from Kabul in 1879 was told for years. They belonged to the 21 Guides Cavalry and 48 Guides Infantry, which were elite regiments of the Indian Army. The 41 belonged to four basic mohallahs, 11 of them from Mohallah Qassaban inside Delhi Gate, nine from Chohatta Rajah Dina Nath in Delhi Gate (now renamed Chohatta Qazi Allah Dad), and 15 from Chuna Mandi Bazaar near the Masti Gate end, and six from Kucha Chabbaksawaran.

All these mohallahs had in the past produced soldiers for the Mughal and Sikh armies, and had rich martial tradition. Even today some of the finest officers of the Pakistan Army, Navy and Air Force belong to the old walled city; they have that special guile, educated and street smart.

First a bit about the fight, then about the actual soldiers, and lastly about what faded memories still exist in the city's winding lanes. The British Residency was in the Bala Hissar in Kabul. In May, 1879, a Treaty was signed between the British and Amir of Afghanistan, Yakub Khan. Under the terms of the Treaty a British Mission was to be established in Kabul. Their safety was guaranteed by the Treaty and the word of the Amir. The Residency was set up in July 1879, and a small detachment of cavalry and infantry belonging to the 21 Guides Cavalry and 48 Guides Infantry, elite regiments belonging to Lahore, were sent as a security measure.

On 3rd September 1879, without warning, Afghan soldiers attacked the Residency and were joined by almost the entire civilian population of Kabul. Urgent messages were sent to the Amir, claiming protection. The messages were ignored. It was to be a fight to the end.

The attackers promised amnesty, which none of the staff in the Residency believed. The attack started even before the time given was over. The worst fears of the Lahori soldiers were proven right. And so four British officers and 69 men from Lahore and its environs faced a raging attack by over 10,000 armed men.

The first to fall was the British Envoy, Major Sir Pierre Louis Napoleon Cavagnari, KCB, originally belonging to the 1st Bengal Fusiliers. Aged just 38, he was an experienced soldier and was serving as the Assistant-Commissioner in the Punjab, based in Lahore. With him was killed Surgeon Ambrose Kelly of the Indian Medical service.

After studying medicine and surgery in Dublin, in 1869 he was commissioned to the Bengal Medical Service and served in the Lushai expedition. He was posted to the 1st Punjab Infantry in 1872. He was working in Lahore when he was selected to join the Embassy to Kabul and was killed treating the wounded in the first wave of attacks.

As the Residency staff regrouped, they were led by the one remaining British officer, a 23-year old dashing soldier by the name of Lt. Walter Richard Pollock Hamilton, V.C., of the Guides Cavalry. At Fatehabad he led the Guides in a charge and was awarded the Victoria Cross. He was selected to command the 75 men of the Corps of Guides who accompanied the British Embassy to Kabul. He was killed defending the second wave of attack. With him dead, command was taken over by the Lahori soldiers.

The Afghans offered amnesty to the Muslim soldiers. The answer from the Lahori soldiers was the battle cry, "Ya

Ali Haider", and an even stranger one the Afghans had never heard, and it was "Lahore Lahore Aye, Maaut Maaut Aye". Regimental researchers were to note this unique battle cry, a cry that was only used again in the 1965 War with India by the Punjab regiment soldiers in the defence of Lahore.

So the third wave of attack started in which the last remaining British officer to be killed was a uniquely gifted 32-year old British 'political officer' by the name of William Jenkyns. Educated at Cambridge, in 1876 he was Interpreter and Secretary to the Embassy at Peshawar for the conference with the Amir of Afghanistan. In 1878 he was a Political Officer with the army in Afghanistan and spoke fluent Pushto. Thus all British officers were dead and the men from Lahore were left to face the final onslaught.

Afghan records tell us that they stood fighting to the last man. One account of the battle tells us that when their bullets had finished, they fixed their bayonets, gave their battle cries and faced the enemy. After 12 hours of fighting the few remaining men fixed bayonets and charged out to their deaths. Over 600 Afghan dead bore witness to the heroic resistance of this small force from Lahore. From this emerged the ballad in Punjabi: "Marrna aye tey dass lay kay marriay". Even today this myth of every Lahori soldier taking ten of the enemy is perpetuated in the regiments of Pakistan and India. Its roots are grouted firmly in the reality of the Kabul of 1879.

When on their own, the men were led by Jamadar Jewand Singh, who belonged to Mohallah Qassaban. He was assisted by Daffadar Hira Singh of Mozang. The cavalry sowars who charged in the final analysis were all from inside the old walled city, they being Gul Ahmad, Khair Ullah, Akbar Khan, Muhammad Akbar, Miroh Badshah, Ghulam Habib, Mahomed Amin, Mahomed Hassan, Amir Hyder, Pars Ram, Amar Singh, Wazir Singh, Ratan Singh, Harnam Singh, Deva Singh and Farrier Amir Ullah.

From the infantry were Jamadar Mehtab Singh, Havaldar Hussain, Naik Mehr Dil, Bugler Abdullah (of Tehsil

Bazaar and great grandfather of Baba Rehmat), Lance Naik Jangi. Among the sepoys were Sonu, Shibba, Sirsa and Tota all of Chuna Mandi. Then there were sepoys Roedad, Akbar Shah, Said Amir, Alam Shah, Mir Baz Khan (all from Kucha Chabbaksawaran), Hamzulla Waddah and Hamzulla Chootha, two brothers from Chohatta Rajah Dina Nath.

The list goes on and on. Last on the list is 3rd Class Hospital Assistant Rahman Bakhsh, who also worked in a Lahore hospital, and went to Kabul for the money and adventure. His great grandson, ironically, still lives inside Bhatti Gate and works in Mayo Hospital, Lahore. But then who remembers all these exceptionally brave soldiers who refused to surrender. Even the families of these martyrs now have little recollection, except for the stories they have heard. Probably in a few years even the songs and ballads will die out.

It matters not who the rulers were, for we have had foreign rulers for almost 1,000 years. The men who died belonged to our soil. In a way, even today, the rulers seem foreign to the poor. The least we can do is to erect a monument for the 'Unknown Soldiers' of our city and land, so we never forget all those, irrespective of time, place, belief and circumstances, who helped shape our history.

A historic 'hole in the wall'

The people of Lahore have a strange sense of humour. If you ever ask anyone living inside the Walled City as to how many gates the ancient city has, they will invariably say 12 and a 'mori', a hole. Now this is not essentially a Freudian way of looking at life, but like all good things there is a story to it.

Between the two main gates to the south, Bhatti Gate and Lahore Gate, there is the smaller Mori Darwaza. This is one of the older gates of the city and was among the original seven that existed when Lahore was hit by the pillaging hordes of Afghans under Mahmud of Ghazni almost 1,000 years ago. It has been a long time since he came, but he started off a tradition of loot, pillage and rape that has never stopped, save for brief intervals.

Mori Gate is soaked in history, for it served as the classic escape route for rulers on the run. But then it also served as a secret entry point for others. It was also the gateway through which the dead were taken for the last rites to the funeral pyres of the majority Hindu and Sikh population of the city. Outside once the river flowed, and nearby on the other side of the moat the dead were cremated. This gate has more history packed into it than any of the other 12 gates of the city. Yes, no pomp or glory, but certainly more mystery and genuine utility.

Almost 1,000 years ago the city walls, then made of huge mud blocks slightly baked and still muddy in colour, had just six gates and a 'mori' a hole of a gateway. According to one account, a man riding on a donkey had to dismount and barely walked through. A horseman had to make his mount manage through with bent knees with difficulty. It was, definitely, a hole that served as a passage for the under-privileged.

At this point, there are some divergent views about why such a small 'hole of a gate' was built in the first place. One view is that the Hindu upper class did not want the 'untouchables' to pass the same way that they did. So for them they built a 'mori' to pass through. Another view is that it was essentially meant for the dead to be taken out and cremated across the river that once flowed outside, though no solid reason for the dead taking this route has been put forward. The river outside soon became a moat. When the Ravi cut its way westwards, it remained just a stagnant pool of water, which then dried, was filled in by the British, who finally levelled it into a garden as part of a defence plan. After partition, the area was encroached upon and now the government just does not have the power to clear the place.

But the British while levelling out the spaces outside, also tore down the original Mori Gate and built a much larger gate, which as an official document says is "now large enough to ensure that a camel cart can pass through with ease instead of the five-foot six-inch hole in the wall." I remember my grandmother telling me that the gate was so small that people had to bend to get through. "The rulers made sure they bowed to them when entering," she once said. Gosh, the stories that people come up with, I remember telling her, and she was annoyed at the comment. But it was a lovely description now that one thinks of it.

Mori Gate shot to fame almost 1,000 years ago when Mahmud of Ghazni laid siege to the city. The ruler, Raja Jaspal, resisted for a number of days, and then decided to escape. He left through Mori Gate. But the Raja's flight did not mean that the people of Lahore took kindly to foreign invaders. They decided to fight on, and Mahmud was shocked at the fierce resistance that the people were putting up. His intelligence people informed him that Raja Jaspal had escaped through a small 'hole in the wall' and he stood outside to see the 'mori' for himself. One can imagine him standing just outside at the crossing of Urdu Bazaar and Circular Road. Then at night Mahmud and his men sneaked into the city after managing to break down the door of Mori Gate. This opened the way for the conquest of Lahore. For seven days and seven nights, as several accounts tell us, the crazed Afghans burnt, raped and looted the city till all its inhabitants either lay dead or fled into the forests to the east. Lahore lay empty and desolate for a good five years.

But that was not the end of Mori Gate. When Babar invaded the Punjab from the west, he also was resisted. In a way all invaders coming from the west had an easy ride on their way to Delhi. It seems the Pathans never resisted anyone, not even Alexander, who met resistance for the first time when he entered the Punjab at Bhera, another beautiful Punjabi town that is almost like a time capsule and needs immediate attention, as it decays and proclaims the end of a fantastic civilization.

At Lahore all invaders were resisted. Babar in a fit of rage decided to burn down Lahore, more out of his hatred of the brave Bhat Rajputs who lived inside Bhatti Gate. But even Babar's troops effected an entry into the city through guile from Mori Gate. The rape that followed emptied the city. From that point onwards every time Lahore was pillaged, the population fled and the city remained empty for years on end.

Many times was the city emptied by the crazed invaders, whose sole aim was, naturally, to pillage, and in the process rape and loot. That is why every time one passes in front of Mori Gate, one thinks of the untold suffering of the people that invaders inflicted, after passing into the city from this point, as also from others. But Mori Gate has a special place in history, one we seem to know so little about.

City Walls under Ranjit Singh

During Maharajah Ranjit Singh's rule the city of Lahore gained a lot. If one were to appreciate his lasting contribution, one would just have to take a look at the northern portion of the walled city and its citadel wall.

To appreciate the logic of the 'one-eyed Maharajah', one would have to understand that he operated in a very masterly and modern manner, especially given the times in which he lived. In Europe, Emperor Napoleon had just been defeated at Waterloo. In India, the British in the guise of the East India Company had managed to entrench themselves in Bengal and were moving westwards. It was only a matter of time that they would have to cross the path of the Punjab. As long as he lived, they were kept at bay. The Lion King, who built Sheranwala Gate and actually tied two live lions there, where the old Khizri Gate once stood, was always a step ahead.

Ranjit Singh

The first European 'armed settlement' in Lahore was French and not British. Several defeated French generals of Napoleon had managed to make it to the court of Lahore, and the Maharajah made judicious use of them. These French generals built Lahore's Civil Secretariat just next to the tomb of Anarkali. These French advisers studied the 'Punjab situation' and advised that not only the walls of the entire city be strengthened, but also that a moat be built around it. That is how the River Ravi was harnessed and drawbridges built.

There was a solid reason for this, a logic grouted in the military considerations. With the coming of the cannon, walls had become easy to knock down and it was essential that an additional barrier be made to prevent intrusions. A moat with a barrier wall was the ideal solution, and the Maharajah went for it in a big way. After 1847, the British filled in the moat and recreated the Mughal era gardens. It was, in fact, a subtle attempt to make sure the natives were not able to defend Lahore in case another 1857 occurred.

But the British did not knock down all the walls. They deliberately, as the Punjab Gazetteers testify, encouraged that those to the south be knocked down, and maintained those in the northern portion of the city. Probably a strategy devised to totally finish off all 'rebels' inside the city if such a situation ever occurred once the south was secured, for that is where the major portion of the British garrison was. It is a sad fact of history that the Punjabi feudal lords played a major role in assisting the British to quell the 'war of independence', and to this day, in both India and Pakistan, Punjabis are dominant in the armed forces of both countries.

The northern portion of the walled city, right from Masti Gate to Kashmiri Gate and on to Sheranwala Gate, formerly known as Khizri Gate, and up to Yakki Gate has a long stretch of well-maintained citadel walls. In those heady days of 1857, the British holed up all these gates and virtually cut off the northern portion of the city. They did so with the remaining ones, too, and only kept Taxali Gate, Bhatti Gate and Lohari Gate open. The idea was that if

Lahore was attacked, these gates could be easily barricaded and a defence of the city undertaken, just like they had done at Lucknow and other northern Indian cities. The composition of the walled city must also be kept in mind. If you were to portion off the Taxali to Lahori part of the city, with the outer point being the haveli of Dhayan Singh near the Barud Khana, the armoury, the Bhat Rajputs, or more simply the Bhattis, who were known as fiercely independent people, inhabited this entire portion. The British secretly feared them and it was this very portion that they left as the safety valve in case things got out of hand. History tells us that it never did, lack of leadership being the main reason the 1857 uprising failed. Some things never change in the sub-continent.

The Yakki Gate, just opposite the Do Moria Pul, was where all the horse and oxen driven carts had a stand. Its name is derived from the 'yakkas' that were used as standard vehicles in those days. From this point, vegetables and other essential goods reached the city, with specialised goods heading towards their own specialized markets inside the walled city. In a way, they still do like they have for over the last 1,000 years. Only the vegetable portion, with the coming of the railways, shifted westwards and today the Sabzi Mandi, vegetable market, is located just near the rail lines as it heads towards the Ravi.

In this portion of the northeastern part of the walled city, the lanes are the narrowest. The outer point being Mohallah Telian, where the mustard crop was brought in carts and oil extracted for cooking. A growing number of people, now more health conscious, are converting back to this cooking oil after the West discovered recently that it actually reduces cholesterol and has all the essential minerals to keep one fit and young. This portion is still the least visited portion of the old walled city, even though it retains, probably, the oldest building still around. It was also the only portion that Emperor Babar did not raze to the ground. In this portion also stands the Wazir Khan mosque, probably one of the most beautiful in the sub-continent.

Sadly, at the time of partition of the sub-continent, a lot of people roasted in fires set by religious zealots, and this sealed portion did not allow escape routes. The damage came from within the city itself. The existence of the Pakistan Cloth Market is testimony to how we have managed to rebuild the very best that we have destroyed ourselves. Just next door is the Purani Kotwali, the old police station of Mughal days, and the contrast is stark if anything could be called that in these days of fast and unmindful change.

Lahore without it celebrated walls

We call our city the 'ancient walled city of Lahore', yet very few of us know that the bricked walls of this city are really not all that ancient. Yet, they are old, very old, but the bricked walls of the city have a history of all their own.

It is important to know that the shape, size and walls of the old city have been changing all the time. In the old walled city there are three basic high points, in the topographical sense, they being the Lahore Fort, the Langa Mandi area, and the Mohalla Maulian, just to the north of Bazaar Mali. The fort is definitely the highest point, with the Langa Mandi mound being the highest point in the old walled city. This area is marked, on the southern side by the Gumti Bazaar merging into Said Mittha Bazaar. You will notice that these are semi-circular streets merging in to one another. The word 'gumti' itself means a curved street. Even the word 'langa' means a thoroughfare.

A study of the streets makes it clear that the Langa Mandi settlement developed, over time, in layers. This could be the very earliest settlement outside the Lahore Fort. The area being the highest point in the entire walled city, it is regarded by experts and archaeologists as the potential site for the very first settlement of Lahore outside the fort. The area to the west of Langa Mandi takes us to the mound we today call Tibbi, originally called a tibba, a mound. To the south is Tehsil Bazaar. To the north is the fort. This area of

Langa Mandi and Tibbi-Tehsil Bazaar can be said to be the original ancient Lahore.

The walls of the Lahore Fort were, till the time of Akbar the Great (1556-1605) built of mud. "The thickness of the mud walls of the Lahore" Fort are said to have been wide enough for horses to run on, as the historian Sujan Rai said writing in 1695. Like the fort there is some evidence to suggest that the mud walls curved to enclose the inhabited areas of Langa Mandi and Tibbi. If this explanation is accepted, and many do not accept this 'creeping theory' about ancient Lahore, then the very first walled city of Lahore was a mud-wall enclosed area just to the south of the fort with Tehsil-Gumti Bazaars being on its southern-most end, and curving in to meet in an oblong shaped citadel just to the south of the Lahore fort walls.

Over time we see more settlement outside this enclosure coming up. The earliest settlements can be traced to inside Lohari Gate, just along the road leading from the south to this enclosed settlement. We see that over time this settlement expanded to enclose the entire area starting from Lohari Gate, probably the oldest gate of the ancient walled city, enclosed on the west by a wall to the east of Bazaar Hakeeman and on the eastern side by a wall just to the west of the main Shahalami Bazaar leading right up to Rang Mahal and heading towards the fort.

This huge settlement is the original ancient walled city of Lahore, the one referred to by Ptolemy in AD 150 as the abode of Lavalke or Labokala. The popular legend of Raja Ram Chandra, of Sita, of Laho and Kasu, as first referred to by Sujan Rai, basically

Sita, Laho and Kasu

referred to popular folklore about the origins of the ancient temple of Lahu, now inside the Lahore Fort. It goes without saying that even 2,000 years ago, the mud-walled city of Lahore, and its mud-walled fort, was a major city (shehr) of the sub-continent, located as it was on the banks of the curving Iravah River, or the Ravi.

The numerous caravans that came to Lahore all camped outside the ancient mud walled city of Lahore on the eastern side. As a major trading city developed a huge settlement began to form just to the east of the mud walls. These traders complained of dacoits harassing them at night, as is mentioned in *Hudud-al-Alam* in AD 982. During this time period small settlements were coming up all along the eastern walls and also at a distance on the southern side. To the west the caravans coming from the west settled and stopped at what we today call Shahdara.

It was in such circumstances that we see the advent of Akbar the Great, who decided to enclose the city in a baked brickwall. This was to protect the business community in order that they carry on their business in peace. It also afforded enough space within the walls to allow for gardens and expansion. Akbar can truly be called the man who gave the old Lahore its present day shape.

The first brick walls to come up were those of the citadel. Built on the original mud walls, they maintained their thickness and were an example of the excellence of the builders of those days. Once the citadel walls were secured, Akbar went about building a larger and new Lahore, all enclosed within solid baked brickwalls. That enclosed Lahore is the existing old Lahore as we know it today. The new areas to the west of Bazaar Hakeeman were included, as were the huge areas to the East of the Shahalami Bazaar. The old mud walls were levelled, though traces of those walls still exist in both places.

The emperor had ten bastions built between every set of two gates. One account describes the measurements of the walls as being ten and a half meters in height and "broad enough to mount guns on the top". The western wall was later rebuilt in a straight line by Aurangzeb in pious intention of bringing the wall in alignment with his Badshahi Mosque.

It was in Akbar's days that the existing gates of the city came up. In every sense Akbar is the first of two great builders of Lahore's walls. It might sound ironical, but the year 2005, some records say the month was just before the monsoons set in, is the 400th centenary of the completion of the walled city of Lahore. Our complete and total ignorance of this unique event is understandable given that there are no longer any walls to celebrate. After Akbar and with diminishing Mughal power, the city was invaded time and again. The walls began to decay. At places there were huge gaps as brick thieves, who still abound, built their houses from stolen bricks, and the law of the land, which is still somewhat similar, just turning a blind eye to these happenings. When the Afghan invader Ahmad Shah Abdali attacked Lahore in 1751, the walls could not withstand the siege and Mir Mannu surrendered. Thereafter the walls began to disappear as disorder spread.

It was 200 years later that Maharajah Ranjit Singh took over in 1799 and immediately decided to rebuild the walls to their old glory. He further had a moat built around the walls, which was fed from the River Ravi. He also made sure that they were maintained and appointed Hukma Singh to further build a second wall on the outer perimeter of the moat. In a way he built Lahore's second wall, though it was not that high. This ensured that Lahore could withstand any siege or attack. Never before had the city been better fortified. On Hukma Singh's death, his son, Deva Singh, took over the maintenance of the walls and moat, which had draw bridges, the last of which was dismantled in 1935. When the British took over in 1849, they set about reviewing the future of the walls of Lahore. After the events of 1857, they reached a policy decision and between 1859 and 1864 they demolished the outer walls completely and reduced the height of the inner walls by half. The moat was filled with mud and a circular garden built on it. The southern wall was deliberately demolished, as was the southern wall of the Lahore Fort. The western gate of Taxali, probably the most beautiful gateway in the sub-continent, was completely demolished. The savagery of the 'enlightened' amazed the inhabitants. The exquisite walls of Lahore were destroyed.

In 1881 the dilapidated inner walls were also destroyed and bricks used to build the Lahore Cantonment in Mian Mir. Some things never change. This went on till 1947 when during the fierce riots the remaining walls of the old walled city of Lahore were destroyed. Today a few sections of the original wall remain, with brick thieves still busy removing the loot. Such is the lay of the land as we see it today.

Every time we write about the walled city of Lahore, we must understand that the walls that were are no longer there. The few yards that remain, though legally protected, have people building their own gates in it. Imagine. There is a need to declare the old city as a protected area. Till then we can just sit back and wait for another enlightened Akbar or a moderate Ranjit Singh to come our way

The old 'walls' within Lahore's wall

Just how did Lahore, in its physical shape, evolve over the ages? Where did the walls of the city originally run? How did major events and invasions, and economic and political happenings shape it as we know it today?

This is a subject of immense interest to people like me, and just over five years ago when one started writing this weekly column, my good friend Sheero *alias* Ghazanfar Iqbal pointed out that he had heard from his father's elders that Lahore had 'walls within walls'. A few weeks ago I reminded him of that peculiar remark, and we both decided to investigate this. Using all the books available to me on the subject, my starting point was a topographical survey carried out of the walled city by the Department of Archaeology in the initial days of the British Raj. The work was reproduced in a book produced, again with assistance from Her Majesty's government, which funded a research project on Lahore in 1959. The point was to find out the high grounds inside the walled city.

It is very clear that the highest point in the walled city is the Langa Mandi settlement. If you have ever been to this place, you will notice that it has a curved road running around it. We have to use the shape of the streets to determine the topographical lay of old settlements. The settlement of Langa Mandi is the clearest to determine, for in an exact semi-circle runs Gumti Bazar. The very name 'langa' means a safe path, for with the Ravi River flowing just nearby, only a mound was a safe path. The semi-circle runs to Said Mittha Bazaar to the west and to Suha Bazaar to the east. The word 'ghumti' means a curved road. Most experts believe that this was the earliest settlement of Lahore.

But then there is a competing site nearby called Mohallah Maulian, just north of Bazaar Mati, to the north-east of Lohari Gate. Judging by the lay of the streets, we form a triangular shaped configuration. At the lower side is Chowk Mati flowing into the Pappar Mandi Bazaar. To the east is Chhapa Gali and to the west is Sootar Mandi Bazaar, which curved with the high ground to form the northern tip joining Chhapa Gali. The shape of this settlement is very important to understand, for it provides us with the shape of old Lahore. This critical settlement stretches from the east of Bhatti Gate to the west of Shahalami Gate.

Here we must pick up some very old references and in the process try to superimpose on these two settlements the rough map of the course the River Ravi ran almost 500 years ago, at least in a rudimentary manner of the course as we know it from reliable references. In 1943, a booklet called *Lahore Qadeem* printed by the Oriental College, Lahore,

Ayaz kneeling before Sultan Mahmud of Ghaznavi

referred to an 1867 writing of Mufti Tajuddin, which states that the eastern portion of old Lahore before Mahmud invaded Lahore in 1014 was called 'Kacha Kot', and that it ran in a long shape to the high ground to the north.

A similar shaped Lahore was first mentioned in the works of Sharif ibn Muhammad Ibn Mansur in his classic *Adab al-harb wa l-shuja*, compiled in 1210-36 and now lying in the British Museum. The lead to this book is in Kanhiyya Lal's *Tarikh-e-Lahore* who picked it from Sarwar Lahori's 1877 publication on the Punjab. This is time for us to first return to the topography of Lahore and let us look at the larger picture, after having determined the two highest points. If we divide the height of the lay of the land in two feet portions, we notice that the mound curvatures all point to an almost 'kabab-like' shaped areas all stretching in a 'north to east' direction being compressed more so from the west, and to a lesser degree from the east. This shape is very important for we see a picture emerging, and very clearly that is, of a few very small settlements way back in antiquity, all perched on relatively safer areas surrounded by the river, with the rulers safe mound to the north (where the Lahore Fort today exists). That is why it is important to look at the shape of the river over time, and to how Lahore was described when the invader Mahmud first came.

We know that there are no traces of some important landmarks from the days of Malik Ayaz (1036-42), like the 'khanqah' of Sultan Shirazade. But then the outer limits of the city definitely make a semi-circle to the east of the present fort, to the east of Bazaar Hakeeman and to the west of Shahalami. It seems there was a 200 yard gap between the mud fort of the ruler and the mud walls to the east. This is the original old walled city of Lahore, as it evolved over time from smaller settlements to a consolidated rich market city (probably a town by modern standards) in the middle of the rich Punjab plains and on the bank of the smallest of the five rivers. It was, from an economical market point of view, the safest place to store grains. That is why, Lahore was such a prized city for all invaders, for it fed their hungry troops well, and where grain exists, so does gold - mouth-watering stuff for any invader. It was not without reason that the wise Akbar thought it prudent to settle and develop Lahore.

Let us now super-impose the map of the old river course on this elongated old Lahore, and we see that from the high mound of the fort with the river flowing outside its northern side, there is a curve. Just along was the old ferry dock which was to later become Khizri Gate, named after the patron saint of fishermen Khawaja Khizr. The river, according to Col. Bhola Nath's 1933 publication *Tarikh Shahr-a-Lahore*, "almost 800 years ago flowed where today runs the main bazaar of Shahalami". We know from *Albiruni's India* (London 1888) that the river was placed "500 steps to the east of the walls" of Lahore.

This means that the river, like all geography students know well, moves in curves, leaving its original course, always shifting direction to suit the flow. It is almost like a politician. The Buddha Ravi is one very recent example most people can associate with. But then like very old politicians all we can do is respect them.

So if the original walls existed to the west of Shahalami, it exactly fits the description of Mahmud's Lahore. Also we know that the area east of Shahalami was described by Maharajah Ranjit Singh as 'rarrah maidan' – barren ground. This was the case right up to Chowk Rang Mahal. The river had moved to the east and outer Lahore was barren by then.

As old small-bricked houses are knocked down for ugly concrete 'creations', the Lahore of old is being destroyed, brick by brick. All over the world legislation prevents such happenings. The line between history and profit has been solidly erased.

Learning to rebuild the walls

As I roamed about the cobbled streets of Florence in Italy, true Tuscany country, vineyards included, gasping at the effort undertaken to preserve the past, for the entire city seems like one huge museum, it made me remember my Lahore, probably one of the oldest cities in the world. It is today an utter mess ... and yet there is just so much to it, the people, the places, the things, the faces ... for that is what memories are made of ... that elusive mental concept that keeps one living here.

As I roamed about in the central square ... the piazza de Doumo ... I met an old English gentleman, rather Victorian in appearance, whose attire seemed more like out of a fading photograph of the sub-continent of a big game hunter. My present day journalistic colleagues in London would call him a "geezer out of tune and time." He had a huge leather-bound book in hand and was giving Florence the once over.

We managed to get talking and what surprised me about the gent was that he knew Lahore very well. He even knew the names of the 13 gates. He shook his head in disbelief at my description of the present-day Lahore. "You will one day regret it," he said, and recommended that I go to Treveso, near Venice, to see how they have managed to rebuild their old walled city, gates and drawbridges included. It is a piece of art, he said. I took his advice and set off on a three-hour train journey to Treveso, and it was well worth it.

As a young school-going lad I had often heard my father lamenting the fact that we were not looking after the Ravi and the Walled City. He was then Editor of that old and famous Lahore daily, *The Civil & Military Gazette* and he wanted, with assistance from friends like Khawaja Zahiruddin, the architect, to preserve Lahore as "the world's largest living museum". The idea then was to make the Ravi the centre of the city by building two huge embankments on both sides lined with beautiful trees and parks, and to decrease the bursting population of the walled city, place strict restrictions on building and demolition, and to preserve each and every house as it then stood. There was a plan to such effect lying in the LIT, or the Lahore Improvement Trust. But then Lahore was hijacked by the 'claim racketeers' or the 47ers as my father used to disdainfully call them. "I suppose one day they will turn Model Town into a commercial proposition," he used to joke. Today that is a tragic reality. Even an 'enlightened' friend has built an office bang in the middle of the quiet G Block, much to the residents' dismay. That is why visiting Treveso was so important. One had to see what they had done, and to try to attempt to make the proverbial flea move an inch in the conscience of the rulers of Lahore, whoever they may be, for these days one just does not know.

In Treveso they have rebuilt the entire walls of the old city that tried, in vain, to defend itself against an expanding Venetian maritime power. They knocked the walls down to deprive them of the ability to defend. This is what the British did to old Lahore after defeating the Sikhs. In Treveso the old walls have been rebuilt. It is, in every aspect, like the original wall, and the gateways are like the original. The moat outside has been dug again, though it remains dry. The streets are cobbled and there are restrictions on house occupation.

It is a marvel of intent and a place of immense peace and beauty. After all, Italy houses approximately 80 per cent of the ancient monuments of Western civilization, and its people are the closest you will find to the Pakistani psyche ... terribly creative, with an immense sense of history, not to speak of other traits. In Treveso lies the answer to many of the problems that face our own Walled city. There is need, urgently to declare all of the Walled City a 'protected city'.

For starters, there is an immediate need to rebuild the entire Old City wall on the Western side, from Bhatti to Taxali gate. There is no reason there should be any problem with that. The moat from the days of Akbar the Great is there, the land is there though slightly encroached, the need is there to protect the residents of old Lahore. It will be a beautiful sight to say the least, and it will be a modest beginning. The walls all around the city can be rebuilt, for the space and need very much exist. Within the old city the population will have to adhere to strict living conditions, not six to a room. Some form of civil living conditions will have to be imposed. This will improve the quality of life of the residents. All this sounds ambitious, dreamlike ... but then what harm is there in dreaming something good for our city. To begin with, the use of the rickshaws within the Walled City must be banned, for the noise level there in the old city is the highest in Lahore, almost 45 per cent above the human tolerance level.

It goes without saying that comparing Venice or Treveso or Florence to Lahore is rather unfair. They have the resources, we do not. We have an uncontrollable population, which they do not have. But then they have the tourists instead and on them the Italian economy manages very well. Then they have the education and sensitivity, which we apparently lack. Even a handful of concerned citizens can change the situation of the "wretched of the earth". It does not take a Fanon to bring home the truth. We can do it within our resources ... that is if we want to. My view is that we can, and we must.

The mucked up city

Even while driving into Lahore one is sad that from the bridge on the almost dry River Ravi, that symbol of purity in our ancient books, one cannot see the domes of the magnificent Badshahi Mosque clearly, just a dull, unfocused image.

The other day, it rained a wee bit. The feeling was great as one saw the city look like a throbbing metropolis again. If this is what it looks like from the road, from the air it is a totally different picture. As one flies over Lahore, one sees a huge dust cover blanketing the city. The aircraft actually enters a dusty cloud and lands in a suffocating environment. This is not the fabled Lahore. Chaucer mentions Lahore as that 'rich city of the East", clean like a babe." Clean my foot! Today we are probably the filthiest city East of Suez. But in the filth and squalor that has become Lahore, there lie genuine solutions. Our forefathers used to say that "filth is money, the dirtier the job the more the money". Let us delve into history and see how genuine solutions lie in the very problems that exist today.

It might interest the 'educated' reader that on the banks of the Ravi alongside Bund Road, there are mountains of filth stacked away by our municipal corporation. The stink and stench stretches for miles. The fashionable word is "open-air waste management". The reality stinks. But humans are beyond comprehension for on these mountains of filth, a colony of Afghans has set up thier own colonies. They are an aggressive lot and have established a 'filth mafia'. It might surprise you that with the willing connivance of our municipal officials, they have the 'unofficial contract' to go through the entire waste of Lahore to finds things that could be sold again. It is just like the skins and hides collection system of Karachi that has been taken over by the Afghans. They now control prices and in a sense the very economic destiny of our leather business.

There have been, of relative recent occurrence, two eras when Lahore's waste was managed in a manner that ensured that the city remained clean and pollution-free. During the Sikh era, the first organized waste collection 'bureau' was set up. Its office was in Tehsil Bazaar. If you enter the famous bazaar from the Bazaar-i-Hakeeman side, about 50 yards ahead to the left is a huge building that even today houses the corporation's clinic. In this building sat the chief sanitary officer and every Thursday sanitary workers would line up for their pay. It is said that for this reason the first use of the phrase *jumarati* was used, though it is today commonly used for those seeking free meals at religious shrines. It is interesting how slang words have a history all their own.

Maharajah Ranjit Singh had warned that if he ever walked the streets of Lahore and found filth on them, he would hang upside down the chief sanitary officer as well as the people of the houses from where the filth was coming. Records show that he actually carried out his threat just twice in the initial period of his rule. The punishments had a 'cleansing effect'. During his rule, French generals helped him to plan a system of waste collection, a system that the British then took over and managed exceptionally well.

The general rule was, and always has been all over the world, that the city is cleaned before the population sets off for work early in the morning. It can be said today that as far as Lahore goes, that rule no longer exists. Even in the 'relatively cleaner' area of the Lahore Cantonment, the cleaners start work at about nine in the morning. Gone is the pride of working for the betterment of the people. Just like law and order is the primary duty of the state, keeping it clean and orderly is the primary duty of the local authorities.

It came as a surprise to me that the police chief and the municipal chief of Los Angeles in the US are the two highest paid public servants in that country, getting more pay than even the president of the most powerful nation on earth. Not so in Lahore where the salary of a constable is a mere Rs. 2800 and he has to beg and steal for his meals. The municipal worker gets almost the same, only his boss manages to take away half his salary. This has become a custom. It should be said that our constables and municipal workers provide more than ample output for the inputs that the state provides them.

In the days of the Sikhs, both these persons got salaries that ensured that they were able to lead lives on a par with the average citizen. The British improved on their conditions of work, and the results were there for everyone to see. What we see of Lahore today, the filth and the squalor is actually a barometer of our respect for the poor municipal worker, whose supervisor robs him of his right to a complete salary. Add to this religiously motivated attitudes towards our minorities who form the bulk of our municipal workers, and we have a picture of a nation that is clean on the individual level, but prefers collectively to live in filth and squalor.

As a child I remember my British mother used to shock our neighbours when after the filth had piled on too much, she would defiantly take a broom in hand and clean the entire street. We ran to hide our shame and our neighbours would run to stop her and promise to get the sweeper to do a better job. "But why does this not move you?" she would ask and there was never a satisfactory answer. Every day as I cross the Ravi, that river of purity that has actually now dried up, and fail to see the domes of the Badshahi mosque, I remember my mother and how she would have reacted to the way we have 'mucked up' the city of our forefathers. But then it does not rain every day any longer.

The Wall and Gates of Lahore

Ancient cities, invariably, have so many turns and twists in their existence that keeping track of them is an impossible task. Lahore's traditions are, essentially, entirely oral. The written word started with the coming of the Mughals. Before that the only written history can be gleaned from the Mahabharata and the Vedas. With the coming of the British, history as it existed began to be written down. Since then the process has improved, even though not at a speed expected of a people interested in themselves.

The ancient walled city of Lahore is the starting point of our interest in the walled city. The story of its gates comes up in almost every story told. It makes sense to write a small piece about the gates and the walls as they emerged over time. What exactly was the shape of ancient Lahore has yet to be determined by scientific research. However, based on the facts as we know them now, it makes interesting reading to describe each gate as a separate entity. We have a picture of what Lahore was like when almost 1,000 years ago the Afghan invader Mahmud, from Ghazni in Afghanistan, struck. We know that after being defeated, the Hindu Rajput ruler, Raja Rana Jaipal the First, committed self-immolation outside Mori Darwaza or Mori Gate.

The word 'mori' means a hole, and most writers have over the time described Lahore's walled city as having not 13 gates, but 12 gates and a mori. This has more to do with superstition and the class-ridden assumption that if the filth left the city through an opening, to be thrown in the river flowing around the city walls, it was not worthy of being described as a gate. But of the very ancient Lahore, Mori Darwaza was one of the five city gates. The 13 gates as we know them today were completed during the Mughal era when the Mughal emperor Akbar built a clay-fired brick wall around Lahore. The next major contributor to the walls was Maharajah Ranjit Singh who built two defensive walls to protect the city from outsiders. Ironically, the British demolished almost all the walls to protect the city from internal rebellion, as was witnessed at Delhi in 1857.

Here it is essential to pre-suppose that the mud-built walls of ancient Lahore in the days of Raja Jaipal ran from the west of Mori Darwaza along the eastern edge of Bazaar Hakeeman to Taxali Chowk, curling eastwards around the northern portion of Paniwala Talaab, which happens to be the highest point of all the mounds of ancient Lahore. From here the mud walls ran eastwards and headed south, almost in a straight line, encompassing the present day Rang Mahal and straight along the western edge of the present day Shahalami Bazaar, from where it headed west again to join Mori Darwaza. This, roughly, is what we can accurately call the confines of ancient Lahore in its mud walls.

The gates that existed then were Mori gate, the present day Lohari Gate, probably the oldest gate of the city and another three or four gates. It is an educated guess that a Taxali Gate existed not where it was when the British knocked it down after 1857, but somewhere near the Taxali Chowk, making it the western entrance of the walled city. Then surely a gate existed near the present Sheranwala Gate and one gate to the east of Rang Mahal, probably the precursor to the present Delhi Gate. When Mahmud from Ghazni ransacked Lahore, these were the five gates mentioned.

When Akbar rebuilt the walled city with clay-fired bricks, the city was definitely expanded and more gates, or Guzars, were added. Much more space was included in the walls and by the time Maharajah Ranjit Singh finally built a double-walled defence perimeter outside the old walls, Lahore was to take its final present-day shape. It seems the very first move was to shift the western wall outwards to include the present-day Bhatti Gate.

The name is derived from the Rajput Bhats, or Bhatias, later to be called the Bhattis, who were the original rulers of Lahore. These Rajputs still live in the villages to the west of Lahore right up to Sheikhupura. The western wall is a straight wall without any gates right up to Taxali, where the old taxal or Royal Mint existed. The present-day Hira Mandi, known more for music, dance and prostitution, did not operate in its present form at this place, but was firmly planted at Chowk Lohari near Suttar Mandi. The taxal itself was to the east of Taxali Chowk. This leaves us with two, maybe three, ancient guzar or gate sites. The present-day Masti Gate is surely one of them for the mere reason that Lahore in ancient times was fed mostly through river transport. At this place was the very first river port, which in the days of Akbar moved to a custom-built dock at Sheranwala Gate. Khawaja Khizr is the patron saint of all fishermen and seafarers, and this gate was once called Khizri Gate. For this reason also we notice that even today all the grain markets are within easy reach of this gate, for the river provided the means to move grains and goods inside the city.To the east was also a gate near the present Rang Mahal, which provided an entry from the east. If we notice the alignment of the road from Delhi gate, we see it curves away to the edge of the city. Most probably at this point existed the eastern gate. Such was the shape and size of ancient Lahore. The present old walled city of Lahore owes its shape and size to Akbar the Great. In its present form it has 13 gates, starting from Bhatti Gate. Moving eastwards we come across Mori Darwaza and then Lohari Gate. In history this is probably the most important and ancient of all the gates of Lahore. This is the gate through which Mahmud of Ghazni penetrated Lahore, and it was also Maharajah Ranjit Singh who broke into the walled city through this gate. Over time it was this, the Achilles heel of the ancient city that proved to be the undoing of the inhabitants. The gateway of this still exists.

Beyond Lohari Gate is Shahalami Gate, named after Moazzam Shah, the second son of Emperor Aurangzeb. Moazzam fought against his brother Azim for the crown after his father's death in 1707, taking the title Qutbuddin Shah Alam. He died in 1712 and the gateway was named after him. The last gate on the southern side to the east is Mochi Gate. The area between Shahalami and Mochi, in some old manuscripts, was known as

Shah Alam

rarrah maidan, empty grounds, and served initially as camping ground for military forces. Inside Mochi Gate are precincts like Mohallah Chabaksawaran, the Cavalry Precinct and other such martial names for various mohallahs. Another pointer is the fact that the majority of the old dwellers of this gate are Shia Muslims of Uzbek and Tajik origin, who were skilled cavalrymen who came from Central Asia along with the various invaders. These open spaces they occupied and built their homes on.

To the east are three gates, starting from the one on the southern side which is the famous Akbari gate named after the emperor Akbar. Moving northwards is Delhi Gate, named after the fact that the road to Delhi meets the city at this point. If we follow the alignment of this road inside the walled city, we notice it is the only road that leads straight to the eastern gateway of the Lahore fort. This leads one to assume that this road existed before Akbar expanded the city, and that the rarrah maidan was almost the entire area to the east of the Shahalami Bazaar road up to Rang Mahal.

The last of the three eastern gates is Yakki Gate, named after the seer Syed Zaki. Most people claim the name Yakki was because it was here that the yakkas, horse carriages, from outside the city came and parked. Even today the main horse carriage tonga stand, and repair facilities of the city are in this area.

To the west are another three gates, they being the Khizri Gate, also known as Sheranwala Darwaza after Maharajah Ranjit Singh placed the statues of two lions there, the Kashmiri Gate, for this gateway pointed towards Kashmir, and the Masti Gate, or Masjidi Gate, built by Akbar in 1566. In 1612 the Empress Maryam Zamani built a mosque there and the gateway was thus called Masjidi Gate.

But the last of the 13 gates is the Roshnai Gate, the gateway of lights and is between the Lahore fort and the city. Here the gateway was always lighted, probably for security reasons, and came to be so called. Each of the gates has a long history, and each is associated with a number of events over the centuries. The stories in this book will often mention these gates, and one hopes some idea of their location and history will be of use to the reader.

The story of Lahore is essentially an oral history. The city was once a great seat of learning, and even today can claim to be such a place. There have been written contributions over the centuries, but none of the quality that can claim a place as essential reading. The first truly comprehensive contribution to writing the history of Lahore was that of Kanhiyya Lal in his famous book *Tarikh-e-Lahore*. He was followed by another contribution Old Lahore by Col. H.R. Goulding. Then came S.M. Latif's book Lahore in 1892. Other writers of note on the subject include B.P. Khosla, M. Waliullah Khan, H. Scholberg, J. Vogel, C.S. Hardinge, and M. Baqir and, of recent, the contributions of Fakir Syed Aijazuddin have brought the subject into the domain of factual scientific research.

In this domain the contribution of the official Gazetteer of the Lahore District from 1883 onwards, especially those under the editorship of Sir Denzil Ibbetson, cannot be overlooked, for they provided the stepping stones of Lahore's written history. With the creation of Pakistan, these gazetteers ceased to be written. With the cessation of such writings, official interest in written history ceased. For half a century it remained a forgotten science. Over the last few years a new interest in Lahore is emerging, with a fresh interest in searching for our past. This is essentially a non-official pastime, and this alone makes sure that it will grow with time. With new developments in information search and retrieve systems, and with better educated younger people around, the future of the science of writing history is bound to emerge. This is good for Lahore.

Lahore Railway Station 142 years ago

The British ruled the sub-continent thanks to the lack of leadership in a fragmented India, and through the railways. The priority given to the railway by the British rulers meant: that they were able to reach parts that no ruler before them could ever have imagined. In a way, had it not been for the railways, the British would have been forced out much before 1947.

The breakdown of civil rule under the crumbling Mughal Empire meant that the only stable portion of the sub-continent was the Punjab under the iron grip of Maharajah Ranjit Singh. India was all red.

Only the Punjab stuck out. Once the Maharajah died in 1839 and his heirs started fighting among themselves, the British walked in and took Lahore in 1846. The Punjabis fought on for three years and by 1849, all of the sub-continent had been subdued. The conquerors knew full well that if they had to control a land-mass stretching from the

Lahore Railway Station

Khyber to Burma, they would have to move about with speed. For this reason, the railways came to the sub-continent much before it came to many parts of Britain. There are two terminal points in the railway network in the subcontinent which stand out, and they are Bombay (now known as Mumbai) and Lahore. I have not seen the Mumbai Railway Station, but a few old-timers who have seen it compare it to the grandeur of the Lahore Railway Station. For that matter few buildings in Pakistan compare to it in sheer scale and style.

The foundation stone of the station was laid, formally, by John Lawrence, the lieutenant governor of the Punjab in 1859. Once the British had managed to get their grip on affairs after the 1857 Mutiny, or war of independence, the very first major decision taken was to lay the foundation of a vast railway network. Within one year, in 1860, the very first train left on its inaugural journey to Amritsar. Within the next few months a train to Delhi was in place. To follow was a line to Multan and then onwards to Karachi. Then work started on a bridge across the Ravi to take the line to Peshawar and on to Landikotal. The Great Game was on.

The Lahore railway station was built by the famous Lahore contractor Muhammad Sultan, a simple man who became rich thanks to the work he undertook in building a lot of military barracks in the Lahore Cantonment, and for the huge market he built in what is today Landa Bazaar. The famous Sultan ke Sarai bears his name to this day. But a civil works of the scale that accompanied the building of the railway station has never been seen or experienced since this city came into existence. Located to the north-east of the Walled City, an area of one square mile was acquired to build a massive infrastructure to support the railway system. Today, 142 years later, the system is still working, even though much needed investments over time have not taken place, especially after independence.

Vast housing colonies were laid for officers, drivers, workers and the entire staff of hundreds of thousands of people. The railway is even today the largest employer after the Pakistan Army and the WAPDA. Then a locomotive workshop was built at Mughalpura to make carriages and steam locomotives. In a way, the setting up of so many workshops and technical centres brought to Lahore engineering as it was known to the western world. The need for mechanical engineers was fulfilled with the building of the Lahore Engineering College, today known as the University of Engineering and Technology. In a way, the building of *the* railways created a new Lahore, with a new social culture and new elite. This had a tremendous impact on life in a city that had changed very little for centuries. It heralded the technological era.

The Lahore railway station is built between two towers, with a massive entrance area. Initially there were five platforms, but as new lines and services increased, more platforms were added. The rest rooms had excellent oak chairs, most of which have since disappeared. It is estimated that the amount of woodwork that had taken place in the completion of the railway system in Lahore was greater than the wood ever used in the Walled City. All this wood was brought from Burma. The removal of this wood is a story in itself.

The architecture has been so designed that in case of disruption, the Lahore Railway Station can be converted into a fortress. The building of the railway station took into consideration the finer points of military contingencies. For this reason for a very long time people were not allowed to photograph any portion of the station. Strangely, this law is still in place, even though people laugh at it. The bricks used were specially made in the Mughalpura area and the specifications used were strictly British. If you happen to visit the station, you will marvel at the quality of the masonry, the carpentry, the ironwork and almost every aspect of construction. The builders took great pride in each and every detail. No room for the dropping of standards was allowed, and the inspectors were strict and very honest. Today what we see is the finest railway station of Pakistan, the result of a unique sense of pride that its builders had in an enterprise that forever changed the shape of Lahore and its people.

Walking down a sacred track

Last week I was in "the zone" as athletes like to describe that special feeling of perfect union of mind and body. Having parked my car near Sherpao Bridge, I decided to walk along the railway track from the Lahore Cantonment railway station to the Walton station, that sacred rail track where thousands of would-be Pakistanis were received dead in 1947.

I was reading this piece about institutionalized "low intensity conflict" that the bureaucracies of India and Pakistan, through mutual 'silent' understanding, nurture. It makes them rich and the people poor, in perpetuity. Dr Mubashir Hasan did a great service by stating the 'unstated'. Silence is sin in every book that I know of. How could such a magnificent set of people hate each other? With these thoughts I walked along wondering at just how much effort had gone into the building of these tracks, the thousands of railways stations that dot the sub-continent, and the trains and the locomotives, and the people who built them.

The railways arrived in the sub-continent in 1850, just one year after Lahore was taken and the entire track from Calcutta (Kolkata) to the Afghan border was under British rule. Mind you, the railways had not been fully laid in most European cities by that time. So it was a revolutionary step by any

Lord John Lawrence

reckoning. By the year 1899, rail tracks had been laid from the south of Madras to the Afghan border, more than 23,000 miles. It was the biggest and the costliest construction project undertaken by any colonial power in any colony anywhere in the world. It was also the largest single investment of British capital in the whole of the 19th century.

By 1863, some three million tons of rails, sleepers and locomotives had been shipped to India from Britain in approximately 70 ships a year non-stop for half a century. Such was their commitment to the railways of the sub-continent. Engineers had looped tracks over the steepest mountains in the world, sunk foundations hundreds of feet into the hot shifting deserts, bridged rivers as wide and as turbulent as the Ganges and the Indus. It was an undertaking the world had never seen, and probably might never see again. Yet today it remains a most unresearched subject, for we just do not have any railway buffs like they do in Britain and all over the world. We simply do not treasure what we have. Somehow it seems to be in the spirit of the times in which we live, in constant low intensity conflict, in constant tension.

The railways also brought about an economic and social revolution. As travel time shrank, the resultant mobility added to the economic development that such mobility brings. Mobility brought with it the feeling of the sub-continent being one huge unified mass. Ironically, a century later, the same railways also made possible the irreparable division of the sub-continent. The partition of India led to what was probably the greatest migration in human history. More than 12 million people exchanged both their homes and their countries. Twelve million souls tore themselves apart from the land of their ancestors.

That very act is still a fresh wound, the severing of a bonding cemented over thousands of years and probably part of our very genes. The railways managed to transport a major chunk of those moving, and in the process over one million people lost their lives in the space of merely 100 days. Never before, and hopefully never again, will mankind see such slaughter, and the rail track between Walton and the Lahore Cantonment railway stations is living testimony of the slaughter that people are even today scared to talk about. Such has been the impact. Such is the intensity of hate. Walking on that track brings forth such thoughts.

It brought forth the question, 'would partition have been possible without the railway?' Many researchers are of the view that it would not have been possible, for millions of people had to be shifted over long distances in a small time space. My view is that partition would have taken place, only the slaughter would have been far greater. It was on the railways that much of the worst violence took place. Lahore station was "the eye of the whirlwind". The fate of Lahore remained uncertain until the final maps of the boundaries between the two nations were released.

In the event the city went to Pakistan, just 15 miles from the Indian border, and the city and its people were instantly torn apart. Thousands of Hindus and Sikhs fought their way to the station to flee to India. At the same time train after train began arriving from the south bringing hundreds of thousands of Muslims to their new homeland. The Lahore railway station became a battleground. This is where the worst slaughter took place.

On the night of Independence the last British officials in Lahore arrived at the station. They had picked their way through gutted streets, many of which were still littered with the dead from the riots. On the platforms they found the railway staff grimly hosing down pools of blood and carrying away piles of corpses on luggage trolleys for mass burial. Minutes earlier a last group of desperate Hindus had been massacred by a Muslim mob as they sat waiting quietly for the Bombay Express.

The late Khwaja Bilal had the unenviable job of being the Station Master of Lahore in August, 1947. He is on record as having said: "On the 14th of August I was on duty. We heard an announcement that partition had taken place. Soon after that the killing started, the slaughter began. Despite the presence of British soldiers, hundreds were being killed on the platforms, on the bridges, in the ticket halls. There were stabbings, rapes, and arson. It was unstoppable.

"At night I could not sleep because of the screams and moans of the dying coming from the platform. Every morning hundreds of slaughtered bodies would be lying everywhere. One morning, I think it was August 30, the Bombay Express came in from Delhi *via* Bhatinda. There were around 2,000 people on this train. We found dead bodies in the lavatories, on the seats, under the seats. We checked the whole train, but nobody was alive except one person who had hidden in the engine water tank. We used to receive one hundred trains a day. There were hundreds of corpses in every one".

When Lord John Lawrence broke the earth on the future site of the Lahore railway station in February 1859, the silver shovel he used bore the Latin motto *'tam bello quam pace'* — better peace than war. Little did he know how things would turn out!

The ice pits of Lahore

Names speak so much about the history of people, their mode of production, and the very land itself. The walled city and its environs have fascinating names, each a story unto itself. Names describe professions and pastimes. One such name that always intrigued me I heard from my younger brother, who spent most of his waking hours playing football in the grounds of the Central Training College, just outside Bhatti Gate.

In the 1970ies we used to live in the Rattigan Road area, once considered a posh locality just outside the old walled city. In the place where today stands the Central Training College just behind the Central Model School, was the residence of Sir William Rattigan, and it might come as a surprise to many that he and his family lived in an old style bungalow with a genuine thatched roof, all very 'old English'. One description of the house compares it to typical Suffolk thatched cottages. The house had the nameplate

"Roselands". It was an imposing residence by any standard. The people of Lahore used to call this area "Rattigan Sahib ki Kothi". Another description terms it "Rattigan Sahib ki Bhooswali Kothi". Later the British formally named it Rattigan Road. This was the house where the first Punjabi regiment formed by the British, the First Punjab Volunteers, was formed. This regiment was to play an important role in the 1857 uprising.

For those not familiar with Rattigan Road, suffice it to say that till just 40 years ago it housed the Parsi Temple, the house of the Syed family of Syed Babar Ali and the Jhang Syeds, the Khawaja family, the Abbasi family of doctors, the massive six-acre house of Col. Ata, the Sheikhs and other city influentials. Almost 100 years ago, it was definitely the most sought after area of Lahore. But even before Rattigan arrived and built his thatched house, the people of Lahore used to call this area 'Purana Baraf Khana'. My brother informs me that the older people still call this area 'Baraf Maidan'.

In the days of the Mughals and the Sikhs, this open area was called 'Baraf Maidan'. When the British came in 1849, they for the first time formally marked this area out in maps as 'Ice Pits'. In these pits, in a virtual pre-historic manner, ice was 'manufactured' in winter and stored underground. In summer it was distributed early in the morning. One description of this activity says: "The big plain was divided into smaller plots or 'kiaris', on which a layer of rice straw was spread. On this straw were arranged a number of shallow pans of burnt clay, all of them containing water. The pits were lined with thick layers of straw and were surrounded by low burnt brick walls. On this wall rested a very thick straw roof, known as a 'chappar'.

"Between the walls and the edges of the pits ran narrow passages which enabled the carriers of ice barrows to distribute their daily loads at different points. At the bottom of each pit were men equipped with rakes and rammers who levelled the ice and consolidated it. The entrances of these pits were always carefully walled up after receiving its full load of ice."

To man these ice pits and to care for them, a large number of poor families formed a sort of 'katchi abadi' just to the east of the shrine of Data Sahib. In these houses now dwell mostly Pathans who have settled in Lahore, and to the farther side is the famous colony of the 'Eunuch Tribe' as they like to call themselves. People of Rattigan Road and Mohni Road have always called this place 'Neutral Zone'. In this colony lives the 'selected' king of the eunuchs of Lahore. But that is another story.

The ice pit families were each allotted a number of pits. It was their duty to place clean boiled water in those shallow earthen vessels, to collect the frozen ice and to take them to the pits that led fairly deeply into the ground. Each family then had to, by the time summer came, collect a given amount of ice, so that it lasted well into the summer. In this manner the people of Lahore were supplied ice from the Rattigan Road 'Baraf Maidan'.

The British also started another ice pit centre in the newly-constructed Central Jail on Jail Road. The entire Shah Jamal and Shadman area constituted the old central jail. Here a new series of pits were made, which supplied the cantonment and the British army with ice in summer. As the quality of water of this area was considered superior to that of the Rattigan Road, the 'jailwali baraf' was slightly more expensive than the 'Rattigan Roadwali baraf'. During the several cholera epidemics that hit Lahore in those days, the European population used only 'jailwali baraf'. At the height of the epidemics special permits were issued to Europeans for this ice.

These virtually pre-historic technology ice pits died after the fist electricity powered ice manufacturing unit sprung up in 1879 on Rattigan Road. For the first time ice was available all the year round in large quantities. This led to the common people also enjoying kulfis in summer, a delicacy that formerly only the rich enjoyed. But though the ice pits of Lahore died away in the late 1800s, a few old-timers even now call the grounds where they existed, as the 'baraf maidan'. One assumes that in a few years even this name will die. Today there exists a swimming pool and some very old banyan trees. In our youth we spent many an evening discussing poetry there, not to speak of several unmentionable pastimes.

The road that was the empress of Lahore

Once the East India Company had annexed the Punjab in 1849 and raised the Union Jack on the Lahore Fort, they set about stamping their 'colonial' mark on Lahore - the 'last major Indian city to fall to the Empire'. No where was this more marked than on the building of Empress Road, the name conjuring up a 'special feeling' in the minds and hearts of the colonial rulers and their supporters.

The Empress Road of Lahore runs from the Governor's House to the Lahore Railway Station, and on its way encompasses the very best that the British offered to the sub-continent, that being a massive rail network and an infrastructure that was, in its days, second to none in the world. A journey down this 'most imperial of roads', as a British soldier was to recall it years later, is even today worth taking, for it brings out some of the major developments that the British achieved during their 98-year stay in this city. It goes without saying that they contributed more to the development of Lahore than any other invader before them starting from Mahmud from Ghazni, almost 1,000 years ago.

A journey in 1917 down Empress Road, as recalled by Fakir Aijazuddin in his book *Lahore Recollected*, makes interesting reading. If one was to walk from the Governor's House back gate towards the railway station one saw the grand Kashmir House, residence of the Maharajah of Kashmir. Then one would 'encounter the residence of Dr. A Jones, dental surgeon, on the left side'. On the right was a beautiful garden. Next to the garden was the residence of Mr. J.F.Rehill of the Indian Police. Then came the massive

Civil Police Lines, a hugé training ground and barracks. Next to it was the residence of the Qizilbash clan, loyal British supporters who had fought with them in Kabul, and assisted them later in the capture of Lahore.

On the right side from the Durrand Road crossing were the residences of Mr. Abdul Rahim, the district engineer, Dr. Francis and Mrs. Anneley, both dentists, Mr. Hammill, a businessman, Mr. W. Pitman, the famous tailor. All of them had beautiful houses with huge gardens. Then came the grand office of what was then known as 'Office of the Manager, North Western Railways'. Opposite on the left side lived, in a huge house, the Meakins family, two brothers one of whom worked in the Punjab Police and the other a Pleader at the Lahore District Courts. Next to them was the Cambridge Hotel, which was "frequented by English ladies and gents of repute" as one description puts it. Then came the auction rooms of Nusserwanjee & Co.

On the right as we went along from the railway manager's office was the St. Andrew's Church, a central hostel and at the Nicholson Road corner the residence of Mr. T.C. Bustard, a piano and organ tuner. Across Nicholson Road was the Kinnaird girls' school and a Christian mission. Facing the railway station were the residences of Rev. H.D.Griswald and Miss Greenfield to the left, and on the right was the residence of Rev. McKee. Of Miss Greenfield one learns that she was "a jolly nice woman who had an eye for style" as one description puts it. That she lived next to the men of the cloth is understandable.

The onset of the First World War saw a change in the very look of Empress Road, as the war and the railways took grip of life in Lahore. A portion of the civil police lines was taken up by the 'Recruiting Officers Office'. The Qizilbash clan managed to get the houses of Francis, Anneley, Pitman and Hammill transferred to their Waqf as they assisted the British recruit soldiers in the areas of Pattoki, Raiwind and beyond. There they also got considerable land to cultivate. Half of the Lahore Division that got killed in the fields of

Flanders and other major European battlefields in Belgium and France in the First World War were recruited on this road. A memorial to them stands at Ypres in Belgium, a most moving remembrance to the sons of our soil.

In 1916, the railways had acquired massive amounts of land along the Mughalpura Road, setting up the Naulakha area, and other railway officers' colonies, including the posh Mayo Gardens, the very peak of colonial luxury. We must not forget that by 1916, there lived in Lahore over 1, 200 Europeans, almost 35,000 Anglo-Indians, another 70,000 migrants from Goa, and an array of nationalities from all over India and the world. Around Empress Road centered their lives, for they all worked for the NW Railway. These people were served by several institutes like the Burt Institute which had swimming pools, billiard rooms, cricket grounds, libraries and coffee rooms. An entirely new world had grown up around the railways, and working for it entitled a special prestige. It was truly cosmopolitan.

But the pride of place along this 'imperial' road was the railways station itself and the headquarters of the railways. It was designed by Chief Engineer William Brunton and constructed at a colossal cost of Rs. 500,000 by Muhammad Sultan (1809-1875), the famous contractor who made a name for himself as a British contractor. He was originally a soap maker, but then died a pauper after becoming probably the richest contractor in British India. Most people ascribe a curse on him for stealing the bricks of the various mosques in Lahore after they had been knocked down during the Sikh rule days. The bricks used in the railway station also came from such mosques. But then it is probably the finest railway station in the entire sub-continent after the magnificent one in Bombay, or Mumbai. "Surely from ruins do rise great empires" as a sage once said.

The story of this magnificent road has taken strange twists as the years have unfolded. Today the old residences, Kashmir House, the Police Lines have all disappeared. In its place is the WAPDA Hospital, the US Consulate, and then there is the Radio Pakistan and PTV buildings where once was the Civil Police Lines. The Naulakha Police Station is all that is left of the largest police lines in the Punjab. The Qizilbash clan has managed to build a huge plaza in its lands next to the railway headquarters. Beyond, the old residences have been knocked down and new commercial premises built. Then comes the Haji Camp. The changes reflect the changed reality. One assumes that the remaining Qizilbash holdings will also disappear as the massive land prices attract the newer generation.

As the role of the railways has been overtaken by aircrafts and motorways, the once grand Empress Road has been reduced to merely "the road that leads to the railway station". Last Sunday I went to receive a guest and stood chatting with the station master. The once grand station is also a shadow of its past, as the roof crumbles and commercial boards block out its beauty. The famous railway breakfast ceases to exist. The teak furniture in the rest rooms has 'disappeared'. In short, the Empress is no more. Even Miss Greenfield faces a Haji Camp (the Almighty moves in strange ways) and the mad rush of inter-city buses. Times have certainly changed.

The old gong at the GPO

If you enter Lahore's General Post Office (GPO) from the main entrance that leads to a massive wooden staircase, you will see, at the entrance, a huge brass bell with the date 1860 written on it. This historic bell was used as a gong when the 'foreign mail' reached Lahore on the 'Government Bullock Train'. The Lahore of the East India Company then stationed at Old Anarkali, would become alive and the question of the day would be: "Did anything arrive for you?"

This bell would ring twice a week. Once when the mail arrived, and secondly, an hour before the 'foreign mail' left Lahore. In the second case, people would rush to post their letters. The story of the post office and Lahore is a very old one, though there is no doubt that the British organized it on scientific lines after almost 200 years of disruption. Sadly, it is a story that is never told, and the Post Office has never made an effort to tell it. The first mention of this service in thé known world are references to a postal system in existence among the Egyptians in 2000 BC.

The first use of a postal system in China was under the Chou dynasty (c. 1111-255 BC). A reference by Confucius in the late 6th century demonstrates that it was already renowned for its efficiency: "The influence of the righteous travels faster than a royal edict by post-station service."

The Thurn and Taxis postal system wás a privately owned network of 20,000 employees carrying post and newspaper in Europe in AD 1505. So the post office is not a very new concept, and there are references to such a service in the Lahore of Raja Jaipal even before Mahmud from Ghazni attacked the city. This and hundreds of attacks that followed disrupted postal distribution for years to come.

In the sub-continent, a system of carrying messages was in existence during the reign of Allauddin Khilji in AD 1296. But credit for the modern post office as we know it today must go to Sher Shah Suri, who during his short reign of five years, built the 2,000-mile long road from Bengal to Peshawar for use by his postal services. This is where the famed 'Pony Express' was actually built, and copied all over the world. He built 1,700 'serais' and relay posts where horses were changed. He died on May 22, 1545.

Later rulers of India improved his postal system. Almost 492 of these 'serais' existed in what is called Pakistan today, with the only existing one in Lahore being located just to the east of the Shalimar Gardens and is known as the 'serai' of Mahna Singh. Even the horse troughs exist and buffaloes use it. I have not researched the other almost 300 in the Pakistani Punjab, but it is a subject that the Post Office can try to 'dig out' ... if they feel so inclined.

During the reign of Maharajah Ranjit Singh, the postal service was revived and the Lahore Fort, where the Maharajah lived, was used as the central sorting office. Every letter was read for any intelligence and then distributed through runners who had an office in the 12 functioning gates of the walled city. People in the city started saying likhan di bhool na karna, a wisdom that continued till British times.

To this date, the 'special branch' of the police have an office there. Communication has always been a threat to the state, just as it is a boon to society at large. The post office thus became a function run by the police. With the British it changed hands, but in a subtle manner, and today it is an independent service with privacy protected by law, or so we think.

The very first 'prepaid' paper stamps to be seen in Lahore were the 1852 "Scinde Dawks" as started by Bartle Frere, the commissioner of Sindh. The stamps bore the East India Company mark. But in Lahore, the very first stamps to be used by the British were simple 'red sealing wax' stamped with the East India Company mark on it.

One such 'stamp' of 1849 exists in the British Museum. For this reason it was called a stamp. Letters were taken to the post office and after payment the 'red sealing wax' was applied, the letter sealed and stamped. Once stamped, it was considered 'posted', though later the word 'stamp' and 'post' were used in varying manners and ultimately as nouns.

According to a description of Lahore's post office by H. R. Goulding: "On the site now occupied by the Public Works Secretariat stood an old barrack-like building constructed in 1849, which was used as the General Post Office until the present handsome building was completed...". The reader might be interested to know that this 'original' post office is just behind the Tollinton Market in Old Anarkali Bazaar, the second food street as we now know it.

At another place he writes: "In 1876, packages were received at the Lahore General Post Office for dispatch by the Government Bullock Train to 24 stations including Ferozepur, Bahawalpur, Rawalpindi and Peshawar". It is clear that Lahore acted as the main postal artery for the entire Punjab and beyond.

The Punjab Gazetteer of 1916 mentions Lahore as having excellent postal services with 132 letterboxes with the monogram of Queen Victoria on them. These are genuine collector's items today. It might interest the reader to know that almost a dozen of the original letterboxes are still functioning today, and as F.S. Aijazuddin mentions in his book *Lahore Recollected*, one can see one of these exquisite letterboxes still in use in Anarkali. I have managed to track down another three in the old railway quarters in Mughalpura.

As the British consolidated and moved their cantonment to its existing one at Mian Mir, a slight change in practices took place. The Punjab Gazetteer (1916,p169) goes on: "Mails are conveyed to and from the railway station in mail carts drawn by horses. Two flags are flown at the GPO, a red one to indicate that foreign mail has been signalled at Bombay, and is expected at Lahore, and a Royal Mail Standard (a white one) to indicate the day of dispatch of foreign mail from Lahore."

Once the mail was received, with the flag up, the traditional gong was used as a matter of routine. With time it became merely a ceremonial gong. Some time in the 1950s, with the railways well established and two to three 'foreign mail' dispatches coming every day, the gong went silent. Today in the din of modern Lahore, the bell stands silent, a testimony to a tradition that is probably as old as our city.

Changing names as the city evolves

Culture and its evolution over time have always intrigued scholars. For those who stick to just one time period, as if that was the "be all and end all" of history, there is the inevitable fear of becoming irrelevant. The history of Lahore suffers from just such a mindset.

There are a large number of scholars who think that the arrival of Mahmud of Ghazni, almost 1,000 years ago, is the time when the history of Lahore begins. Their reasons are understandable.

The Ramayana, written in approximately 300 BC, tells us about Ram and Sita and their sons Lahu and Kasu, and how they set up home on the mound where the Lahore Fort stands today. The story of Ram belongs to a far earlier era. Since then Lahore came to be called by many names. There is also the comparatively recent theory that the 'real Lahore' was actually at Icchhra, and that it was the growth of inhabitants around the grain market on the banks of the Ravi, the present grain market inside Akbari Gate, that led to the growth of what we call Lahore today. But the time period is too recent to be taken seriously, especially since archaeological finds from the inner city offer evidence of pottery and iron instruments dating to almost 1,500 years back.

An interesting analysis of culture has been presented by Faiz, that culture keeps evolving in line with what the people of a land actually do. The modes of production and the social changes that take place because of it are all important and need to be considered. This is our evolving culture. Let us examine one aspect of the changes that have taken place in the names of the gates of Lahore's Walled City.

It is amazing how little people know about their own city, their own locality, its history and myths. It is only by actually walking through the streets of the Walled City that one appreciates just how important names are. Most of us think that the Shahalami Gate, which no longer exists, thanks to the carnage of partition, was named after Emperor Aurangzeb. One Sunday while walking through the area, I kept asking people living there why was Shahalami so named, and almost all of them gave the same answer. The facts are different and there is considerable irony about the characters involved and what they did. After the death of Emperor Aurangzeb in 1707, he was succeeded by the Emperor Shah Alam, by all accounts an unpredictable person.

The new emperor, while in Lahore to crush the growing menace of the emerging Sikhs and the raiding Khokhars of Sheikhupura, thought up the idea of adding words to the 'Kalima', which the majority of the Sunni population of Lahore found totally unacceptable. The preacher who had obeyed Emperor Shah Alam and announced it was hacked into pieces and delivered at the Lahore Fort.

This act of defiance enraged the emperor, who for some bizarre reason issued a number of decrees, among them that all dogs of Lahore should be killed. The people took this as an insult to their defiance of his first decree. So they hid their animals indoors and the next morning, so an account of the event tells us, hundreds of people could be seen swimming across the River Ravi taking their pets to safety. This amazing decree earned him the nickname *kuttaymaar,* a popular slang to this date in the Walled City for anyone or anything that is extremely crazy. But this decree also helped Shah Alam become a jocularly liked person, for the people of Lahore could expect just about any decree, depending on his mood. The grand Mughuls had become the laughing stock of the people. For this reason historians, mark the end of the Great Mughuls with Aurangzeb's death. So marked was the change that the feared became the mocked.

It is said that people actually awaited Shah Alam's decrees and immediately jokes were invented about them and the emperor. On his death in 1712 the area to the south east of the Walled City and the gate serving it was named after him. The death of Shah Alam is actually the time when the slow destruction of the cultural heritage of Lahore began. It continued for a good 50 years after the British had taken over from the Sikhs.

On the subject of the changing names of the gates of Lahore, the current Sheranwala Gate was always known in history as Khizri Gate. When the Ravi flowed to the north of the Walled City, this was the point where the river ferry used to touch the Walled City. This was an important stop for the Ravi ferries. In a way, this was also the point through which most invaders from the north used to enter the city. But then along came Ranjit Singh, who initially tied two live lions outside the gate and renamed it Sheranwala Gate. Later, he had two lions carved in stone put there. With the river having moved westwards and the ferry transport naturally disappearing, the name Khizri Gate vanished from the minds of the people. During my Sunday stroll, I found out that nobody knew the old name of Sheranwala Gate, though almost every one knew why it was now so called. Recent history probably has a higher recall.

Another gate of Lahore whose name was changed in the Mughul days was Taxali Gate. It was originally called Lakhi Gate, meaning thereby that this was where the 'millionaires' lived. In a way they still do. But as the Mughuls built their mint just near the Lahore Fort, the taxal, probably the word 'tax' has some connection to it, the gate was renamed Taxali Gate. Today not a single person living there is aware of the word Lakhi Gate, and yet for many years, this was the name of Taxali Gate.

In a way even Akbari Gate had another name. Though Emperor Akbar built this gate, originally outside it was the 'nakkhas mandi' or the 'horse market'. This was serviced by a 'mori', a small gate recorded at a few places as 'nakkhas darwaza'. Just along is Yakki Gate named after the horse carriages that stood there to serve people going to villages and areas outside the Walled City. But no one in Akbari Gate has ever heard of those times. This is nothing to be sorry about, for so rapid has been the change that Lahore has seen, and also so frequent the destruction, that names, places, things, faces, everything has changed. Some for the better, some for the worse.

Walking to Charing Cross

During our school and college days in the late 1960s-early 1970s, it was considered fashionable to go for a walk on The Mall in the evening. We would invariably end up at Charing Cross for an ice cream at The Chalet, after which we would walk back home briskly before 'light time' to listen to the radio, or watch the one-hour television transmission in black and white.

The New Lahore, which was 'new' at the turn of the 19th century and just before the First World War, had a 'new' focal point, the new centre of modern Lahore. To the west lay the walled city and the nearby old Anarkali cantonment, to the east lay the new cantonment at Mian Mir, to the north the Railway Station and its huge colonies, and to the east was the last 'chungi' toll station outside the city at Mozang. In the middle was Charing Cross, the place where everyone wanted to be seen. It had restaurants, hotels, tailoring shops, cigarette manufacturers, piano saloons, and all the other ingredients of a modern city.

The term Charing Cross was first used, in the context of Lahore, in 1908 in a publication by G.R.Elmslie titled *Thirty Five Years in the Punjab* (1908, Edinburgh). A 1918-19 'B&R Report' refers to it as the 'Charing Cross Scheme'. However, this area was earlier known as Donaldtown, after Mr. Donald McLeod, who was later to become the lieutenant governor of the Punjab (1865-70), and after whom we, even today, thankfully, call McLeod Road. He was earlier the president of the Lahore Improvement Committee, which then became the Lahore Improvement Trust, later to be renamed the Lahore Development Authority. What's in a name.

The crossing became a point of importance with the building of the new Masonic Hall, which replaced the old one on Lodge Road, where today stands the Lady Maclagan Government High School. Opposite this was built the Shah Din Building, which now is, thankfully, a protected one.

The Punjab Assembly building was started in 1935 and completed in 1938.

Thanks to the new book by Fakir Syed Aijazuddin on Lahore, a map of the Charing Cross area, drawn by the British in 1867, makes interesting reading. The area from the crossing, going eastwards, has nothing but gardens on the right. Where today stands the Masonic Hall was a beautiful circular garden. The area where the Lahore Zoo came up is also a garden, named 'New Garden', which has a huge water tank in the middle. Then starts the 'Agricultural and Horticultural Society Garden', in the middle of which were placed the Lawrence Hall and the Montgomery Hall.

From the crossing of what was to be later named Racecourse Road, start more gardens and then comes the house of Major Hutchinson, a huge mansion. On Racecourse Road is the lone house of Mrs. Purdon. Probably she was the wife of Mr Purdon, the architect, the person who designed the King Edward's Medical College along with Kanhiyya Lal. All around her house were green fields, for today's GOR estate were agricultural fields.

But on the left side from Charing Cross onwards, going eastwards first came the Punjab Club building. Today at this spot stands WAPDA House. Then came agricultural fields and more gardens, with Jwalla Sahib's Garden, which was renamed Royal Park, where today no signs of any park, let alone a single tree, remains. Probably the excellent 'halwa puri' shop there is its hallmark, a sign of our times. Beyond is the Tomb of Syud Nurdeen Bukhari and the Kothi of Jamandar Khushhal Singh, which was then being used as the Government House. That was Lahore in 1867, nothing but gardens and greenery.

By the time the First World War started, 'Great Britain' felt the time had come for the Empire to stamp its authority on India, and in Lahore, this came in the shape of a grand statue of Queen Victoria at Charing Cross. This was be "the most prominent monument of the British presence for many years". A marble pavilion was designed by Bhai Ram Singh Mistri, then deputy principal of the Mayo School of Arts. The bronze statue of Queen Victoria, wearing her Imperial crown on "a veil of her favourite Honiton lace, cradling the scepter and holding the orb" was cast in London by B. Mackennal in 1900, a year before her death. The statue remained there for over 50 years, when in 1951 it was removed and taken to the Lahore Museum. In its place now stands a model of the Holy Quran.

But by 1914, the time when the First World War started, the shops from the Regal Crossing to Charing Cross make interesting reading. To the left at Regal was Ranken & Co., civil and military tailors and outfitters. This tailoring concern had branches at Calcutta, Simla, Delhi, Rawalpindi, Lahore and Murree. Established in 1770 in Calcutta, it was among the first tailoring concerning "on Special Appointment" to the Company, and later on the governor-general. Then came the Civil & Military Gazette Press, followed by Cutler Palmer & Co., wine merchants. A few shops later came Smith and Campbell the Chemists and then was Richards & Co., drapers and tailors. Next door was Walter Locke and Co., gunsmiths and then was the shop of Mr. J.D. Bevan, the piano dealer.

On the right side going eastwards was Varcados & Co., cigarette manufacturers, Hakman & Co., hairdressers by appointment, then came Prince Edwards & Co., the opticians and then was Fred Bremner the photographer. Then came the Savoy Hotel and way up was E.L. Stiffles the confectioners, next to whom was C. Steirt & Co., music saloon. Finally, was Max Minck & Co., jewellers and watchmakers, now known as Goldsmiths & Co. Today all signs of British Lahore up to Charing Cross have disappeared.

The days when Charing Cross was the place to be at have long since gone. New high rise commercial buildings of character and style are certainly much needed, as much as there is a need to preserve the past. A beautiful future awaits Charing Cross, provided the will not to forget the past exists. There is no need to name this crossing by any other name but by its original name.

Road names are not just about history

There is an old saying that "a nation lost tends to loose old names". In the old walled city changing names is not easy. The government in its zeal to Islamise street names managed a few during the Zia days, but people still use the old names, leading to the new ones being discarded – unofficially.

During the British era most names were of British origin, the reason being that they built the streets and roads in the first place. They, however, made sure that the old name remained. Take the case of Company Bagh, the beautiful garden built by the East India Company. With the 'company' departing and the Crown taking over, its name was officially recognized as Lawrence Gardens. Come Pakistan and its name was again changed to Jinnah Gardens. But the fact is that most old folk still call it 'company bagh', while everyone else calls it Lawrence Gardens. With no disrespect to Mr. Jinnah, it would make sense if the old name was restored and the history of the garden be written, along with the fact that the British brought in almost every known plant species from all over the world to make this exquisite botanical garden.

Take the names of Sir James Abbott, after whom is named Abbott Road. Its new name no one knows, for everyone calls it by its original name. Sir James was a famous frontier administrator who managed to tame (if that is ever possible) the NWFP. It was after him that we have the name Abbottabad, which thankfully has not been changed. Then we have two well-known soldiers in Chamberlain and Nicholson, after whom two well-known roads were named. People still call the roads named after them by their original names, even though two Islamic names have replaced them – officially.

Then there are roads named after former deputy commissioners, they being Nisbet Road, Beadon Road, Brandreth Road, Cooper Road, Cust Road, Lake Road and Hall Road. These names endure, even though officially they have all been changed. If today one was to ask for directions using the new names, one would never be able to locate them. Then there are the names of former Commissioners of Lahore, they being Davis Road, McLeod Road, Egerton Road, Montgomery Road and Durand Road. These are well-known and all the new names just do not click in the minds of the people.

The names of former Lieutenant Governors of the Punjab have been used, as development went ahead, to name Beadon Road, Brandreth Road, Cust Road, Lake Road and Hall Road. Take the example of Maclagan Road, named after Maj. Gen. Maclagan, a former Secretary of the Public Works Department and who contributed so much to Lahore and its rebuilding after the Sikh era. Should we forget his good work? So what if they were foreigners, but then so were all our rulers 800 years before them. The point of this piece is that we must learn to accept them as part of our history, and to lend them their due respect, just as there is a need to accept that we had a history before Mahmud from Ghazni hit Lahore and burnt it and looted the entire population. We know that the Afghans came as invaders to a more prosperous sub-continent. Some settled here, forever, while the rulers looted and raped and took massive wealth to Kabul. One has just accepted that they are part of our history, just as we must accept that before Mahmud, we were, for thousands of years, a Hindu city. Such is the plurality of Lahore.

Take other names like Temple Road being named after Sir Richard Temple, a brilliant barrister of Lahore who went on to become the Governor of Bombay. Thornton Road was named after another brilliant bureaucrat in Lahore who planned most roads. The Roberts Road, opposite the Civil Secretariat, was named after the first Commandant of the Punjab Volunteer Corps. The Roberts Club, office of the special police, is also named after him. He went on to become the highest ranking soldier of the British Raj. One is not interested, solely for the sake of writing our history, in the ethics of an invader, just as we cannot wish away the armed forces of Pakistan capturing political power and becoming the biggest corporate power in the country. It is a happening, that no civilized people should endure, but it is the reality we live in. So why wish away the reality of our past. It will not go away, no matter which times we live in.

Back to tracking our history through the names we live with. We have Lytton Road, named after the famous soldier, Lord Lytton, who stayed in Lahore when planning and conducting the Afghan war that the British fought, and deservingly lost. It might interest the reader to know that this road was specially made to facilitate troop movement from Ferozepur toward the G.T. Road and onto Peshawar. When the British were routed, most people in the city ascribed it to the graves in Mozang that were flattened for the road. But that is another story, one in which Capt. Hodson played a part.

Then we have a few more famous names like Lawrence Road, Mayo Road and Napier Road, all named after former Governor Generals and Viceroys. All these names have been changed. It seems we have a fixation with the present, especially with the names of Jinnah and Iqbal, both famous men without doubt. Lahore has 21 Jinnah roads and 23 Iqbal roads, or at least this was the count when last taken by the municipal authorities. They are spread all over in almost every new colony or estate that are sprouting up. It would make better sense if one major road each was named after them, and the history of the road with regard to the name written and displayed for everyone to read.

The point of this piece is not to belittle any name, for each one is as important as the other in its own context, but to try to make our 'rulers', removed as they are from the past and the people, understand why our history is not another country. It is the route we all have to travel to reach the present and to speed away into the future. So let old names live again for they have a charm that adds class to life.

The curse of the trees

Every time and age has its own outstanding men and women, ones whose influence remains after they are dead and gone. Greatness is how lesser mortals describe such persons. But on Mother Earth besides the homo sapien erectus, other species also exist, and their impact on life is probably greater.

No other living species has impacted our world greater than a tree ... that static, silent living species that serves us so much and so well. No other species has been more ravaged by man than the trees of this world. For the city of Lahore trees have a profound and historic connection, and probably no where on earth have we treated them more shabbily. There are stories about the trees of Lahore that need to be told. Here are just three of them.

In the beginning there was a mound, and around the mound flowed a river, a holy river. On the mound was a tree, a banyan tree, the very symbol of wisdom and stability. The old holy books say that Ram and Sita sat on the river edge and their conversation was concentrated on setting up home. "What better place than under the banyan tree on top of the mound, for here we shall have shade and also will be able to have a good view of the land all around." And so that is where they settled, and that is where Sita conceived her son Lahu, and that is where she gave birth to a son and to a city. The holy book actually says Ram predicted that as long as this banyan tree stood, so would the hamlet. That hamlet became Lahore, the city of Lahu, and if you are interested in that banyan tree, then in all probability its offspring still stands.

If you ever have the chance of visiting the Lahore Fort, take time out and find the temple of Lahu. Besides the temple is a massive banyan tree. This tree, so the experts inform me, is the oldest living tree in the entire sub-continent. Now that is a hard one to swallow, for beside the old banyan tree are a number of other ones, all having sprung up in the course of centuries from the seeds of the original. Does the curse of the banyan tree still hold true today for the city of Lahore? That is a question that is best left unanswered, for the tree is still there and so is our ancient city.

But then such myths have a habit of also multiplying. Many centuries after Lahu was born on the mound under the banyan tree, another great Lahori by the name of Sir Ganga Ram, an engineer without peer and the man who probably contributed more to the development of Lahore as a city than any other person, assisted Sir Riwaz in planting trees all along The Mall and in the Cantonment. He calculated that the point from which the Lahore Cantonment started was the corner of The Mall as it winds its way into the cantonment and the corner of Tufail Road, just opposite the house of the Corps Commander. On that corner, a sumbal tree was planted and was blessed by the clerics of many a religion. The high and mighty of these times were all in attendance, and it was said then that as long as that tree stood there, so would the Lahore Cantonment.

Over the years the tree grew to be the most magnificent and the tallest tree in the city of Lahore. The locals used to call it badshah, and it was this strange name that attracted me to it. Over the years I would pass by and nod a silent 'hello' to the massive badshah, and just as one grows found of children one was attracted to it for its sheer majesty. Then one day the men in uniforms moved in and in the name of 'development', cut it down. It took a total of five days to fell the old badshah, and every time I would pass by I would curse those felling him.

Today that spot is an isolated place, like a desert. One wishes that our subconscious mind is not trying to recreate images of deserts all around us, as we try so hard to create within ourselves the sensitivity that reflect the harshness of a desert. Will the curse of the badshah sumbal tree hold good? It is too soon to say, but given the sway of history and the extremist bends that our rulers pander to, the portents seem all ripe. After all, if Kasur could come to

Bulleh Shah, what could the arrogant rulers, pushed by the logic of religious fanatics, do about it? Precious little, history tells us.

But how is justice done to the species that we have shown so much disrespect to? Therein lies our third tale, the tale of justice and truth. If you have been unfortunate enough, as a litigant, to have visited the Lahore High Court, you will notice that it has two massive banyan trees. One is in the middle of the central courtyard, and the other is just outside the Bar room. So the bench and the bar both have their own banyan trees.

According to local legend, the banyan trees begin to dry when justice is at its lowest ebb, and flourish otherwise. This tale was told to me by none other than M.D. Khalid, a court clerk to the late Justice Kiyani. If there ever was a court clerk who knew how to write good, well punctuated English, MD was one such person. When I returned from England and wanted to rejoin the sole English-language newspaper then, he put his foot down and said; "Now reporters write their English in Urdu, and you will die of grief." MD would go on and on about the banyan trees and how Justice Kiyani used to salaam them every time he passed them. Probably that is why I started saying 'hello' to the good old badshah.

Perhaps even now we can make amends by planting trees in our amends dry. Let us honour those who did so before us. If you have noticed, the remaining trees of the Main Boulevard, planted so fondly by the late Zafarul Ahsan, are being cut down in the name of development. Probably we do want to turn our land into a desert, for only then, it seems, will our subconscious dreams come.

Lahore Cathedral

Great crosses of Lahore

Our culture is what we have on the ground, the fort, the mosques, the walls and the gates of the old city, the houses, the tombs, the graveyards, the churches, the colleges and schools. It is an endless list. The poet Faiz put it very aptly. "Everything we have is our culture. Full stop".

The city of Lahore has so much that one lifetime is not enough to cover everything. It is like French cheese, for they have one cheese for every day of the year, and a different one for every part of the day, and even then over a thousand varieties are left over, each more delightful than the other. So it is with Lahore, for here there is a story under every brick, each more amazing than the last one.

I set off with my friend 'Tipu' Al-Makky to walk over and see a few memorial inscriptions of the British era in the Cathedral of the Resurrection on The Mall, for it is one of the oldest churches in Lahore.

We sought permission from the bishop's office, and walked through the Cathedral School and the church. On entering the main gate, I remembered, from our youth, the house of Mr Castro Alonso, a former principal of the school. He was a great friend of the family and was a favourite friend of my father's, for he respected him for being a veteran fighter from the Spanish Civil War, for opposing fascism, and most importantly, he admired the three great Pablos of modern times, they being Picasso the painter, Neruda the poet, and Casal the celloist.

My old man, who was a former BBC war correspondent, knew all three and had spent long hours listening to Casal in France. Castro Alonso was an institution in Lahore, just as today is Cecil Chaudhry of St Anthony's High Schools, an upright man if there was one. The house of Mr Alonso is just the same as we saw it in our youth.

As we moved towards the cathedral, in the centre of the lawn is a huge red stone cross. On the plaque is its brief history, but there is much more to this cross than meets the eye. There is a legend that this cross was the original one on the very first church that came up in Lahore during the reign of Shah Jahan.

The strange thing is that even though Akbar is known as the liberal, yet it was he who refused to let them build a church. With Aurangzeb came the decline and even Maharajah Ranjit Singh refused to let them build a church. All he allowed his French generals was a chapel inside the shrine of Anarkali. When the British came they found this cross and placed it on the tomb of Anarkali.

When the British consolidated themselves in Lahore in 1849, they initially used the tomb chapel. However, as the military grew in size, they built a number of churches. The Cathedral of the Resurrection was built in 1887. The construction of the cathedral was supervised by the famous architect, John Oldrid Scott. The bishop of Lahore then was a French. Scott chose to build it in the Gothic style, its towers and red brick and pink sandstone exterior, being visible from several points in the city.

The church bells have been a subject of great interest. Originally, the frame for the bells was made to accommodate eight, but only six of them arrived from England. They were cast in 1903 by John Taylor & Co. of Loughborough. In the world of church bells, the Lahore bells are classified as rare and "priceless" as one church website states.

Inside, the church is a picture of serenity. We set about reading the plaques. That day we were interested in the one set up for Gen Sam Browne, the man who 'invented' the Sam Browne belt. As we walked along the walls, we were amazed to see memorial plaques of almost the entire Raj. There was one for Lawrence, for Montgomery, for McLeod, for Goulding. You take any name that was important during the Raj, and his name and special plaque is up there.

As we walked along, we stood at one for the police office Saunders, the man shot dead by the freedom fighter Bhagat Singh. It was an amazing experience. Before us, in the city of Bhagat Singh, was the plaque for Saunders "whose life was terminated by assassins". It is an amazing experience to see the flip side of history. But the church was then, like the mosques of today, an arm of the establishment. It seems rulers need a religion or cult to peg their morality on.

At every turn there is history. There are a lot of plaques for the brave men of the Punjab Regiment who fell in Mesopotamia. Almost 80 years later, there is a remote chance that the Punjabis might yet to go to that unfortunate land, even if it is under the guise of the United Nations. There are a number of other plaques of other battles in which men from this house of God fell. In death, they are remembered. It is a sobering experience.

But then the masterpiece of the visit turned out to be a small cross on one side of the cathedral. It is a replica of the original. This is an amazing find from an era in which the cross was not even known as a symbol of Christianity. It is a cross from a necklace worn in approximately 200 years after the death of Jesus Christ. Based on pure historical data, it might well be the oldest cross in the world, and could be the one worn by one of the original disciples of the prophet who is to return on the Day of Judgment. There is a story to this effect, but not much evidence to warrant its narration. It is good that the original is safely tucked away elsewhere, for this is a priceless relic in the history of Christianity. Outside stands the oldest cross of Lahore. A truly amazing collection, and one for which Lahore should be proud of its churches, as it is of the great men who have run them so far.

The Model Town that lost its ideals

In the 1950's going to Model Town was almost always a two-day affair, for it was considered so far away that one slept the night there. As all my father's uncles and aunts resided there, it was like second home. We called it the "town in the forest". But if ever there was a dream 'town' that the people of old Lahore built for themselves, this was it.

Model Town, which was originally conceived as an ideal town, was the brain child of a lawyer of Bhatti Gate called Dewan Khem Chand. He claimed that the idea came to him as a 'vision' when he was only 14 years old... for he did not like the narrow winding streets of the old walled city. He dreamed of an open city in the middle of the forests where: "one could run with no end in sight". During his studies in England Dewan Khem Chand put his idea on paper in January 1921 and titled it 'My Scheme'. His dream was to buy 1,000 acres of land and to build a 'modern town'.

On his return to Lahore, he improved on his original 'My Scheme' and wrote another paper titled 'Ideal Town', a place where people of every religion and faith lived in perfect harmony. "To achieve this, it is essential to allow humans to have sufficient space to achieve a serene state of mind". With this in mind he went to meet the original Father of Modern Lahore, Sir Ganga Ram, a man we today love to forget.

Sir Ganga Ram was a very practical and generous man. He immediately rejected the idea of having this 'ideal town' on the other side of the River Ravi near Shahdara, saying that his 'ideals' would be swept away by flood every third year. Seeing him so dejected, Sir Ganga Ram got up and took Dewan Khem Chand in his car to see the 'Rakh Kot Lakhpat Reserve Forest'. Later Khem Chand was to write he "immediately" fell in love with the place.

On the advice of Sir Ganga Ram, Dewan Khem Chand applied for 1,963 acres of land from the government, after a new society was formed as a company and was registered under the Co-operative Societies Act. The Forest department would just not agree to the scheme of this "town in the middle of their forest". For two years Dewan Khem Chand ran from pillar to post. In the end he asked Sir Ganga Ram for ideas. We do not know which string Sir Ganga Ram pulled, but within days he got his permission. On January 5, 1923, the land was handed over to the Model Town Co-operative Society.

The first meeting of the society was held in the Lahore Town Hall on February 27, 1921, in which Sir Ganga Ram was elected the first chairman and Dewan Khem Chand the first secretary. In this meeting the word 'Model Town' was suggested and adopted "till such time a more suitable name was found". After the meeting the plan was presented to Raja Narendra Nath, who on reading the 'scheme' threw it into his waste paper basket. It was when Sir Shadi Lal mentioned that it was very practical, and that Sir Ganga Ram thought it was an excellent idea, that he sent for a new copy and backed it to the hilt.

For the planning of Model Town, an advertisement was placed in the local newspaper with the stipulation that it should incorporate the best of our "own culture, as well as the best of Western culture". A grand prize of Rs.1,220 was offered. A total of 32 plans were received. They were placed on The Mall for public comment. Four plans were selected, and as the 'selection committee' liked all four they divided the prize money among all four.

The second prize winner was paid an additional Rs.500/- to incorporate all the four plans into one. "The town is square in shape with a circle in the middle. Four rectangles link the square to the circle, with eight triangles making up the residential quarters". The society bye-laws stipulated that there could be only one house per plot allotted with two-thirds being left for open for lawns and gardens. The plot sizes were also planned as being of six kanals, four kanals and two kanals only. They were classified as A,B and C class plots.

The membership was selected with great care. Dewan Khem Chand was to write later: "All members are literate, belonging to the upper and upper middle class, and people with clean records". The society hired a well-known architect by name of M.C. Khanna, who designed a total of 100 houses. The first 'flush system' houses in Lahore were introduced using the 'Kéntucky pattern', which worked with great efficiency. Dewan Khem Chand himself built a 'C' class house in 1930 within a record 32 days at a cost of Rs.6,500.

The Model Town Society banned all commercial advertising as it "debases residential living". They banned beggary in the society. A massive community services plan was launched which included a dairy farm, a poultry yard, an orchard and six acres were reserved for children to play in a nursery.

The most remarkable aspect of Model Town was how well they integrated people of every religious community. Special funds were raised to built a Mandir for Hindus, a Mosque for Muslims and a Gurdwara for the Sikhs. A cremation ground was set aside, and a graveyard planned.

Over the years, Model Town has undergone a dramatic change. From the original 184 members in 1920 with a population of less than 2,000 persons, by 2002 the population of Model Town had grown to 70,000 plus. Crass commercialism has taken over and even commercial establishments allowed within residential houses. Like the rest of Pakistan, commercialism has beaten back the private space and lives of the citizens of this ideal town.

Recent attempts to reverse this commercial thrust have been beaten when elected office-bearers were ousted by political-cum-commercial interests. Slowly and steadily, the original dream of Dewan Khem Chand is being pushed back, as house sizes get smaller, residential spaces are being used by commercial offices... the movement to reach a slum status is approximately half achieved. The bus service has ceased to exist. The dairy closed long ago. The Father of Modern Lahore, Sir Ganga Ram, had no idea just how badly the city he loved so much would be pushed back in time.

Taslimpur that became Lahore Cantonment

There is a rumour that the Lahore Cantonment is moving out, and that a new site has been selected for development. Such a rumour hit Lahore exactly 150 years ago when "Sir Charles Napier decided that the Anarkali Cantonment was to be moved". The reason then was that the cantonment was becoming 'unhygienic'. The reason today can correctly be said that it has become "too civil and less military". From a military man's point of view, even that is 'unhygienic'.

In the days of the East India Company in 1857 just when the war of independence was taking place, the cantonment existed in the Anarkali area. There was a small village called Taslimpur near the shrine of Hazrat Mian Mir. This area belonged to Prince Dara Shikoh, who acquired it during his lifetime and gifted it to his 'pir' Mian Mir. The Company acquired it on assuming power, and the first troops that had moved in from Amritsar in 1849 when Lahore fell from the Sikhs, had camped on the field between the Shalimar Gardens and the grounds of Taslimpur. These camping grounds proved to be the foundations of the new cantonment, and the area that is today called Saddar Bazaar is where the first troops rebelled in 1857 and were 'put to the cannon'.

When Sir Charles Napier decided that a new cantonment was needed, it was Henry Lawrence and John Hardinge who rode out one day on a 'mystery gallop' to Mian Mir – or 'Meean Meer' as the books refer to it – and on their return announced that a spot had been found for the new cantonment. The year was 1850, just after the British had managed to establish their control over the Punjab. Between the Shalimar Gardens and the tomb of Mian Mir, sizeable British troops were camped. The Anarkali Cantonment had virtually no space to house them as the clerks of the

Company had moved in to establish trade houses. So when a selection of the site was announced, it was decided that a straight line be drawn right from the gates of Shalimar to the "outer limits of the new cantonment". Military people love straight lines, and they call it the 'no nonsense approach'. So at one end of the road was the grandeur of a Mughal garden, while at the other end was the "epicentre of the new British Cantonment" – the Garrison Church of St Mary of Magdalene.

So keen were the British to establish their way of life, that the very first major building to come up was the church. After taking over from the Sikhs in 1849, they had selected the site for their new cantonment by 1850, and that very year work on the church started. In 1857, the year the War of Independence started and ended, the church was consecrated. Suffice it to remind that the marble 'flagstones' were taken from the gardens of the Dewan-e-Khas inside the Lahore Fort. The church cost a huge sum of Rs. 90,000/- of which Rs. 43,000/- was provided by the government as a grant, while the remaining was 'donated by supporters' of the Company.

By the time the church was established, the war of independence had made sure that Lahore was to become an important military station, and so the heavy guns were all brought to this 'safe station'. The officers had established an 'Officers Colony' midway between the Shalimar and the church. This was the principal site of the cantonment. It came to be called Saddar, or main cantonment. Another straight line, parallel to the first, was drawn between the housing area at Saddar and the newly established Royal Artillery establishment just a mile to the south of the church. This road was called Artillery Road. Here sprung up the now famous R.A. Bazaar, or the Royal Artillery Bazaar. All military activities, or regiments, were established, initially, along these two roads, and the arteries that connect them. Then in 1867 a complete and 'comprehensive' plan for the Lahore Cantonment was made, and every detail mapped out. Since then all military commanders have followed that plán and map.

The very first activity that the British undertook was to plant trees along the roads. They brought in a small canal to water these areas, which in the old days ran along today's Sarfraz Rafiqui Road, for the old Artillery Road. Today it is a dried channel. By the time 1857 had come, this area was the greenest area of Lahore, and still remains so, even though of late massive tree cutting exercises have taken place. With the trees came up a number of barrack buildings. Almost all the bricks for these barracks were provided by Muhammad Sultan, the famous contractor, who collected all the bricks from destroyed mosques from inside the old walled city. They say Sultan died of a "curse for stealing the bricks of Lahore's mosques" and died a pauper. Among the barracks that came up, the soldiers gave them strange names. For example the barracks that housed bachelors were called "chummery", slang for 'chums'.

If we examine an old map, dated 1867, of the Lahore Cantonment area, we see that the road from Lahore, that narrow horse track that ultimately became The Mall, shows that the area that today constitutes St. John's Park, opposite the Fortress Stadium, was originally where the military 'Ice Pits' existed. The map shows this as being next to the 'Meean Meer Railway Station' on the Amritsar Line. All the year round, ice frozen because of the night cold was stored underground in an ancient method of collecting ice. In old Lahore, the Mughal and Sikh era 'ice pits' were located just next to Rattigan Road on the grounds next to Central Model School and the Central Training College. Opposite the military 'ice pits' was the bungalow of the Sergeant, where today stands the Fortress Stadium.

Another map of 1927 shows the Saddar Bazaar as the most developed portion of the new cantonment, with the R.A.Bazaar also developing into a sizeable area. The other areas also grew and developed. Then came, initially, the Aircraft Park, which was renamed the Lahore Aerodrome, and then renamed the Lahore Airport. With time it has grown in commercial importance. Today it is called the Allama Iqbal International Airport. Initially it was the RAF Base at Lahore. Today it is the PAF Base at Lahore. If we follow the 1927 map, and move from Saddar to R.A.Bazaar, we have the Officers Colony, then the Indian Officers Club, then 'Magazine Cells', a name for an ammunition depot, then comes the Chitral Lines and then the RAF Headquarters. Then there was a Grass Farm for the cavalry horses, and then came the huge barracks of the famous Probyn's Horse. All that has changed, and in its place are hundreds of houses, including the Jinnah House, one that belonged to the Quaid-e-Azam, but gifted to the Pakistan Army to house the Corp Commander of Lahore.

The Lahore Cantonment has a history all its own, steeped as it is with history. There is a need to preserve that to the maximum extent. If the Lahore Cantonment moves on to another place in the next few years, it will surely be because today lax military rules have allowed civilians with military roots to inhabit this area. Today it is more civilian and less military. Maybe, the time has come for them to move to their own secluded 'hygienic' corner in national life. Even this is history in the making.

The grandeur that makes up GOR-1

In all non-democratic societies the 'rulers' have preferred to live apart from the people. Just as Mughalpura was built for the Mughal elite 600 years ago, and the Officers Colony at Lahore Saddar, near Mian Mir's tomb, served the British East India Company before the present cantonment was built, so was the GOR, or Government Officers Residences, built for the white officers of colonial Lahore.

The story of the Lahore GOR, or GOR-1 as it is officially called, has a unique history all its own. Its greenery and grandeur remains unsurpassed in any residential colony in Lahore. With the coming of the railways, the glorious Mayo Gardens served as an example of how the elite railway officers were housed in utter luxury. They had the very first golf course for themselves, a 'facility' the present military regime promptly have got rid off in the name of 'restructuring'. Sounds sensible on paper. The officers are now refused permission to the privately-owned place.

The very first military officers colony came up on the Dharampura Road, now called Zarrar Shahid Road, in the Lahore Cantonment. It served the new British military elite of the East India Company. In the 1857 war of independence three British soldiers who were killed in this place - an event we just do not observe to remember the thousands of Muslim, Hindu and Sikh soldiers and civilians of Lahore. But the very first civilian officers of the Company found civilian quarters in the Old Anarkali area. All of them were rented premises from the local population.

Then the Company decided to build a number of houses in the Rattigan Road area. If you happen to walk on the road in front of the College of Veterinary Sciences, past Rattigan Road, onto Tap Road curving onto Lahore Road, you will notice the entire area, still, full of old British-era houses, most of them crumbling. All these magnificent bungalows comprised of the very first civilian officers residences.

With the building of the new cantonment at Mian Mir, the civilian administrators felt that they had to move 'up market'. Their first move was to build a 'gazetted officers' residences' in an enclave between the Jail Road and the Racecourse. It is a triangular piece that had a scenic view of the park and the races. The British ladies would go for walks in the park between the Racecourse and the Punjab Club on the Mall. As is the habit of all bureaucrats, they have an eye for acquiring the best 'plots' and for inventing the correct logical excuse to build on it. A British journalist wrote in 1920 in a Lahore newspaper: "The fun is the bureaucrats suggested and the bureaucrats decided. They love playing judge and jury with such innocence".

In 1914, the Secretary of State for India got a brief which stated: "Government of the Punjab was informed of an excellent site that could house government officers in an environment suitable to their temperament, safe from the heat and dust of the city of Lahore". The reason was the same given to Akbar the Great by his courtiers hundreds of years earlier when Mughalpura was built. The British officers had built a golf link at the present Lahore Gymkhana site. So there existed another 'plausible' reason why the present GOR-1 site was suitable for residences. So in 1914, "a tract of land equal to 192 acres was acquired for Rs. 3,24,369" and handed over to the Buildings and Roads Department.

In 1918 the department reported having built six houses, making an effort to cut out any expense that could be termed as 'luxury'. The interesting aspect of the work was that the roads were first completely built for the entire GOR. Then came tree plantation, followed by the telegraph office. Then came the markets with shops and last to start were the first six houses. The housing committee of the department approved the designs, as were all houses that were to follow.

In 1919 another three houses came up taking the number to nine. So work went on with new houses being built for specific posts. The housing committee made clear "no construction should be undertaken unless it fulfils the needs of a specific permanent post". The emphasis was on not constructing to specific demands of persons in positions of authority. In 1936 the Commissioner's House was built at a cost of Rs. 50,100/-, a sum that caused considerable concern in official quarters. The Deputy Commissioner's House was completed soon afterwards at a cost of Rs. 44,700/-. Then came the beautiful house for the Punjab Chief Secretary.

In 1936 the beautiful house of the Chief Justice was completed at a cost of Rs. 67,100/-. This was followed by the house of the Punjab Minister of Finance, which cost Rs. 80,486/-. This house today houses the Chief Minister's official residence. So with time specific residences for posts came up. A series of A-type houses were built for the Secretaries of various departments.

The GOR came to be seen as the 'elite area' of Lahore, where as one sage put it "all power resides". Most importantly this is where all the judges of the Lahore High Court live in "seclusion, not meeting anyone, to concentrate only on justice to the people". But then with time the bureaucracy has grown in a geometric ratio, and more GORs were needed. So a second one came up when the old jail was knocked down. Today six GORs exist, sadly each new one of a lower standard than the one built before.

In a free Pakistan why are GORs needed? In my days as a journalist in England, I remember travelling on a train to work in London, sitting next to the British Education Secretary going to Whitehall to work. He travelled, like all British bureaucrats, on public transport and lived in his own house. But like the Mayo Gardens which might be sold off one day to build commercial plots, it seems one day GOR-1 might also go the same way. That, at least history tells us, it should.

Lahore's Last Frontier

The other day, I spent almost the entire day in the Ferozewala kutchery on the banks of the Ravi in Shahdara. It is probably the wildest, roughest, toughest place on earth where every third man has a gun. I recall reading a saying of Maharajah Ranjit Singh, who, when praised on his iron grip on the whole of the Punjab, commented: "I will accept that compliment only when I control Pakhtiala in Sheikhupura."

The truth of the matter is that no one has ever been able to control Pakhtiala, save once when a crazy English deputy commissioner decided to take on the wild dacoits of the area and lived to regret it. The 'Thug Movement', which the British crushed also, bore no fruit in Pakhtiala. Our very own Pakistan Army in 1999 tried to take on the villagers of Pakhtiala, after a young captain in the company of his troops surrounded the area in an attempt to force the people of this village to pay their electricity dues, their land revenue and their 'abiana' or water tax. It is a well-known fact that the captain used his common sense and left.

Pakhtiala is a place no one in Lahore, let alone from the district of Sheikhupura, goes to. For centuries, the ruler of Lahore has had Pakhtiala, at least ethnically, for standing on top of the Lahore Fort it can be seen through binoculars. But no ruler has ever had the guts to go there. Even Maharajah Ranjit Singh preferred to avoid the place. It is not that the people of Lahore today do not know about it. The fact that they refuse to pay any taxes or utility dues is also well known, for it has been acknowledged during question hour in the Punjab Assembly. It has even appeared as a question in a PTV television quiz programme.

Many call this the 'Last Frontier of Lahore' and the goings on in Pakhtiala can best be judged by watching the proceedings in the Ferozewala kutchery. As I sat at the lawyers' stump in the open, I asked the 'munshi' why everyone carried a gun here. "Oh, it's because the people of Pakhtiala have cases here," he said in a casual way. The name rang a bell in the mind's eye, for Maharajah Ranjit Singh had mentioned that he always avoided Pakhtiala. I sat in stunned silence.

The 'munshi' was wearing two iron rings on his leg. "What are these?" I asked in simple urban innocence. He looked at me in surprise and said: "I am not 'Ahle Tashee' it's the rings my dead mother made me wear when I was in prison." After a long silence I asked why he was in prison. "Oh, I murdered three people who tried to tease the women in our village. Five were killed and 14 injured seriously in that fight. I was released after three months when I paid the other party eight lakhs." Yes he also belonged to Pakhtiala, but has moved out to lead a normal life. He also carries a pistol just in case old enmities break out again.

What is Pakhtiala all about? Ask anyone to the West of the River Ravi about the place, and they will immediately catch their ears. It is important that this aspect of Lahore be narrated. For centuries the people of the lands to the west of the River Ravi have always lived off people who came and left Lahore. The entire area has, and most lands still have, 'Idkkar' forest, a small hardy tree that defies any abuse we humans can throw at it. Like the people it survives. With extreme poverty, the people had no option but to take to dacoity. During the Mughal era, the Rajputs of this area lived their own independent way of life, never surrendering to any authority. When the army set off after them they hid in the forests and in the scrubs along the river.

It is perfect land for guerilla warfare, and it was these very lands on which the gallant Sikhs carved their kingdom. Their misls developed into a potent force that ultimately crushed Mughal and Afghan power. It goes to their credit that they managed to develop strategies that no army could match, groups of 10 or 15 on horseback, a classic hit and run tactic, nay, hit, loot and then run tactic. Looting the Afghans was their favourite pastime, and they through sheer grit and guts managed to wear down the Afghan hordes, who in the name of Islam actually themselves came to loot. So in a way they returned to the land what foreigners had stolen from us. Only they allowed them to pass to Delhi in peace, but on the way back they broke even.

Today Pakhtiala stands alone, that last frontier of Lahore where people still do not pay their electricity dues, nor do they pay any land revenue, or water cesses. When Wapda tried to cut off power, no officer worth his salt had the guts to switch off the main line. No 'patwari' has been able to tax them, and when irrigation SDO tries to stop water going to their lands, a submachine gun burst does the trick.

It is not without good reason that the Lahore-Sheikhupura Road and the numerous roads that go inside the district have been declared as the most dangerous areas in the entire country. The British decided that it was best to leave them alone, but only when any prominent person from Pakhtiala came to Lahore, they just locked him up for questioning. Such tactics are still followed and that is why the people of this village are so suspicious of their 'rulers' in Lahore.

Sitting in Ferozewala kutchery reminded me of my cousin Usman Turi who, as a Sui Gas officer had the nerve to disconnect the factory gas connection, for non-payment, of a gent from this village. Early one morning he was physically lifted from his Gulberg home and was found in the Ferozewala lock-up two days later. A case had been filed in the Ferozewala kutchery and he was blamed for some obscure crime. Usman watched in horror as a burly policeman tortured a thief by placing his hands under the legs of a 'charpoy' and sitting on it. I managed the needful through a bail application. That gent still runs his factory a la Pakhtiala.

Pakhtiala is no myth. It has been a grim reality for the numerous rulers who have managed to make it in Lahore. It is part of Lahore, but it is truly the last frontier of the area immediately to the west of the walled city. It is the true homeland of the Sikh movement. To the south is Nankana, where Guru Nanak was born and his family dwelt. To the north-east the Ravi snakes through. Along the banks and in the shrubland around Pakhtiala is where the Mughals murdered thousands of Punjabis, but the brave always returned to win. Such is the territory, such are the people. It is truly Lahore's 'Last Frontier'.

Walton: The 'Greatest Airlift Ever'

If you have ever visited the Walton Railway Station, it would make sense to stand there in silence and just imagine hundreds of blood-soaked trains coming in from the eastern parts of the sub-continent in August, 1947, the doors would open and out fell hundreds of human bodies, all hacked to death. Something similar was happening in Amritsar a few miles away. An entire sub-continent, Hindu, Muslim and Sikhs, all of them, had just gone mad.

The blood-soaked events of the Partition of the sub-continent seem to have been forgotten. So great was the shock that we have still not broken out of it. If you walk through the old walled city of Lahore one comes across scores of old men who sit and discuss almost every event under the sun, but never the events of 1947. It is, as if, there is a conscious effort to 'partition' the past. I know an old aunt who just refused to tell what happened to her, and she walked bare feet from Chawinda with her two sisters, her house in flames. It seems, like her, we all just refuse to record our history. The practice of recording our past has been poor in the sub-continent save for the folk tradition of songs and ballads, but now that we are a 'literate' nation, there is a need for a conscious effort.

To my way of thinking Walton is sacred soil, as is also the Shahalami Gate area, which was burned down completely, gate included. In one mohallah alone over 4,000 Lahoris were locked in and burned alive. "I saw burning children jump from roof tops and we clapped in delight", informs a grim old man in Tehsil Bazaar. He was with the crowd that torched the place. It was in retaliation to a Muslim women's hostel in Amritsar being attacked, the inmates raped and burned alive. It was a gruesome event, as were all the ones, hundreds of them, that followed. It was unstoppable. Humanity had gone mad. The greatest exodus in human history was underway. The murder and rape that accompanied has seldom been equalled by any civilization. Even that was unrivalled. Yet all this remains unrecorded. There are no monuments to the grief and suffering through which everyone went and emerged as a 'free nation'. Makes you think.

The idea is not to blame any one sect or religion, for that is a futile exercise. Everyone is equally to blame. The point is to stop and think and then to record. There is very little that we can do about what happened, for what has happened cannot be undone. Two nations were created, which within a quarter of a century became three nations. Some even now joke that the 'two-nation' theory actually turned out to become the 'three-nation' one. The secular among us blame communal politics for the hate. "Communalists need to be faced and defeated in both countries if we are to have a relationship", says an Indian expert.

But then historians in all three countries, India, Pakistan and Bangladesh, agree on one thing, and that is that the geography of nations was ultimately decided by their market access. In the end economic progress, non-communal as it is by its nature, and market access proved to be a greater binding force than the hate of beliefs. All this creates an even great need for information about what happened. That is why recording the events of 1947 is very critical today, for given just one more generation, and none among us will be eye witnesses to the event.

There is a need for several small museums dedicated to special events. For example, how many people know that from Walton Airport, most of which is now armed forces plots and buildings (another misguided pastime of those with muscle), the largest airlift ever took place. It was an event that has never been recorded. However, a former RAF pilot has written an interesting piece about what he calls 'The Biggest Airlift Ever'. Ft. Lt. Michael Kidd, from Ashcott in England, is a famous aviator in his own country. "Aviation was my life," he says. After serving in the Fleet Air Arm during World War II, he joined BOAC as one of just six trainees, and served as Station Manager for the corporation all over the world. One of his most interesting postings took him to Walton in Lahore in 1947, the year of partition, when he took part in the biggest human airlift ever, the flying of refugees to and from Pakistan and India.

Mike Kidd himself flew the Dakotas designed to carry 28 people. By removing the seats they were able to take an average of 69 people each trip. He remembers refugees lighting fires in the cabin to cook their 'chapattis'. He is proud that there were no accidents and no loss of life, except for one memorable flight, this time with a Bristol 170, capable of carrying 119 people, when one woman died en route and another had a baby; this meant that on arrival the pilot was able to report the same total of living people on board as when they started. The British Museum is said to be preparing an exhibition about this event, and Walton Airport will be the focus of international attention. I wish they also show the army houses that have sprung up in the 'aerodrome' area. Such is our history.

But one cannot live on wishing to undo what the army has acquired by means that are highly questionable. What we can do is to stop the drift by creating houses to learn our past – museums - about our struggle for Independence in all its aspects. If a small museum at Walton Aerodrome recorded the 'Biggest Airlift Ever', and another one at Walton Railway Station recorded the 'Biggest Rail Movement Ever', the shifting of millions, burying hundreds of thousands in the land of their dreams, or another one at Walton where the refugee camps once stood, or yet another one at Shahalami Gate to record the manner in which Lahore burned down and its citizens killed by one another. There is a need to record the thousands of stories of our elders, so that future researchers can piece together just what happened where. We owe it to our children, as we do to our parents for they suffered so that we could live free. Now that the basics have been accepted by one and all – minus the lunatic fringe – it is time to tell and record and keep them to remind future generations of the collective madness that the entire sub-continent went through.

Why Hazuri Bagh?

The garden between the Lahore Fort and the Badshahi Mosque is known as Hazuri Bagh. Why is it called Hazuri Bagh? This question has always puzzled me. There are many versions to this name, and like all things, good, bad or ugly, in Lahore, there is always a story to it.

There are two credible versions to the use of the name Hazuri. The first one is that all courtiers who mattered, the 'Jee Hazuri' type (flatterers) waited for their turn in this beautiful garden. The old folk in the walled city still jokingly call it

Hazuri Bagh

the 'Jee hazuri bagh', and they point out to the grave of Sir Sikander Hayat in the garden who they claim was the chief 'flatterer' of the British rulers.

If you head from Garhi Shahu across the canal towards the Mian Mir Graveyard in Dharampura, to the left you will come across, in a lane on the road that heads towards the CMH, a small graveyard which is built on two levels. The main structure has a green dome. Through the main door one comes to an open space with a lot of graves enclosed by a wall. In the middle is a small tomb built of small bricks. Inside is the grave of Syed Mahmud Hazuri. There are two graves in this tomb. One of Syed Mahmud and the other of Syed Shah Nuruddin, the son of Mahmood. Next to this small tomb is yet another small tomb, again with two graves, of Syed Jan Muhammad Hazuri and his son Syed Sarwar Din. Next to them is a small mosque of the same period.

The name Hazuri comes from this great family, who claimed to have direct lineage from Imam Ja'far Sadiq. This is a tall claim to say the least, but then the family claimed, in writing, the exact lineage.

On one side of the tomb is the exact lineage given, and it seems reasonable to accept it as correct. Every year a small Urs is held in which on the first day people come to pray and light mustard oil lamps in the traditional clay 'deevay', while on the second day 'qawwalis' are held.

Our piece is about which exact 'Hazuri' was the garden outside the Lahore Fort named after. This calls for a short history to be told. The story goes that this famous family of Musavi Syeds had their origins in the mountains of Ghaur in Afghanistan. They were considered a very pious family, and in their tradition of learning they wrote out copies of the Holy Quran and also excelled in the art of bookbinding, almost always in leather. Two copies of their works can be seen in the British Museum, excellent specimens of calligraphy and leather bookbinding. This family of Musavi scholars moved to the sub-continent and settled in Uch Sharif in Sindh, where the environment was conducive. The exact time period of this migration one cannot dare to mention, as the oral tradition seems to vary so much.

From Uch Sharif during the period the Mughal Emperor Shah Jahan was in power, this family moved to Lahore, as in those days this city was the main seat of learning and scholarship. They lived, initially, inside the walled city in, as one account puts it, near Akbari Mandi. Which exact mohallah or area one does not know. But they definitely soon acquired a reputation for scholarship, and also, more importantly, as being "masters of the known and the unknown" sciences. This was a very good reason for them to become well known to the royal court, which kept an eye for such people to cover all options, or threats, to their power. In a way, this still goes on as we read in newspapers about various saints and seers.

The royal court is known to have been deeply influenced by the learning of Syed Jan Muhammad Hazuri, a man who refused to accept any money or gifts from the Mughal rulers. He was a humble man and saw it best to come and go to the Lahore Fort as an unknown seer. That this great man of learning may have waited, or dwelt in Hazuri Bagh, one cannot say with any certainty, but he surely would have passed this way, or waited here. Jan Muhammad Hazuri died in AH 1064. In the graveyard also exist the graves of a number of leading personalities of Lahore, including the poet Mufti Ghulam Sarwar.

Over time this graveyard has fallen into disrepair, and along with the graveyard next to the tomb of Mian Mir, it has become an encroachers' delight. Every year a few houses creep up, with the living building on the dead.

One account describes Syed Mahmud Hazuri as the person after whom Hazuri Bagh was named by the Mughals. But then one piece by a scholar names Jan Muhammad as the person after whom it was named. It would be futile to pinpoint the exact person. It seems that the entire family, for several generations, continued with the tradition of learning and 'advising' people on how to solve their problems by following the ways as described in the Holy Quran. It might come as a surprise that even today there are four persons claiming direct lineage from that family who are today working as holy men. It seems that the garden was named after the family, not one person, all of whom acquired the name Hazuri in Lahore, being described as 'hazoor' as is normally the manner in which such people are addressed. But that the name has a mystery to it is all the more alluring. After all, that is what Lahore is all about.

The Shalimar Gardens remarkable hydraulics

It might seem to many merely 'a grand dream of heaven' desired on earth by the Mughal emperor Shah Jahan, just as he wanted his bride Mumtaz Mahal to be remembered forever in the magnificent Taj Mahal at Agra, but the building of the Shalimar Gardens in

Shalimar Gardens

Lahore in the period 1641-42 was much more than a mere dream, it was an engineering feat few would even dream of attempting today.

The emperor put in years of planning before he gave the go ahead for the Shalimar Gardens, and midway when he realized that engineering hitches would mar his project, he threw in fresh minds and more money to overcome niggling problems. The story of the building of the gardens, and, more importantly, its engineering components, is one that we must know more about. Situated in the north-east of the city of Lahore and spread over 40 acres, the Shalimar Gardens structures include the 'Aaram Gah' (Resting Garden), the 'Khwaab Gah' (Sleeping Garden), the Aiwan (Courtier's Garden), these being the three terraces of the famed garden. Then to these are a series of gateways, kiosks, pavilions and wells. Then there is, to one side, a 'Naqqaar khana' and the 'Chahar Bagh' (Paradise Garden).

The real story of the Shalimar Gardens is about how water was brought to it. The challenge was to bring natural flowing water, with all its nutrients, to feed the massive lawns on the three terraces of the gardens, as well as to have clean sand and mud free water to flow at the exact pressure and amounts to run the 410 fountains planned on the three terraces. Remember we are talking about the year 1640, so we have to keep in mind the technological realities of that age. There was no electricity to power pumps, so it all had to be a very controlled and calculated use of available water.

For the gardens a massive water canal was planned. This was named the 'Shahi Nahr' (Royal Canal). The best water available was 160 kilometres upstream to the north at a place called Madhupur where the once beautiful River Ravi left the mountains and entered the plains. A special canal, running parallel to the river, was dug at a level always higher and to the left of the flowing river. Along the way 'stilling reservoirs' were made to deplete the mud content of the water. After it had travelled its 160 kilometre course, the water level was eight metres higher than the top terraced garden of the Shalimar.

This canal was designed by Ali Mardan Khan and cost in the year 1640 a sum of Rs. 150,000/-. The project, a marvel on to itself, did not meet the exacting high standards expected of the Shalimar. The job of rethinking the entire 'Shahi Nahr' project was handed over to a young Mulla Ala al-Mulk Tuni, who at an additional cost of Rs. 50,000/- fixed the problems of the canal and got it ready in record time. Water started flowing from Madhupur to Lahore. During the British era it was called the Madhupur Canal, then changed to Hansli Canal, and finally was referred to as the Shalimar Distributory. In 1960 when the Indus Water Treaty was signed the once 'Shahi Nahr' ceased flowing.

The 'Shahi Nahr' irrigated the complex of gardens and filled the canals of the upper terraced garden and the main tank on the middle terrace. But the water for the fountains was had from a hydraulic complex to the south of the garden. Situated outside the walls of the garden, it was fed by a series of Persian wheel wells. A series of natural water filtration tanks were made. The water lifted from the wells was deposited in a tank (19 metres by 5.5 metres). Near the top were three holes each ten cms in diameter that took the water to a second filtration tank. From here the water travelled to two chambers with four holes vertically positioned. The depth of each tank was 1.4 metres.

Each of the tanks was built of solid brick masonry with red sandstone blocks. On the western side a 15 cms diameter pipe went underground and emerged inside the garden. The simple terracotta pipe was all hand-moulded and all collared together in Hessian and limestone. This simple structure has endured time and pressure. The cavities have been filled in by jute threads dipped in a white lime cream which has a waxy feeling. What this substance is we do not yet know, but what we do know is that it has managed to survive almost 400 years of a functioning water hydraulic system.

The perfect planning of water pressure to the fountains defies imagination today. The upper terrace has 105 fountains, the middle 152 and the lower terrace 153 fountains. Each fountain works to such perfection that water just laps the edge of the tanks in which it is located, never spilling over. It is almost like a fast flowing stream in the mountains from where the Mughals came, flowing on always, yet never out.

The beauty of the Shalimar is the 'Sawan Bhadon' waterfall at the edge of the middle terrace. The sound of the flowing water into a massive series of tanks and fountains reminds one of the monsoon season in Lahore, where rain and sound make up for such a beautiful day. On a holiday, as young children, one remembers going there with buckets full of mangoes. The mangoes inside the gardens, once owned and managed by the Mian family of Baghbanpura, were famous all over the sub-continent. It is a picture of perfect harmony, a place in heaven.

The laying and placement of the 'unseen' water pipes had always been a mystery. A few years ago nuclear scientists had to use radiation technology to locate a massive leak. That for the first time revealed the manner in which the pipes have been laid. At one point it is in the middle of 20 feet of rock solid lime masonry. Today the hydraulic engineering feat of the Shalimar is largely unknown. It is an engineering marvel we just do not like to own up to.

Some modifications were carried out during the period Maharajah Ranjit Singh ruled over the Punjab in 1799-1839, and also during the British occupation of the Punjab from 1849 to 1947. But the greatest damage has been caused to the entire garden and its unique engineering works through neglect and other reasons in the period 1947 to date. Most of the original flora has been destroyed. The hydraulic system has been damaged immensely and the 'Mughal vision of a paradise' lost, maybe forever.

In 1999, the Shalimar Gardens and the Lahore Fort, were placed on the list of 'World Heritage Sites in Danger' following the demolition of the Garden's unique hydraulic works by the Nawaz Sharif government in its hurried attempt to build a better road to Amritsar, from where the Indian Prime Minister was to come on a 'peace bus', the real beginning of the India-Pakistan peace process. In Pakistan seven 'world heritage' sites have been marked by the world, and, sadly, none has seen any major conservation work undertaken so far by either the federal or the provincial governments. It is reflective of the times in which we live.

The Federal Department of Archaeology undertook various works on 'preservation and restoration' of the Shalimar Gardens, which commenced in 1973-74 and continued until 1988-89. A master plan for the preservation and restoration of the Gardens was prepared in April 1998 by the Department of Archaeology and Museums and covers the 1998-2003 periods. Nothing noteworthy emerged from these half-baked unfunded attempts.

In the end the United Nations organization UNESCO, with assistance from the USA's Getty Conservation Institute Program, decided that the Shalimar Gardens was far too important for the entire world to be left to the mercies of the Government of Pakistan, and they have set into motion a conservation plan for the Shalimar, a project that is scheduled to be completed by the end of December 2005. What the UNO had not calculated in was the Pakistani bureaucrat. If there is nothing in it for him, it cannot be undertaken.

Jadoo Ghar and its enduring mystery

For the people of Lahore, no other building or place holds greater mystery than the Freemasons Hall, known to the locals as Jadoo Ghar. With this building is associated a secret powerful society whose meetings took place with a human skull placed on the podium and the members wore eerie costumes, holding daggers.

This chilling description was provided in a story printed in a local Urdu newspaper in 1895 after a waiter, living in the Old Anarkali area, blurted out his version of what happened inside the headquarters of the Free Masons Hall at Charing Cross. Today, the nameplate reads, 90 Shahrah-i-Quaid-i-Azam. The next day, so the newspaper later alleged, the waiter disappeared never to be seen again. That added to the mystery with people alleging that the entire thing was a Jewish conspiracy. Others alleged it was a weird Christian secret society that was actually anti-Christ. But no one has really written or researched much about 90, The Mall. One book does provide a fair bit of detail about the building plans taken from official records of the Punjab government, but beyond that, not much information is available.

It so happens that as a young reporter in 1974, I was deputed to go along with government officials who took over the building when the organization was banned. The Peoples' Party, then in power, took it over to set up their own headquarters. Many believe that was the day when the party came under a curse and its upward growth stopped. But the real restrictions on the Freemasons came about during the 1965 Pakistan-India War. Its activities were curbed and during the disastrous 1971 war, there was a lot of suspicion that they were actually spies of the enemy. Such has been the mystery of the Freemasons Society that the people of Lahore have never been sure as to what it actually stands for.

Let me describe my visit to 90, The Mall, when it was taken over by the Z.A. Bhutto government. On entry, there were a number of swords, and on the sides of the staircase going up were a number of skeletons and human skulls. All sorts of strange mallets and weapons and silken clothes almost like the ones worn by the Ku Klux Klan of the US were lying all over the place. There were gongs and brass bowls and huge tapestries hung from the wall. The place was eerie, as if human sacrifices had taken place there. But then, so strong was the myth of the Freemasons we had grown up with, that seemingly innocuous items on display appeared to be part of a sinister plot. It was clear that it was a club of elite persons, all of whom met to discuss what was dear to them. The building also has a lot of history to it. But before one delves into that, let us look at how Freemasonry came to the city of Lahore. The first Freemasons of Lahore are said to have been Ventura and Avitable, two French generals in the Army of Maharajah Ranjit Singh, who had escaped from France after the defeat of Napoleon at Waterloo. The first meeting of the Freemasons in Lahore was held inside Sheranwala Gate in the last days of the Sikh ruler. This site was to be used later in the initial days of the British rule.

In 1859 Lodge 'Hope and Perseverance' No. 782 was formed and the very next year a building was constructed in the Old Anarkali area. Till recently, that road was called Lodge Road, for on it was the District Grand Lodge of the Freemasons Society. The members were called Brethren of the Lodge. On September 6, 1859, H.D. Sandeman, who is better known as the man after whom Fort Sandeman is named, laid the foundations of the lodge. The brethren called the lodge their 'temple'. With time the lodge was extended and soon it was felt that a new and better 'temple' or lodge was needed. It was then that in September, 1914, the original lodge was sold to the government of the Punjab for the setting up of a public library, and a new plot of 13 kanals and 126 square feet was purchased for Rs. 32,590 out of the then Deer Park corner of the Lahore Zoo. It was here that the Freemasons Hall was built.

The consulting architect of the Punjab government, one Mr. Sullivan prepared the drawings and plans, which the government approved. The foundation stone of the new building was laid on April 1, 1916. The interesting thing is that the foundation stone laid by Sandeman in 1859 was relaid. The lodge was housed in the Goldsmith building just opposite the hall. It was then known as the Max Minck Building. By the end of 1917, the new temple was completed. This is the brief story of the hall building.

But what has happened to the Freemasons Society of Lahore? It is generally assumed that it has stopped functioning. But those in the know say that it still functions. Legally speaking, the hall belongs to the society, and very few know that a writ was once pending in the Lahore High Court in which the society had asked that their building be returned to them. What happened to that writ, no one knows.

A Freemason of Lahore informed me that all these stories about the Jadoo Ghar were hogwash, and that the society basically worked for the betterment of the people in which the lodge was located. The only difference between them and others is that no one knows what 'welfare' work they do. But the 'brethren' insist that is all they do, and keeping such work a secret is essential if it is to be meaningful. Well, it must be said that the spirit is genuine. The problem is that in this age of openness, even genuine good work for the poor is looked down upon if it is not publicized. Now where does one go from here?

Gymkhana: the sacred ground of the sahibs

If ever the British left behind a part of their countryside, it was in the shape of the Lahore Gymkhana cricket ground in the Lawrence Gardens, or Jinnah Gardens. My father used to tell me that it reminded him of the Worcester cricket ground, probably the most beautiful in Britain, with The Hove in Sussex being a close second.

One of my favourite pastimes on a spring Sunday is to take my tea and sandwiches to watch cricket at this virtual temple of serenity. The old eyes cannot make out the fine cuts or glances without binoculars, but one can, after honing my senses in the Minto Park of old, take the measure of the man at the wicket. My late father had seen Don Bradman play his last innings for a duck and one never tired of listening to the excitement of the tragic event. He missed his average of 100. Finally, it was proven that he was mortal.

But then so is Tendulkar, at least I think he is. It is sad that Tendulkar will not play at the Lahore Gymkhana cricket ground, for little does he know that he will be missing an experience that might make him love Lahore. Nehru called it the cultural capital, the 'real heart', of the sub-continent. Bhagat Singh lived out his immortal act here. Yet in the turmoil of history, one that goes back in antiquity, did finally emerge a game that the people of the entire sub-continent learned to love, more so in Lahore than anywhere else.

The Lawrence Gardens were created after the turmoil of 1857 was over. The 'desolate land' is where the British forces camped and finally overcame 'our disorganized ancestors' against great odds. In the disorder, in these gardens, was born the famous Club Sandwich. In an area covering 112 acres were organized the gardens. The vow of the East India Company was that it would bring 80,000 saplings of 600 different species from every corner of the world, where in those days, the sun never set. After collecting money from the sale of Badami Bagh, the Soldier's Bazaar at Anarkali and from a grant by the 'Company Bahadur', was purchased the land where today stands the cricket grounds of the Lahore Gymkhana Club. This was the year 1860.

To start things off, a top gardener from Kew Gardens in London was shipped over and he began to train the local gardeners - 'malis' - and set about laying "the most beautiful gardens in the Punjab and Upper India". The Government College, Lahore, took over a major portion of the place to set up a botanical garden. The very first tree was planted by a beautiful young daughter of the commissioner of Lahore, Mr. Forsyth, on a crisp January morning in 1862. So thanks to the young Miss Forsyth began Lahore's most beautiful tradition.

She was later to become Mrs George Parker, who was to build the first house on the Racecourse Road. She died in Lahore and is buried in the cemetery on Jail Road. The garden was fed water from the Lahore canal. The three main gates were called Victoria Gate (on The Mall), Rivaz Gate (on Lawrence Road), and Montgomery Gate (on Racecourse Road). Today they remain nameless.

In the middle of the Lawrence Gardens was built the Lawrence Hall, designed by the chief engineer, Mr. G. Stone, and built in 1861-2. It was here that the Lahore Gymkhana Club was housed. I remember in my youth using the club and signing the 'chits' with relish. With my brothers we once ran up a monthly bill exceeding Rs 2,000. What followed one cannot describe. The old waiters used to keep us in check, short of looking behind our ears to make sure we had had a bath.

But the pride of place in the entire garden must surely go to the cricket ground. The expert from Kew Gardens did a splendid job, for he laid out a turf the equal of which has not been found in the country. So true is the flatness, almost as if one could play a game of billiard on it. The pitch is another story. One legend has it that the entire mud was brought over from Worcester, and for one whole year it was cured and rolled and "not a lice was allowed to crawl on it". The result has been an exceptionally true wicket, with a 'true bounce'.

But to suit the beautiful trees that surround the ground and the lush green turf, is the exquisite pavilion, made from British oak. Many years later the cricket-crazy prime minister Nawaz Sharif got another one made of brick and cement, a sign of our times.

The first major match played here was in 1911 between the British Army and a World XI. The World XI comprised players from Gloucestershire and Lancashire, while the army team was drawn from the 87th Punjabis, 17th Lancasters, 15th Sikhs and the King's Regiment. The World XI team won by 61 runs. The match had its desired effect and a strong team led by D. R. Jardine played here in the 1930s.

It was followed by a Jack Ryder led team that included 'Governor-General' Charlie Macartney in which Ryder, a former Test cricketer, hooked Muhammad Nisar, then one of the fastest bowlers of the world, at will. Lahore did not take well to their very own Nisar 'Gooli' being hooked. The seeds of competition had been sown.

Pakistan's first unofficial Test against the West Indies was played on this ground from Nov. 27 to 30, 1948, resulting in a draw. The Lahore Gymkhana cricket ground is where the very first 'official' Test between India and Pakistan on Pakistani soil was played from Jan. 29 to Feb. 1, 1955, making it the 35th Test ground in the world. The result was a draw.

Miani Sahib Graveyard and the crazed Sikhs

It was a sad day when my grandmother, Syeda Begum, died. She had been a teacher in Victoria School of Mochi Gate in the 1920s, and went to school in a *doli*. It was sadder still because I was not in Pakistan when it happened. She was buried in the Miani Sahib graveyard of Lahore, probably one of the largest burial grounds in the sub-continent. There is something strange about the place, an eerie past that needs to be told. The saddest part about my grandmother's death has been that I have never been able to find her grave. She had willed that five years after her burial all traces of the grave be erased and they were erased. My father also willed the same, only he wanted it ploughed after five years. But we never let that happen. There is a strange fascination in clinging to the dead, and that is why in the burial grounds of every civilization lies its story. Anthropologists unravel its secrets and tell us all about a people and the age in which they lived. The Egyptian pyramids are basically burial mounds, their unique quality makes one marvel how every aspect of almost every science has been combined to produce a wonder of the ancient world. No such marvel exists at Miani Sahib, but there is a story that merits consideration.

The story of Miani Sahib begins from Emperor Jahangir's reign, during which came from Sirhind a scholar and sage by the name of Sheikh Muhammad Tahir Qadri Naqshbandi. He settled down away from the Walled City of

Lahore in the 'remote' mauza (hamlet) of Mozang, a settlement almost two miles from the nearest gate, Shahalami. A toll station, a *chungi,* was established a furlong along the road, and Mauza Mozang had an independence of its own, near the city yet detached in a way. A forest separated Lahore and Mauza Mozang, and one can imagine that it must have been a peaceful place. Sheikh Tahir Qadri was a scholar and a Sufi fakir, and he did not want officialdom to disturb his peace. He set up his own madrassah (school) and within a few years he had a large following of admirers and students. Very soon, this remote hamlet became a sizeable village in which the madrassah of Sheikh Tahir Qadri and its huge grounds were the focal point.

The reputation of Mozang grew primarily because of this madrassah and the excellent religious scholars it produced. The Punjabi language has a word, *miani,* which means a learned preacher, and because of the Sheikh, the madrassah and its grounds came to be known as Miani Sahib; a name given by the local population out of respect for Sheikh Tahir Qadri. As long as he lived, he taught Islamic *fiqah* and *hadith* free of cost to anyone interested in it.

It was a very liberal environment in which the teachings of Ibn Arabi reigned supreme. Sheikh Tahir Qadri died in the year AH 1040, and it was during this era that Muslim rule in the sub-continent was coming to an end and the rule of the Sikh misls was on rise. We all know that for a fairly long time the entire area around Lahore was run by gangs and dacoits, streaks of whom still operate in the remote areas with abandon.

A few years after the death of Sheikh Tahir Qadri Naqshbandi, Mauza Mozang was raided by a massive Sikh misl, with one account putting the raid down to the Nakkai misl, and the entire treasure of Holy Quran's copies, a huge library of rare books and papers were removed. They had been informed by roaming fakirs that a "treasure beyond measure" lay in the madrassah, Sikhs went for it. When they were informed that they were all sacred texts and that portions of it were included in the Granth, they tore all the books into pieces and scattered them all over the area. Piles of books were set on fire and papers were burnt and scattered. One estimate puts the number of copies of Quran and its 'qaidas' and various books on the fiqah and hadith at well over 30,000. Not a single one was left intact by the furious Sikh raiders. They also set on fire every house in the village, leaving behind a scene that was to determine the future of Miani Sahib.

The religious scholars of the madrassah soon recovered from the shock of the pillage and managed to restore the institution, which to this day is still run on the same lines. The problem lay in the torn and burnt copies of the Holy Quran and other books that lay strewn all over the place. It was decided to leave these grounds alone till the flood came and all the desecrated texts were washed away.

For many years no flood came and the ground around lay abandoned. The people of Lahore decided that the best way to use this place was to bury their dead here, and so without much ado this became the favourite burial ground of Lahore.

During the rule of Maharajah Ranjit Singh, the Muslims of Lahore, on the orders of the maharajah, chalked out the exact area where lay thousands of desecrated copies of the Holy Quran and the entire area was given to the madrassah and converted into a burial ground. So the wise Sikh had, in his own way, repaid for the misdeeds of his coreligionists. One popular version, and one that does not have much evidence to support it, tells of fakirs predicting that after the copies of the Holy Quran were burnt and torn and scattered all over Mozang, that only the dead would 'live' there. It seems more of an emotional sentiment of a hurt population that respected the spirit and work of Sheikh Tahir Qadri Naqshbandi of Sirhind. Ironically, the grave of the sage still exists on one side of the madrassah, a simple grave without much adornment. Probably that is how he would have liked it.

A French barrack, an American church or a gymnasium?

A better part of the school and college days for us five brothers was-spent either in the swimming pool or the gymnasium of the Government College, Lahore. The pool we called the 'frog's cesspool' and the gymnasium we called the 'god house of the fit,' both names we picked up from the employees who looked after these two places.

We had access to these places in our school days because two of our uncles, Dr Muhammad Ajmal, the famed psychologist and principal, and Dr Ahsanul Islam, the famous zoologist who almost won a Nobel prize for his discovery of the 'Ahsan Method' in embryology, were professors who lived on the campus.

In the swimming pool, three families dominated life, the Hashmi, the Lashari and the Burki boys. They were all excellent swimmers in their own days, and we were definitely no match for them, and when they were not dominating the pool, we would have a field day. But life in the 'god house of the fit' was very different, it had history written all over the place. There was a mystery about its origin, and then there was the myth that whoever tried to knock it down would be knocked down himself. This was not true of the swimming pool, which has already been knocked down. One hopes a new one with the architectural features of the old comes up soon, and in all fairness the Hashmi, the Lashari and the Burki families owe it to their college to assist in rebuilding just such a place.

But our interest today is in the now sealed Government College gymnasium. The Buildings Department has declared it 'dangerous' and sealed it. Today it stands neglected and deserted and in a state of disrepair. In a way, history has been sealed in this unique building, the story of which must be told if we as Lahorites, and Ravians, are to do justice to our past. Not only must we tell this story, we must also do something about our past.

After having researched considerably on the subject, going through Kanhiyya Lal's *Tareekh-i-Lahore* and Syed Mohammad Latif's *Lahore,* and after reading a piece based on reports from the Lahore Gazetteer, 1894, Goulding's *Ravi, 2001* called 'The Story of the Union Church,' as well as reports of 'Public Instruction in the Punjab, 1908-9,' the mystery deepened further. I had spent the first 21 years of my life playing around this building, and little did we know its origin and history. With the building now in a derelict state, there is an urgent need to piece together its history, so that steps are taken to ensure that its future is brighter and better than its past. Before the British came to the Punjab, under Maharajah Ranjit Singh this was the most powerful nation in the subcontinent, and experts from those days rated the Punjab army as the finest and best trained in Asia. When the British first tried to enter the Punjab, the *Fauj-i-Khas* of Maharajah Ranjit Singh, led as it was by French generals of Napoleonic experience, crushed them with such force that the East India Company resolved never to enter the Punjab as long as the Maharajah was alive. This *Fauj-i-Khas* was barracked in a series of buildings stretching from the present civil secretariat, incidentally also built by the French and not the British, right up to outside Bhatti Gate to where now lies the Central Model School. This was the first planned military cantonment in Lahore, and the one initially used by the British, who shifted it later to Mian Mir.

One source, writing in the times of Maharajah Ranjit Singh, does state that a barrack was also built on the mound opposite the line of barracks, for it was there that the officers of the French contingent, as well as the Maharajah, spent their days with the troops. However, as they already had their headquarters near the tomb of Anarkali, it seems that this building could have been their training centre. Later, when the

G.C. Lahore

British built their first 'dak' bungalow just opposite the gymnasium, this building already existed, at least the account of the contractor as given in the initial Gazetteer states. The 'dak' bungalow was later to become the principal's lodge of the Government College in 1864. Today the Principal's Lodge has been knocked down to make way for an impressive new building in the same style as the main building, which has a majesty all its own, and a walk up the road past the Oval green transports one to another level of nostalgia.

The marble slab on the gymnasium building states that it was converted into a church by an American Presbyterian mission in 1858, one year after the Indian war of independence, or Indian mutiny as it is called, took place. The plaque states that they built it. One source, however, puts it down to the building being handed over to the church in an attempt to spread Christianity, and the Americans were known as the 'bible punching' type, not that they have changed much since. The Government College, Lahore, was set up six years later and in 1890, the acting principal, E.S. Robertson, purchased the building from the Americans for a handsome sum of Rs. l5,000. It seems that once the British had established themselves well, they felt that their American cousins needed to be politely nudged out from a critical area. In 1891, it was converted into a gymnasium by the principal, Prof W. Bell, who decided to give the barrack a Gothic look. "Modern machines were installed to drill the students into good shape" and "paid instructors regularly train the students" said a report of those days.

So the very best gymnasium of Lahore got going and in 1932, the principal, the famous Professor Garrett, extended the building to the southern side by 40 feet to allow for more space for still more machines. Another major renovation took place in 1937 by the principal. Professor Dunnicliff, where the entire gymnasium was modernized. All these names sound familiar to me as my late father used to mention them with awe. The gymnasium was functioning when we grew up and in our college days, we used to spend the afternoons trying to prove that Tarzan was no match for our skills, only to end up going home bruised, and to be scolded by out mother: "Stick to cricket and swimming" she used to say, "one will make you a gentleman, the other will keep you fit and out of harm's way." I never could understand till this day what she meant. In 1982, the gymnasium was finally closed after being in service for almost 125 years as a building and 100 years as a gymnasium. Since then it has been sealed. Local legend has it that it is haunted, but the present principal, Prof. Dr. Khalid Aftab, who may rate among the finest principals of the College, has other plans. There was a time when the prime minister, Mr Nawaz Sharif himself an old Ravian, wanted to knock down the building, but the principal refused to permit such blasphemy. The idea now is to raise funds to 'save the gymnasium' and to convert it into a museum dedicated to the history and traditions of the college. What better end-use could there be? The problem is that people do not have time for the higher pursuits of life. In this effort a lot of money is needed, a lot of expertise is needed, and a lot of humble, selfless effort has to be made. In true Ravian traditions this effort has to be a faceless one, only then will the spirits of Garrett, Dunnicliff, Sondhi, Karamat and Nazir smile upon us. Lahore needs a new start, for the Age of the Inquisition must now end.

Lahore's Seven Forts

The known and recorded history of Lahore is basically just about 2,000 years old. Beyond that one has to depend on the myths and stories that we have, some grouted in genuine fact, some opaque with factual trimmings and some based on legend that come to us through the oral tradition.

Lahore is a genuinely old city, though not ancient, in the academic sense. The site of the mound where today stands the fort of Lahore, rebuilt seven times as the legend goes, is definitely ancient. Legend has it that this site always had a fort. Local folklore tells us that the present fort is the seventh one built on the site of the older ones, some destroyed by invaders, others just crumbled through neglect. We all know that the present fort of Lahore was built (rebuilt) by the Mughal emperor Akbar. The one before it was destroyed by his grandfather Babar, whose troops murdered and looted the local population for seven days and nights, as was the Mongol tradition once a major conquest was achieved. Before him Timur did the same, as did Genghis Khan before him.

In a way, Lahore has suffered a major upheaval every 75 years on the average and major destruction every 150 years. The last one, the Partition of the Punjab, was probably the greatest upheaval the city has ever faced, with major portions being burnt to the ground. The entire area of Shah Alam Gate was razed to the ground in a fire many times greater than the great Fire of London. In our case the 'plague' was the plague of sectarian hatred, which still continues to rule the way we think and act. Only in 1947 the people of the Walled City turned against themselves. It remains the least analyzed period in our land's tortured history.

As a young reporter it the 1980s, it came in my 'beat' to cover culture and archaeology. I ended up believing that the sector was more criminal than the 'crime beat' my Editor had managed to take away from me after constant complaints from the police chiefs. It all started after the Department of Archaeology had announced at a press conference that they had dug a portion of the Lahore Fort, and had discovered the remains of the fort that existed before the present one was built. During the Press conference, one that I also attended, it was suggested that in the findings that there was a possibility that the remains of an even earlier building had been 'found', and they were confused as to how many times the fort had been rebuilt.

Bappa Rawal

Now this is a story that must never be allowed to die out, for our very history would die with it. But by then a puritanical streak had taken over the manners in which the affairs of State were run, and history 'officially' started just 1,000 years ago. That is why it is important to take up the case of tracing the origins of Lahore and its people. Having done that, it makes greater sense to discuss the history of the old forts of Lahore.

The origins of the original people of Lahore have many starting points. In my view, and many might differ, we must take up our case from the time the forces of Islam led by Muhammad bin Qasim, first landed on our soil. Who were the people who lived here then?

We all know that the origins of Lahore, without any shadow of doubt, lie in the high mound on which the Lahore Fort is built. This mound is important for the simple fact that it was the highest ground in the landscape, and when the River Ravi, or Irrawadi as it was originally called, was in full flood, this was the safest place to be in. And so it was here that we learn that the Hindu deity Rama existed. There is a view that Rama was born here, as were definitely his sons Loh and Kasu. In a way, the entire fuss over Ayodhya is all humbug.

I would like to introduce you to a sterling character in our forgotten history at this stage, the Rajput warrior king called Bappa Rawal whose real name was Kalbhoj (b. Prince Kalbhoj, ca 713-d. 753, possibly at Eklingji), the eighth ruler of the Guhilot Dynasty and founder of the Mewar Dynasty (734-753) alleged by Hindu genealogists to be 80th in descent from the Hindu god Rama, a man who lived ,and belonged to Lahore, as did his son Lahu, after whom Lahore is named. Bappa Rawal was one of the most powerful and famous rulers of the Mewar Dynasty. He went on to become a celebrated hero on battlefields near and far. His father, Rawal Mahendra II had married a woman of the Paramara Rajput clan, possibly from Mount Abu or Chandravati, both Paramara centres at the time.

Bappa Rawal is best remembered, historically and in legend, as a great warrior, especially against India's Muslim invaders. When the armies of the Arab caliphate breached the western borders of Rajputana, Bappa Rawal combined his army, which included his Paramara vassals, with those of the rulers of Ajmer, Jaisalmer, and other smaller Rajput kingdoms. They liberated Lahore and drove the Muslim invaders across the Indus River to the border of Sindh. Some accounts say he conquered many countries west of the Indus, including modern Afghanistan and Iran. It is believed that, to celebrate his victories, Bappa Rawal married several Persian princesses. Ultimately, members of his family advanced south, retook the Guhilots' ancestral city of Vallabhi, and re-established their line there. Others settled in Sorath, Marwar, and several other centres throughout Rajputana.

In Hindu mythology there are many ends to the life of Bappa Rawal. One has him living in Iran with a large new family. Another has it that he settled as a hermit near the foot of the 'golden mountain' which legend has it is one of two probable sites, either Rawalpindi or at Mewar in India. But the legend of the man also establishes for us the fact that Lahore was, without doubt, a truly Rajput city, ruled by the Bhat Rajputs, a fierce warrior people. When Mahmud Ghazni first came to Lahore just over 1,000 years ago, the Rajput ruler, Raja Jaipal, opposed him, and in a rare rite burnt himself alive after facing several defeats at a place just outside Mori and Bhatti gates.

The myths that flow to us from the times of Bappa Rawal determine the fact that there was a fort even then at Lahore. How and why did the walls of the fort fall so many times, this is something we will continue to find out.

The Shahi Hammam and Noor Jahan's foot

The other day we had guests over from India, all educationalists, and it made eminent sense that they see the beautiful mosque of Wazir Khan, as well as the exquisite Shahi Hammam (Royal Baths) of the master builder, located inside Delhi Gate, just next to one another. The appalling state of disrepair and decay of these outstanding architectural masterpieces made me regret my decision to show them to my guests.

Noor Jahan

For me the mosque of Wazir Khan stands for Lahore at its very finest. So it is also with the Shahi Hammam. Over the last five years these two building have been in progressive decay. It is almost as if the reign of the Sikhs has returned. The property of Wazir Khan, which he converted into a Trust before he died, stretched from the Delhi Gate right up to the mosque and approximately 50 yards beyond. The mosque premises had an outer gate, portions of which are still intact. Between the outer gate and Delhi Gate was the Shahi Hammam area, surrounded by a beautiful garden. One description tells us: "on one side are the mosque and its garden and fountains in the square. To the other side is an open space for the caravans of merchants from all over India. At the gate are the Royal Baths, beautiful beyond description and forbidden in its lush gardens".

Today the creations of Wazir Khan are in ruins. Take the Shahi Hammam as a case, for the mosque deserves a separate piece. The main entrance has exquisite floral paintings on the walls. The Government of the Punjab leased it out to a gentleman to use as a 'Shadi Ghar', Wedding Hall. He, in his wisdom, plastered wall paper on the ancient wall paintings. This happened just nine years ago.

The Shahi Hammam has a total of 21 rooms. Of these eight were used as fresh water baths, for they had marble pools to bathe in. Another eight were hot water baths, while five rooms were steam baths built on the lines of Turkish Baths.

The walls and roofs had exquisite floral paintings, while the roof centres have natural light openings. Along the sides water ran and fell in cascading fashion in specially designed sitting areas. The oxygenated water ended in a central pool, where the elite would bathe in utter luxury. There are special rooms where the bathers would lather themselves, and special servants would scrub and oil the bathers. To one side the water would pass through a series of revolving brass pipes, under which log fires would heat them. A portion of the water also flowed towards another set of brass pipes, under which fires would convert them into steam. It was a very exact science. This steam would be fed to rooms in the central portion of the Hammam. One account describes the experience as being hot enough to 'peel one's skin'. From here they would jump into a cool bath and a massage room. The experience would surely be an exhilarating one.

The Shahi Hammam has a special female section, which also has similar facilities, which was managed by a special female staff. In those Mughal days the rulers and their families took their health very seriously. The heating chambers and the water pumping section were destroyed in the initial days of Sikh rule. The British did not bother much to redeem them. Instead, they filled in the bathing and swimming pools to convert them into living quarters. In the era immediately after the fall of the Mughals, the Shahi Hammam fell into neglect. They have never since seen better days.

In the initial rule of Nawaz Sharif, an attempt was made to redeem the Hammam, but the damage has been so extensive, that unless a massive investment is made, there seems no hope of it being redeemed. But the entire structure, massive and well-built, is in place, and there is a need for a huge investment to be made to bring it back to its glory.

A word about the builder. Nawab Wazir Khan lived during the era of Shah Jahan. His real name was Sheikh Ilmuddin Ansari, and he belonged to Chiniot. He trained as a 'Hakeem' and started his practice there. When things got bad for the young 'hakeem', he moved to Lahore, and then on to Delhi and settled in Akbarabad. Soon his fame as a 'hakeem' spread and once he cured the Queen Mother, the mother of Emperor Shah Jahan when he was just a prince. The royal family honoured him with gifts and gold.

But the break for Hakeem Sheikh Ilmuddin Ansari came when Jahangir's Queen, Noor Jahan, had a huge ugly bloodshot blister on her foot, and she was afraid that giving it a cut would disfigure her foot and would scar her. Sheikh Ilmuddin wanted to inspect the foot, and a novel way was created for him to inspect the foot in detail. He made her walk over the Royal cot and back again in such a fashion that she cut her foot slightly. This cut he immediately closed and within days her foot was back to its original beauty.

So pleased was the Queen that she gave him all the jewellery that she was wearing, plus seven lakh rupees. The entire jewellery of all the women in her harem was also given to the hakeem. Overnight he became an immensely rich man, and he promised the queen that he would build her a special Shahi Hammam, so that she and her family could have steam and hot baths to enhance their beauty. So the Shahi Hammam that now lies in utter ruins, was the beginning of the rise of Wazir Khan.

Along the way he made sensible choices in the court of the Mughals and soon was made the Subedar of Lahore, where he built his mosque and other buildings, each more splendid than the last. But the Shahi Hammam definitely is among his finest. It is a tragedy that today we live to ignore what is our finest achievements. Probably a sign of our times.

Havoc of Mohallah Dai Laado

"The Bhangis of Gujrat blatantly looted one mohallah and the Kashmiris at the cattle market (gowalmandi) actually stole the bricks of the other mohallah, reducing it to the ground." In this way two of Lahore's finest mohallahs outside the walled city ceased to exist.

The history of Lahore has some amazing events, most of them unreported or unrecorded.

One has to walk the streets and to hear the names of streets and buildings to connect them to events in history. The other day, I set off on Ganpat Road, trying to locate a merchant who sold 'handmade paper'. It was once a huge business on the banks of the River Ravi, and Lahori paper was used in the finest manuscripts that lie in museums all over the world.

As I moved eastwards towards Shahalami Gate, avoiding the main road and walking through the back streets, I came across the mosque of Dai Laado. The name seemed to ring a bell and it reminded me of a clash I had read of in a book between the Kanhiyya and the Bhangi clans of two Sikh misls, in which the battle was stopped after the Bhangis won the right to pillage as long as they did not transgress onto Kanhiyya land. After that pact, the people of Lahore began to say: "Likh kay na dayo, khas taur Kanhiyyan noon" (Give nothing in writing, especially to the Kanhiya dan).

During the Mughal era, the portion between the Shahalami and the Lahori gates, opposite the walled city, had a magnificent residential area known as Mohallah Dai Laado. It was the largest and the richest mohallah outside the walled city and covered major portions of where, much later, the garden and tank of Rattan Chand were built. Today, the Bansaanwala Bazaar passes through the old mohallah that once was. As I stood before the very small old mosque that has now been "rebuilt" with concrete one can see the thin old bricks to one side. During the Sikh era when this mohallah was attacked by the Kanhiyya Sikhs, the merchants of Lahore got together and paid a price for protection. But then the Bhangi misls had grown in size and they attacked the mohalla-burning it down and kidnapping the young women. The Kanhiyya misl was approached for protection, but they refused to acknowledge their own document.

When the Sikhs captured power in the Punjab, during the reign of Maharajah Ranjit Singh the mosque of Dai Laado was occupied by a Hindu Sadhu and his followers. They installed their statues on one side of the mosque and converted it into a mosque-cum-temple where both Hindus and Muslims could come and pray. It was seen as a gesture of friendship by a sadhu who did not like the fact that the Bhangi Sikhs from Gujrat had burned the mosque. For many years, this was known as the Dai Laado 'ibaadatgah'. The Muslims called it a mosque. The Hindus called it a 'mandir', and the 'sain log', both Muslim and Hindu called it an 'ibaadatgah'. Many Sikhs also came to use this unique mosque of Dai Laado. The place was known as where the 'sain log' lived.

Then one day, just out of the blue, came a Muslim 'fakir' and hundreds of his followers, all armed with swords, and they took over the mosque, removed all statues and named it the mosque of Dai Laado. The Hindu sadhu, so accounts tell, watched the scene and walked away in utter disgust. He was never seen again. The damage done to this magnificent mohallah, that once boasted of the finest buildings outside Lahore was too much for the inhabitants to bear. They all moved to either inside the walled city, where they were better protected, or to remote villages. All that was left were burnt buildings and empty streets.

Just next to the Mohallah of Dai Laado was the Mohallah of Zain Khan, who happened to be the naib subedar of the Punjab. This was an extension of Mohallah Dai Laado, and where Zain Khan and his family built huge new havelis. The entire strip from the edge of Anarkali Bazaar opposite Lahore Gate right up to the area opposite Mochi Gate was known as 'new' Lahore in the Mughal era.

The royal family had built their own 'Mughalpura', a detached magnificent city. But the landed elite lived in these two areas. The fall of the Mughals saw the rise of the Sikhs, and the first clan to attack the areas outside the walled city was the Kanhiyya misl, led by Jai Singh Kanihyya. The population collected Rs. l0,000 and gave them to the Sikh chief as protection money. In gold terms, this comes to about 2,000 *tolas,* as one account puts it. But then the Bhangis had attacked the next mohallah of Dai Laado and ventured onto this mohallah. The Kanhiyya misl again went back on their word. They were shown signed documents, at which, so one account goes, the Sikh chiefs laughed and said: "There is a difference between a piece of paper and a sword".

At Mohallah Zain Khan lived mostly people of Pathan origin, and they decided to make a fight of it. The Bhangis slaughtered them, and soon they saw it more prudent to flee. So the entire beautiful strip opposite the Mochi Gate and Lahori Gate lay in total ruins for almost 20 years. Empty buildings and empty streets. By this time Maharajah Ranjit Singh had started his Kashmir campaign, and to Lahore came a lot of Kashmiris. All of them threw up 'katchi abadis' at what is today Gowalmandi. They started stealing the bricks from Mohallah Zain Khan, and later from the Mohallah of Dai Laado.

By the time Rattan Chand had managed to get his piece of land from the maharajah, the once empty space had been razed right down to the ground. The area that we know of as Gowalmandi had come up and the land up to the walled city had become one huge open ground. The destruction had been complete and total. One clan from Gujrat had destroyed an entire way of life, and another group of migrants from Kashmir had stolen everything that remained. The way was opened for Rattan Chand to build his garden and his tank, which with time was again vandalized during the partition of the Punjab. It has been a deadly mix of clans, money, religion and power. They tend to destroy the very history through which we wade, for our culture is what we have, and we love to destroy our culture.

How the Pari Mahal was destroyed

Almost 195 years ago, on Rabi-us-Sani 9, AH 1232 to be exact, Maharajah Ranjit Singh, dressed in his finest robes and seated on his finest horse, one of over a thousand, left the gates of the Lahore Fort and headed towards Shahalami Gate. He told his ministers jokingly that he was going to meet a pari, a fairy.

On arrival, he was received by the custodians of the house of the late Nawaz Aliuddin Wazir Khan, the subedar of Lahore during the Shah Jahan era. The house had acquired the name of Pari Mahal. So lavish was the entertainment and so varied the programme, that the Maharajah granted a massive Rs100, a huge sum in those days, for the upkeep of the house. Whether he met his pari or not, that we will leave to the reader's imagination, for the maharajah loved horses and women with gusto. But the fact remains that he had visited what was one of the finest houses — havelis — of Lahore, and that of a man whose contribution to the city of Lahore remains, by all counts, outstanding even to this day.

There is nothing left of Pari Mahal today, for in the period just before partition, the grand building was being knocked down and its bricks sold off by a contractor, and in the fire of partition, everything went up in smoke or was removed with callous abandon in the name of development. In the area that we today call the D-point parking lot in Shahalami stood the palace of Wazir Khan. Next to the Pari Mahal, even today, a small, partly destroyed, yet beautiful mosque stands with two minarets. This is the Pari Mahal mosque.

The palace was a huge and grand haveli that housed Wazir Khan's family. It had its own small gardens and fountains. The subedear of Lahore made a name for himself in Shah Jahan's reign by building in Lahore the finest mosque that stands today, named aptly as the Wazir Khan mosque. How did the name pari come about? According to one source, the Afghan women who lived in this palace were beautiful and fairer than their neighbours, and everyone mentioned them as fairies, a common use of the word for a fair and beautiful woman even today.

Maharajah Ranjit Singh took possession of the house after he effectively ended Muslim rule over the city and used it for his own 'creative' ends. He made sure the building was kept in top condition. Just before him the three joint-rulers of Lahore, Lehna Singh, Sobha Singh and Gujjar Singh, between them stripped the Pari Mahal palace of its beautiful stones and sold them. It is said the Maharajah managed to retrieve some of the stones and repair the Pari Mahal. Even though he used a major portion of the huge house as a gunpowder store, he still maintained a portion for himself. When Sikh rule ended a lot of people occupied small portions of the palace and started paying rent to the Maharajah of Kashmir, who by then, thanks to the British, claimed ownership.

By the time partition came, the entire building was set ablaze and then razed to the ground in the name of development. However, the small mosque next to it remains, a testimony to the master builder of Lahore. The entire mosque does not stand today. Just a small portion and two minarets are intact. On both sides of this small mosque one can see the old Mughal-era walls, a testimony to the once grand palace and mosque that surely deserve a mention in the history of the ancient city.

Wazir Khan's main feat shall remain the grand mosque he built, undoubtedly the finest in Lahore, and of far greater beauty and significance than the Badshahi Masjid opposite the fort. Wazir Khan's biggest contribution was the opening of a school and university of religious learning on the side of the mosque. He set aside a huge fund to ensure that the tradition of learning continued after he was no longer there. For this, a series of shops were built to contribute funds to the upkeep of this seat of learning.

And so ended the legend of Pari Mahal, the finest haveli that existed in Lahore. The Sikhs plundered and misused it, the British turned a blind eye to it, and the flames of partition consumed it, with the new-era 'claim generation' selling off its bricks to put an end to history. Half a century has gone by and now it is being realized that the Walled City of Lahore needs to be protected. My father used to tell me that this was the world's largest living museum, and live it must to have a meaning, for the people of Lahore, who in all their shades and hues, make up the real Lahore. Special laws are needed to stop the new soul-destroying constructions that are taking place. If we are ever to rebuild our 'pari mahals,' a special effort is needed over a long and sustained period of time.

The 'hotspur' of the Lahore Darbar

One of the most intriguing incidents in the entire history of the Lahore Fort has been the manner in which an important archway between the Hazuri Bagh and the fort at Roshnai Gate collapsed in 1840 without any apparent reason. There are several versions to the collapse, as well as some folk legend.

The collapse took place just after the cremation of Maharajah Kharrak Singh, the son of Maharajah Ranjit Singh, just outside the Lahore Fort. As the ruling Sikh elite walked back to the fort after the cremation, the heir-apparent Naunehal Singh, accompanied by Udham Singh, son of Maharajah Gulab Singh of Kashmir, led the procession.

As soon as they reached the archway, it suddenly, and mysteriously, collapsed, killing both princes of Punjab and Kashmir in a tragedy that shook both States and led to their ultimate collapse. Was it intrigue or was it sheer accident, this is a question that has vexed many an expert. Let us examine the folk legend that still makes the rounds of the old walled city of Lahore.

It exists in the shape of a phrase: "Whether it fell or was made to fall, for in it perished Naunehal". Such old sayings are now dying out themselves, and need to be recorded for the sake of future research. But the few that can be recorded in such columns add so much to our understanding of how people felt in those days.

According to a description of the incident by Kanhiyya Lal, once Maharajah Kharrak Singh became the ruler, the Dogra family that was so powerful in the Lahore Darbar, started intriguing against the new Maharajah. The death of the all powerful Maharajah Ranjit Singh, who ruled for a full 40 years, had left a massive power vacuum. Anyone of any consequence was trying to read just in a more powerful slot. Intrigue reigned supreme.

The powerful Dogras had managed to find a power ally in the heir- apparent, Prince Naunehal Singh. After they managed to murder Chet Singh, a pretender, they created circumstances that led the prince to force his father into confinement at his haveli inside the walled city, and himself became the effective ruler.

Maharajah Kharrak Singh never forgave his son for this treatment, so much so that when he fell ill he refused to let his son come to meet him. In turn, Prince Naunehal Singh began to portray his father as a crazy man, which he certainly was not. He had turned into a mystic, and kept uttering deep meaningful sentences, which most people were not able to understand. Others thought they were wise utterances of a very wise man.

It is a fact that the people of the walled city began to take a liking to the imprisoned Maharajah Kharrak Singh. In his confinement he would go round the mohallahs of Lahore knocking on windows of Muslims, waking them up to say their prayers. The phrase "Kharrak Singh kay khattaknay say kharrakti hain khirkian" is still uttered by almost all school-going children in Lahore.

The sardars of the Lahore Darbar found this to be 'utter madness' and they wanted a patch-up. Maharajah Kharrak Singh refused to entertain such thoughts and started telling anyone who came to meet him. "He is stupid if he thinks I will go to the Lord alone. When I go, he will go too". Kanhiyya Lal records as having met a lot of old people in the walled city who had heard of this.

Another source, a Sikh history website, states that "Kharrak Singh was a mystic who could predict the future and he accurately, to the very date, predicted his own and his son's death". Yet another source describes Kharrak Singh as letting out a loud laugh when told that Naunehal Singh was the effective 'Maharajah'. "That day will never come", he would laugh.

There is every reason to believe that Naunehal Singh was party to the slow poisoning of his father. When Kharrak Singh died in 1840, he was cremated just next to where his father was. After the cremation as the hyperactive Naunehal Singh was walking back to the Lahore Fort for his certain enthronement as Maharajah of the Punjab, the archway under which he was passing collapsed and he was buried alive along with Udham Singh. Here it would be interesting to take up the description of Col. H.R.Goulding. The British called him the hotspur of the Punjab.

"The fall of the archway has been attributed to some design.... as the sikh courtiers tried to conceal the injuries to the heir-apparent, conspiracy was feared. But the precise timing of the fall certainly does not seem accidental. Gulab Singh is feared at having engineered it. But then his own son perished, which is inconsistent with the motives of Gulab Singh."

Yet another scholar has described the death of Naunehal Singh in the following terms: "Once the cremation of Kharrak Singh was over, a gun salute followed which shook the grounds of the fort. At this moment the heir-apparent was in a hurry to leave and start his enthronement. The vibrations of the cannons dislodged the already damaged archway, and it so happened that it collapsed just when Naunehal Singh and Udham Singh were passing under it. The theory of a conspiracy is most unlikely." Sounds a logical theory, even though archways as strong as those of the Lahore Fort are not known to collapse from the thunder of a cannon. But then the mystery remains.

The samadhis of Kharrak Singh and Naunehal Singh are both in the same room, where their ashes are under two small domes just next to that of Maharajah Ranjit Singh. Together rest three generations of the most powerful family ever seen in the Punjab. The first was a pragmatic ruler, the second a mystic and the third a 'hotspur'. In modern terms he could be called a misguided missile that helped end the very dynasty that raised him. In Lahore the first is still admired, the second is loved by those who know about him, while the third has been forgotten.

Bradlaugh Hall in History

The year 1929 is very important in the history of Lahore, of Pakistan and of the sub-continent. It was an event that took place in Lahore that kicked off the final events that led to the partition of the sub-continent.

In 1929, the Indian National Congress (INC) resolved, in a meeting held at the Bradlaugh Hall in Lahore, that India should have complete independence from British rule. Very few of us know that the headquarters of the Indian National Congress at Bradlaugh Hall still stands today, but only refugees from that "most massive exodus in the history of mankind" inhabit it. How many of us have ever seen this hall, lying as it does in utter disrepair? This piece is about this hall and about how several resolutions that emerged out of that meeting there shaped the sub-continent.

Bradlaugh Hall stands just behind the Central Model High School and the Central Training College on Rattigan Road. If you head from the Lahore district courts towards Bilal Gunj, just a hundred yards ahead on the left a small lane turns in. This is Rattigan Road, once a posh area of Lahore where the elite lived. There were only 17 houses on this road. Today, this same area has well over 300 small houses. To the right of this road at the very beginning, a narrow lane heads towards a cul-de-sac, where only one massive building exists. From the main road this building is not visible, but once you enter the cul-de-sac the sheer size of the hall overwhelms you. This is the original office of the Indian National Congress, the central point from where the struggle for independence in the Punjab was planned and monitored. Till the time of partition, it served its purpose, and when the division took place, it became irrelevant.

The Bradlaugh Hall is not a structure of any notable significance, but in the history of our country and the sub-continent, it certainly has a place. The scholar and the bigot would have different interpretations, but the fact remains that there is a need to rescue the building and convert it into a museum of significance. In this lies the maturity of the way we look at history.

The INC resolution of 1929 sparked off a split in the Congress, with Mr Tilak taking a hardline towards attaining independence, and Mr Gandhi preaching a 'non-violent' approach. Till then Mr Jinnah was all for it, and it was only following the INC's Lahore resolution, that when a "future constitution" for a free India was drafted that Allama Iqbal dwelt on the need for a State for the Muslim minority. Mr Jinnah, however, followed the legal route by suggesting changes in the proposed constitution, changes that the INC rejected leading Mr Jinnah to choose his own path. Ironically, the first soundings of this separation were in a speech in the Bradlaugh Hall. So this hall saw the seed and fruits of Pakistan ... little that we are willing to accept. What has happened to Pakistan can well be gauged from the condition of Bradlaugh Hall today. Probably the resurgence of our country could begin by taking a much more enlightened view of this building, and changing it into a place where we should be reminded of our past in a much more meaningful and secular manner. The fallout of the 1929 INC resolution was seen just a mile down the road at the Minto Park just 11 years later in 1940, where a resolution of the Muslim League demanded a separate homeland for the Muslims. It took another seven years for it to become reality. It was a declaration in the open, and that declaration was celebrated in the shape of the Minar-i-Pakistan. There is a general belief among the older people of Lahore, those who have lived with the Hindus that the partition of India would never have taken place, had the INC been a genuinely secular party.

In the city there are a lot of buildings that are related to the freedom struggle. There is the Barkat Ali Hall, there is the Mochi Gate ground, there is the Bradlaugh Hall, and there are a number of other such sites. It seems only fair that we should convert them into meaningful places of learning. Somehow building new concrete structures to house the freedom struggle have never made sense to a layman like me.

There is need to study the 'secular' period till 1940, as well as the remaining portion. Each has its own heroes and its own villains. Today Bhagat Singh is more relevant to Pakistan than he is to India. The same goes for Lala Lajpat Rai. We must learn to be fair to each hero, and only by doing so can we truly honour the legacy of the Quaid.

The 'staging bungalow' with a history

In the beginning, on the mound outside the old walled city of Lahore, there was a staging bungalow, from where stagecoaches would leave for other cities. In even older times it was a staging area where troops would train and then leave for battle. Today many a career takes off, and, hopefully, will do so in the centuries to come.

In the days when Maharajah Ranjit Singh reigned supreme (1799-1839), on the mound where today stands the Government College, Lahore, there was a military training centre. Just next to the mound, where the troops of the elite 'Fauj-e-Khas' trained, was the staging area. On the mound was built a bungalow, which was, as the records of the Sikh-era show, called the 'staging bungalow'. A 1867 map of Lahore confirms this fact. On the left was a chapel that was latter to be incorporated into the college as a Gymnasium; a derelict building that today needs considerable funds to convert it into a 'Government College Museum'. But more of that later.

According to a well-known writer on Lahore, Latif, the first classes of the King Edward's Medical College, Lahore, were held in 1860 in this staging bungalow, while the hospital was established in the stables of Raja Suchet Singh's haveli in the main Tibbi Bazaar near the Taxali Gate. When the British for 'military reasons' demolished the beautiful Taxali Gate, this hospital was also lost. But by then it had moved to the present Mayo Hospital.

In 1856 the East India Company approved the establishment of a Central College in Lahore. Towards this end the Punjab's Director of Public Instruction entered into 'correspondence' with the Dean of Carlisle and with the Rev. G.E.L. Cotton, the Headmaster of Marlborough School, England, "with the view of selecting two suitable graduates from Home for appointment as Principal and Physical Tutor of Natural Philosophy." A 'handsome' salary of Rs. 600 and Rs. 400 was offered.

The 'handsome prospects' did not attract the correct candidates, and so the East India Company decided to constitute a board comprising Rev. Cotton, Rev. A.P. Stanley, Canon of Canterbury, and Mr. T. Walround, Fellow of Balliol, Oxford, who suggested that only graduates from Cambridge, Oxford, Dublin or Durham should be considered as this would be a 'prestige posting'. So from the very beginning Government College, Lahore, was, and is still, considered to be a very special institution, or at least it has so proved as the years pass.

It was then considered that for excellence in philosophy, a Professor of Mathematics was essential. The Lt. Governor of the Punjab, Sir John Lawrence, who considered it premature, rejected this proposal. In these circumstances the board selected Dr. G.W. Leitner, as the very first Principal of Government College, Lahore.

You might be wondering as to just what happened to the Central College, Lahore, proposal. That also saw the light of day, only it was called the Central Training College, Lahore, built just opposite the Government College, Lahore, and next to the Central Model School, Lahore, which was built in 1883. This set of school and teacher training college also proved to be a 'centre of excellence', much that they are ignored today.

The original Government College, Lahore, opened in the spacious haveli of Dhyan Singh inside Taxali Gate on the First of January, 1864. The present building, a Gothic masterpiece of W. Purdon, the Superintending Engineer of Lahore, was started in 1870. It took five years to complete costing Rs. 320,537/-.

The construction was undertaken by Rai Bahadar Kanhaiyya Lal, a genius and dedicated builder who has written a marvelous book on Lahore, not to speak of building almost all the well-known buildings of that era. Over the years various blocks have been added to this college. It has a huge Botanical Garden next to the Lawrence Gardens (now called Jinnah Gardens), it has an Atomic Physics Laboratory opposite the Civil Secretariat, next to which it has its own cricket ground.

An important part of the college is its hostels, of which it has two. One is the Quadrangle (now called the Iqbal Hostel), which is inside the college premises and is meant for Intermediate students. The other is the original Government College Boarding House, which was later named the New Hostel. In one description of this hostel, a Punjabi Gazetteer places its location as being "next to the house of Mr. H. Brandon, Pleader, and the Punjab Association Club".

No trace of the 'pleader' remains, though in our school days I do remember my late father mentioning "Khoona pleader", an Anglo-Indian lawyer who lived next to the hostel. For that matter to the north of Government College was the DAV School, which is today called the Government Muslim Model High School.

But then Lahore is not all about building and history. Its people have always been more important than the institutions that it has. The Principals of Government College, Lahore, have all been 'great' men so to say. Starting from Leitner, the great names just do not cease. There was Garrett, Dunnicliff, Sondhi, Bukhari, Nazir, Rashid and now Dr. Khalid Aftab, just to name a few.

Each educationalist was outstanding in his own right. In the post-Independence era Patras Bokhari definitely stands out, as does the great Dr. Nazir, Prof Rashid, Dr Ajmal and Dr. Khalid Aftab. Their mark on the finest educational institution of Pakistan definitely remains. As a student I remember Dr Ajmal immensely. I once asked him why he wrote only 'Muhammad Ajmal' on his board and not Dr. Ajmal. He smiled, rolled his cigarette and in a shy dragging style said: "Otherwise people start showing me their pulse".

But then so have been the students. Name any discipline and the list of names of its illustrious students is mind-boggling. The poets Iqbal and Faiz stand out. Among scientists there is the Nobel Laureate Dr Salam. In zoology there was the Nobel nominee Dr Ahsanul Islam whom my father always called "aandawala doctor" - the 'Egg Doctor'.

He determined the cell formation of embryos, a lead that was to take others to discover just how genes and DNA function. He was the man who unlocked 'the secret of life'. I knew him well and was very fond of him. Whenever I asked him about his life work, he would remark: "Allah ka kamal hai". Many feel that by coming back from Imperial College, England, he gave up his Nobel nomination. But his sick mother was more important to him.

Such have been the great teachers and students of Government College, Lahore. Today it has managed to achieve the status of a university. As it meanders its way to new heights, we return to the question of the museum in the making. One assumed some old Ravian would one day leave a fortune for this project. Maybe we forget what Bilal the Slave from the Holy Prophet (pbuh) learnt: "A drop of a scholar's ink is more sacred than a martyr's blood".

The red stones of Dara Shikoh

Of all the monuments of Lahore, nothing represents the city more than the Badshahi Mosque. It might not be as beautiful as Wazir Khan's mosque, but it certainly is the trademark of the city, and, probably, represents the last of the great Mughal buildings to be built in the city.

Built in the year 1084 Hijra under orders of Aurangzeb, the last of the great Mughal emperors, its history has many strange twists and turns. Before Aurangzeb became emperor of India, his brother Dara Shikoh, after whom is named Shahdara (or correctly Shah Dara), was named the ruler, or prince, of Lahore by his father Shah Jahan.

Dara Shikoh

He was a very well educated person, interested in poetry and the mystics. His love for the saint Mian Mir was well known. Shah Dara first got constructed the famous Chowk Dara Shikoh outside Akbari Gate, and from there he planned a red stone-lined walkway right up to the grave of Hazrat Mian Mir.

The idea was for him to walk barefoot every morning after prayers to offer 'fateha' at the grave of Hazrat Mian Mir. The massive amount of red stone needed for this royal walkway was all collected and construction started. It was planned that on the way would be fountains, trees and water tanks. Probably it was the most unique walkway ever planned in the world, or the known world then.

Barely had work started that Aurangzeb imprisoned his father and got murdered his brother Shah Dara Shikoh.

He then ordered Fadai Khan Kooka, his 'doodh bhai' - for Aurangzeb had been suckled by the mother of Fadai Khan, and kooka is a Turkish word meaning to give milk - to shift all the red stone meant for the walkway of Dara Shikoh and to build a mosque opposite the Lahore Fort.

So under the guidance of Fadai Khan was built the Badshahi Mosque. It was specifically ordered that the mosque must be bigger than the famous Jamia Masjid in Delhi, and the finest craftsmen were brought in to complete the work within his lifetime. The result was an exquisite mosque. But then no sooner had the mosque been finished than the western most minaret collapsed after an earthquake had struck Lahore.

The myth was then created that it was Providence's revenge for the murder of Dara Shikoh. The minaret was repaired, only to get hit again by another earthquake. This was enough to ingrain in the minds of the people of Lahore the 'saintly intentions' of Dara Shikoh. Many called it the revenge of Hazrat Mian Mir. But all these were nothing compared to what was to follow.

Turmoil followed the death of Aurangzeb and the mosque began to lose the numbers who came to pray there. Very soon, it was difficult to muster a reasonable number to pray. The people of the walled city avoided the mosque out of sheer affection for Dara Shikoh. By the time the Sikhs seized power in 1799, the Badshahi Mosque lay in ruins.

Maharajah Ranjit Singh immediately converted it into stables for his horses, and by the time he died 40 years later, it had over 1,000 of the finest horses. To one side he made an ammunition dump, and initially many of the Sikh soldiers who conquered Lahore barracked there.

Maharajah Sher Singh

Thus for the next 50 years, the Badshahi Mosque lay in ruins, trampled by horses, soldiers and used for drunken bouts of the freeloaders of the Khalsa army of the Lahore Darbar. The minarets, which had beautiful white marble domes, were damaged, as was most of the red stone. Very soon, the grandest mosque of Lahore lay like a skeleton denuded of its beautiful exterior. The Maharajah got the three undamaged minarets of the mosque partially knocked down for security reasons.

After the death of Maharajah Ranjit Singh, the next ten years saw the very worst period. Once when Maharajah Sher Singh came from Patiala to capture the Sikh throne in 1841 from Rani Jindan, he mounted cannons on the top of what remained of the 143 feet high minarets and bombarded the Lahore Fort where the Rani was.

In return the gunners of the Rani pounded the mosque. For three whole days and nights the pounding continued. The floors of the mosque were damaged, the side buildings were all hit. This reduced the mosque to a state where there was a suggestion that it be razed to the ground to ensure the future safety of the Sikh rulers.

But then a few years later when the Sindhianwalia sardars took the Lahore Fort and Raja Hira Singh surrounded the citadel, the mosque was again used to pound the fort, and in return the gunners inside the fort returned fire. The mosque was then, as one account puts it, reduced to a mere skeleton. One account jokingly described it "like the face of the pockmarked Maharajah Ranjit Singh, whose one eye was blind". Ironically,

Lord John Lawrence

yet another earthquake hit the mosque in 1840. The curse of Dara Shikoh, or Mian Mir, call it what you like, had returned.

When the British East India Company moved into Lahore before the final demise of the Khalsa rule, they preferred to respect the feelings of the Muslim of Lahore, who had a considerable hand in assisting the British get rid of Sikh rule, and removed the horses and ammunition from the mosque. They held their Sunday services in Hazuri Bagh. In 1856, Sir John Lawrence, who was instrumental in keeping all British forces out of the mosque, handed back to the Muslims of Lahore possession of the mosque.

The document was signed by the 70 'most influential' Muslims of Lahore, and by the representatives of the Company. Its opening paragraphs needs to be reproduced: "Whereas from time preceding the Badshahi Mosque situated in the citadel of Lahore had been used for worship by the Muhammedans, and under Royal mandates the ancestors of Syud Boozoorg Shah, son of Kazee Ghoolam Shah, were custodians and priests of the mosque Syud Boozoorg Shah has been appointed custodian and priest of the mosque..."

And so the mosque was returned to the Muslims in 1856, and from then onwards started a long period of reconstruction. It must be said here as the record shows, that the British Government did, from time to time, donate considerable amounts for the restoration of the mosque. Also influential Hindus, Sikhs and Muslims donated reasonable sums over the next 80 years. But the bulk of the money came from the poor of Lahore.

There was a time when the mosque was called "Chooani nikah" (four annas per nikah) Masjid. This was a cess on marriages taking place in the mosque, and the funds all went to its repair. What one sees today is the over 140 years effort to restore this grand mosque, whose stones were brought by Dara Shikoh, stolen by the Sikhs, partially recovered by Lawrence, and now, finally, restored to its original glory by the Government of Pakistan. May be, if just one symbolic red stone was removed and placed at the tomb of Hazrat Mian Mir, the uneasy soul of Dara Shikoh would rest better... maybe.

The crazy maharajah and the mosque

Two of the most fascinating incidents in the torturous ten years after the death of Maharajah Ranjit Singh pertain to his son and grandson, Maharajah Kharrak Singh and his son Kunwar Naunehal Singh. Two kings of Lahore who died within a day of each other in an intrigue that saw the end of Sikh rule.

Maharajah Kharrak Singh

The two maharajahs had a fascinating relationship with the Muslims of Lahore, and, in a way, that relationship still persists, little that we know about it. This is a tale of two tales, each linked by fascinating utterances by a weak, and some would say, crazy, Kharrak Singh, the son of Maharajah Ranjit Singh. Born on Feb 9,1801, he was married to Chand Kaur, daughter of Jaimal Singh Kanhiyya, in 1812. The Maharajah brought him up in the family's martial tradition and assigned him to a variety of military expeditions. While barely six years old, he was given the nominal command of the Sheikhupura expedition (1807); was placed in charge of the Kanhiyya estates in 1811; and deputed in 1812 to punish the rebel chiefs of Bhisnbar and Rajauri. He was invested with the command of Multan expedition (1818) as well as of Kashmir (1819). He was also sent on similar campaigns undertaken by Ranjit Singh for the conquest of Peshawar and against the Mazaris of Shikarpur. It was during the reign of Maharajah Ranjit Singh that Kharrak Singh decided to build a house for himself. He summoned the chief architect and ordered him to find the most distant point from where Maharajah Ranjit sat daily. This was said within the hearing of his father. The architect did not know what to say. Maharajah Ranjit Singh smiled and said: "The mad fool wants to die away from his home." "No, I will be killed where I stand today, but till then I want to live as far away from this point as is possible," retorted Kharrak Singh. The Maharajah surely thought his frail son was crazy.

So a suitable place was selected at the very beginning of the Lahori Gate Bazaar. The plot selected had a mosque to one side. A few Sikh advisers wanted the mosque knocked down, but Kharrak Singh refused to touch it. Instead, he ordered the Imam of the mosque to come under his protection, had a Rs10 monthly salary made official, and exhorted the Muslims of Lahori Gate to use the mosque more frequently. Other houses in the area were cleared for the royal haveli of the crown prince, and work started on a beautiful building, which took two years to complete. The people of Lahore, who used to come to see this exquisite haveli, naming it 'Dingi Haveli', and all because Kharrak Singh had approved a dent in the design to accommodate the little mosque. It was in this house that Maharajah Naunehal Singh was born on Feb 11,1820.

Kunwar Naunehal Singh

There were times when prince Kharrak Singh would walk out after hearing the 'azaan' and would start knocking on the windows of his Muslim neighbours, ordering them to come to pray. The frightened Muslims would promptly turn up for prayers, and a pleased prince would then distribute sweets.

The 'Dingi Haveli', or the Haveli of Kharrak Singh, was to become the centre of power for a few years in the last days of Maharajah Ranjit Singh. Prince Naunehal Singh was a much more aggressive person like his grandfather. The frail Kharrak Singh ascended the throne in June 1839 on the death of his father. From the very first day he had to encounter the envy of his powerful and ambitious minister, Dhyan Singh Dogra, whose haveli inside the old walled city still stands. Dhyan Singh resented the ascendancy of the royal favourite Chet Singh Bajwa, a trusted courtier who had also been Kharrak Singh's tutor. The Dogras started a whispering campaign against the Maharajah as well as against Chet Singh. It was given out that both were surreptitiously planning to hand over the Punjab to the British and that the Sikh 'Khalsa' army would be disbanded. To lend credence to these rumours, some fake letters were prepared and discreetly intercepted. Gulab Singh Dogra, Dhyan Singh's elder brother, was charged to work upon. Prince Naunehal Sigh, then travelling in his company from Peshawar to Lahore.

Matters came to a head when, on the morning of Oct 9, the conspirators entered the Maharajah's residence in the Lahore Fort and assassinated Chet Singh in the presence of their royal master, who vainly implored them to spare his life. Maharajah Kharrak Singh was removed from the Fort and he remained virtually a prisoner in the hands of Dhian Singh. Prince Kunwar Naunehal Singh took the reins of government into his own hands, but he was helpless against his powerful minister, who continued to keep father and son separated from each other. Doses of slow poison were administered to the Maharajah, who died on Nov 5, 1840. One well-known account claims Kharrak Singh telling his son: "If you think you will be a maharajah, time will show you that you will never be one."

But the plot did not end there. After Maharajah Kharrak Singh was cremated along with four wives and seven servants just next to where the samadhi of Maharajah Ranjit Sigh exists outside the Lahore Fort, the new Maharajah of the Punjab, Naunehal Singh, was returning to the fort when the doorway to the fort mysteriously collapsed, killing the new Maharajah of one day. The crazy sayings of Kharrak Singh all seemed to be coming true. The Muslims of Lahori Gate pledged to serve the family of Maharajah Kharrak Singh, who had saved their mosque.

When the wives of three Maharajahs of the Punjab, Ranjit Singh, Kharrak Sigh and Naunehal Singh, died, they were all cremated outside the old walled city far away from the fort and near where the River Ravi once flowed round a bend at a point where today stands the Islamia College, Civil Lines, just opposite the office of the SSP of Lahore. The samadhis of the wives of the three Maharajahs are all at the same place. The biggest in the centre is that of Datar Kaur, mother of Kharrak Singh. To the right is the samadhi of Maharani Chand Kaur, wife of Kharrak Singh. To the left is the samadhi of Ghulab Kaur, wife of Naunehal Singh. A contribution for these samadhis came from the people who prayed at the little mosque inside Lahori Gate. Sadly, today the offices of the college operate inside these three samadhis.

But the tale has an even sadder tail. One of the first acts of the British on capturing Lahore was to order the razing of the beautiful haveli of Kharrak Singh. It was ordered that 'Dingi Haveli', a building Lahoris loved, be razed to the ground. In the process, the little mosque was also razed. The bricks were removed to build houses in the new cantonment of Mian Mir. A stark open space was left. Though new houses came up, that open space in our collective memory must always remain.

Lahore's exquisite mosques inside its walls

With the coming of the Muslims to Lahore approximately 1,000 years ago, the old walled city has had a curious relationship with mosques. While the hugely beautiful Badshahi Mosque attracts the most tourists, the more exquisite of these places of worship are tucked away inside the walls of the old city.

Now this is not to belittle the unique history of the Badshahi Mosque, which was primarily an exhibition of the grandeur and authority of the last of the great Mughals. Their empire just withered away, thanks mostly to growing illiteracy and intolerance. In a way the situation then is somewhat similar to today's. The condition of most mosques reflects the reality of the growing mass illiteracy and intolerance to other religions, and now even to Muslim sects. Only we do not have insight of time to understand what is happening to us today. That is where history comes into play to guide us through these difficult days.

The initial steps taken by the Muslims in Lahore were by scholars and saintly persons, who preferred to debate and discuss, and to learn in the process. The end result was a very happy mix.

Toleration assisted considerably, both the native population and the new converts, not to speak of the series of invaders who found Lahore silently lapping them up. Ali Hujwairi, popularly known as Ganj Bakhsh, was the first of the saints that came to this city, and stayed on. And with Islam came mosques. Today, there are 123 mosques per square kilometre, or one every 100 yards. The interesting thing is that the mosques of various sects tend to move side by side. There has always been a competitive edge to mosque making in the city.

If we begin a brief journey along the Bazaar Hakeeman deep inside Bhatti Gate, we reach the crossing of Tehsil Bazaar. Just before this junction is the famous Fakirkhana, well known but not maintained as such an institution should be. Just next to the newly built school of miniature painting is the Imambara Mubarik Begum, and bang opposite at the beginning of the narrow lane is a 200-year old mosque maintained by a Wahhabi imam. A few yards ahead at the crossing of Tehsil Bazaar are two mosques, both over 100-years old, one a Sunni mosque maintained by Sheikh Mubarik, and the other a Shia mosque maintained by the Ali family. Along Tehsil Bazaar, just 50 yards ahead is another set of two mosques, again a Sunni-Shia combination.

If one were to follow Tehsil Bazaar right up to the point where it meets the street coming from Mori Gate, but technically in the precinct of Lahori gate, one would in the 300 yard walk find 11 mosques and three madrassahs. None of the mosques or madrassahs are new, for all of them are well over 100-year old. But the beauty lies not in the mosques themselves, but in the way in which the local population has maintained a fascinating balance of toleration. Yes, there is the odd sharp remark here and there, but it is basically to restate their own stand. Never does it spill over into hatred, for that is not what Lahore is all about.

Two of the 11 mosques mentioned in this street are over 300 years old, and one is from the Mughal era with exquisite brickwork. Mind you, this is just one street bang in the middle of the city. If you were to begin walking from Chowk Rang Mahal at the end of the Shahalami, and if you turn to the right and walk along Kashmiri Bazaar, you would be heading towards Delhi Gate. Along this stretch stand three of the most beautiful mosques in the entire sub-continent. At the crossing of Rang Mahal is the Sunehri Masjid, and this is not the one inside the Lahore Fort. Immediately to the right turn towards steps that lead up to a white mosque with huge domes covered with brass. It is an exquisite mosque in the grand Mughal tradition. The sheer simplicity of the design, which incorporates classic Mughal architecture, against the brass domes, stands out.

If you further walk up the bazaar another Mughal era mosque stands out for its exquisite brickwork, certainly a superior finish to the Mughal marble finish that is its hallmark. Further up comes the exquisite mosque of Wazir Khan, a magnificent piece of architecture and without doubt one of the most beautiful mosques in Lahore. Much older than the Badshahi Mosque, it stands out as a testimony to the excellence of its planning. Just outside is an open space where travellers used to set up their tents and sold their wares. In a way, one can almost see the same environment there, minus the crude plastic pots that jar the eye.

But that is not all. Just opposite is another brick-finished mosque of outstanding beauty. Smaller in size, but with a history all its own. The sheer sweep of variety in architecture inspires awe. And my old city has hundreds of streets and lanes, some through which one can barely pass. Yet in the dark alleys mosques abound. The sad part is that almost all the other places of worship of the Hindus and the Sikhs have been razed, or converted into living quarters. This is in sharp contrast to the tolerance Lahore always has shown. The years of Zia-ul Haq saw to it that the very best of this ancient land and city lost its bearings. We shall always remain the poorer for what we have inflicted on ourselves.

But there are bright spots too. Just opposite Lahori Gate is the Anarkali Bazaar. Almost 50 yards down the ancient bazaar, to the left, is the oldest church of Lahore. Portions of it are made of wood. This was allowed and funded by Emperor Akbar on the request of a Portuguese priest. Its interior takes you back to an era when toleration thrived. It was the golden age where a million flowers bloomed.

'Sunehri' Mosque and fading myths

Of all the mosques inside the Walled City, there are two that stand out as outstanding in their artistic content and architectural value ... these being the Mosque of Wazir Khan and the Sunehri Mosque. The Badshahi Mosque is huge, very huge, but definitely not in the league of the first two in terms of beauty and finesse.

Of the two mentioned above, the Mosque of Wazir Khan is definitely in a class of its own. Its intricate brickwork and marble settings are unrivalled in the entire city of Lahore and the northern part of the sub-continent. But then it also goes without saying that the Sunehri Mosque is not only exceptionally beautiful, but is unique in its simplistic beauty. On a rainy moon-lit night, its golden-coated brass covered domes shine for miles around.

Its simple lines and golden domes stand out. If you happen to have lived inside the Walled City, it serves, from the roof tops, as the compass for the rest of the old city. But there is much more to this unique mosque, for the stories associated with it add to the myths that abound among the old folk inside the old Walled City.

Located in Chowk Kashmiri Bazaar, off Rang Mahal, the mosque was planned and built amidst controversy. Built by Nawab Mir Syed Bhakari Khan, the naib subedar of Lahore in the period when the subedar was Mir Moinul Mulk, also known as Mir Munnoo, in the reign of the Emperor Muhammad Shah. This was the year 1163 Hijra, almost 340 years ago. Syed Bhakari was a simple Sufi and religious-minded person interested in literature and the fine arts.

Sunehri Mosque

He requested Mir Munnoo that a piece of land in the middle of Kashmiri Bazaar be allotted to him to build a mosque. The problem was that the people of the area objected to the building of a mosque in the middle of the crossing as it would hinder the flow of traffic, slow as it was in those days. We must not forget that Lahore was the largest grain city in northern India, and the caravans passed through this crossing to the 'caravanserais' inside the old city.

The subedar was unable to oblige Syed Bhakari, and instead decided to seek a 'fatwa' from top religious scholars of the Walled City. A meeting was held by the 'religious leaders' at the site, and they informed the local population that "as all land belongs to Allah, no one had the right to stop the construction of a mosque". So they cleared the way to build the mosque.

But the old folk of the Walled City are certainly no meek creations of the Almighty. They informed the "religious leaders" that if all land belonged to Allah, it was also wrong to build two mosques in the same place. This they argued because at the crossing of Kashmiri Bazaar another mosque existed, and was functioning. The meeting ended in commotion, and the matter stood in abeyance.

One account in Maulvi Nur Ahmad Chishti's book *Yadgar-i-Chishti* describes the mood in Lahore over this issue as not divided, but that most people were against the building of yet another mosque in the busy crossing. A second description of this very incident in Kanhiyya Lal's *Tarikh-i-Lahore* states that the matter went back to Mir Munnoo, who though weak as a ruler was not in a position to annoy Syed Bhakari.

So the seers of the court, just like the modern-day bureaucrats, set about trying to win the high moral ground to pave the way for the building of the mosque. The 'religious leaders' of Lahore then issued a fatwa stating that as the new planned mosque was not being built inside the old mosque, the land outside was also Allah's land, therefore, it was permissible to build the mosque, even if everyone was against it. So in these circumstances, the Sunehri Mosque's construction started.

It must go to the credit of Syed Bhakari that he tried to please the local population in every way, so much so that when people objected to the design, he made sure that the Kashmiri Bazaar crossing kept functioning, and that the shops under the mosque paid for the upkeep of the new building. He promised that the end result would be worth all the trouble.

He made an attempt to incorporate the old mosque in his new scheme of things. The local people resisted this move. The local mullahs issued a fatwa which made clear that the doorway of the new mosque could not open in front of the old mosque's doorway. The Nawab was most upset by this fatwa as he was himself a very learned religious scholar. His plan for a grand doorway had to be shelved, and he asked his planners to now plan two entrances both of which avoided the doorway of the old mosque.

The domes of the mosque were covered with gold-plated bronze, and they added to the beauty of the otherwise exceptionally beautiful mosque that emerged. The local population did accept that the effort was worth it, but they never let go of the fact that a much smaller, older mosque could be razed just to accommodate the wishes of a rich man. Such remains the ethos of the people of the old Walled City.

But it seems Allah did finally listen to the wishes of the pious Nawab Mir Syed Bhakari Khan, for after his death and with the coming of the British, Lahore came under the rule of the wise Captain Nisbet, who was the deputy commissioner of Lahore. The family of the Nawab described the story of the Sunehri Mosque to him, and he set about creating circumstances to get the wishes of the founder carried out.

Nisbet passed an order stating that as the old mosque no longer had any keeper or worshipper, it makes sense that it be knocked down, and not incorporated in the Sunehri Mosque. Also those two mosques were hindering the flow of traffic. "It makes sense that the small mosque, which is lying vacant, be knocked down and the main gateway of Sunehri Mosque be built as was originally planned. This will increase traffic flow and add to the beauty of the Golden Mosque."

Captain Nisbet got the gateway built in record time, and opened traffic to run around the mosque. It goes without saying that it proved to be a wise move. The area people still hold strong opinions about this exquisite mosque with golden domes. But then with time such opinions weaken and become myths or do they?

In search of the city's oldest mosque

Over the last one thousand years, Lahore has seen an increasing number of mosques built, destroyed and rebuilt. Their numbers keep multiplying. But which is truly the very oldest mosque in Lahore? This is a question with no clear answer, but the evidence is interesting.

The records say that when the Walled City and its fort, then made of mud, was conquered by Mahmud of Ghazni in AD 1025, he built a mosque and a tower inside the Lahore Fort. The whereabouts of this mosque are not known. To celebrate his victory, he established a separate mohallah which over time came to be called Arab Mohallah. In this was built the very first mosque which got the name Khishti Masjid. No exact location has been given of the mosque, but it was believed to be located somewhere near the present day Chuna Mandi. The Ghazni rule lasted till AD 1191, so one is not sure when this mosque was built.

But then we also have the first mosque built just outside Bhatti Gate by Syed Abdul Hasan Ali bin Usman of Hujwair, popularly known as Data Ganj Bakhsh who is Lahore's patron saint. His book *Kashf-al Mahjub* says he died in AD 1107, and that he had in his lifetime built a small mosque just outside Bhatti Gate. 'The mosque was later to be a model for fixing the direction of the *qibla* in the centuries to follow. The original mosque was completely destroyed in The Great Floods during Emperor Aurangzeb's reign and had to be rebuilt. This rebuilding process has been going on ever since, with a grand mosque being completed recently. So the original mosque of Data Sahib can safely be said to have been built sometime around the year AD 1095 to 1105. The site is certainly one of the oldest. The original building is not.

But then besides Data Ganj Bakhsh, also to Lahore came another Muslim sage by the name of Syed Ismail Bukhari in the Ghaznavid period. He died in Lahore in AD 1057 and was buried just off Hall Road where the Cathedral

School and its church today stands. There are remnants of his grave and a single room mosque in one corner of the school. If this is correct, and one research paper claims this to be so, then this small crumbling quarter is probably the oldest mosque of Lahore, built around AD 1050.

So these three mosque sites can truly claim to be the very first mosque sites in Lahore and its environs. Probably none of the three original mosques stand as they were built, but it is the Data Ganj Bakhsh mosque which can safely claim to exist at its original place. The very first one surely was the one built inside the Lahore Fort, and tradition has it that after a number of Mongol hordes swept through Lahore destroying everything, the Emperor Akbar rebuilt the Mahmud Ghazni mosque in the Lahore Fort. Ironically no trace of the mosque exist today.

But during the early reign of Akbar a mosque known as Oonchi Masjid was built inside Bhatti Gate in Lakkarhara Bazaar. That mosque stands even today in its original form. During the same period, Akbar built another mosque in AD 1614 in memory of his mother, Maryam Zamani. The place exists even today just to the east of the Lahore Fort and is known as Begum Shahi Mosque. These two can claim to be the oldest original mosques existing in Lahore and its environs standing in its original sites. Which of these two was built first is difficult to say, with a difference of opinion existing over the issue. Probably some scientist can carry out carbon-dating experiments to determine the oldest original existing mosque of Lahore.

But then there is yet another contender for the title of Lahore's oldest mosque. Just off Rang Mahal near the tomb of Khwaja Ayaz and to the eastern side of Kucha Chabbak-sawaran is a grave known as Ganj Shahidan. The myth is that this is the collective grave of the very earliest Muslims who were martyred for spreading Islam in Lahore. Next to it is a small mosque known as Masjid Ganj Shahidan, and tradition has it that this is the oldest mosque inside the Walled City. But then there is also the Chinianwali Masjid, built originally in AD 1078 and reconstructed every time Lahore was put to the torch. It stands in its original position, though the age of the building is certainly not AD 1078. But this is where the debate starts, and solid scientific proof is needed to determine the exact age of the mosque.

There are some other very old mosques that are of considerable interest. There is the one at the grave of Said Mittha who died in AD 1263. Then there is the mosque at the grave of Pir Balkhi in Kashmiri Bazaar. There is a story about this mosque. When the Sunehri Mosque was built, Kashmiri Bazaar was realigned to accommodate the mosque, which affected the Masjid Sufi Wali. It is said this mosque, built in around the same period, was built on the foundations of some older mosque. Research into this is needed to determine what originally stood here. As the foundations are original, it would be interesting to know its date and origin. Perhaps this is our oldest mosque!

Also in our search for the oldest mosque in Lahore, we must consider the claim of a mosque at the site of the grave of Syed Yaqub Zanjani, also known as Sadr Shah Zanjani. He was among the many preachers who came to Lahore during the Ghaznavid period. A small mosque exists next to his grave just behind the Lady Aitchison Hospital. Though the present day mosque is a huge rebuilt one, portions of the original structure still exist. No time period is mentioned, but it certainly could be a serious contender as the oldest existing mosque. Another Zanjani, but of a later period, Shahanshah Husain Zanjani, lies buried in Khui Chah Miran in Misri Shah.

But given the array of probable oldest mosques, the major determinants of being the oldest is that the mosque building itself must be present, even if it is in rudimentary shape. The originality of the site does not matter as much as the existence of the building itself. From that point of view, it seems that if it can be scientifically determined that the small mosque of Shah Ismail Bukhari on Hall Road is the original building, then that must surely rate as a forerunner. If not then the evidence is there for everyone to research. But it would be nice if our scholars, equipped with scientific methods, could help us track and trace our very oldest mosques and other buildings. I'm sure the one above would love to see which one of His beings finds just one of the millions of mysteries that Lahore offers us to unravel.

Tombs, graves and Wazir Khan's mosque

If there is one spot inside the old walled city of Lahore that has the largest collection of tombs and graves of 'saints' and 'sufis', it is inside, and in the immediate environs of the beautiful mosque of Wazir Khan. Each grave has its own story and mystery, laced as they are with the twists and turns of the chequered history of Lahore.

In this piece we shall touch on just five important graves. We have already touched on the grave of Syed Ishaq Gardoni, who lies inside the mosque itself. He is also known as Miran Badshah, and his grave existed a few hundred years before the mosque was built in 1044 Hijri, almost 375 years ago. Gardoni belonged to 'Faras' Persia or modern day Iran, then known as Paras, from where the word Parsi comes and migrated to the sub-continent during the upheavals in that part of the world. It should come as no surprise that the sub-continent played host to all its Muslim saints and Sufis from the immediate West because it was the land of peace and plenty. When Gardoni died his date of death was recorded on the tombstone as 786 AH. It is a symbolic noting and nothing to do with the reality of his death in Earthly terms.

When he was buried the area was an empty space, and next to the grave grew a huge Pipal tree. The miracle of this tree was that its roots surrounded the grave, leaving it untouched, yet spreading in every direction, or so the story goes. The saint was called Pir Sabz, and the people of the city, of every religion, used to pick the leaves of this Pipal tree and eat them to have the cures they sought. With time a huge annual 'Mela' took place here and on every Thursday people came to pray and pick leaves for various cures.

The grave of Syed Ishaq Gardoni reached its zenith when the new conqueror of Lahore, Maharajah Ranjit Singh, along with his favourite courtesan Moran, came to the mosque in 1799 and spent the whole day drinking and 'enjoying' themselves on the minaret. By the evening the maharajah fell very ill and his Sikh 'occult master' informed him that his actions in the mosque had annoyed the saint. The next morning the maharajah came to the grave of Syed Gardoni, sought his pardon and donated 500 rupees to the keeper. He also allotted an annual tribute to the saint. On her part Moran and the courtesans of Lahore promised to dance to Sufi music every Thursday. As long as she lived this tradition was kept alive. It continued till the time of Gen. Ayub Khan, who in a 'fundamentalist martial' mood banned the pastimes of Hira Mandi. Later Zia-ul Haq was to enforce this agenda.

Just near the grave of Gardoni lie the remains of Imam Gamoon. This saint died in 1244 A.H. and his real name was Imam Ghulam Muhammad. He was a pupil of the Sufi saint Abdullah Shah Baluch Qadri of Mozang. His son became the imam of the mosque, and then his grandson. Imam Gamoon is said to be a man with considerable learning, and when he died he was buried just next to the mosque wall, where he preached.

Just opposite the front entrance of Wazir Khan's mosque is the grave of Syed Sauf. Legend has it that he was the real brother of Gardoni, and came with him from Iran. He was a man of considerable learning, and Syed Ishaq Gardoni is said to have the greatest respect for him. Syed Sauf is the man who started the tradition of writing books in a small dwelling near the place his brother sat. He is also said to be the person who leather-bound his books, one such sample of which is available in the British Museum.

From this tradition sprang an interest that made the Wazir Khan square a centre of learning, book writing, leather book-binding and storytelling, a tradition that died out with the expansion of the city after 1947 and the crackdown on creative books, posters and pamphlets by various military regimes. During the British era, the famous contractor Sultan built a small mausoleum on the grave of Syed Sauf. Every Thursday people still come here to say 'fateha', while some make 'promises' to the saint for wishes they want granted from the Almighty. People living in the area respect Syed Sauf as a man who was not only a very learned man, but had great powers granted to him by the Almighty. That could explain the interest of Sultan the Contractor, who after the fall of the Sikhs, removed most of the bricks from destroyed mosques to build houses for the British in the Mian Mir Cantonment. Some claim he belatedly sought pardon for his actions, as his fortunes declined and this richest of contractors died a pauper.

There is another grave near that of Syed Sauf, and that is the one of Syed Sarbuland. One version puts him down as a friend and disciple of Syed Ishaq Gardoni, while another source puts him down as yet another brother of the saint. Tradition has it that he spent most of his time with Syed Sauf, and assisted him in his book writing work, training young boys how to write in the traditional Persian style. Not much more is known about this seer, though every Thursday people still come to say 'fateha' at his grave.

There are a number of other important graves, all of which have their own value in and around the mosque of Wazir Khan, but the fifth most interesting grave is that, so the tradition goes, of Pir Zaki. If you are familiar with the old walled city, you will immediately point out that the grave of Pir Zaki, after which Yakki Gate is named, is at Yakki Gate itself. This is where tradition comes in. The tradition is that Pir Zaki while fighting to defend Lahore against a Mughal invasion was killed at Yakki Gate as the gates were knocked down. Zaki stood his ground and fought against the intruders. In a pitched battle Zaki's head was cut off and fell to the ground. But the headless Zaki kept fighting on and was forced to retreat. When he retreated till the grave of

Gardoni, he was blessed and fell, headless, to meet his Maker. So his head was buried at Yakki Gate, where there is even today a grave, while the body was buried just outside where today stands the mosque of Wazir Khan. That grave also exists today.

So two graves of the man exist, with the one at Wazir Khan's mosque being declared that of a 'pir'. Logic dictates that the probable scenario would have been that the headless body of Zaki was removed by his followers from the scene of the battle and buried. History tells us that the head of Zaki, as per Mughal tradition, was hung up on a lance and buried where he fell once the capture of Lahore was complete. There is a need to detail all the graves inside the walled city, and to write down the history of the great seers and saints of our city. If our history is to live, then the deeds and lives of the dead need to brought alive.

The Chuna Mandi haveli mystery

There is no doubt that Lahore as Chaucer mentions in an epic poem as "Magnificent Lahore where streets are paved with gold" has been magnificent at times. At other times it was reduced to dust. At times it stood deserted as invaders approached to loot its immense wealth. Probably no other city has seen so much turmoil as has this truly old city.

One does not mind saying that old man Chaucer had an imagination beyond the ordinary as far as the "gold paved streets" of Lahore went, for its practical dwellers would know full well what to do with its 'gold pavings', just as the other day I saw a beautiful granite tombstone of an old British soldier (Sgt. Thomas - died 1877 in Lahore) being used in a book binding factory as a pressing bench. I was told that Lahore is littered with such tombstones, for the old and original British East India Company graveyard outside Yakki Gate has been robbed of all its statues, tombstones and other funeral decorations. It is a sign of the times in which we live. If they can try to knock down the Lahore High Court, whose beauty lies in the fact that every brick is custom-made and its architecture so very special, then what chance does an old forgotten graveyard have? But today we must dwell on things more splendid than graveyards or even imaginary 'gold pavements'.

The coming of the Sikhs to power in the Lahore Darbar in 1799 brought with it immense destruction, especially of priceless Mughal buildings. From the ruins certainly did rise some excellent buildings, mostly havelis of the Sikh chieftains who backed Maharajah Ranjit Singh. The shrewd maharajah never did try to stop the terrible destruction, except in a few cases where he felt that divine punishment was possible. It is almost like present-day governments trying to undo what the earlier rulers had done. The concept of continuity does not seem to be in the genes. But then some monuments do manage to survive, and today let us look at one small area of old Lahore where some truly magnificent havelis still survive.

If you map out the triangular area between Gali Chuna Mandi, Moti Bazaar and Jamadaran-walley Gali (now called Gali Said Sakhi after a saint who lies buried there) you will find a complex of six magnificent havelis, each more beautiful than the other. The triangle is cornered by three crossings, they being Chowk Chuna Mandi, Chowk Begum Shahi Maseet and Chowk Karri Sikander Khan. If one day a truly representative tourist guide is written about old Lahore, this triangle of havelis will surely be among the top five places to visit. It can be approached from Masti Gate and also from Kashmiri Gate.

The largest haveli is the Haveli Jamadar Khushhal Singh which occupied the south-western corner of the triangle. Next to it is the haveli that comprised three havelis, allegedly built by Raja Dhyan Singh, the prime minister of Maharajah Ranjit Singh, for his three wives. This is a popular belief in the old walled city, and there seems to be some mysterious story to this, for in British times this haveli was called 'Haveli Jamadar Khushhal Singh'. Even the mohallah opposite it was called the Mohallah Jamadaran, a word then not used in the sense it is today. The famous Kanhiyya Lal in his book *Lahore* written in 1884 describes the buildings as: "Two gateways have been provided for the outer parts of this haveli. One opens in an open *maidan*. The southern gateway has a 'farrash khana' on the first floor. The northern gate has several 'kothis'. The magnificent gate opens towards chowk Chuna Mandi. Built by his brother Teja Singh, it is now occupied by Harbans Singh, his successor".

Jamadar Khushal Singh started off as a doorwayman of Maharajah Ranjit Singh. So impressed was the maharajah by the courtesy and loyalty of the doorman, that he raised him to high office. He was originally a Hindu Brahman from Aikrri near Sardhana, and his liquid flowing praise of the maharajah finally took its toll.

One day the maharajah in a happy mood called him to court and said that as he was such a 'wise man', if he converted to Sikhism he would be made a Jamadar and have his own haveli with his own doorman. The Brahman turned out to be truly wise and he converted to Sikhism. He was made 'lord chamberlain' of the Lahore Darbar and named Khushal Singh. When the maharajah died, he got involved in the family feuds over succession and his luck rode out as the wild Sikh kept removing one another by force. The shrewd Brahman died in 1844, some say he was poisoned, and was cremated outside Masti Gate on the Ravi as it then flowed.

It is said that Khushal Singh built this magnificent haveli by appropriating the property of several Hindu and Muslim owners, who were evicted without compensation. He built the haveli like a fortress. The date of building this truly beautiful haveli can be judged from a correspondence sent to the 'peshwa' of the Marathas at Poona from the court of Maharajah Ranjit Singh in a letter of 22 Ramazan 1232 (4th August, 1817) which mentions the maharajah gifting Khushal Singh 500 wooden beams for the construction of his haveli.

On the death of Khushal Singh, even though his three sons were alive, it was his nephew Teja Singh who inherited the property. He was the person who betrayed the Sikhs in major battles that changed the fate of the Lahore Darbar. When the British captured Lahore in 1849, he was made the Raja of Sialkot. They also had considerable property in Sheikhupura.

After Khushhal Singh died, Teja Singh built on the haveli and added to its magnificence. There is evidence that suggests that this triangle was owned by Asaf Khan, the prime minister of Mughal emperor Shah Jahan, and that a magnificent building existed on this site at a cost of Rs. 2 million in those days. Many thought it was more splendid than the Lahore Fort itself. In this citadel-like house of Asaf Khan were presented gifts to the emperor worth Rs. 1 million. Saleh Kamboh, one of Shah Jahan's courtiers writes in *Aml-i-Saleh:* "Yamin-ud Daula has built these lofty and superb edifices in the direction of the Fort on the boundary of the horse-market plain where traders every day assemble". This area has been described in Latif's book as 'Nakkaskhana'.

One research on this subject suggests: "Local tradition, historical authority, location and the physical characteristics of the Khuskhal Singh haveli complex and other havelis in the triangle suggest that under the Chuna Mandi havelis lie the ruins of the palace of Asif Khan. During the days it was occupied by the CIA, some excavation work was undertaken. Newspaper reports claiming mosques etc. were refuted by the authorities. Then it became a girls' school. It is about time that the correct history of this Chuna Mandi complex of havelis be researched. We certainly do owe ourselves this much ... surely.

Mubarak haveli and its remarkable history

If ever there was a haveli that could be labelled as among the oldest, and also the finest, without doubt it would be Mubarak Haveli, just off Bazaar Hakeeman inside Bhatti Gate. It was here that the Koh-i-Nur Diamond was recovered from a trapped Afghan king. This 'haveli' has stories galore, ones that make history so interesting.

Our story begins with three brothers by the name of Mir Bahadur Ali, Mir Nadir Ali and Mir Bahar Ali. All three were well placed and on the death of their father, a well-known 'tabeeb' and 'hakeem', they decided to build a colossal haveli to house all three brothers. This was the time of Mughal emperor Muhammad Shah. It took three years to build and when the three brothers moved in, Bahadar Ali's wife gave birth to a son. This was seen as a good omen and the haveli was named Mubarak Haveli.

The family continued to prosper in the field of medicine and business. With time they branched off into two major components, the Fakir family and the Syed family. The Fakir family built their own havelis near the Mubarak Haveli, one of which stands even today and is known as the Fakirkhana in Bazaar Hakeeman. There are three other properties of the Fakir family still near Tehsil Bazaar-Bazaar Hakeeman crossing.

The Syeds owned the properties from both sides of the right edge of Tehsil Bazaar right up to the entrance of Mubarak Haveli. The land going right to the back of Lohari Gate Bazaar formed their western edge. So the haveli, in its original form, was between the main Bhatti and Lohari bazaars. One could call it the prime land in the old walled city of Lahore.

With the start of the Sikh period began years of pillage and looting. Sikh mobs would come and loot whatever they could lay their hands on. While the Fakir family, because of their influence in the Lahore Darbar remained in power, it was seen that the Syeds had to flee. The grand Mubarak Haveli remained empty for a few years and people inside the city began to steal the bricks of the western portion of the haveli. It presented a deserted look, prompting Maharajah Ranjit Singh to take it over, for himself and his guests.

The Maharajah is said to have held wild parties here. One account tells us that a seer informed him that as the original owners were Syeds, it would bode badly for him.

Being a man who heeded caution, the Sikh Maharajah decided to use it as a guest house.

It was during his reign that the Afghan king Shah Shuja and his family, who were fleeing from Kabul because of fighting over the Afghan throne, were his 'guests'. The crafty Sikh ruler made them his prisoner and decided to release them only after they gave him the unrivalled diamond called Koh-i-Nur.

Initially the Afghan king refused to admit that he had the diamond, but a team of Sikh spies informed him that it was hidden within the clothes of a Royal Afghan princess. This led him to ask his female khalsa warriors to search each and every woman, but to no avail. It was decided to make them prisoners in the Mubarak Haveli till such time they yielded the diamond.

This tired the Afghans, who wanted to move to British India in order to mount a challenge to the throne of Kabul. Eventually the diamond was produced and the Maharajah finally smiled. It had been an immense game of patience. But the Maharajah decided that they still had other gems and jewels, and he again decided to harass them.

Over the next three weeks the Afghan royal family women escaped dressed as local women, while the remaining men one night knocked down a wall of the western portion of the haveli, and escaped from Lohari Gate. Five days later they landed at Ludhiana and began their conspiracy with the British to regain the Afghan throne. The Maharajah was very upset at this escape and decided that he did not need Mubarak Haveli any longer, and handed it over to Sardar Khar Singh Sindhuwala.

But Sardar Khar Singh also did not want to handle the property of the Syeds lest bad luck comes his way. He handed over the property, on lien, to Ghulam Mohyuddin Shah Quraishi, who managed to build a few houses for himself on the south-western portion of the huge lands of the haveli. With the coming of the British the Mubarak Haveli was taken over and handed over to Nawab Ali Raza Qizilbash. The Nawab, out of respect to the original owners, rebuilt the haveli and converted a major portion into an Imambargah, which is considered among the finest in Lahore.

The haveli then went on to his son Nawab Nawazish Ali Khan and his brother Nawab Nasir Ali Khan. These brothers also managed to rebuild major portions to help the old haveli regain its original glory. But this time the ancestors of the original owners moved to regain their rights of a property abandoned out of fear for their life. They managed to get the haveli back. But the number of owners was so large that it was decided to sell it off as one block to pay off all those who claimed a slice of the cake.

It so happened that Syed Maratab Ali Shah, one of the descendants of the original owner decided to acquire the entire property of his mother's family. His own wife's name was also Mubarak Begum. So the Syed, in this grand gesture of preserving their family property, regained what was originally theirs. Syed Maratab Ali decided to form a trust, and the property now belongs to this trust, whose objective is to preserve the main haveli, to further the traditional skills that made Lahore among the eight great cities of the old world.

Syed Maratab Ali's son, Syed Babar Ali, has proven his immense love for Lahore by building a School of Calligraphy at the edge of the entrance of Mubarak Haveli. Built in small brick, it is a testimony to the creative genius that the man is. Two years ago another school inside the haveli, dedicated to preserving the paintings and old art forms of Lahore, was completed. Today it is, without doubt, well kept and is a testimony to the immense respect this very old Syed family have for Lahore and its history.

The missing havelis and the hukamnama

When the Mughals were at the height of their glory, the elite preferred to establish a small city just outside Lahore. The havelis and gardens which they built there represented the wealth that truly was Mughal. Chaucer described this wealth in a verse:

"Magnificent Lahore, where streets are paved with gold." This clean and spacious place was Mughalpura.

This was the main reason why the Emperor Shah Jahan built the magnificent Shalimar Gardens just outside Mughalpura. He expected the elite to be entertained there to the choicest food and wines, and Mughalpura boasted of excellent 'raisin wine', which even the English aristocracy visiting the court of Maharajah Ranjit Singh professed as "being smooth, soft and with a deep mellow strength."

Even though Mughalpura had the Shalimar Gardens and an array of fine Mughal buildings, it were the magnificent havelis, grand in every respect, that attracted the most attention. In the Mughal court there was a saying that there are more bricks, of mud and gold, in Mughalpura than in the entire walled city of Lahore. History was to prove this to be correct. Mind you, the place is still full of magnificent buildings, if you are the wandering type and care to explore.

During the reign of Akbar the Great, it was decided to build Mughalpura on the Lahore-Amritsar road. Probably the idea had two basic motivating factors, they being an attempt to be away from the common man, and, more importantly, to be just far enough away when invaders from the West attack Lahore. This provided the elite with enough time to leave to safer havens at Delhi, for Lahore represented the western edge of the settled portions of the Mughal Empire.

Almost all the leading lights of the Mughal court purchased large tracts of land in Mughalpura, and set about trying to build residences of excellence. The haveli of Nawab Zakariyya Khan is recorded as having cost Rs. 1.2 million in its day and encompassed gardens and entire sections for various uses. The haveli of Shahnawaz Khan is said to have cost Rs. I.I million and mind you in those days an excellent house cost rupees five to six thousand to build. The entire area from Wagah to Lahore had hundreds of brick kilns operating, where the small bricks used in those days were baked. Some of the finest builders were employed and workers' colonies sprung up at Dharampura and at Jallo. The area was well known as vegetable producing and some of the rich Arain families of the area also built their havelis there. Even today, the old families of Mughalpura still have possession of their old havelis, like the families of Mian Iftikharuddin, or that of Mian Misbah-ur Rehman.

By the time the Mughal Empire was declining sharply, the invaders from Afghanistan came on their annual pillaging raids, their sole aim to loot and plunder. By the time Ahmad Shah Durrani was on the throne at Kabul, his forces invaded India, and based on their intelligence, they attacked Mughalpura and not Lahore. When asked why they avoided Lahore, he is said to have remarked: "The money and gold is in Mughalpura, the guns and grit are in Lahore." And so they hit Mughalpura, and the entire army went on a wild looting campaign. All day and all night they looted, so one account goes, and by the next morning each and every soldier was laden with wealth they could never imagine, or even lift. The army decided to forget about invading India or attacking Lahore, for they had more gold and wealth than they could carry, and so they decided to return to Kabul.

By the time the Sikhs came to power, they also attacked Mughalpura three times, each time managing to take away what was left. By the time the Sikhs had decided to ransack Mughalpura, the entire city was empty. Not a soul was left in the magnificent havelis. It was a ghost town. By this time, when Maharajah Ranjit Singh came to power, the town of Mughalpura was virtually without any population.

He decided to tear down the place and, so the legend goes, find the gold buried in the foundations of Mughalpura.

It took almost ten years for him to take away the bricks of Mughalpura, and from these, so an account by Kanhiyya Lal says, he built a thousand havelis. It seems a rather exaggerated account of the number of bricks stolen, but one account says that the bricks used in the huge haveli of Maan Singh inside the walled city were taken from Mughalpura. Another account puts down these bricks and the marble as having been stolen from the grand graveyard of Nawab Zakariyya Khan, the area now called Begumpura.

And so lay Mughalpura waste, its glory being the reason it was destroyed. But so many were the havelis of Mughalpura that they had become part of the local folklore, depicting grandeur and glory in style. It truly is mind-boggling when one thinks of the immense destruction that once took place, and if we are to imagine just what the original Mughalpura was once like, we can picture a small city of the Mughal elite. While wandering through the streets of Mughalpura, it was interesting to find that in a small simple house lives Zahur Ahmad Khan, a descendant of Ghani Khan who, along with his brother, Nabi Khan, saved the life of Guru Gobind Singh at Machhiwara, living in abject

Guru Gobind Singh

poverty, this man possesses the original Hukamnama of Guru Gobind Singh that was presented to Ghani Khan and Nabi Khan in AD1704. The hukamnama is kept wrapped in silk and has been passed on from generation to generation.

A translated version of the 10-line hukamnama reads: "The Sikhs may know that Ghani Khan and Nabi Khan are as sons to me. They have saved me. He who serves them would be blessed Service rendered to them would be service done unto me." The Shiromani Gurdwara Parbandhak Committee on April 13,1928 (letter No. 3046/16) certified that the hukamnama was authentic. Besides this, Zahur Khan has with him the Farman of Maharaja Ranjit Singh conferring a jagir on his family, a jagir that was confiscated by the British. Research tells us that such a hukamnama was indeed issued by Guru Gobind Singh, and it was nice to know that it is safe in the hands of the family. I advised them to put it away in a bank locker, but they do not 'trust' banks. I am not surprised.

Lahore's first English-medium school

With the British conquest of Lahore in 1849 came the first English-medium school. It is ironic that the first English-medium school was not set up by the British, but by an American missionary called Rev. C.W. Forman, the man who was to go on to found the Forman Christian College in Lahore.

The Rev. Dr. C.W. Forman, along with a colleague, John Newton, set up, within a few months of the defeat of the Sikh army, an English-medium school outside Bhatti Gate, in one of the abandoned barracks where today stand the district courts of Lahore, with the help of the local administration on December 19, 1849. India's governor-general, the Marquis of Dalhousie, donated Rs 4,238 to the cause. This was the very first English-medium school of Lahore.

In October, 1852, the American Mission in Lahore, led, as it was by the Rev. C.W. Forman, applied to the British commander for permission to set up a school inside the Rang Mahal, a historic building built in the reign of Shah Jahan. The building was originally used as a courthouse. The Sikhs used it as a police station or a 'thana'. With the British take-over the reverend suggested that it was about time that "it should be put to nobler use". The board of administration of the East India Company sent an evaluator, who put the price of the building at Rs 4,000, "and nothing less, for given its historic value, it definitely should be priced higher". The value of the land was estimated at Rs 627, and the old building materials were "five times the value of the land".

But Rev. Forman put in a price of Rs 1,000 and the Company decided to accept the offer with the comment "the economic value cannot hold true for the noble cause put forward". And so the very first English-medium school was set up. This school was to grow with fame, and soon it grew into a college and was called the Forman Christian College, which then shifted to outside Anarkali at Nila Gumbad. This college was then to shift to its present location along the Lahore Canal.

However, the East India Company felt that there was need for a school for the European and 'Eurasian' children of its employees that "should remain detached from the goings on inside the walled city". So they decided to fund "the Lahore High School". This school was set up inside the Lahore Fort in August 1858, exactly nine years after the American mission had started to function in Lahore. The Chaplain of Lahore, The Rev. C. Sloggett, headed the school and the initial enrolment saw 24 boys and 20 girls. Most of the students belonged to soldiers and employees of the Company, or were orphans of its employees who had been killed in action, or had died of the "various sicknesses that plagued British in India" as one account puts it.

This Lahore High School then shifted to one of the old barracks near Anarkali, from where it shifted to a house on Lower Mall near the 'Pipals House'. Then a new building was made for the school on Temple Road near the old Masonic Hall. The Rev. E.H. Gulliver, M.A., Cambridge, headed this school. Today, both the old Masonic building and The Lahore High School do not exist. The former shifted to its present building on the corner of The Mall and Queens Road, opposite the Shah Din Building, which was later taken over by the Punjab Government after the club was banned for reasons that are as mysterious as was the club itself. A case for its restoration is still pending before the Lahore High Court.

But the Lahore High School just disappeared after a decision was taken to absorb it in the Lawrence College,

Ghora Gali, near Murree. The records of the East India Company state that "the teachers of the Lahore High School were the very best obtained in the whole of India". However, the girls' section of the school was shifted to join the Cathedral High School, also on The Mall.

These two schools, the Rang Mahal Mission School started by the Americans, the Lahore High School started by the East India Company with the assistance of the Church of England, were the very first English-medium schools of Lahore, With time other planned schools were put into place. For example The Primary and Middle Anglo-Vernacular School was built outside Bhatti Gate in 1883 with the aim of training teachers for English-medium schools all over the Punjab.

However, at the other end of the spectrum for the elite came up the Punjab Chiefs' College in November, 1886. This huge school was built on a design submitted by Lockwood Kipling and Bhai Ram Singh of the Mayo School of Arts (now called the NCA). The Viceroy, Lord Dufferin, later decided to call it the Aitchison College, Lahore.

In this way English-medium schools began to spring up all over Lahore and the Punjab. The central idea was to produce 'brown sahibs' for the Raj. It would not be out of place to mention that it was Maharajah Ranjit Singh who effectively stopped the British from even sending their missionaries to the Punjab. He allowed the American Mission to establish a small base on his border with the British at Ludhiana in 1839. Probably he saw in the Americans a neutralizing force to British interests. Within two yeas of his death, the American Mission had managed to get to Lahore. The rest is history.

The city's first medical school

Very few of us know that the first modern school of medical education in the Punjab was set up during the last years of Maharajah Ranjit Singh. He relied a lot on the Fakir brothers for they were excellent hakeems, but he was wise enough to know that the future belonged to modern medicine.

His spies in British India, from Delhi to far away Calcutta, informed him of what the British were doing in the field of medical education and sciences, and he was well briefed on how the institutions in England, Scotland and Ireland were producing doctors and surgeons. His French advisers in the Lahore Darbar had educated him about the progress medical education had made in Europe and he wanted a similar institution set up in Lahore, more so as a support to his immensely powerful army, then the "finest in Asia".

For this, the Maharajah asked his French generals to seek out Europeans to teach local hakeems something of the medical sciences. Medical books were translated into Persian in this regard. He set up the first medical education school in the French-led barracks of the Fauj-i-Khas located outside Bhatti Gate where today stands the Government College University, Lahore. The small school had barely taken off when the Maharajah died and things came to a grinding halt. Within ten years of his death, the British moved in, violating every treaty signed with the Punjabis.

The first Indian war of independence in 1857 brought forth before the victorious British forces the problem of inadequate medical services in the sub-continent. Even before Delhi fell, after several false alarms and several false celebrations in London, the East India Company had put forth the proposal for a medical institution "of the same quality as those existing in Britain" in Lahore. They were picking up the work left by the late Maharajah.

Though one existed in Calcutta, they were of the view that it was too small in size to cater to the immense needs of the entire sub-continent. The siege of Delhi brought with it a very large number of casualties and even before the siege ended the proposal was ready for implementation once the "company re-established its writ over the rebels".

Orders for "the establishment of a medical college" were in place in 1857 itself and materialized in 1860. The Lahore Medical School was started in the artillery barracks at the site of the Government College University, Lahore, with the hospital located in Taxali Gate. Mind you, the barracks were the same where Maharajah Ranjit Singh had set up the first medical school, and which ceased to operate after he died. The barracks were originally constructed by the Maharajah for the elite Fauj-i-Khas, commanded as it was by the French generals Allard and Ventura, who were assisting him in the scheme.

To complement the Lahore Medical School, a huge hospital was also ordered, and that came up in the shape of the Mayo Hospital, the largest hospital in northern India. The Mayo Hospital building was completed in 1870 and was named after the Earl of Mayo, who was then viceroy of India. The architects were Purdon and Rai Bahadur Kanhiyya Lal, that famous chronicler of Lahore's history, was the engineer in charge. In 1886, the Senate of the University of Dublin granted the students of the Lahore Medical College "privilege similar to those granted to students from English schools".That privilege still stands.

The post-mortem room and pathology building were constructed in 1895. Every crime reporter of Lahore has to do a stint visiting this 'ghostly' place if he hopes for a scoop story, and I spent many nights going over dead bodies trying to find the real story behind the corpses.

A major civil works programme was completed in 1911 and at the time, the Lahore Medical School was named the King Edward's College, Lahore. The official affiliation of the College with the Punjab University came in 1906. At the time of partition, 228 students joined the King Edward's College, Lahore, with Dr. Col. Ilahi Buksh as the first Muslim Principal in 1947. He was also the personal physician to the Quaid-i-Azam. This meant having almost 45 students a year. The present annual intake is 232 and the total number of student is 1,194, 628 male and 566 females. Things have changed a lot over the last 55 years, and changed they have for the better.

We have forgotten the great principals of this great medical institution, just as we have forgotten all our great professors, scientists and teachers. In fact, we have forgotten that doctors are without frontiers, for humanity is their religion. The fact is that we have completely forgotten that during the Sikh era, the literacy level in the Punjab was well above 65 per cent, better than what it was in most European countries nearly 200 years ago, and three times higher than what it is today. But then the Punjabi 'qaida' alphabet book — then an essential in every Punjabi village was abolished by the British, converting rural Punjab into a completely illiterate expanse. Things have not changed since. The slide continues.

The decay of a great library

When the subedar, or governor, of Lahore, Nawab Wazir Khan, started building his famous and exquisite mosque in 1634 inside the walled city in the reign of the Emperor Shah Jahan, he also started laying an equally beautiful garden half a mile eastward from Lohari Gate. It was known then as Bagh Wazir Khan.

When asked why he was trying to copy the famous Shalimar Gardens being built then by his emperor, he said: "I am a humble subedar. The mosque is for man to try to appreciate the unseen beauty of Allah. This small garden is to help man to appreciate Allah's beautiful nature." Many experts believe the original bagh of Wazir Khan was a much more beautiful garden than the legendary Shalimar. It is almost like comparing the Badshahi Mosque to the mosque of Wazir Khan. But today that garden is no more. The only trace of that exquisite creation is the Baradari of Wazir Khan. Every time you cross The Mall opposite the museum,or the old campus of the Punjab University, you are trampling on where the garden once was. The baradari remains, a testimony to that great builder of Lahore. It eventually got to be the starting point of one of the finest libraries of the sub-continent.

The story of the Punjab Public Library is one that must be told, again and again, and lessons extracted, and action taken, concrete action, by private and public persons and institutions, for these actions could, eventually, determine our place in history. The baradari of Wazir Khan has seen the history of our city unfold since 1634. The Mughals collapsed, the Afghans pillaged and raped, the Sikhs suffered immensely and ultimately rose to power.

The beginning of their zenith started in the baradari of Wazir Khan, where the aspiring Sukherchakaria chieftain from Gujranwala waited before his troops stormed into Lahore in 1799. The baradari watched 40 years of utter pillage as it served as a garrison building for the Sikh elite officers of the French-trained the Fauj-i-Khas. The garden was looted of its fountains and flowers.

Then came the British and they also camped in the baradari. After the British took over in 1849 it first served as a Settlement Office as the East India Company set about expanding its writ in the Punjab. It next served as the first telegraph office in Lahore,connected directly to a point on Jahangir's baradari in the River Ravi at Shahdara. Once consolidation was complete culture returned and it served as the very first building to house the Lahore Museum, which moved out after it got its own beautiful building just behind it.

The British then started the 'Anarkali Book Club', and the board stated, as one account of Goulding tells us, 'for Europeans only.' When the Lawrence Hall was built and became part of the Lahore and Mian Mir Institute, now called the Lahore Gymkhana Club, the library was moved there. Thus the baradari

Mayo Hospital

became available once again. At this stage the Lt. Governor of the Punjab, Sir Charles Aitchison, wished that a library to reflect the immense history and literary traditions of Lahore be built in the baradari. This was named the Punjab Public Library. The committee formed to undertake this project met for the first time on November 12, 1884, in the French-built Secretariat building. Sir Charles donated his entire library and other well-connected people followed likewise. Well-known collections from Munshi Naval Kishore, from Sardar Attar Singh and the huge and rare collection of Fakir Syed Jamaluddin, came the library's way. It was an impressive start. On the December 21, 1885, Sir Charles Aitchison inaugurated the library.

But the greatest contribution of Sir Charles was the fact that he made sure that it remained out of the clutches of the bureaucracy. He got the library registered under the Charities Act, declaring its intentions as being 'non-profit oriented'. This single step guaranteed its success. Great librarians then headed this unique library, which was seen as one of the finest libraries in northern India.

In 1886, the great Lala Kirpa Ram became the chief librarian, setting the highest standards of service and working day and night to make sure Lahore had the finest library in the entire sub-continent. He served for 27 long years and was followed by Lala Labbha Ram who served another eight years till 1921. By then these two had collected the finest set of rare manuscripts and books in India.

In 1921 another well-known librarian, Vidya Sagar Gorewara joined and served for just two years. In 1923 came Lala Ram Labhaya, who worked till the midnight of August 14, 1947, a solid 24 years of effort work that made sure Pakistan inherited one of the finest libraries in the world. In 1947 the first Pakistani Chief Librarian of the Punjab Public Library, Khwaja Nur Elahi, took over and served for 19 years till 1966. His greatest contribution was that he managed to keep the bureaucrats at bay, expanding the library in the process. As the library grew, so did the need for space. New buildings were built in 1924 and 1939. In the space of 80 years, just five librarians headed this great institution, which is testimony to its solid growth and direction.

The martial law of Gen. Ayub Khan had by then set in a new malaise, a sort of aversion to learning and knowledge. Come to think of it, no library worth the mention, let alone an excellent bookshop, has managed to raise its head in Lahore over the last 40 years. Today the Punjab Public Library has a massive collection of 375,000 books, most of them rare ones.

For example the well-known book 'India: the Transfer of Power 1942-47,' in 12 volumes, edited by Nicholas Mansergh, lies in the chief librarian's office. That alone is worth a fortune. The very rare collection of ancient manuscripts number well over 850 collections, each one definitely worth more than money can measure. There is so much more in this library that only a massive effort of the donor agencies can help to save, what to my mind, is our finest institution gone all wrong.

On the dusty floors of the library rest some of the rarest books and manuscripts in the entire sub-continent. It is our history left to die. There is just not even enough money to get old and rare books rebound. The use of modern paper preservation techniques is missing. The lack of space, absence of funds and expertise, let alone a passion to save the true and rare heritage of this ancient city and the land, add to the tragedy called the Punjab Public Library.

The real malaise set in when the Punjab Government took over the library and placed it under their 'education' department, a violation of the trust in which it was set. The baradari still stands out for it houses the facilities to read newspapers and magazines. It watches in silence the decay. Even the young sensitive students of this city no longer protest, or feel, or even see, the slow, very slow, and silent death of one of Lahore's greatest institutions.

The book writers of Lahore

The city of Lahore did not have any printing presses till the British arrived in 1849. The first printing press arrived in 1850 and was owned by Munshi Harsukh Rai, who launched a weekly English publication by the name of Koh-i-Nur, which was also the name of his press. The age of printing had arrived in Lahore.

But before the printing press came, Lahore had a unique place in the world of book publication. Books hand-written in Lahore were much sought after, and traders exported books to far off places like Iran and Khurasan and even to Constantinople and beyond. The museums of almost all these places have hand-written books from Lahore as unique samples of excellence. The story of that tradition needs to be told.

There was a time when the trade caravans from all over the world used to reach Lahore. Their normal place of rest was in the huge open space just opposite the mosque of Wazir Khan. Around this area were the famous 'Karvan serais' of Lahore. A few names from antiquity of these serai's are Maula Bakhsh Ki Serai and Babu Ki Sarai. This space was the collection point, the melting pot of ideas from all over the world. To one side of the 'maidan' was the Nakkaskhana, or the Horse Stables, and just near it were numerous water troughs. Even today one such trough, probably dating back to the 1700s is still functional. The ideas of the changing world came from this place, and it is this very place where the institution of the kissakhawan, or storyteller, emerged.

From this institution or practice of narrating the tales of strange lands and people grew the industry of story writing, and Lahore excelled in this. There is no doubt that at Delhi, Peshawar, Samarkand and Bukhara the tradition of the storyteller existed. But then at all these places, just like they existed in the Europe of old, the written word followed the spoken one. The written word meant that the business of publishing existed there, and it might interest those in the habit of reading that of the shops that ringed the maidan outside the mosque of Wazir Khan, over two dozen book publishers did excellent business. A brief description of these businesses merits mention, for it provides us with reasonable clues as to what Lahore meant to the world of books and scholarship before the printing press arrived.

One of the largest publishing houses of old Lahore was owned by Mian Muhammad Bakhsh Sahaf, who had over 50 calligraphers who copied books and sent them for binding.

Epics like *Alif Laila* and numerous other Punjabi, Persian and even Turkish tales (when it was written in the traditional Turkish script) were written here. The sheer beauty of the Sahaf publications made them expensive copies. Besides the usual commodities that traders purchased, books also did excellent business and were purchased from all over the world.

Besides this group, other well known publishing houses were owned by Chiragh Din, who in the year 1815 sold books worth over one thousand rupees every day, as one account puts it. In the initial Sikh conquest of the walled city of Lahore, another account states that "the book sellers of Lahore had more money than the goldsmiths, a fact that shocked Ranjit Singh".

Fakirullah, who was a Sadhu by caste as one description puts it, owned another major book publishing concern. He had employed over 65 calligraphers and he specialized in publishing religious texts like copies of the Holy Quran. Copies of the Quran with the Fakirullah sign are among some of the prized copies in the British Museum.

Yet another major publishing concern was owned by Sheikh Elahi Bakhsh. He also had over 60 calligraphers working for him. He also specialized in religious texts, though some samples of traditional folk stories are known for their sheer beauty. The artistry of the outer spaces show the high level of expertise and taste that the books of Elahi Bakhsh were known for.

All these numerous publishing houses had their own specialist binders, and all these hand-written manuscripts were leather bound and done in a style that was in later years to be copied by many experts in the West. The leather used in bookbinding is of a special type with specific properties to make them last. Today, there are only two families that specialize in leather bookbinding, with both devoting their energies to binding copies of the Holy Quran.

If we visit the Wazir Khan mosque even today, we can visualize the scene of numerous caravans, with storytellers helping the tired traders pass the time as the night approaches. The book business has always been good business, and still remains a major industry in all sane societies. In Lahore the habit of reading has touched an all-time low, let alone the tradition of hand-written manuscripts and leather-bound editions. The old city of Lahore had libraries in virtually every mohallah. Gone are the libraries, the calligraphers, and the leather bookbinders. Not that the printing presses ruined their trade. If anything it enhanced it, and gave it a new respectability.

Lahore's pavements of gold

Whenever I get the time on a Sunday, when the begum is in not too possessive a mood, I drive over to the Anarkali Mall crossing, park in front of the old Tollinton Market, and spend my happiest two to three hours browsing through old books, buying a few and reading delightful portions from others.

My father did this, as did all his friends, from Faiz the poet to Ali Asghar the daredevil reporter, now working as a broadcaster in Germany, indulged in this pastime. I passed on this 'habit' to my daughters, who now, whenever they are home from abroad, plan a day out with me in Anarkali. The old books are spread out from the gates of The Government College (now called a university, though Dr Khalid Aftab has done a great job of restoring the glory of old to our alma mater), towards the front of the old campus of the Punjab University, and to the right up to the Nila Gumbad crossing. In the thousands of books up for sale, one finds rare ones, and even manuscripts. The prices are very reasonable, thought not dirt cheap, and it all depends on how well you bargain and just how desperate you look to the seller, for they can make out quickly how educated you are and then the 'supply-demand' principles get into play.

Lahore was once known for its libraries. Today we see that the few libraries that are left are without enough people to use them. The 'mohallah libraries' of old have almost died out, and even great institutions like the Punjab Public Library of Lahore is in virtual ruins. Recently, I visited the Lahore Museum Library searching for an old map of Lahore, and was shocked to see the condition of the library, a dark dingy place that was once the pride of Lahore. The famous library of the College of Oriental Languages and Studies is also sparingly used, and the people manning the new Quaid-i-Azam Library mention the low numbers interested in books. It seems that our environment, and its true worth, is reflected by the state of our libraries.

But this is borne out by the fact that no new bookshop worth its name has sprung up since partition. One can name two notable exceptions on The Mall, but they are exceptions born out of the fact that their owners were interested in books and used tactics to make sure a profit existed. That is why the roadside bookshops have become, over the years, a trade mark of the city. My father always used to drum into our ears the fact that the 'written word', no matter how much communication developed, could never be replaced.

Over the years, I have managed to pick up several excellent books. If I happen to come across a rare book, or seems, like one worth purchasing, one looks up rare book sites on the internet. That adds to the satisfaction of buying a book that adds, in its own way, to one's life. In an era where one is willing to spend thousands on a meal, spending a few hundred on books is seen as waste of money. Such is the mindset of a nation which prints only one million newspapers for a population of over 140 million in all languages. Probably Pakistan has the world's lowest 'functional literacy' rate on earth. That is why every book acquisition is an event, an event I would like to share with you.

The other day I purchased the well-known Introduction to the Middle Ages by Ephraim Emerson. The original was printed in 1898 and is considered a collector's item valued at over $ 1,500, or so says the Amazon internet site. Only five books of that original manuscript came to Lahore, all of them in the five major libraries of the educational institutions of the city. The one in the Kinnaird College Library was sold in 'raddi' as waste and ended up in a roadside shop. It was from there that I purchased the original print. This book was later scrapped because it described in detail how during the Crusades the Christian forces actually used to eat, as cannibals would, their enemies. In 1929, the British authorities decided to withdraw this book. The college library discarded this book and sold it as waste. I have no idea where this book went after the clean-up, but two years ago it ended up on a Lahore pavement shop. Their loss has been my gain. I purchased the book for Rs. 40 only.

Another interesting acquisition has been a leather-bound original 1873 edition of the *Punjab Record,* Volume IX. This was printed, and published by W.E. Hall, successors to the Punjab Printing Company. Its veritable store of knowledge of British Punjab is amazing. An expert has valued this book at anything over Rs. 50,000. I managed to buy it for Rs. 50. But the one major acquisition that I managed was an original hand-painted 1899 original hand written version of *Hir* by Waris Shah. I would estimate its value at anything over Rs. 500,000, and there it was lying among scores of Punjabi books for a mere Rs. 150 and the bookseller thought that he had me trapped when I refused to pay even Rs. 150 he was stuck at. Being a true Sheikh, I haggled for a two digit figure, and then grudgingly paid his price. But these are my major finds. There are other important books I have and all because we as a nation have forgotten the value of the printed word.

Two other libraries, which have lost some very rare books, have been one in the Freemasons Hall and one in the Lahore Gymkhana Club. The first lost books to some very influential vandals while the latter lost books in several clean-ups, all of them officially justified. But then all these books turn up on the roadside on The Mall and in the streets of Anarkali. It is a vast storehouse of knowledge that lies on our pavements. Chaucer was not wrong when he wrote about Lahore that its streets were paved with gold.

Remembering the paper makers

There is no doubt that Genghis Khan wreaked havoc on Lahore, pillaging it, raping the women who did not manage to flee the walled city and butchered all able-bodied men who remained. But then if he can be said to have made one positive contribution that lasted, it certainly must be the introduction of paper to Lahore.

The Chinese were the first to use paper, an invention that goes back almost 2,000 years. In those days a thin strong fabric was used in the Punjab, as paper did not exist here. If you have ever seen the 'farmans' of old in the Lahore Museum, you will notice that the older ones are all on fabric. When Sher Shah Suri revolutionized the land record system, he made it compulsory for each 'patwarkhana' to have two fabric copies of the entire record of the relevant area. The tehsildar certified the copy with his seal and signature and kept the original. But then came paper, and paper came to Lahore from two routes: from Samarkand *via* Kashmir, and from the south, thanks to Arab traders who initially came to Multan. In both cases, the initial route was *via* Samarkand.

We have to thank the Mongols for forcing paper to come to Samarkand. The Chinese prisoners of war, brought to Samarkand after the battle of Atlakh near Talas, first introduced (AD 751) the technique of paper-making from linen, flax or hemp rags based on methods used in China. Ibn-i Nadim observed in *Al-Fihrist*: "The Chinese write on paper made from a sort of herbage. The Arabs learnt the technique of paper-making from the Chinese captives at Samarkand and diffused it westward".

After the paper technology reached the Arabs, the latter improved the technique and supplemented linen with flax and other vegetable fibres. This was the beginning of the modern paper industry. With the conquest of Sindh by the Arabs, Khurasani paper was first introduced in the eighth century AD, and it continued to be imported for several centuries.

The paper-making industry in the sub-continent was established in Delhi and Lahore, the two chief political and cultural seats of the Sultanate period. Generally, Indian paper-making centre produced the glazed variety. One research categorises ancient paper into seven types — Kashmiri, Ahmadabadi, Hyderabadi, Faizabadi, Khasah-i-Jahangiri or Lahori, Kanpuri and Aurangabadi.

While Kashmiri paper was stout and glazed, some Kashmiri centres produced superfine paper called silken. Khasah-i-Jahangiri, or Lahori paper, was made here though later on Sialkot also acquired a reputation for quality paper. The paper was glossy, thin, polished and bluish white. The Lahori variety was a class product in that it was the most flexible of all papers produced in the sub-continent. However, one researcher thinks paper came to Sialkot from Kashmir and from there to Lahore, which also makes sense.

The oldest recipe for making Lahori paper has been described as follows: "To make the pulp, use old clothes, old tents, the bark of certain shrubs and trees. Wash well and soak in water for a few days. Beat these materials with wooden hammer. Mix the pulp with a little limewater. The mixture, when lifted out, would become paper".

The description further states: "Once removed, each sheet is drawn through a second reservoir of water and then hung up to dry in the sun. A quantity of gum Arabic was dissolved in water and then the beaten pulp was placed. The water in the second reservoir, through which the sheets were drawn, also contained gum in the form of mucilage, as well as some alum dissolved in it. The moulds or forms used by the workmen were generally made of bamboo. The gum Arabic was obtained as an exudation from the babool tree".

In the old Indian technique of paper-making, the main tools used were: dhegi (hammer), chhapri (screen), and sacha (teakwood frame), kunchawas (soft date-palm brush), and polishing stone. One expert describes the process: "The process of making paper from such pulp was not very difficult. The pulp was moistened with water, taken to the river Ravi and pounded with stones, and washed for three days. It was then taken to a cistern about 7ft x 4ft x 4ft deep, half - filled with water. The pulp was thrown into this cistern.

"When it was thoroughly dissolved, the workman sitting on the edge of the pit, bending over the water, took in both hands the square frame which held the screen serving as a sieve, passed it underwater and drew it slowly and evenly to the surface; such that as the water passed through, a uniform film of pulp was left on the screen. The screen was then lifted up and turned over, and the film of paper was spread on a rag cushion. When sufficient layers had been heaped on this cushion, about 9-14 inches high, a rag was spread over them and a plank weighted with heavy stones was laid over it.

"When this pressure had drained the water and some of the moisture out of the stock of paper, the stones were taken away and two men, one standing at each end of the plank, see-sawed over the bundle of paper by hand. When it was well pressed, the paper was peeled off, layer after layer, and spread to dry either on the walls of the building or on rags laid in the sun. When dried, each sheet was laid on the polished wooden board and rubbed with a shell till it shone".

In this way, paper was made on the banks of the River Ravi, as it was on the Indus near Multan. In the

Punjab, very fine quality paper began to evolve, thanks to the use of cotton, though normally the last pick, slightly rusty in colour, was used.

One researcher claims that paper came to Lahore before it had reached the Arabs. But no matter how it came, there is no disputing that this is the one contribution to learning that Genghis Khan unwittingly made. It would take another 600 years before printing on paper started in the sub-continent, with the 16 pages of *Doctrina Christina* in Tamil by Fr Henriques and Fr Manoel de Sao Pedro. This was printed in the Malabar coast in 1578. This little work, known only from one copy in existence, is the earliest example of printing in the characters of one of the languages of India.

The 16 pages of *Doctrina Christina* are printed on a single sheet, in conventional octavo format, the pages measuring approximately 14x10 cm. It is the famous Khasah-i-Jahangiri, or Lahori paper, which goes to show the immense contribution to the fast evolving industrial world that the sub-continent was becoming before it was colonized and thrown into mass poverty. Because of the alum used, it is still intact, a remarkable contribution of the local genius of Lahore. There is need to recognize the early paper-makers of Lahore and Sialkot, for they in no small measure contributed to the spread of knowledge.

Lahore's first 'Company era' businesses

Once the British had defeated the Sikhs in 1849 at Chillianwala Bagh near Gujrat, the Union Jack went up at the Lahore Fort. The Lahore Darbar ceased to exist. Rani Jindan and her family were effectively removed. The Company era had started in Lahore.

As is true of all expanding powers, business concerns come first, because that is the real intention. The military and the wars and the 'heroes' are all there to assist business interests. As we look at Lahore, it would be interesting to see how the British entered its business markets. The Anarkali

Bazaar had yet to come up, and all development started from the base of British power, the cantonment. This was initially established in the Anarkali area. This area can be described as present day Anarkali Bazaar, old Anarkali up to the French military mission that we now know as the Civil Secretariat, Lower Mall outside Bhatti Gate, which includes Rattigan Road, Government College and the Punjab University. It was here that the first business houses opened.

According to one account written in 1924, "Mr William Bell may be described as the pioneer of European business enterprise in Lahore. Apart from his timber trade with Kashmir and Chamba, of which Mr M. Ter Arrotoon was the originator, he set himself up as superintendent of the government printing press, left it and set up his own press, auction houses, booksellers shops, stationery shops, general stores." He even set up tailoring shops and piano shops. William Bell, who also printed the Punjab Record, started all the beautiful old leather-bound books that we see with lawyers today. When Bell grew old, he retired to his impressive bungalow at the Lower Mall, and his son-in-law, J. J. Davis, took over and set up his business at Court Street. If you even today happen to drive on The Mall, in the YMCA Building you will see, at one corner, an old board that reminds us of the presence of J. J. Davis. His printing press grew in size and ended up becoming the Civil & Military Press. Their survival lay in doing government printing. The various businesses that William Bell set up, he sold to other European businessmen, who all developed them into thriving concerns.

But strange as it might seem, with the shifting of the Lahore Cantonment to Mian Mir, that is where the big shops first opened. After they had established themselves, they all moved back to the Anarkali area. Among the first shops in Mian Mir was the shop of Jamsetji and Sons, which was established in 1862. They ran a 'general European store' as the expression went then, and sold wines and spirits, toys, ammunition. Initially, they even sold "black powder in flasks, percussion caps and bags of shots," as the flintlock era was still on. The old and original Jamsetji and Sons shop is on Sarwar Road next to the present day Zakir Tikka Shop. They opened a branch in the Commercial Building next to the old Tollinton Market. They built a beautiful house at the northern end of Lower Mall called 'Rose Cottage'. This exquisite house was demolished to make way for the Government College Hostel.

The standard of tailoring irked the officers of 'Company Bahadur' as the East India Company was locally known. They encouraged the best tailors of London to move here. The very first to set up business was Messrs Philips & Co., which was situated at the present Nila Gumbad building at the corner. Among the three most prominent tailors of Regent's Street in London to set up branches in Lahore were Messrs Clarke & Co., Messrs Adlard & Co. (which still exists in London), and Messrs Davidge & Brothers. Initially they felt secure at Mian Mir, but within a few years, they shifted to the Anarkali and Mall area. All of them did well. However, their method of doing business was very different from how tailoring is conducted today.

When a gentleman wanted a suit tailored, it would normally be more than one suit. Strange as it might seem, getting "just one tailored" was the unacceptable thing to do. A message was left at the shop by the gentleman and the European tailor, accompanied by a bhangi would visit the house of the person concerned, have tea, and after social niceties would measure him up. The bhangi would be carrying fabrics for shirts and undergarments. A complete array of orders had to be given to "dress and drape" a gentleman. It was almost like a mini social event in the life of a European. For this reason, tailors liked to get an official certification from as high an official as was possible. That, in many ways, determined the professional skills of the tailor. The local population also learnt these tailoring skills and tried to open up small shops in the lanes of Anarkali. The officers of the Company called them 'Cheap Johns' and it was a social insult to be seen near such a shop.

Then there were the professional photographers. Among the first and most famous photographers of Lahore was a person by the name of Mr William Bartholomew. He originally lived in the Lahore Fort when the conquest of 1849 was completed and was an 'apothecary'. He then became an adviser to the Raja of Faridkot and moved his studio to Lower Mall. With his death his shop closed. But by then another photographer, Mr James Craddock, had moved from Simla to Lahore. He set up studio on the Lower Mall, for then the limits of The Mall were at the GPO crossing. With Craddock's death the shop also closed. Much later another shop opened up at the same place by the name of S. Rollo & Co., with the grandfather of the last surviving Rollo being an apprentice. The old Mr Rollo died about 10 years ago, and his apprentice now runs the concern by the same name.

Also in 1872, the first European chemist shop opened on the Lower Mall. This was called Richardson Chemist, which went on to be called Messrs Peake, Allen & Co. This shop managed to do well and then was named, as owners changed, as Messrs Plomer & Co., with the original Plomer shop being at The Pipals on the Lower Mall. Later it shifted to its present location opposite the Lahore High Court. This is one business that has never seen a downturn, and Plomer & Sons still remains a very viable and historic shop. In a way, this is probably the oldest European shop of the Lahore that emerged with the British Raj, though I am ready to accept evidence of any older shop, as Jamsetji & Sons no longer functions in its original shape or calling.

Lahore's Kakkayzai 'horse traders'

The original precinct of horse riders in the old walled city of Lahore is known as Kucha Chabbaksawaran inside Mochi Gate. This area was inhabited by people who were, in one way or another, involved with horses, be it riding, manufacturing saddlery, riding boots, reins, belts, whips, or simple horse trading. Anything to do with horses has always had a 'chabbaksawar' connection.

Horse trading was the 'natural' business of the Kakkayzai clan of this 'kucha' - precinct, and they operated through the various 'nakkaskhanas' of Lahore, especially the one opposite the Wazir Khan's mosque. These horse traders were known as 'chabbaksawars', though the very name itself means 'horse riders'. In earlier times this is where the cavalry soldiers dwelt, especially during the Mughal period. But by the time the Sikhs took over power in 1799, various other traders linked to the cavalry started moving in. By the time the British came in 1849, Kucha Chabbaksawaran had an array of traders, manufacturers and officers of the Sikh cavalry living here. But it is the Kakkayzais and their horse trading that had always dominated the area.

A number of detailed accounts exist about horse trading in Lahore, but none as colourful and detailed as the one in the book *Yaadgar-i-Chishti* by Maulvi Nur Ahmad Chishti, who also wrote the famous *Tehkeqat-i-Chishti*. The Kakkayzai horse traders all acted as one, with the profits being added to a pool. The normal profit rate was four per cent, which was deposited in a collective fund, and on the first Thursday of the new moon week, the collective fund would be distributed equally among all the horse trading Kakkayzai clan. This clan had their own strict ethics, and they had a tradition whereby they never uttered a word during the entire dealing, except when praising or condemning a horse.

The method they used was unique. Whenever the price of a horse was asked, after ascertaining the seriousness of the buyer, they would throw a handkerchief over their hand and use a unique sign language. The price was always told through a sign, never through words as that was considered inauspicious. The sign language was the movement of fingers informing of an acceptable price.

Once a deal was struck, the piece of cloth was thrown over the horse and the deal finalized. Once the price was paid, the cloth, the reins, some green fodder and the basic saddlery went with the price. Giving green fodder was considered a sign of good luck. No horse was ever sold without the seller providing some green fodder.

The Kakkayzai clan had an ethics all their own, and it goes without saying that the people of Lahore never did quite swallow their working methods. They had a reputation for being very tough negotiators, and people have, over the years, been rather wary of them, at best trying to avoid getting into any fray with them, for once they get into a fight, the Kakkayzai clan seem to all unite. Yet they have proved to be the biggest enigma, as a people, that have ever lived in the walled city.

These horse dealers had an exceptionally aggressive attitude towards their customers, yet when it came to their womenfolk, they are placid walkovers. The Kakkayzai women are known, even today, as a set of women who fight, sometimes over trivia, for hours, using a language that would make hardened criminals blush. They keep a verbal fight going for days and weeks and even months.

They start arguing in the morning after putting their kitchen utensils upside down, and then a slanging match starts. Such is the colourful language that no man in the walled city would dare to pass through their area. They all use the side streets, blushing at the invectives as they rush through. As I have experienced this scene once in my college days, I can assure you that one would rather be shot dead than face these aggressive women.

But then besides horse dealing, the Kakkayzais of Kucha Chabbaksawaran were known for their infidelity. Their fondness for the 'good' things of life were legendary, and some say that their pooling of resources was one way of ensuring that they all had an equal fling at life. There is an old saying in the old walled city, that "a Kakkayzai sleeps best after selling a horse", probably because he is assured of some good time in the very near future. It is, therefore, understandable, why their womenfolk have gained such legendary status, for they are known to even tease their 'fellow opponents' about the impotence of their husbands.

Such have been the ways of the Kakkayzais of Kucha Chabbaksawaran. Their customs also need to be studied, for, according to Chishti, unlike other clans in Lahore, they celebrate a woman's pregnancy throughout the nine months of expectancy. Every month they send sweets to the house of the expecting mother, even if she is involved in a fight with a neighbour. The men strictly keep out of this activity, preferring to pool resources and enjoy themselves collectively. It makes eminent sense. Once a child is born they then react in extreme behaviour, depending on whether it is a male or a female. Need one say more?

But then times have changed since the Kakkayzais of Kucha Chabbaksawaran were horse dealers almost 150 years ago. They initially moved out of the walled city towards Shahdara, where a Basti Kakkayzaian exists. There, even today, the daily ritual of verbal fights among the women takes place. Others spread out to other parts of the city. Some remained, working in the leather trade. Today this clan, like all others, works in the diverse trades that are available today, though still known as aggressive and tough to tackle. It is probably in the genes, for one source puts down their origins to the tough Cossacks of Russia that came to Lahore over 600 years ago with the Turkish invaders, all horsemen that they were.

There is an area in Turkmenistan that is called Kakzai. But the word Kakkay is from the Greek word 'Kakophnos' meaning 'bad'. The word 'kaka' has Indo-European roots like 'kratia' is from kratos meaning 'strength, power, rule'. So these tough Cossacks, the men who rode in on horses, remained with their horses till such times machines replaced them. It comes as no coincidence that over 50 per cent of all racehorse owners in Lahore are Kakkayzai, as are the jockeys and trainers. Till this day they are, like their womenfolk, not easy to deal with. It's the genes without doubt.

More than just a boss

The corporate world of Pakistan lost Azhar Ali Malik. To me, he was much more than merely the big boss of ICI in Pakistan. He was a friend since we were five years old and for the last 47 years we followed each other's fortunes closely. His story is one of how a life should be lived, to the hilt, in excellence, bordering on brilliance, yet as a human being simple and earthy.

Azhar Ali Malik

We first met in 1957 in Class One in the St. Anthony's High School, Lahore. On the first day at school we were all strangers, scared. He sat on the desk next to me and confidently stuck out his hand and said: "I'm Azhar Ali Malik".

It was the beginning of a lifetime association. He was very young when his father died. Instead of going into a shell, he became an extrovert, but a very sensible one. The military government had nationalized the Nazar Stud Farms that belonged to his family, and he was angry over that. He wanted to kick President Ayub.

His uncle, the politician, Malik Ghulam Jilani (father of the woman's rights activist Asma Jilani, now Jahangir) was in the news those days. He was very much influenced by him and every other day we would have a discussion in class where he kept predicting that if we keep on behaving like this, Pakistan would collapse. But, more importantly, he always emphasized that we must do something about it. To fight back was second nature to him, but always in a positive way. Added to this was the inborn gentleman in him. He was a class act. His cousins, Asma and Hina, are, in this sense, very much like him, optimists, fighters and correct to a fault.

Strongly built and athletic, he loved an argument. And when words flew, he would be the first to calm things down with a patent sentence: "If we cannot settle this matter in a sensible way, I am willing to wrestle anyone". That was the end of the matter, for he never let anyone leave with a bad taste in the mouth. We matriculated and joined Government College, Lahore. There he was a natural leader. He took to squash and his friendships were varied and many. In academics he excelled and most of all he loved to argue with our professor of economics, Shoaib Hashmi. We participated in our first protest demonstration against Ayub Khan on The Mall, where, in our college blazers, the police beat the daylights out of us.

So Azhar Ali went on to become a debater par excellence, an academic, he was in the college swimming team with Kamran Lashari, in the college squash team with Azhar Iqbal, in the debating team with Imran Aslam, he wrote in 'The Gazette' of which yours humbly was editor.

In those days I used to stammer like only a champion could. One day Azhar Ali suggested that I join the college debating team. "You must be mad". "No, I am serious, I am worried about you. Your pen flows so well, so must your tongue". He was joined by Imran Aslam who insisted on taking me to an All-Pakistan contest in Islamabad. Both managed to drag me, a champion stammerer, to a topflight debate. Azhar physically pushed me towards the dais. There I started, timidly. He stared me hard in the eye with a smile. Words, just like magic, flew forth. I have never looked back.

When I was given a consolation prize Azhar Ali Malik stood up to protest. There was instantly complete chaos in the hall. Chairs flew from all directions, and Azhar soon had the mike in his hands. Imran Aslam was furious, his hands flying in all directions. I was given a Special Consolation Prize. He cursed them all the way back to Lahore. But it was the beginning of a reasonable debating career in which I won many a prize.

By the time we were both in our MA economics classes, he was arguing with the teachers no end. In the canteen, he was always saying: "These teachers know bugger all about economics". So with him in class one always expected a verbal contest. Then he took off for

England to become a chartered accountant. It was only when I went to England to study and work that we used to meet in his London flat. Help of the right sort was available and the food and refreshments were plentiful. He loved good food.

We then went our ways and met again in Lahore when he was in the ICI office in Gulberg. One day he rang to call me over. "Bloody well come, its important", he said. So I drove there only to find a crowd waiting for me. "What's going on?" I asked. "Nothing, I am just going to beat my driver up". The poor chap had given a lift to a 'woman' in an ICI car, and that was not done. Azhar Ali actually bashed him up and asked: "Did you do anything?". "No Sir". "That is even worse", he said and gave him another blow on his back. Back in his office I told him he was mad, why not sack him. "No, he has seven kids. But imagine, he never did anything to the bloody woman". That was Azhar Ali ... always an enigma.

In between he went to Malaysia, and that is where he honed his skills as an entrepreneur. In London, he got a taste for the mergers and acquisitions game. He loved it and was very skillful at corporate analysis. We often discussed creative solutions to corporate matters when we met, and there he was, always with his feet firmly on the ground.

There was a time when the ICI bored him and he wanted to leave. By this time I had left a cushy job and was venturing into the corporate world, so he wanted to learn the realities I faced. We discussed the issues at stake and I counseled that he must learn to wait. And wait he did. I am sure he consulted wiser persons than me, but he had a habit of returning to old friends. Within a few years he was to head the ICI and set into motion a strategic plan that was to save the company in Pakistan. His plan was daring and brilliant just like him. Today ICI Pakistan is the multinationals' highest profit centre globally. He had higher plans for ICI. But the Almighty had other plans for him. We last shook hands over lunch at the PC almost two months ago.I was discussing the education of his son. We left with a firm handshake and his last comment was: "Sheikh, want to wrestle?"

The oldest Muslim shop that closed

Exactly two years ago, the oldest Muslim-owned shop in Anarkali, approximately 102 years old, closed down, because it had run out of owners. The illustrious Chishti family of Lahore had run out of 'men' interested in taking forward a brand name that still, even today, stands for courtesy, quality and reliability.

We all grew up learning to trust 'China Mart', that famous shop on Dhani Ram Street in Anarkali Bazaar. When it opened in 1899, it was the first Muslim shop in Anarkali in the superstore category. Muslims in the walled city of Lahore used to come, every evening, to just see it from outside. Its owner was Maulvi Hamid Ali Chishti, a scholar in his own right who kept trying to convince the Muslims of Lahore to get involved in entrepreneurship. "This is the only way forward if we are to be an honest and respected community in the modern world," he wrote. In those days 'business' was a dirty word for the landed elite, and, surprisingly enough, the Muslim clergy.

Maulvi Hamid Ali belonged to a family of outstanding scholars. One was a freedom fighter, an expert at blowing up trains. He preferred the gallows to enslavement. The question of Pakistan did not exist then. But for Hamid Ali "only by being economically strong could the Muslims of the sub-continent expect to have a fair deal in the free days ahead." Such was his vision as described in papers of the East India Company.

The brothers and cousins of Maulvi Hamid all made a name for themselves. One of them, Maulvi Nooruddin Chishti, wrote the magnificent *Tahqiqat-i-Chishti,* a well-known reference book on Lahore. In a way, the Chishti family was immensely modern, in tune with the times and progressive beyond doubt. He set about writing books in

Persian and Urdu for the East India Company. He writes: "I accept that the British are an over whelming military power who are here to stay. I also accept that our religious leaders are essentially illiterate. In this situation, it makes sense that the British understand us better, so that over time they assimilate faster. In this way, the goal of freedom will come nearer." Could anyone today be as far-sighted as him?

But then so were his sons, his grandson, and even his great grandson. They were a class act. The British by then had chosen to follow a policy of "separate development" from the natives. Assimilation ceased to be a policy, for they feared "getting lost in the immense and diverse crowd that is India" as one scholar put it. This meant a new approach had to be thought of. It was then that Maulvi Abdul Hamid Chishti, the son of Hamid Ali, came up with the idea of Muslims becoming the "businessmen of the world, with their roots firmly in the lands to which they belonged." In one pamphlet he wrote: "The Holy Prophet was a businessman, and his honesty grew out of his fair trading practices. A Hadith exists where he ordered all Muslims in the days ahead when he has gone, nine out of ten, to be businessmen, so that you may dominate the world with your fair name."

In the end, it was having a "fair name" that mattered so much, and it was in this spirit that China Mart emerged as the one shop in Anarkali where a Muslim would outdo everyone else in honesty, courtesy beyond the ordinary, and reliability that is difficult to find today. Then came the son, Maulvi Abdul Qadir Chishti. During the bloody riots of partition, he was the sole shopkeeper who protected hundreds of Lahore Hindu businessmen, converted their goods into gold and saw them across that "bloody line of hate". His immense contribution to dampen the "hate and hurt" was never officially recognized.

The role of religion in the affairs of state always worried Maulvi Qadir, who in disgust dropped the use of the name 'Maulvi' and insisted that he be called only Abdul Qadir

Chishti. During the late 1960s, he saw hope in the young Z. A. Bhutto as the only way out for Pakistan to become a modern self-reliant Pakistan. He was the sole businessman in the whole of Anarkali Bazaar to back him. In him ZAB found an immensely powerful ally, one who silently worked, unnoticed, refusing to accept any office, or any form of gain. One shopkeeper remembers him even today: "When Chishti Sahib walked through Anarkali, every shopkeeper would stand up to shake his hand. He was the very picture of dignity."

If you happened to visit Anarkali during the 1950s and 1960s, you would have noticed a clean-cut man in a neat sherwani and an impressive Jinnah cap, sitting at the counter of China Mart, always a smile on his face. Whenever we visited him, he would order for us refreshing drinks, and we all loved going there. One thing we just can never forget about Abdul Qadir 'mamaji' as we all called him, is that whenever we got up to leave, he would call us over and whisper in our ear: "Your mother is a very fine and hardworking lady, respect her and look after her. Allah will be most pleased." When I think of the hundreds of times he must have repeated that line in my ear, it brings tears now that the old woman is not around. Such was the magnetic power of Abdul Qadir Chishti.

The great man died just ten days before my own father, and my grandmother always used to say that he died because he loved his 'mama' very deeply. China Mart was taken over by his son Abdul Quddus Chishti, an absolutely magnificent man just like his father. He was kind and considerate to a fault. He kept alive all the family traditions of his ancestors. We kept visiting China Mart with Abdul Quddus Chishti sitting there on his father's chair. Like his father, he worked silently, never accepting any gain from anyone. "The beauty of business is that it forces you to become an honest man."

There must be hundreds of people in Lahore who still remember Abdul Quddus Chishti. I was sitting in the Allied

Press the other day and Jawad Almakky mentioned: "They do not make people like Abdul Quddus any longer. He would drop in once a week to see how we were. A truly caring gentleman."

After Abdul Quddus Chishti no one was interested in the "most famous Muslim shop", the place that opened the way for Muslims in Lahore to be entrepreneurs in their own right. The old haveli in which the family lived in Mozang was sold off. The remaining family moved on. The great tradition of the Chishti family, progressive and modern, died with him. The shop and the great men who ran it have a unique place in the history of Lahore.